Inside the Castle

*

Inside the Castle

LAW AND THE FAMILY IN 20TH CENTURY AMERICA

*

JOANNA L. GROSSMAN

AND

LAWRENCE M. FRIEDMAN

PRINCETON UNIVERSITY PRESS

PRINCETON AND OXFORD

Copyright © 2011 by Princeton University Press
Published by Princeton University Press, 41 William Street,
Princeton, New Jersey 08540

In the United Kingdom: Princeton University Press,
6 Oxford Street, Woodstock, Oxfordshire OX20 1TW

press.princeton.edu

Grossman, Joanna L.
Inside the castle : law and the family in 20th century America / Joanna L. Grossman
and Lawrence M. Friedman.
p.   cm.
Includes bibliographical references and index.
ISBN 978-0-691-14982-0 (hardcover : alk. paper) 1. Domestic relations—
United States—History—20th century. 2. Marriage law—United States—History—
20th century. 3. Parent and child (Law)—United States—History—20th century.
4. Children—Legal status, laws, etc.—United States—History—20th century.
5. United States—Social conditions—20th century. I. Friedman, Lawrence Meir, 1930– II.
Title.
KF505.G77 2011
346.7301'5—dc22
2011002661

British Library Cataloging-in-Publication Data is available

This book has been composed in Palatino

Printed on acid-free paper. ∞

Printed in the United States of America

1 3 5 7 9 8 6 4 2

FOR GRANT, LUKE, BEN, AND MILO

—J.L.G.

FOR LEAH, MY SISTER, IRENE,

AND ALL MY LINEAL DESCENDANTS

—L.M.F.

*

Contents *

* *Acknowledgments* *

THIS BOOK is the culmination of a longstanding shared interest in family law and a wonderful friendship. We are grateful for this opportunity to collaborate with one another in exploring such a dynamic and important field. We are also grateful for the support from friends, colleagues, and family members, especially Maxine Eichner, Mary Grossman, and Grant Hayden, who read the entire manuscript and provided helpful comments. We appreciate the very useful critiques and suggestions of two anonymous reviewers and the enthusiastic support of our editor, Chuck Myers. At Hofstra, Dean Nora Demleitner has supported this project through generous summer grants and course relief. Joanna's friend and colleague, John DeWitt Gregory, funded the research scholarship that freed up valuable time she needed to finish this project. Patricia Kasting and other members of the Hofstra Law Library staff were cheerful, prompt, and resourceful in chasing down sources. A long line of research assistants provided superb help with research and footnotes, including Andrea Caruso, Ashley Lane, Sasha Minton, and Leah Saxtein, with special thanks due to Sarah Crabtree, Andrew Ford, and Bryn Ostrager, who devoted substantial time and effort to this project. At Stanford, thanks must go to the Dean, Larry Kramer; to Mary Tye and Stephanie Basso, who assisted in so many ways; to Andrew Shupanitz and David Oyer; and especially to the wonderful people at the Stanford Law Library, Paul Lomio, Erika Wayne, Sonia Moss, Sergio Stone, Kate Wilko, and George Wilson. Finally, we both thank our own loving families, who remind us every day that there is no place like home.

Inside the Castle

*

Introduction

Everybody, in every society, is born into a family. Even a newborn baby, unwanted, abandoned as soon as it is born, perhaps wrapped in a filthy rag and left on a doorstep, will eventually wind up in somebody's family. A child without a family is likely to die. But there are families and there are families. They come in all shapes and sizes. There are loving families, unloving families, crazy families, saintly families, families made up of nothing but men or nothing but women, nuclear families and extended families, small families and large families. Even a person who lives alone has a family—somewhere; and can be defined as a family of one; or a fragment of a family. Human beings, like wolves or termites, are social animals, family animals. The family is the fundamental unit of society. Families are the molecules that together make up that huge compound we call a community, or a society. In this society, in this day and age, families still matter enormously—even though modern life has, in many ways, weakened the family and instead has placed enormous emphasis on the individual, the isolated, naked self. This emphasis is one of the themes of this book. This is because individualism has had such an overwhelming impact on families and family life. Nonetheless, the family remains a vital social institution. What we will try to show is how individuals and families interact, how the equations of family life shift and contort, and the role that law plays in these complex equations of family life.

Families are also *social* institutions. Family structure and family life are different from place to place, time to time, and culture to culture. In some societies, one man can have a flock of wives; in a few rare societies, a woman can have a flock of husbands. There are societies where the core of the family is a mother's brother, or a mother-in-law; where women have a lot to say or very little to say about marriage, sex, children, and family power; there are societies where blood relationship counts, no matter how far-fetched, where distant cousins have significance and assert claims on people's lives; while in other societies (like ours), even brothers and sisters often have nothing to do with each other once they leave the nest. The ways in which law and the legal system impact the family—regulate it, affect it, mold it, challenge it, or perhaps even ignore it—are, naturally, as variable as the forms of families themselves.

This book is about family law in the United States in the twentieth century and the first decade of the twenty-first century. Or rather, it is about law and the family. "Family law" is the name lawyers give to a particular branch of the law—mostly about marriage, divorce, child custody, family property, adoption, and some related matters. This book deals with all these subjects; but it tries to consider other parts of the law that touch on the family in an important way: inheritance, for example; or the intersection between criminal law and family affairs—domestic violence and marital rape.[1]

We do not, however, claim to exhaust the subject. In some ways, it would be more accurate to say that this is a book about middle-class family law. There is another, vast field, which deals with poor families. This too is not usually classified as "family law" and is not covered in the usual treatises and articles. But it is a significant factor in American law, and has a huge literature of its own. Its history, among other things, is the tortured and depressing story of the way in which the state, in exchange for welfare payments, has claimed and exercised rights to meddle with the family lives—even the sex lives—of poor mothers and other women, in ways that would be legally and socially intolerable with regard to middle-class families. We will refer to this alternate system of family law from time to time, but we do not deal with it in much detail.

We have already mentioned our most basic assumption. Family law follows family life. That is, what happens to families, in this society, determines what happens to the law of the family. Law is not autonomous; it does not evolve according to some mysterious inner program; it grows and decays and shifts and fidgets in line with what is happening in the larger society. The relationship between law and society is tight, but it is not always transparent. This is, in part, because family life, in a big, bustling, diverse society, is a tangle of complexities; its essence (if it has one) is also not always immediate and transparent. No single formula, no lapidary sentence, describes the American family, as it was in 1900, as it was in 1950, as it is in 2011. When family life is intense, multiplex, and conflicted, then family law is bound to be equally intense, multiplex, and conflicted. The story we want to tell is therefore quite complicated. But the main lines of development, we think, are reasonably clear.

CENTURIES OF CHANGE

The twentieth century was a period of constant and dramatic change in society—it was a century that began with the invention of the automobile and the airplane and ended with the computer and the Internet. It began with the world divided, pretty much, among the great European empires; and it ended with a world in which tiny islands were sovereign nations, and the mighty empires had crumbled into dust. It was a century of genocide and war, a century of human rights, and a century of incredible technological development. The world, at the end, was bursting at the seams with people, as the population grew and people lived longer and longer. All of these developments made their mark on the law, and indeed in some ways all of them took place in and through law. The sheer volume of law, in all developed countries, grew even more rapidly than the sheer volume of people.

What happened to family law (in our expanded sense)? In part, the changes were continuations of trends that started in the nineteenth century; but in part they were completely new. Perhaps the single most important trend was the decline of the traditional family, the family as it was understood in the nineteenth century, the family of the Bible and conventional morality. The traditional family, in the twentieth century, came under greater and greater pressure; and, in some ways, it came apart at the seams.

"Traditional family" evokes a certain image. It is a picture of the family in a Norman Rockwell painting. Here is the cozy home; in it, a man and a woman, married and faithful to each other, sit at the head and foot of the table; he is the breadwinner, and the head of the family, ruggedly masculine, in charge, ruler of the roost, but a benign despot, firm but understanding, an object of respect and not of dread. She, on the other hand, inhabits a "separate sphere." She is the homemaker, the soft and delicate core of the family, neat and feminine, the loyal and trustworthy wife, obedient and helpful, darning the socks and baking the bread; the primary caregiver of the children; a warm and tender

3

presence, who teaches the children religion and ethical values, who instructs them to honor their father, and blankets them with the unique blessing of mother love. And the children too—the apple-cheeked boy and girl—are enveloped in sweetness and affection, as they grow up in the image of their parents. And, of course, the family is middle class and white.

This was always something of an ideal type—or perhaps always something of a myth. Most families never fit the description.[2] Poor and non-white families, in particular, never lived this idyllic life. Moreover, death and dissolution destroyed thousands of families in the nineteenth century. It was also a century of desertion, drunkenness, and orphanages. But the law respected and supported families that conformed to the central image, insofar as it could, and coerced or ignored the families that did not conform. Law gave the father the right to command. The wife and the children were supposed to obey. He had custody of the children, if it came to that. Divorce was appropriate only if he was a vicious brute, a philanderer, or simply abandoned the family. He controlled the family's money and its business affairs; a married woman, well into the nineteenth century, had no right to buy and sell property, could not own a farm, a house, a lot in the city; or execute a will. Her position in law was little better than that of a lunatic or a slave. Husband and wife, as Blackstone put it, were "one flesh." But it was his flesh, not hers. He was the manager and owner of the flesh.

Of course, nineteenth-century law was not static. Society was changing rapidly, and so was the law. Both formally and informally, law gradually changed to conform to what was happening to men and women and to family life. From about the middle of the nineteenth century, the states began to pass married women's property laws. These laws gave the wife the right to own property, to buy and sell, to earn money in her own name. The courts were sometimes hostile to these laws, and some courts parceled out rights to married women rather stingily, but in the end the changes took hold. The changes in the law of marital property did not result from a dramatic rights movement; it was not because men had their consciousnesses raised, but because of concrete economic and social needs and demands.

New developments in inheritance law, for the most part, improved the position of women—especially women who lived longer than their husbands. In the common-law system, widows chiefly had to make do with the ancient right of dower. This gave her a lifetime share in some of her husband's land, but nothing much else. New laws gave the widow a fixed portion of the whole estate, and it was hers to do with as she pleased. Again, this was only in part (if at all) an act of generosity or social equity; but it helped ensure a more orderly disposition of land, by freeing estates from the threat of possible dower, which might act (in the law's apt metaphor) as a "cloud" on the title to land.

In the early nineteenth century, divorce was rare and cumbersome. In some states, mostly in the south, only the legislature could grant a divorce. The northern states instituted a system of judicial divorce: divorce as a regular courtroom procedure. The formal rules of divorce, in many states, danced back and forth between toughness and leniency; for most states, in the end, toughness won out. Divorce was not to be encouraged. That was the posture of the law. It was the view of most ethical elites. But the reality of divorce law soon made a mockery of the toughness. In the last third of the century, all sorts of ways to get around stringent divorce laws developed. Some states turned themselves into "divorce mills," where divorce was quicker and easier to get. Above all, there was collusive divorce: divorce as a lie, as a charade.

In theory, there was no such thing as an agreement to get a divorce. Husband and wife had no right to make any such agreement—no right to decide to call it quits. Divorce was a privilege granted to an innocent spouse—a woman, say, whose husband beat her, or deserted her, or committed adultery (in New York, only adultery would do). But in practice, most divorces in the late nineteenth century were in fact products of some sort of agreement—in other words, collusive. They were (legally speaking) frauds. They depended on lies told in court. Yet the legal system accepted them. The judges saw through the charade, but played dumb.

In custody disputes, the father lost ground between 1800 and 1900. Children no longer belonged, almost automatically, to the father, which was the original rule: as head of the family, he was also the natural guardian of children in case of separation or divorce. By the end of the century, a new rule prevailed: the child's "best interests" were paramount. In practice, this usually meant (for young children at least) a mother's loving care.

So, at the dawn of the twentieth century, family law had already undergone tremendous changes. What did the twentieth century bring? A great deal more. A massive evolution. Dramatic change—more dramatic, perhaps, than anything in the nineteenth century. It is not easy to sum up these changes in a few crisp sentences. Many of them, however, like much of the development in the nineteenth century, led even further away from legal arrangements that mirrored, more or less, the Norman Rockwell picture of marriage and family life, toward more fluid, more complex, legal arrangements. One major development has already been mentioned: expansion and redefinition of the legal concept of the "family." Marriage lost its monopoly over legitimate sexual behavior. By the end of the century, there was no such thing, legally speaking, as a bastard; children born out of wedlock had more or less the same rights as children of married parents. This development was linked to another one, which would have startled the good citizens of Victorian America: cohabitation was not only legal, it was as common as dirt. Sexual freedom had gained both social and legal acceptance. Moreover, in some places, gay couples could be recognized as a kind of family.

A second development was the transfer of responsibility for family welfare, in many situations, from individuals or families, to the government: Social Security and Medicare are outstanding examples, and so are the laws concerning pensions and pension funds. The federal government also made its first forays into child welfare law in the twentieth century, with deep involvement in the law of child support, as well as issues of child abuse and neglect. Government programs have aimed at strengthening family life; but whether they did—or further weakened the family—is an interesting question. In any event, tax laws on the whole tended to favor families: homeowners, for example, got to deduct their mortgage payments from their income tax, and there was no estate tax on money left to a dead man's wife, or a dead woman's husband. In the twentieth century, the state took responsibility for educating children, at state expense. Children had to go to school, and parents had no right to say no. To be sure, there were disputes and arguments over home schooling, private schools, and the rights of small, discrete groups (like the Amish) to control how their children were brought up and taught. But these were marginal. There were such programs as Head Start for good children; and juvenile courts for delinquents. The laws with regard to children became, in many regards, denser, more complex, and in a sense tighter than before; but at the same time, restraints on the family's grown-ups became looser and looser. No-fault divorce, cohabitation rights, and protection for non-marital children are clear examples of this second trend.

This book will describe some of these dramatic changes in family law. The question is, what brought them about? There is no point looking at the law itself for answers. The key lies in larger movements of the larger society: dramatic changes in relations between men and women, the particular mass culture of the late twentieth century, and the influence of the media, among other factors. The precise way in which these factors played themselves out in connection with the law is the subject of the book. Thus, the dependent variable (to use social science jargon) is the law that affected the family. Changes in family life itself act as the independent variable—the motor cause. Many of these changes in family life are obvious. For example, changes in sexual mores led very notably to changes in legal rules, on such subjects as cohabitation, unwed parenting, use of new reproductive technology, and same-sex marriages or civil unions. There evolved more ways of constituting a family, more ways of constituting "relationships," than had been true in the past. And family law reflected all of these things going on in society.

A few of the obvious factors that had an impact on family life in the twentieth century are worth mentioning. There were, to begin with, technological changes—methods of contraception, the pill, in vitro fertilization. These made possible a wide variety of family forms that never existed before. Other technologies had more subtle, indirect effects on family life. The automobile made families more mobile, and helped the trend to leave the crowded streets of the city. The automobile has a lot of responsibility for that great innovation, the suburb; the suburb in turn encouraged families to live in the single-family house, the house that sits by itself in a puddle of flowers and grass, fenced off from its neighbors, and relatively private. Suburbia, and the general restlessness of Americans, also helped accelerate the flight away from the so-called extended family. In many or most families, grandma and grandpa no longer tended to live with the kids, or even anywhere near them.

There were also demographic changes of a pretty fundamental nature. People lived longer—because of antibiotics, better nutrition and sanitation, and modern medicine in general. Longevity changed the dynamics of inheritance enormously. As John Langbein has pointed out, it is one thing to inherit money in your twenties or thirties; quite another to have to wait until your last parent dies at age ninety-five. Lifetime gifts—down payments on a house, college tuition—became critical forms of transfer of wealth within the family, more critical on the whole than the money that came from estates of the dead.[3] Longer life spans have also changed the dynamics of divorce. As Lawrence Stone observed, most marriages endure about as long today as they did one hundred years ago; divorce has become a "functional substitute for death."[4]

Above all, there was the influence of money on families and family law. This was already a rich country, relatively speaking, in the nineteenth century. In the twentieth century, and especially in the last half of the century, it became an immensely rich country. The Great Depression was, as things turned out, an interruption in a long-term cycle of growth (at least we hope so); this book, however, was written during one of the deepest recessions (2008–2010) in memory. Still, over time, a bigger and bigger proportion of the public left the ranks of the poor and entered the house of the great middle class. Middle-class people, everywhere in the world, have fewer babies than poor people. They organize their families differently from poor people (or the very rich). They have some leisure (that is, extra time) in which to spend their money. They have separate rooms for each of the kids, and bathrooms with stall showers. Attitudes toward privacy—and toward nudity—change. These attitudes, in subtle ways, affect sexual behavior; and whatever affects sexual behavior impacts the family as well. They also accelerate the trend toward "expressive individualism"[5]—the radical individualism of our times—and this too has had a crucial impact on family life and family law.

All of these developments in society are linked to each other in chains of cause and effect. Technology produced wealth, wealth produced leisure, leisure encouraged consumption and advertising, and all these, together with demographic trends, fostered a culture of personal growth and individualism. The traditional family tottered under the weight of these powerful forces. The media played a special role, spreading the message of getting and spending and developing the self. They were a powerful outside influence on the family. Children were exposed to the big world sooner and in a more vivid, intense way than in the villages and cities of the nineteenth century. Now, in the age of television, children were a market, a target, an army of potential and actual consumers; and the conditions of social life made them draw closer to their peers than to their parents. Adolescence became a time of turbulence. At the same time, the civil rights movement—and the civil rights idea—strengthened an already strong movement of women to claim their half of earth and sky. Opportunities—jobs, professions, careers—began to open up for women. The role of women in the economy, as it grew steadily, reverberated, naturally enough, within the family. The family became (relatively) less of a unit, more of a collection of individuals, each with his or her own rights and obligations. It is no accident, then, as we shall see, that in the late twentieth century one began to hear not only about women's rights, but also about "children's rights," a concept our great-great-grandparents would have found unsettling and strange.

Butting In and Butting Out: The Law of Marriage

In the early part of the twentieth century, the law of marriage became in some ways more intrusive than before. The state asserted more claims to regulate marriage. That old American institution, the common-law marriage, was already in retreat at the end of the nineteenth century. A common-law marriage is a marriage without any formalities at all—no license, witnesses, judge, or minister (not to mention bridesmaids and a wedding cake). Two people simply agree to be married. Most states at one time recognized this sort of marriage, that is, they treated a common-law marriage as no different from a ceremonial one. But state after state later decided that the time had come for common-law marriage to go.

One reason for this change was a heightened concern for the country's gene pool. The early twentieth century was the heyday of the "science" of eugenics. Marriage was the door to sex and children (for respectable people). Controlling marriage was a way to make sure that diseased, criminal, and feeble-minded people were unable to marry and to breed. But common-law marriage was beyond state control. In this period, some states experimented with sterilization as well—an even more radical way to improve the stock. Marriage across race lines was also forbidden—between blacks and whites; and, in the West, between Asians and whites. One point was to prevent the birth of "mongrels." There was, in fact, plenty of sex across race lines— mostly white men and black women, in the south; but the point of the laws was to keep that sex illegitimate and unrecognized. There were also "marriage mills," as increasing mobility challenged the ability of states to enforce their own strict rules on who could marry; and a complex set of doctrines developed, on the recognition (and non-recognition) of out-of-state marriages.

In the latter part of the twentieth century, the laws of marriage reversed course dramatically. The legal controls loosened. The civil rights movement doomed the laws against miscegenation. Sterilization laws were wiped off the statute books. And marriage lost one of its most sacred aspects, the monopoly on legitimate, approved-of sex. "Cohabitation" (it used to be called "living in sin") became so common in the late twentieth century that in some circles, and in some parts of the country, it had pretty much become normal. Millions of couples "cohabited," living together in a kind of trial marriage. Or as a substitute for marriage—a form of family life (or sex life) in itself.

If behavior changes, can legal change be far behind? The answer is no. In the second half of the century, many states did a general housecleaning of their penal codes, and in the process got rid of fornication laws. The laws survived (on paper) only in the Bible belt; and even there they were hardly enforced. The next dramatic step began, as usual, in California, in the famous case of *Marvin v. Marvin* (1976).[6] The gist of this decision was that cohabiters did or could accrue rights against one another. A "contract" to live together, and share money and property, was not illegal (as it once was), just because the partners shared a bed as well as a life. The *Marvin* case caused a stir in legal circles, was widely reported in the papers, and was a topic of nervous humor on talk shows and in magazines. Its practical impact was probably much less than advertised; but it was striking evidence of the way in which morals and mores had changed; striking evidence, too, of the sensitivity of courts to changing styles of life. Generally speaking, the line between marital and non-marital families blurred.

The serious attack on "traditional values" toward the end of the century was nowhere more obvious than in matters of marriage and sex. This was, apparently, the weak link in "tradition." Other "traditional values" were as strong as ever: norms against killing or stealing, for example. But what was good and right and moral and acceptable in matters of lifestyle and choice was radically redefined. The old ways still had passionate defenders, even at the end of the century, and were even claimed to be the views of a "moral majority." But any claim of a moral majority was probably based on shaky statistics. Millions of people—perhaps most—had given up on at least some of the "traditional values." They chose to get married or not, without endorsing the notion that marriage is the only "relationship" worth having. They chose to have children—or not—as they saw fit. Contraception and abortion came out of the closet. The Supreme Court helped, particularly with regard to abortion. At the end of the century, abortion was still wildly controversial (but common); contraception, basically, was not controversial at all. Sex outside of marriage came out of the closet, too; the Supreme Court, in *Lawrence v. Texas* (2003), extended the constitutional right of privacy to encompass whatever "intimate relations" consenting adults chose to engage in privately.[7]

In short, marriage was no longer a sacrament. If anything, it was a commitment. People still lusted and loved, of course, and they still wanted family life, they wanted "relationships"; but old forms of marriage had given way, first to companionate marriage, then to post-companionate marriage. Companionate marriage was marriage as a partnership, a sharing. It was a marriage between two equals. It replaced (for many couples) an older, more patriarchal form of marriage. Marriage was also no longer simple and monolithic, with its rights, roles, and obligations dictated by the state. The parties had more freedom to customize their marriages. In a companionate marriage, the fiction of marital unity—or "one flesh," with the husband in charge—was definitely gone. Marriage was a union of two more or less equal people, whose roles were complex and ambiguous. Mostly, the husband still ruled, but with less than absolute power.

In the last part of the twentieth century, something different seemed to be evolving, something we might call post-companionate marriage, or—to use Andrew Cherlin's phrase—individualized marriage.[8] Equality was still a goal, but marriage was also thought of as an intensely individual matter, a road to self-realization, to personal fulfillment. Companionate marriage failed when companionship failed, when partnership failed, when sharing lost its zing. Post-companionate marriage failed when it no longer contributed to personal growth and fulfillment, for either partner. At any rate, if marriage no longer satisfied the hopes and dreams of bride or groom, he or she felt a right to end it, then and there.

Of course, these changes in attitudes came on gradually. There was a "sexual revolution" and a "gender revolution" and a "gay rights revolution," but, unlike the Russian or the French revolutions, there are no dates, no battles, no uprisings to pin these revolutions on. There were all along straws in the wind. The attack on the cause of action for breach of promise to marry was an early sign of change in attitudes. An engagement was legally a contract; backing out was therefore a breach of contract. Women brought these lawsuits—often women who had had sex with their fiancés; or even gotten pregnant and given birth. The real action, then, was for seduction, and for loss of respectable status. By 1930, this attitude was something of an anachronism; and a movement arose to repeal the "heart balm" laws. A number of states abolished breach of promise to marry and other dinosaurs—the torts of seduction, "criminal conversation," and "alienation of affections." Some states allowed these causes of action to limp along until the 1980s and 1990s, when they were put out of their misery, either by the legislature, or by the courts themselves. A few states still cling to them, along with the archaic notions of marriage and sex that shape them.

Perhaps the most startling development has been the movement to legalize gay marriage. In 1900, not only was this unthinkable, but in every state same-sex behavior was a crime, and quite a serious one. A growing gay rights movement and changing public sentiment led state after state, in the late twentieth century, to remove the onus of criminal penalties. After one false start, the Supreme Court put an end to all sodomy statutes in 2003 in *Lawrence*—a dozen or so had survived until then. And gay couples began to demand more positive rights: civil unions and gay marriage. In some cities, by ordinance, committed couples, of whatever mixture of sexes, could enjoy at least some of the financial benefits of marriage, and other benefits as well—rights to visit sick partners in the hospital, or bury dead ones, and the like, as if the survivor were a spouse. Some created statuses that mimicked marriage—civil unions and robust domestic partnerships. And in a few states, gay marriage actually became legal. But the mere thought that gay marriage might spread set off something like a moral panic, and led most states—as well as Congress—to rush to "defend" traditional marriage against this alien interloper.

DIVORCE AND QUASI-DIVORCE

More and more, Americans in the twentieth century, who felt trapped in an unhappy marriage, wanted the right to end that marriage and start over. But divorce was controversial—and the law was a tangled and conflicted mess. There was strong opposition to easy divorce, or divorce at all, on religious grounds. Hardly anybody thought divorce was a good thing in itself. At best, it was a necessary evil. But there was, undeniably, a great demand for divorce. As we saw, in the nineteenth century, even though the formal law was on the surface unyielding, there were ways to give people their divorces. This "dual system" continued well into the twentieth century. It led to some bizarre results. Women with money and time went to Reno, Nevada, to establish residence (quickly) and get a divorce. Men in New York faked evidence of adultery (posing with a hired woman in a hotel) so that their wives could prove adultery, the only available grounds for divorce. Some people tried getting divorces in Mexico or elsewhere, with questionable legal results.

But in the twentieth century, as the rate of divorce moved steadily upward, the old order started to crumble. A few states, gingerly, allowed divorce for "incompatibility." Other states, ·

around the middle of the century, began to tolerate, in effect, no-fault divorce. Couples who were separated for a certain number of years could get a divorce, without any other "grounds."

For most of the century, the old system stayed alive, fighting bitterly against its enemies. To be sure, nobody liked it. It gave off a rancid smell of collusion and fraud. Time and again, there were proposals for reform. Experts wanted to allow consensual divorce—usually only after attempts at conciliation, and some sort of cooling off period. But all attempts at "therapeutic" divorce, and "therapeutic" family courts, ended in failure. And the forces aligned against easy divorce managed to block or stalemate major change.

The end came suddenly and dramatically. The no-fault "revolution" (if we can call it that) completely destroyed the old fault-based system. This was, to use Herbert Jacob's phrase, a "silent revolution."[9] Politically speaking, it seemed to come out of nowhere. In fact, the old system had been for a long time in decay—it had become a house of cards, which the slightest breeze could knock over. The new system, no-fault divorce, began in California, in 1970. It spread like wildfire in the next decade or so. Eventually, all states adopted some form of no-fault divorce. No-fault was not just consensual divorce—divorce by agreement. It went far beyond this. It became divorce on demand—for either side.

No-fault solved one problem; but family lawyers did not have to close up shop and look for other business. Support payments, property disputes, custody arguments: these became, if anything, more common than ever and more complicated. Officially, men and women were equal, by constitutional fiat; and equal in marriage as well as outside of it. But gender roles persisted. This made property issues more difficult. Some couples entered into premarital and separation agreements, to give them control over the consequences of broken marriage. But most left themselves to the mercy of the law. There also remained a lively argument about whether no-fault made women better or worse off. Beyond a doubt, divorce hurts women (in general), whether or not no-fault aggravates the situation. But courts have had to balance men's belief that ex-wives should go out and earn their own living (without alimony), against women who argued that their help in putting their men through college, or in starting a career, entitled them to a good chunk of their husbands' money.

Custody, too, is a burning issue. Some states experimented with "joint custody," splitting the children in two (legally speaking), and giving each parent equal rights. (In real life, "joint custody" is apt to be an illusion.) States also fretted and legislated about the problem of the "deadbeat dad," the man who welshed on his child support payments. In a mobile country this was, in fact, a national problem. Deadbeat dads helped give rise to a federal bureaucracy, designed to force parents—married or not—to support their children and keep them off the welfare rolls. This level of federal involvement in domestic relations was unprecedented.

No-fault had carried the day, but not everyone was happy with the results. Millions of people, after all, had never bought into the changes—never felt swept along by modern attitudes toward sex and marriage. Many were appalled that divorce had become so cheap and so easy. At the very end of the century, there was something of a movement to revive the corpse of traditional marriage. A small backlash, starting in Louisiana, aimed to discourage divorce; the state enacted a new form of marriage, "covenant marriage," for couples who felt totally committed, and who rejected the no-fault idea. So far, however, covenant marriage has not been much of a success. But the culture war is far from over.

What happened to divorce thus ran parallel to what happened to marriage. In both cases, arrangements became much looser. It was easier to marry (or not marry); and easier to break up. A couple who cohabited did not have to "divorce" at all to break up. Packing a suitcase was enough. For a married couple, divorce was more complicated than for live-in partners; nonetheless, under no-fault, divorce was, as we saw, quite simple and cheap. The whole fabric of attachments had become unstrung, relatively speaking. But this was not a simple, linear development, as the movement for covenant marriage shows. And, of course, even at the end of the twentieth century, some couples did not believe in divorce, usually for religious reasons. Legal separations and annulments are an alternative, although, compared to the vast number of divorces, they remain fairly uncommon.

Even though fewer couples, at the end of the twentieth century, chose to get married, wedding bells nonetheless continued to ring. And ring again. Easy divorce may be a sign of the breakdown of the traditional family. But it is also a sign of the strength of marriage as an institution. Divorce paves the way to a second, perhaps better or more ideal marriage. As Samuel Johnson quipped, remarriage represents "the triumph of hope over experience."[10] Despite massive changes, marriage still meant something: a commitment, perhaps; or a bow in the direction of old-fashioned respectability. People still wanted weddings, with presents, and a banquet, and a gown and a veil. Marriage also still carried with it numerous legal and financial advantages— tax advantages, during lifetime, and (for widows and widowers) after death. Long-time girlfriends, partners, cohabiters, enjoyed no such advantages. But even here, at the end of the twentieth century, there were some signs of change, as we have seen, in the form of domestic partner laws and civil unions, and the right of cohabitants in some cases to make financial claims against one another.

DEATH AND TRANSFIGURATION

Families, like people, are born, grow, and die. In some societies, whole generations live together, in big houses, under a single roof—aunts, cousins, grandparents, kinfolk of all sorts. American families are, on the whole, much smaller. The typical family is the nuclear family: a mother and father, and kids. And even this sort of nuclear family made up less than half of all "families" by 2000. It is less and less common for old folks to live with grown children. It is less and less common for grown-up children to keep on living at home. Their job is to move out, leaving the old family like a queen bee to start a new hive. More and more, it is the pattern, then, for a family to shrink as the children grow up and move on, until only mother and father are left; then one of them dies, survived by a widow or widower; then comes final extinction and family death.

But by then, of course, the family has renewed itself, in the next generation (for most families). Death has legal significance, however, because at that point, finally, whatever the old folks owned and enjoyed passes on to the next generation. Here the law of wills, trusts, and inheritance comes into its own. These institutions are crucial to family life—and to society in general. Rich families stay rich because they inherit money; poor families stay relatively poor because they do not. The social structure renews itself each generation, as money, goods, stocks and bonds and other assets flow through the generations. These matters are not conventionally treated as part of "family law." But they are important to millions of families. Money keeps families together, or drives them apart. Families squabble over who should inherit, and how much. Meanwhile, the old folks live longer and longer lives; and this, as has been pointed out, increases the significance of lifetime transfers and gifts.

And what of transfers the other way? For most people, inheriting from old parents is less of an issue than taking care of old parents. The emotional strain is hard to shift to the government; but the financial strain is something else. Nothing has more significantly affected families, family life, and family structure than the Social Security Act (1935) and Medicare (1965). What makes these programs so untouchable, so popular, is their impact on the middle-aged as well as on the old. Medicare and Social Security are a lifeline for seniors; but their adult children benefit almost as much. The financial burden of parent-care has been lifted from their backs.

The Children

Families do not need to have children, but children need to have families. In this society (as in most societies) it is parents who have the job of conceiving, bearing, feeding, clothing, raising, and teaching children; and controlling them until they become adults. In the United States, basically only parents have this job; in other societies, the extended family has a role in everything but pregnancy. One of the primary rules in this society—so basic we never think much about it—is that the state, government, collective, or whatever one calls it, leaves child-rearing essentially alone. There are no legal rules about how to raise children. The parents will decide what toys to buy, and what schools, religions, clothes, food, and standards of conduct to impose. Early in the twentieth century, this was elevated to a constitutional right. Fit parents were entitled under the Constitution to make decisions about the "care, custody, and control" of their children. In all but exceptional cases, the state could not interfere; and neither could unwanted third parties, even grandparents. But this simple rule is under increasing pressure, in an age of complex families, in which multiple adults have parent-like relationships with children.

Despite a general hands-off policy in the twentieth century, the federal government more and more tried to guarantee (bare) minimum standards for the care of children. It mandated basic definitions of child abuse and neglect, to be imposed on the states, and set up a national center to study and document the problem. It established a new framework for child support awards.

The state intervened where parents were unable or unwilling to take care of their children; or cases where parents abused their own flesh and blood. Failure to provide for children, or abusing children, was a crime under local laws. The state as *parens patriae*, as an institution standing *in loco parentis*, had the right, indeed, the duty, to take children out of homes where they were beaten or tortured; or in which they were starved or neglected. The problem is that this power was easily misused. Torture is torture; but neglect is not quite so obvious. State policy in this area can be controversial—as it was when the state took children away from their Sioux, Navajo, or Hopi parents, and put them in foster homes or boarding schools. It misjudged the customs and habits of immigrants; it was intolerant to parents whose main sin was poverty. On the other hand, the state was often castigated for its failure to act. Particularly later in the century, there were many scandals—horrendous cases in which children or foster children or adoptive children were beaten, abused, burned, starved, or murdered; and nobody had seen fit to intervene, or had intervened too little and too late. Social work agencies were obvious scapegoats in these scandals.

It is easy to forget that parents sometimes wanted state intervention. The juvenile court is essentially a twentieth-century institution. The first juvenile court was set up in Cook County, Illinois (Chicago) at the turn of the century. It spread from there to every other jurisdiction. The juvenile court handled problems of neglected and delinquent children. Often the parents themselves turned their children over to the state. They wanted the state to take care of "incorrigible" or "unmanageable" children. This was particularly true of immigrant parents. Juvenile justice was a replacement—wanted or unwanted—for a family that had somehow failed. Modern "baby Moses" laws serve a narrower, but similar function: mothers can abandon newborn babies in a safe place (rather than a dumpster) without fear of criminal consequences.

In one area, the state's role is far from marginal: education. In the twentieth century, education for children was universal and compulsory. Child labor was generally abolished. For almost all children from the age of five or six onward, a large part of the normal day was spent in school, away from the family and under the guidance and control of civil servants. Even those children who went to private schools (mostly religious schools) followed a curriculum dictated by the state. School—along with the peer group, and with such outside influences as television—may have eroded parental authority. This was part of the larger process— one of our central themes—in which the family tended to dissolve into a collection of unique individuals, each with its own zone of power and authority.

ADOPTION, REPRODUCTIVE TECHNOLOGY, AND THE NEW FAMILY

The state could at times break up a biological family, and shift the children around. The law could also create an imitation biological family through adoption. An innovation of the nineteenth century, adoption is a strictly legal procedure. It brings a genetic stranger into a family, and makes that child the same as a "natural-born" child, for almost all legal purposes. In the twentieth century, control of adoption was an issue. There were state rules, but also private agencies, and a sort of black market in babies. One issue was whether children had to be placed only in families with the same racial and religious backgrounds. Another significant issue was secrecy. In the first decades of the twentieth century, states moved first to close off adoption proceedings from public scrutiny and later to insist on anonymity among the parties themselves. By the 1950s, virtually all states treated the "true" parents and the circumstances of birth as deep, dark secrets. This attitude changed dramatically toward the end of the twentieth century. Adopted children demanded the right

19

to search out their "roots" and uncover their genetic history. For whatever reason, hundreds of adopted children, often to the dismay of adoptive parents, dug into old records, papers, documents, in search of mothers or fathers who might or might not want to confront their own distant past.

Illegitimacy was once a terrible stigma. (Most adopted children were, at birth, illegitimate.) But the stigma of illegitimacy, like the stigma of divorce, weakened considerably in the twentieth century. As early as 1921, an Arizona law declared that every child was "the legitimate child of its natural parents," just as if the child had been "born in lawful wedlock." The Supreme Court, in *Levy v. Louisiana* (1968), gave constitutional protection to illegitimate children.[11] Even the word "illegitimate" itself gave way to "non-marital"; and nobody spoke about "bastards" any more. If there was nothing wrong with cohabitation, it followed that there was nothing wrong with "illegitimacy." In 1985, 22 percent of all children were born to mothers who were unmarried; in 1997, that number had increased to 32 percent; and by the end of 2008, it was an astonishing 40.6 percent.[12] And a large majority of black children were technically illegitimate. The increasing social acceptance of unwed motherhood caused a decline in the supply of adoptable babies; and increased the pressure for foreign adoptions, among other things.

It was no longer the case that only married people were entitled to have children. There were by the early twenty-first century forms of families that the nineteenth century could not have imagined. In the 1990s, surrogacy burst on the scene. Women were paid money to conceive and carry babies for families that could not have children. Science developed techniques of in vitro fertilization. There were egg mothers who were not womb mothers, and womb mothers who were not egg mothers—women who carried somebody else's (genetic) child inside their belly. A child could have an egg mother, a womb mother, a sperm donor father, as well as a mother and father who intended to raise him or her. There were gay couples who adopted a child or made use of a surrogate mother; and lesbian couples who had babies through artificial insemination. There were even children whose biological parents had died before the children were even *conceived*. All of these variations on the theme of motherhood, fatherhood, and family life posed legal problems and called out for legal solutions—which were often ragged and inconsistent.

. . . . .

This is a book about changes in American family law; and their social backgrounds. That is a huge subject in itself. It is a huge subject in every major country. And, to be sure, each country— indeed, each city and each state—has its individual culture, and its individual story of how family law developed. But most of the large social forces that propel American family law are not unique to the United States; and consequently, the law follows a common pattern elsewhere as well. For example, the trend toward looser divorce can be found all over the Western world. It took longer in England, or Italy, than in the United States; and was very late in arriving in Chile; but as of 2011, only Malta still refused to countenance absolute divorce; and no-fault divorce had taken over in many countries. Cohabitation not only swept across the United States; it swept across Europe as well. The sexual revolution was not a one-country affair.

Yet, in some regards, the United States deviates from the patterns common to developed countries. More Americans marry—84 percent of American women marry by age forty, compared to 70 percent in Sweden, and 68 percent in France.[13] Americans form relationships easily, it seems; but they also break up easily. There is more marriage, more divorce, and more remarriage. American children leave home earlier than Italian children. An unmarried Spanish man or woman is likely to live at home; an adult American, man or woman, is likely to move away, whether married or not. Another structural point: family law, despite certain federal initiatives in the twentieth century, is basically the law of the states. There is, in the United States, as Mary Ann Glendon notes, no cabinet minister "charged with responsibility for family affairs," nor an "explicit national family policy," as there is in some other countries.[14]

Throughout the book, we try to relate legal to social change— to put family law into historical and social context. A man's home is his castle, as the old phrase put it. It is no longer only a man's; and it is no longer (if it ever was) a castle. But the home was always the seat of the family. Our aim is to look inside the home, inside the castle; to map a century's worth of dynamic change. In the following chapters, we will consider in more detail, first, problems involved in the making of a family—the marriage contract itself and the legal regulation of marriage. We also examine in this section the legal and social meaning of marriage, including its treatment by tax and immigration law; and also domestic violence, a potent destroyer of marriages. We look then at the margins of marriage, including the rise and fall of both common-law marriage and "heart balm" laws. A separate section will deal with modern challenges to traditional marriage and traditional notions of sex life—sexual freedom, cohabitation, and same-sex marriage. We will also consider family breakup: separation, annulment, and the relatively complex story of twentieth-century divorce. We explore the aftershocks of divorce: custody, child support, property division, and support payment issues. We will briefly deal with older members of the family—aged parents, in particular; and with the younger members, too, both natural children and adopted children. In one chapter, we will treat questions about inheritance and other issues that arise when death dissolves a family. Throughout, we will have our eye on the "new new family": families created outside the traditional mold—through cohabitation, or with the aid of reproductive technology, or with the involvement of multiple adults. In the last chapters we look at the formation of parent-child relationships and parental rights.

In the century or so that we cover in this book, the family has changed enormously. What lies ahead is something we cannot know; but eternal constant change seems to be the fate of this most vital and intimate branch of law. Much has happened, in the course of the twentieth century. Is there a single theme, a single line of development, which ties the whole fabric together? Perhaps not. But, to repeat, it is striking how much the social concept of "the family" has moved in a single direction. The old family has been melting away; what was once a tightly knit unit is now more and more a cluster of individuals, all more or less on their own. Family members are selves who choose (or think they choose) their own path through modern life. They marry as they please and divorce as they please. They feel free to indulge their own intimate desires; and the law allows them to do this, so long as there is no collateral damage. Even children are treated, more and more, as miniature selves. They are no longer the slaves of their parents. Parents can choose or not choose to have children. Children, of course, cannot choose their parents; but they can choose to break all ties when they reach majority; and they are not financially responsible for their family of origin, as they would be in many cultures. Government—law—has moved in to fill some of the gaps in the social fabric, as the traditional family dissolved.

This is the main event, the great show in the center ring. It is important to recognize that the changes are relative, not absolute. Through all of this, the family remains: changed, modified, twisted in some cases beyond recognition, but still the bedrock of the social order. What we experience today was the product of a legal and social evolution; it was a long time growing; and with many detours and sideshows, and only with effort and struggle. The rest of the book fills in the details.

PART ONE

TYING THE KNOT: MARRIAGE AND

PROMISES TO MARRY

*

Marriage and the State

O<small>N</small> M<small>AY</small> 2, 2008, Mildred Jeter Loving died at the age of sixty-eight, in her home in Central Point, Virginia. Ms. Loving, a woman of mixed race, was the widow of Richard Loving. She was survived by a son, a daughter, eight grandchildren, and eleven great-grandchildren. Richard Loving was a white man, and their 1958 marriage, which was illegal in Virginia, forced them to live in exile from their home state until the Supreme Court struck down the law in 1967.[1]

Foneta Jessop was also sixty-eight when she died in 2009. At the foot of the open casket, in Colorado City, Arizona, was her husband Merril, a member of a polygamist group. At his side were also his "numerous other wives, all wearing matching white dresses." Some members described life in the group as "idyllic"; but one of Merril's wives, Carolyn, who had broken with the group, painted a different picture of Foneta, Merril's first wife: "deeply unhappy … an overweight recluse who fell out of favor with her husband and slept her days away"—shut up in her room, except for eating, doing laundry, and watching "old Shirley Temple movies on television."[2]

Two deaths. Two marriages. Foneta and Mildred had very little in common—except that each was touched by the law of marriage. In this initial chapter, we take up that law—rules and doctrines that define and control marriage. That body of law, like most aspects of family law, is primarily left to the states. Each state lists its impediments to marriage, and declares that prohibited marriages are either void (invalid per se) or voidable (subject to annulment). Some marriage prohibitions—such as incest and bigamy—are reinforced through separate criminal bans. States also lay out the procedural requirements for marriage. Although it is no longer the case that there is *no* federal law relating to marriage, states are generally responsible for crafting their own provisions about the right to marry and the mode of marriage. Here we ask some basic questions: Who can marry and under what circumstances? Who is forbidden to marry and why? How are valid marriages contracted? We explore the rise and fall of marriage restrictions rooted in racism and eugenics, as well as the persistence of other, more enduring, impediments to marriage, like bigamy, incest, and youth. Central to the story of state marriage regulation is the establishment, beginning in the 1960s, of constitutional protection for the "right" to marry, which limited, at least at the margins, the freedom of states to impose certain restrictions on marriage. But also central, in a system dominated by state law, are the rules of interstate marriage recognition, which dictate whether marriages travel across state lines. In broad brush, we will tell a story of increasing marital freedom, reined in only by a handful of seemingly immoveable social norms.

POLYGAMY

Polygamy—at any rate, Mormon polygamy—was a burning issue in the nineteenth century. It was denounced from one end of the country to the other, with enormous vigor and outrage, along with lurid fantasies of the wild sex lives of the Mormon patriarchs, whose wives were supposed to be little better than slaves.[3] In 1890, the Mormon Church renounced polygamy. Polygamy, of course, had always been illegal. The Morrill Act of 1862 made bigamy in U.S. territories a *federal* crime.[4] Federal law also made "unlawful cohabitation" a crime; this too was aimed at the Mormons. In *Reynolds v. United States* (1878), the Supreme Court upheld the bigamy law, despite the claim that it violated the free exercise of religion protected by the First Amendment.[5] To top it off, Utah's statehood was conditioned on its banning polygamy.[6] Every state today provides that bigamous marriages are void.

The church's renunciation of polygamy spelled the end of polygamy for mainstream members of the church—at least officially. There is little question that some members of the church secretly continued the practice into the twentieth century. Joseph F. Smith, head of the church, who died in 1918, had several wives, and forty-three children. When Reed Smoot from Utah was elected to the Senate, in the early twentieth century, he was accused of polygamy (he denied it); and an attempt was made to prevent him from taking his seat. The church continued to denounce polygamy, but small splinter groups, living at times in remote towns in Utah and neighboring states, kept up the practice.

One of these communities was Short Creek, which straddles the Utah-Arizona border. Here polygamists freely practiced their faith and their lifestyle. On the whole, they adhered stubbornly to their beliefs, despite persecution, raids, lawsuits, and attempts by the authorities to take their children away unless they renounced the dreaded practice of plural marriage.[7] An investigation in 1935 found that the men in the group, known as the Brethren of the United Order, had from "2 to 6 wives and from 5 to 29 children." The investigation had been touched off when women in the community "identified themselves as 'plural wives' in filling out applications for relief."[8]

Polygamy, then, did not simply curl up and die—neither among Mormon splinter groups, nor among other small sects. When Rulon Jeffs, president of the Fundamentalist Church of Jesus Christ of Latter Day Saints (FLDS), died in 2002 at age ninety-three, he left behind as many as twenty wives and hundreds of grandchildren; thirty-three sons served as pallbearers at his funeral.[9] He lived in Short Creek, which is still filled with plural-marriage households. This sect was the subject of a front-cover story in the February 2010 issue of *National Geographic*, with pictures of polygamous life and in-depth interviews with members.[10] According to the story, about 38,000 "breakaway Mormon fundamentalists" still practice "plural marriage." FLDS is the largest group, with about 10,000 members. At least one "patriarch" had eighty wives. As one might imagine, the birthrate in the group is staggeringly high.[11]

The legal battle against polygamy did not curl up and die either. A Utah man, Thomas Green, was tried and convicted of four counts of bigamy in 2001, and sentenced to five years in prison.[12] He had numerous wives, several of whom were related to each other, and twenty-five children at the time of his conviction, plus four more on the way. He and his wives appeared on popular talk shows, touting their lifestyle and proclaiming a constitutional right to pursue it. Although local prosecutors had long since ceased pursuing polygamy cases, Green provoked them to go after him.[13] His was the first major polygamy prosecution in Utah in nearly fifty years, even though thousands of Utah residents still live in polygamous households.[14] But the stress in recent years has been less on lust and sex, or the immorality of polygamy, than on the exploitation of women and children. The habit of marrying very young girls has been an especially thorny issue. Tom Green's youngest wife was only fourteen when they married, but the girl—whose mother he had also once married— was already pregnant. While the marriage was legal, he was later convicted of child rape for the premarital sex that led to the pregnancy.[15] Because he divorced each woman before marrying the next (while keeping them all as his functional wives), the child-rape victim was his "only legal wife" when he was freed from prison in 2007.[16]

These issues were front and center again in 2008 and 2009, when a huge media blitz focused on a raid of the Yearning for Zion ranch in Eldorado, Texas, a settlement of the FLDS sect that was founded in Short Creek. One leader of the sect, Raymond M. Jessop, was arrested, along with other men in the group. They were accused of marrying and having sex with girls who were under age—some as young as twelve. There were attempts, too, to remove some of the children from the ranch. The case against Jessop was difficult because the women were unwilling to cooperate; but in November 2009, Jessop was convicted of sexual assault on an "under-age girl whom the church elders had assigned to him as one of his nine wives."[17]

Still, in the age of the sexual revolution, a few people have begun to wonder: what is so wrong with polygamy—not, of course, of the Yearning for Zion variety, but a more civilized form. Men can legally have a whole stable of women, provided the women agree; and having a mistress or two, or six, would not violate any law in most states. (Utah and Colorado are unusual in that they define the crime of bigamy to include purporting to marry or cohabiting with another person while already married to someone else—a measure expressly designed to preclude the kind of manipulation engaged in by Tom Green and other modern-day polygamists.)[18] What, then, would be so terrible about marrying these women, instead of simply living with them? That is perhaps the question for viewers of a new reality show, *Sister Wives*, which depicts a "normal" polygamous family currently living in Utah. There is no underage marriage, no sexual predation, no dependence on welfare. There is just Kody, who lived with his three wives and thirteen children in a house specially designed for polygamous marriages; and in the course of the show, marries a fourth wife (with three children of her own from another marriage). He opens the show with this admission and promise: "I'm a polygamist, but we're not the polygamists you think you know."[19]

Of course, there are answers to the question of what's wrong with polygamy. Letting a man have several wives would make hash of the laws about marital property and child custody. It might create a legal tangle of heroic proportions. And the problem of male supremacy persists. Muslims are allowed four wives; and some African societies practice polygamy as well.[20] A Kenyan polygamist, whose nickname was "Danger," recently died in his late nineties. He left behind one hundred widows and two hundred children, for whom he had established two separate schools.[21] Immigrants from these countries are now found everywhere in Western society, including the United States. In all of these societies, polygamy is clearly a symptom and a form of male domination; and in an age of (official) gender equality, that simply will not do. There is also the effect on those men who are not part of the leadership group of alpha males. Hundreds of young men have been expelled from FLDS, ostensibly for "being disruptive influences," but more likely from a "cold-blooded calculation by church leaders" that they had to limit "male competition for the pool of marriageable young women." After all, if one man can have eighty wives, then seventy-nine other men are unlikely to find a mate.[22]

At the Yearning for Zion ranch, the subjugation of women was more than a rumor; it was reality. Seen on TV, dressed in identical long dresses, with identical hairstyles, the women seemed mindless, strangely robotic, as if drugged. A breakaway member of the church, Rebecca Musser, testified in the Jessop trial that the founders and leaders of the church, Rulon Jeffs and his son Warren, "controlled every aspect of the women's lives, including how they dressed and what they ate ... who they married and when."[23] Warren Jeffs was convicted of rape as an accomplice for compelling a fourteen-year-old to marry her cousin with the knowledge that nonconsensual sex would follow.[24]

But that anyone besides members of these sects can even ask whether polygamy should be permitted is in itself definitely a sign of the times. Of course men, not women, ask the question.

Nobody speaks up for polyandry.[25] If harems ever come to be legalized, they would presumably follow the usual pattern—one man, many women. The other way (on Tuesday she sleeps with Claude, on Wednesday with Stephen, on Thursday with Max, and all of this legitimately) seems out of the question. True, the United States is more and more a sexually permissive society. But it is also more and more a society committed to gender equality, and, whatever the theory, polygamy in practice is a glaring affront to this last ideal. Both feminists and Christians would agree on this point, though perhaps for different reasons.

MISCEGENATION

Laws that prevented interracial marriage were for a long time a major form of state control over marriage.[26] These laws went far back into the nineteenth century; and indeed, even further; there were precursors in the colonial period. As of 1913, no fewer than thirty of the forty-eight states had laws on the subject.[27] In all thirty, blacks and whites were forbidden to marry. But there was always the problem of defining what "black" meant, for purposes of miscegenation laws. In Virginia, a "colored" person was defined, until 1924, as someone with "one-sixteenth or more of negro blood." In 1924, the statute in that state went further, and established the so-called one-drop rule. A person was non-white if he or she had any traceable African ancestry whatsoever.[28] Nebraska expanded the racial scope of the prohibition, making a marriage void if one party was white and the other "possessed up to one-eighth or more negro, Japanese or Chinese blood."[29] On the West Coast, this focus on Asians was the main thrust of the miscegenation laws. In Oregon, for example, marriage between a white and anyone with more than one-quarter of "Chinese blood" was void.[30] California extended this ban to include marriages between whites and members of the "Malay race."[31]

Feelings against interracial marriage were strongest, no doubt, in the Southern states. Ironically, all the propaganda against "amalgamation" and "mongrelization," the shrill cries that the white race was in danger, that the country faced "[c]omplete ruin," and that the "white population will be crowded out," seemed to ignore the fact that it was white men, especially during slavery, who produced the bulk of these persons of mixed blood.[32] But deep emotional reaction to such marriages was not confined to the South. When Jack Johnson, the black boxer, married a white woman, Lucille Cameron, in Chicago, it was something of a national scandal. Seaborn Roddenbery, a Congressman from Georgia, introduced a bill to amend the Constitution to outlaw marriages between Caucasians and "persons of color," which included anyone with "any trace of African blood."[33] Roddenbery referred specifically to the Johnson-Cameron affair—"a white girl of this country made the slave of an African brute"— and fulminated against such marriages: "No more voracious parasite ever sucked at the heart of pure society, innocent girlhood, or Caucasian motherhood."[34] But the bill died in Congress.

Opposition to interracial marriage was surprisingly strong, even in the North. When, in 1919, Mabel Puffer, a white woman, and Arthur Hazzard, a black man, took out a marriage license in New Hampshire, it set off a minor tempest; relatives of the bride moved heaven and earth to prevent the marriage. Hazzard was arrested, and accused of stealing money from Puffer; the family also tried, successfully, to have Puffer declared mentally ill and locked up.[35] All this despite the fact that New Hampshire had no law against interracial marriage. In the end, the harsh tactics were successful—the marriage never took place.[36]

One of the sensations of the 1920s was the so-called Rhinelander case. Leonard Rhinelander, the wealthy son of a real estate tycoon, had married a girl from the other side of the tracks, Alice Jones. The Rhinelander family was incensed, and put pressure on Leonard to end the marriage. Leonard did leave Alice, and went to court to ask for an annulment. On what basis? Fraud: she had hidden the fact that she was black. The trial made headlines. *Was* Alice black? At one point, she had to undress and show her body to the jury. Leonard lost the case—the jury thought Alice was black, but they felt Leonard must have known this before he married her. Alice was, partially, vindicated. But she and Leonard never lived together again. And it was assumed that Leonard's suit would have been justified if Alice had concealed the truth about her race.[37]

The miscegenation laws persisted for many years. Slowly, imperceptibly, they lost some of their normative power. And they were clearly out of step with the world as it was, in the years after the Second World War—at least in the Northern and Western states. Thousands of blacks migrated out of the South, into Northern cities. This gave them a certain measure of political power, since in the North, unlike the South, they were allowed to vote. Some Northern states enacted the first weak, crude "fair employment" laws. In *Perez v. Sharp* (1948), the California Supreme Court struck down the section of the Civil Code that outlawed marriages between whites and non-whites.[38] Andrea Perez was Mexican American (officially white in California); Sylvester Davis was black. They were both Roman Catholics. They petitioned the California Supreme Court for a writ to compel the issuance of a marriage license. The Court granted the writ, and voided the miscegenation statute. It was the first court in the twentieth century to do so.

Perez began or stimulated a trend. Other Western states voluntarily repealed their miscegenation statutes: Oregon in 1951, Montana in 1953, Colorado and South Dakota in 1957, Nevada in 1959; still others in the early 1960s. Changing views about race—and the reaction against "racial prejudice as practiced by the Nazis," who also prohibited "marriage across racial lines," may have been a factor.[39] The Southern states, to be sure, made no such moves. But the writing was on the wall. Even without a legal mandate, opposition to interracial cohabitation and marriage had significantly diminished within public and private institutions. In 1963, the U.S. Air Force stopped asking personnel whether they had married a person of another race during their overseas tours, and a resolution condemning state laws against interracial marriage was presented to convention delegates for the Young Democratic Clubs of America.[40] In the same year, the advisory board of the Family Life Bureau of the National Catholic Welfare Conference adopted resolutions deploring "the attitudes and cruel behavior of American society which penalizes and ostracizes those persons who exercise their fundamental right to free choice of a marital partner by entering into interracial marriage."[1] Two years later, delegates to the General Assembly of the United Presbyterian Church considered an uncontroversial recommendation to urge repeal of all remaining miscegenation bans.[42]

McLaughlin v. Florida (1964),[43] a Supreme Court case, concerned a Florida statute that made interracial sex, in essence, a crime. If any "negro man and white woman, or any white man and ne-gro woman ... habitually live in and occupy in the nighttime the same room," they were liable to be fined and jailed for up to one year. Lewd cohabitation, fornication, and living in adultery were also offenses for same-race couples, but the law required proof of intercourse to sustain a conviction. The Supreme Court declared this statute unconstitutional. Florida could use the criminal code to preserve "sexual decency," but could not single out offenders for harsher treatment based solely on race. The Court did not, however, express "any views about the state's prohibition of inter-racial marriage." Not in that case, at any rate.

But three years later, in *Loving v. Virginia* (1967), as we have seen, the Court took the final step.[44] Richard Loving, a white man, had married a mixed-race woman, Mildred Jeter, in Wash-ington, DC. The couple then returned to Virginia. In Virginia, a white person was not allowed to intermarry with a "colored per-son." Law enforcement officers "entered the Lovings' bedroom, shined a flashlight on them, and demanded to know why Rich-ard was in bed with 'this lady'."[45] (The sheriff, in a later interview, defended his action: "The Lord made robins and sparrows, not to mix with one another.") The couple was arrested, convicted, and sentenced to a year in jail. The Lovings were told, however, that their sentences would be suspended if they left Virginia and did not return together for twenty-five years. Accordingly, the Lovings settled in nearby Washington, DC. But later, they de-cided to return home and to try to overturn the judgment against them. The American Civil Liberties Union took their case and fought it all the way to the Supreme Court, which unanimously held in their favor. The Virginia law, according to the Court, was nothing but a device to "maintain white supremacy." The Court talked about the freedom to marry, which we take up later in more detail. But the main thrust was against miscegenation laws. No state should or could control the choice of a marriage partner, in the name of a racist ideal. This was the final nail in the coffin of state restrictions on interracial marriage.

Loving was, for the most part, quietly accepted. Two months after the Court handed down its decision, Virginia's first legal interracial marriage was scarcely noted.[46] Months later, the first interracial marriage in Tennessee was celebrated on the steps of the Nashville City Hall and Courthouse.[47] Alabama was the last

35

state to repeal its dead-letter prohibition against interracial marriage officially—amending its constitution in 1999.[48] One writer observed on the eve of the vote on the constitutional amendment:

> [I]n the state nicknamed "The Heart of Dixie," the land of Bull Connor and George Wallace, the movement to relinquish this searing symbol of the past has caused barely a ripple. There are no billboards on the highways, no marches for or against the repeal, no yard signs or bumper stickers. Articles about Amendment 2, as the ballot measure is known, are few and far between in the local press.[49]

There were some speed bumps along the way, but the larger trend was toward acceptance. In 1970, a judge in Calhoun County, Alabama, refused to grant a license to an interracial couple. A federal court had to order Alabama to comply with the new legal regime. There was resistance in Georgia and North Carolina, too.[50] Eventually, every state had to comply; and provisions in state constitutions forbidding interracial marriage were eliminated. No doubt some true believers still think such marriages are a violation of some divine plan, but their numbers are dwindling, and their political force is completely spent. A Louisiana justice of the peace's refusal, in 2009, to issue a marriage license to an interracial couple, out of concern for any children the marriage might produce, was met with genuine shock.[51] The civil servant, Keith Bardwell, told reporters that he was "not a racist. I just don't believe in mixing the races that way. I have piles and piles of black friends. They come to my home, I marry them, they use my bathroom. I treat them just like everyone else." But, he believes, children of interracial couples suffer because neither black nor white society accepts them.[52] The incident triggered a complaint to the federal Department of Justice, and the couple easily found another official. The case blew over, but clearly some would still agree with this reluctant justice of the peace.

Just as legal bans on polygamy did not fully eradicate the practice, overturning miscegenation bans did not completely normalize interracial marriage. The Court's ruling allowed the Lovings to return to Virginia and allowed Richard, for the first time, to "put my arm around her and publicly call her my wife."[53] (They lived together as husband and wife for only eight years before Richard was killed by a drunk driver in 1975.) But it is hard to say whether the ruling had much impact on the practice of interracial marriage. Despite the firm establishment of a legal right to marry someone of a different race, the number of people exercising the right remained (indeed, remains) small.

There had been a rising trend of interracial marriages during the years leading up to *Loving*; black-white marriages had "increased more than six times between the 1946–55 and 1956–65 span."[54] The trend continued into the 1970s, but most Americans today still marry partners of their own race.[55] Interracial marriages account for only 6 percent of all marriages in the United States,[56] and African Americans remain the "least likely of all racial/ethnic minorities to marry whites."[57] The "social boundaries between African Americans and whites nevertheless remain highly rigid and resilient to change," especially when it comes to "romance and marriage."[58] *Loving* did change the formal law, but, as Rachel Moran observes, "it would be naïve to think that the Court could instantly undo the informal assumptions and practices that developed during three centuries of a 'separate but equal' principle in sex, marriage, and family."[59] It did give "ordinary Americans the freedom to rethink the role of race in their intimate relationships."

THE CONSTITUTIONAL RIGHT TO MARRY

The Supreme Court's decision in *Loving* was important beyond its impact on the law or practice of interracial marriage. Disputes among states over the proper regulation of marriage and divorce had made their way to the high Court on occasion.[60] But the Court's role in those cases was limited to referee: resolving conflicts that arose because states imposed different restrictions on marriage or divorce.[61] Before *Loving*, the Supreme Court never said what the rules *should* be. It had never invalidated a state's marriage or divorce law. And while the Court sometimes mused on the importance of marriage, it had never suggested that individuals had some kind of right to marry, nor that states faced consitutional limits. As Justice Field wrote in *Maynard v. Hill* (1888), "Marriage, as creating the most important relation in life, as having more to do with the morals and civilization of a people than any other institution, has always been subject to the control of the legislature."[62] States were left to draw their own moral lines, consistent with the federalist tradition in domestic relations law more generally.[63]

The Lovings had challenged the constitutionality of the Virginia law under both the Equal Protection and Due Process Clauses of the Fourteenth Amendment. They won on both arguments, ushering in a new era in which state marriage laws had to comply with developing federal constitutional norms of equality and privacy. On the claim that the ban violated the Equal Protection Clause of the Fourteenth Amendment, Virginia's defense was that its racial classification "punish[ed] equally both the white and the Negro participants in an interracial marriage," and thus, did "not constitute an invidious discrimination on the basis of race."[64] Virginia contended that the law needed only a "rational basis" to survive.[65] The Supreme Court roundly rejected Virginia's "equal application" theory and applied the "most rigid scrutiny" to the law.[66] It found no sufficiently compelling purpose to justify Virginia's racial classification. Quite to the contrary, the Court concluded:

> The fact that Virginia prohibits only interracial marriages involving white persons demonstrates that the classifications must stand on their own justification, as measures designed to maintain White Supremacy . . . There can be no doubt that restricting the freedom to marry solely because of racial classifications violates the central meaning of the Equal Protection Clause.[67]

The Court could have ended the case there, but went on to hold that the miscegenation ban also violated the Due Process Clause of the Fourteenth Amendment. The Court drew on *Skinner v. Oklahoma* (1942), a case in which the Supreme Court struck down, as an infringement of a fundamental right, a state law imposing compulsory sterilization as a penalty for some forms of theft but not others.[68] Like the right to maintain reproductive capacity, the Court concluded in *Loving* that the "freedom to marry has long been recognized as one of the vital personal rights essential to the orderly pursuit of happiness by free men." "Marriage," the Court wrote, "is one of the 'basic civil rights of man,' fundamental to our very existence and survival."[69]

Henceforth, state restrictions on marriage could be analyzed on federal constitutional grounds. *Loving* may have been a case about racial equality, but it spawned a right to marry that soon took on a life of its own. The Court revisited the federal constitutional right to marry in two important cases after *Loving*. In *Zablocki v. Redhail* (1978), the Court struck down a Wisconsin statute that prohibited noncustodial parents who were behind on support obligations and whose children were on welfare from marrying without prior court approval.[70] Between *Loving* and *Zablocki*, the right of privacy had been broadened dramatically to include rights regarding abortion, living with extended family, contraception outside of marriage, and so on.[71] The plurality opinion in *Zablocki* called marriage a right "of fundamental importance"; any law that directly and substantially interfered with it warranted "critical examination."[72] *Zablocki* signaled that state marriage laws could be challenged on grounds other than race. The defendant in *Zablocki*, after all—a Caucasian, teenage father of an out-of-wedlock child with a new, pregnant girlfriend—was part of no "suspect" class.[73]

Almost a decade later, the Court again took up the right to marry, in *Turner v. Safley* (1987).[74] A Missouri prison regulation permitted inmates to marry only with permission of the prison superintendent, to be granted only for "compelling reasons."[75] But the Supreme Court ruled that marriage was a fundamental right that could be taken from prisoners only as necessary to serve legitimate penological interests—a standard the prison failed to meet in that case.[76] *Turner* completed the trilogy of right-to-marry cases. How far this right extends, however, is at the core of the debate over same-sex marriage, which we discuss in chapter 7.

OTHER RESTRICTIONS ON MARRIAGE: HEALTH CONTROLS, FORMALITIES, YOUTH, AND INCEST

Until the last decade of the twentieth century, when the same-sex marriage controversy arose in earnest, miscegenation was the hottest flashpoint in marriage law history. But states imposed many other impediments to marriage, some of which were nearly universal, others the source of interstate conflict.

With the rise of the eugenics movement in the late nineteenth century, states began to pass laws to prevent people who were sick or considered "defective" from marrying.[77] We explore the reason for this in our discussion of common-law marriage in chapter 3. In brief, states relied on marriage law to control reproduction. All states had, and still have, some restriction on marriage by the mentally incompetent. The "insane" were generally prohibited from marrying, as were the "imbeciles."[78] States did not generally restrict the impotent from marrying, though this could serve as a basis for annulment by the other party.[79] The state of Washington passed a law in 1909 that ruled out marriage for any "common drunkard, habitual criminal, epileptic, imbecile, feeble-minded person, idiot or insane person," and those with "hereditary insanity," as well as "pulmonary tuberculosis in its advanced stages, or any contagious venereal disease."[80] The statute applied to women under age forty-five, and the men who married such women; the thrust of the statute is obvious.

The statutes also applied in many instances to people with epilepsy—Connecticut and Michigan had such laws before 1900; Minnesota in 1901, Kansas in 1903, Ohio in 1904; and it was a feature of the Washington statute quoted above. As late as the 1950s, seventeen states still prohibited epileptics from marrying. Some of these laws were also specifically restricted to people of childbearing age. In *Gould v. Gould* (1905),[81] a Connecticut case, Marion Gould applied for a "divorce or a decree of nullity"; her husband, Roy, had epilepsy, she said, and had concealed that fact when they got married. Roy did not contest her claim, but the trial court refused her petition. The Connecticut Supreme Court reversed. Epilepsy was a "disease of a peculiarly serious and revolting character," which tended to "weaken mental force." It was passed on from parent to child; and the children were often "of an inferior type of physical or mental development." Needless to say, by the end of the twentieth century, these statutes had all been repealed.[82]

A number of states began early in the century to require couples to get medical examinations. Many prohibited people with venereal diseases from marrying. Some called for specific laboratory tests for syphilis and gonorrhea. As of the end of the 1930s, eight states had statutes that mentioned syphilis specifically; six more added gonorrhea.[83] In the days before antibiotics, to be sure, there was a strong and rational case against allowing people with syphilis or gonorrhea to get married or, more to the point, have sex. Men often contracted the disease from prostitutes, and then passed it on to innocent wives and children. This was the theme of Ibsen's famous play, *Ghosts*, and of *Damaged Goods* by the French playwright, Eugene Brieux. The Brieux play, in translation, had trouble finding theaters in which to perform, because of its shocking subject, but there was a showing in Chicago in 1913.[84] The same term, "damaged goods," was used in a column in 1918, in the *Chicago Defender*, the African-American newspaper. "If you have syphilis and are engaged to marry a beautiful, innocent, charming girl.... Postpone indefinitely the marriage, or break the engagement." You are "damaged goods" and "if you marry her you are a deceiver."[85]

These fears were widespread; and it is not surprising, then, that the courts generally upheld these statutes. In *Peterson v. Widule* (1914),[86] the Wisconsin Supreme Court upheld a law that required men to get a medical certificate, stating that they were free from venereal disease, before a marriage license could issue. Society, said Chief Justice Winslow, "has a right to protect itself from extinction and its members from a fate worse than death." What about the fact that the statute applied only to men? It was, he said, "common knowledge ... that the great majority of women who marry are pure, while a considerable percentage of men have had illicit sexual relations before marriage." Hence, the "number of cases where newly married men transmit a venereal disease ... is vastly greater than the number of cases where women transmit the disease."[87]

These requirements for blood tests and the like were gradually repealed. Ohio, in the 1970s, still required a doctor's statement affirming, based on a "standard serological test," that the applicants either did not have syphilis, or the disease was "not in a stage of that disease which is communicable."[88] Today, only a few states still require blood tests or other health certifications before marriage. In Mississippi, for example, the couple is required to take a blood test for syphilis and it has to be analyzed by a state-certified laboratory and recorded on the state's form.[89] In Indiana, a woman under age fifty has to provide a statement to show whether or not she is immune to rubella, a disease that can lead to birth defects if contracted by a pregnant woman. In Idaho, each of the parties has to receive a "confidential AIDS educational pamphlet" and "certify" that he or she has read it and answered a "confidential questionnaire" on the subject.[90] In the late 1980s, Illinois briefly required marriage license applicants to undergo an HIV-AIDS test, but backed off because of public objection and the exorbitant cost.[91] Given the expense of the testing and the low rate of positive results, the state was spending "approximately $243,000 for each HIV-positive identification."[92] The requirement also had a stark impact on marriage practices; Illinois residents went elsewhere to marry rather than submit to the mandatory test.[93] Most states have eliminated the old health restrictions altogether. Pennsylvania dropped the requirement of a test for syphilis in 1997; Oklahoma in 2004; and the District of Columbia in 2008.[94] In New York State, for example, all it takes to get married is a $40 marriage license and a twenty-four-hour wait after the license is issued. (In many states there is no waiting period; a couple can rush out and get married immediately.) The loosening of these requirements is consistent with the broader trend: the states are giving up control over marriage and the gene pool—and transferring more power to individuals to customize their own arrangements.

In all states, ceremonial (as opposed to common-law) marriages must be solemnized by a recognized official. Any member of the clergy can perform the marriage; and judges as well. There have been minor variations in some states. In Ohio, for example, along with clergy and judges, mayors of municipalities can perform marriages, and also the "superintendent of the school for the deaf."[95] New York permits leaders of the New York Society for Ethical Culture, a group that provides "non-theistic services in a congregational setting," to perform marriages.[96] Many states specifically accommodate Quakers, who believe that every member is a minister. Few of them would meet the typical definition of clergy, which requires ordination by a recognized religious body and a congregation or following.[97]

Lawsuits have questioned the validity of marriages solemnized by ministers ordained through the mail or, more commonly today, on the Internet. These ministers generally fail to meet the definition of clergy in marriage laws. The Universal Life Church (ULC) is a non-denominational church founded in Modesto, California in 1962 that has ordained more than 20 million ministers, according to its website (including one of the authors of this book).[98] The ULC has no set doctrine and does not require its ministers to believe in God. Its website boasts that it provides ordination with "no religious hurdles, no hoops to jump through, no tests of loyalty, no religious rings to kiss, and no fees to pay."

The siblings of Cobert Blackwell challenged Nadine Fortenberry's claim for a widow's elective share of Blackwell's estate, claiming that their marriage was invalid because it was solemnized by Claude Clark, a constable and Methodist with "Credentials of Ministry" from the ULC. At the time they were married, Blackwell was a fifty-eight-year-old widower in Walthall County, Mississippi. He and Nadine obtained a marriage license in November 1984, and the "next day, a Friday, our couple set sail for Jackson (of all places) in search of legal blessing for their bliss." They were referred by a local judge to Clark, who performed their marriage the following day. When Blackwell died less than three months later, his seven brothers and sisters stood to inherit everything except the share designated for a surviving spouse under Mississippi law. They zeroed in on Clark's credentials. Only a minister, rabbi, or "other spiritual leader of any other religious body" could solemnize marriages in Mississippi.[99] The Mississippi Supreme Court, however, upheld the validity of the marriage. While the majority conceded that the "ULC is hardly a conventional church by Bible Belt standards," it was "enough of a religious body," and Clark was "enough of a spiritual leader" to validate the marriage.[100] (One justice concurred only in the result, criticizing the majority's "enough of" standard as "horseshoe jurisprudence.")

Courts in other states have not all been so forgiving of ULC's unorthodox ordinations. Courts in New York and Virginia have invalidated marriages that were solemnized by ULC ministers.[101] The Supreme Court of North Carolina voided a bigamy conviction in *State v. Lynch* (1980) on the grounds that the defendant's first marriage was performed by a ULC minister, and was therefore invalid.[102] A year later, the state legislature amended its marriage laws to validate ULC marriages retroactively, but was silent on whether new ULC marriages would be valid.[103] Utah passed a law prohibiting ministers ordained by mail or online from solemnizing marriages, but a federal court struck down the provision as a violation of the Equal Protection Clause.[104]

At one time, too, it was common for states to make people wait some decent interval after a divorce before remarrying. The first judgment of divorce was "interlocutory"; it became final only with the passage of time. This was the case in California, under a statute of 1903. These laws went hand in hand with attempts to deal with migratory divorce, which we address in chapter 8. Remarriage waiting periods served to maximize the possibility that spouses victimized by a "secret" divorce in another jurisdiction would have a chance to contest the suit or appeal it—or at least discover it—before the harm was compounded by remarriage. The divorced couple was in limbo, unable to marry, until the decree became final—a situation exploited, for example, in the wonderful movie, *The Awful Truth*, with Cary Grant and Irene Dunne, in 1937. But these restraints too have all but vanished; a person generally can marry the moment the divorce goes into effect. By the end of the century, there were only a few exceptions—Wisconsin, for example, still disallows remarriage within six months of a final divorce decree.[105] Providing an easier way out and a smoother path to the next marriage is of course part of a larger trend in the law.

A few restraints on marriage do remain. The most obvious one has to do with age. In the past, a distinction was made between males and females; and the minimum marriage age varied somewhat from state to state. Thus, in Nebraska in the 1920s, males over eighteen, and females over sixteen, were allowed to marry; minors, however, needed parental consent.[106] In New Mexico, the age for males was twenty-one, for females, eighteen; for those younger than these ages, parental consent was needed, though a marriage of a male under eighteen and a female under fifteen was always invalid.[107] In South Carolina, into the 1960s, a girl of fourteen and a boy of sixteen, could marry with parental consent.[108] Such gender distinctions seem invalid today. The Supreme Court has declared that sex-based classifications are "suspect" in a series of cases beginning in 1971. But the age minimums have been upheld against constitutional challenges. States can adjust the constitutional rights of minors in light of their unique stage of life.[109]

Today, there is a statutory minimum age for marriage in every state but California and Massachusetts.[110] Kansas was a third outlier; until 2006, girls as young as twelve and boys as young as fourteen could marry with parental consent.[111] Matthew Koso, age twenty-two, and Crystal, fourteen, crossed the line in 2005 between their home state of Nebraska, which prohibited marriages by anyone younger than seventeen, and Kansas. Wearing jeans and carrying pink carnations, the couple was married by a judge in Hiawatha, Kansas. Crystal's parents consented to the marriage, which Kansas law required, but Matthew was nonetheless prosecuted and convicted of statutory rape in Nebraska. Their infant daughter was the key piece of evidence.[112] Nebraska did not challenge the validity of the marriage; it simply refused to treat the couple's subsequent marriage as a defense to statutory rape, which had occurred *before* the marriage. Koso served fifteen months in jail before returning home to his daughter and his wife—who had just turned sixteen, the age of consent in Nebraska.[113] In the wake of bad publicity about this case, Kansas amended its marriage law. The state now prohibits marriage for anyone fourteen or under, permits marriage by a fifteen-year-old only with a court order, and permits sixteen- and seventeen-year-olds to marry only with parental consent.[114] In other states, the age restrictions are mostly unisex, and generally higher than they were a century ago. Typical statutes permit minors ages sixteen or seventeen to marry with parental consent, and some permit those younger than sixteen to marry upon proof of pregnancy, birth of a child, or with judicial approval.[115] In every state but Mississippi, individuals must be eighteen to marry without parental consent.[116]

Every state had, and still has, restrictions on incestuous marriages. These do not differ, in any material way, with regard to members of the immediate family. Oedipus could not legally marry his mother in any state. Nor can brothers and sisters marry, nor uncles and nieces, nor aunts and nephews. Many states prohibit marriages between any direct lineal ancestor and descendant, regardless of the number of generations dividing the parties. For these relatively close relationships, most states not only prohibit marriages, and declare them void from the start, but also criminalize the underlying sexual relationships. There is much less agreement in state laws as to marrying in-laws and ex-in-laws, or stepparents.

The incest laws in this country have largely religious origins. In England, incest was punishable only in ecclesiastical courts, which ostensibly applied the law of *Leviticus* prohibiting persons more closely related than the *fourth* degree to marry. This ban applied equally to relations by blood and by marriage, based on the canonical maxim that husband and wife were one, and therefore equally related to each other's kin. American jurisdictions departed from English law by declaring incest a crime, as well as a basis for invalidating marriage, though the criminal laws often defined incest more narrowly.

The primary modern justification for banning incestuous marriage is the fear of genetic complications for offspring. There are, however, other justifications for incest laws. Margaret Mead felt the "incest taboo" was "among the essential mechanisms of human society." It had clear benefits: children can "wander freely, sitting on laps, pulling beards, and nestling their heads against comforting breasts—neither tempting nor being tempted beyond their years."[117] Claude Levi-Strauss argued that the taboo benefits society at large, by forcing families to reach outward and connect with other families—connections that make society function.[118]

While some incest restrictions are universal within the United States, others vary from state to state. As of 1930, at least twenty-seven states prohibited the marriage of first cousins.[119] Twenty-four states prohibit them today, while six more permit them only in certain circumstances, when procreation is impossible.[120] Utah, for example, permits first cousins to marry only if both spouses are over age sixty-five, or at least fifty-five with evidence of sterility.[121] The *social* taboo against incest is a bigger obstacle to first-cousin marriages than law. Though famous Americans like Jerry Lee Lewis and Albert Einstein were notoriously married to their first cousins, first-cousin marriage is far from the norm in the United States. Most countries, including most of Europe, permit first-cousin marriages without restriction; cousin marriages are the norm in parts of Africa and Asia.[122]

The concern over defective offspring still permeates marriage law and makes first-cousin marriages dubious. But a 2002 study in the *Journal of Genetic Counseling* concludes that first cousins do not face much higher risk of producing children with genetic abnormalities than "normal" couples.[123] Children of first cousins have only a slightly higher risk of a serious birth defect than children of unrelated parents. There have been no constitutional challenges to first-cousin marriages, but the state would be hard pressed to show that a categorical ban is necessary to achieve any "compelling" state interest. Modern genetics, and the fact that most first cousins in the United States do not grow up in the same household, argue against the ban. In general, American family law is moving away from categorical rules, toward letting individuals make decisions—even bad ones—about vital aspects of relationships and family life. Yet, the traditional bans on incestuous marriage have held steady. A few courts have invalidated incest laws with respect to couples with no blood relation, like a sister and brother related only by adoption.[124] But there have been surprisingly few challenges given the more general trends.

MARRIAGE IN A FEDERAL UNION

States have residency requirements for divorce, but not for marriage. You can get married anywhere and anytime you please—on vacation, at home, wherever. This opens the door for "marriage mills." The most prominent is Nevada. Las Vegas and other cities in Nevada are full of "wedding chapels"; the idea is not only to catch those people who went to Nevada for a divorce (and remarriage), but also everybody else who wants a quick and painless wedding. There are marriages for all tastes. The "Wee Kirk o' the Heather" offers "a simple Las Vegas Wedding," but also an "elaborate Las Vegas Wedding, or a fun-filled Elvis wedding."[125] The "Shalimar Wedding Chapel" can provide, among other types, a "Grand Canyon Helicopter wedding"; first comes the ceremony, then the helicopter ride, then a trip by "horse-drawn wagon" to a Ranch House, where "real working cowboys" will entertain the couple "with ... their myths, legends, [and] songs."[126] "Destination weddings"—those in which the couple, perhaps with guests, travels to a vacation destination to say their vows—reportedly increased 400 percent between 1996 and 2006, in part a response to the development and expansion of a vast wedding industry that can suck the life savings out of bride and groom alike—and their parents.[127] The average cost of an American wedding in 2009 was more than $28,000.[128]

When the honeymoon is over, though, couples return home and expect that their marriages travel with them. They expect the same when they move or travel after getting married. And for the most part, they are right. States generally give effect to marriages validly celebrated elsewhere. But, as we will see in chapter 7, most states have drawn the line at gay marriage. There are other exceptions as well.

As Fred Hall and Mary Richmond said about marriage laws in 1919: "After all these years of endeavor and experimentation, look at the diversity—the chaos even—of laws!"[129] The lack of a residency requirement for marriage gave rise to the practice of "marriage evasion"—traveling outside of one's home state to marry, in order to evade some marriage restriction. Early in the twentieth century, the National Conference of Commissioners on Uniform State Laws (NCCUSL), an independent body that proposes model statutes for states to adopt, flirted with the idea of uniform marriage laws. But, in a 1907 report, it deferred the issue in favor of trying to agree on a uniform law of divorce.[130] NCCUSL did propose the Uniform Marriage and Marriage License Act in 1911, but it was focused primarily on procedural requirements for marriage. It urged some substantive changes, including the abolition of common-law marriage and a higher age for minors to marry without parental consent, but even there it left the age blank so states could set their own.[131] Later uniform acts also avoided the basic question of who could marry.[132] There were also several unsuccessful attempts to amend the Constitution, either to give Congress general authority to regulate marriage and divorce, or specifically to ban polygamy or interracial marriage nationwide.[133]

A nationally uniform marriage law would have resolved these interstate conflicts, but states were simply unwilling to relinquish their control over marriage. The hodge-podge of laws on marital impediments was, instead, addressed indirectly through rules about *recognition* of the marriage laws of other states and countries—rules that tried to balance respect for the laws of sister states and foreign countries, while also limiting the impact of "lax" marriage laws here or abroad. The general rule was the "place of celebration" rule—a marriage valid where celebrated was valid everywhere.[134] And a marriage void where celebrated was void everywhere else. But if a marriage interfered with an important public policy or interest, a state did not have to recognize even a marriage that was valid where it was celebrated. Marriages that violated "natural law" or a state's "positive law" fell under the exception. No state, for example, would recognize the second, third, and fourth wives of polygamists, even if plural marriage was perfectly legal in the home country. Polygamous and incestuous marriages were "universal" exceptions to the rule of recognition.[135] Before *Loving*, there were always at least some states that allowed interracial marriages. Could those marriages be recognized in other states? Perhaps not if the marriage was truly evasive;[136] but if the couple was originally domiciled in a state that allowed the marriage, it was likely to be recognized elsewhere.[137]

The positive law exception gave legislatures the power to preclude judicial recognition of a particular type of marriage by deeming it "void." A prime example of this kind of "positive law" was a statute aimed at banning marriage evasion. Indiana's evasion law, for example, declared that, "If persons residing here, with intent to evade the local law relating to licenses and prohibited marriages, go outside to marry with the intention of returning and do return, such marriage is void."[138] As of 1931, seventeen states had such a law, some patterned after the Uniform Marriage Evasion Act, which was proposed in 1912.[139]

The general rule and narrow exceptions meant that states sometimes recognized marriages they would not themselves permit. In *Estate of May* (1953),[140] a New York case, an uncle and niece of the half blood, "both of Jewish faith," were married by a rabbi in Rhode Island. Jewish religious law allows this kind of marriage; and Rhode Island law allowed "any marriage which shall be solemnized among the Jews, within the degrees of affinity or consanguinity allowed by their religion."[141] Fannie and Sam May, the half-uncle and half-niece (who were, incidentally, the same age), lived together for thirty-two years, and produced six children. One of the couple's daughters was recognized by the probate court as the "administrator" of her mother's intestate estate. But Sam objected on grounds that a surviving spouse has superior claim to that post. The daughter contended that her parents' marriage was invalid because they had deliberately evaded the marriage laws of New York, a state they had recently adopted as their home and where they continued to live for the next thirty-two years. She argued thus that her father was not a surviving "spouse." The court rejected her claim. Despite New York's prohibition on all uncle-niece marriages, the marriage could be recognized since it was valid in Rhode Island—and no strong policy stood in the way. First-cousin marriages have also been recognized by courts in states that prohibit them;[142] so, too, for common-law marriages, which we discuss in chapter 3. Courts also sometimes recognized a particular marriage for some limited purpose. A Mississippi court in 1948, for example, permitted the surviving spouse of an out-of-state, interracial marriage to inherit from her husband's estate, even though such a marriage was considered against the state's public policy.[143]

Over the course of the twentieth century, variations in state marriage laws lessened. A confluence of social and legal forces left us with a virtually uniform set of restrictions and requirements.[144] Marriage laws, like family law in general, headed in one general direction: toward more freedom for the partners—freedom to marry who they liked, for example. The only exceptions were cases where strong social norms still governed: laws against incest and polygamy, for example. As we will see in a later chapter, freedom to marry whoever one likes has reached an important frontier: same-sex marriage. This issue has not only split the trend toward uniformity—Massachusetts and Mississippi are not traveling the same path—but has also engendered an entirely different approach to interstate marriage recognition.

Marriage, Law, and Society:
A Tangled Web

W HEN MAYME VAIL'S husband became critically ill with tuberculosis in 1948, she promised to go to church every day, a sort
of bargain for his return to good health. She probably did not
anticipate that she would be attending mass daily for at least
sixty more years, or that she and her husband, Clarence, would
make it to the Guinness Book of Records for the longest marriage recorded by a living couple as of 2008. At ages 101 and 99,
respectively, Clarence and Mayme celebrated their eighty-third
anniversary in White Bear Lake, Minnesota, surrounded by their
big and loving family, which included six children, thirty-nine
grandchildren, one hundred and one great-grandchildren, and
forty great-great-grandchildren.[1] When asked by NBC's *Today*
show in 2008 for secrets to their long-time wedded bliss, which
began when both were teenagers, Mayme spoke in practical
terms: "You take your vows, for better or for worse, for richer
or for poorer. I guess you just stick to it, come what may."[2] (She
claimed their last argument had taken place in 1946.) When
asked whether he had ever considered divorce, Clarence simply
said: "I don't remember."

This is the kind of marriage praised by lawmakers, judges,
politicians, and advocates. But of course marriage in real life is
more diverse and complex. At the other extreme from the Vails,
there was Zsa Zsa Gabor, an actress and socialite who married
nine times, and who, when asked how many husbands she's
had, quipped: "You mean apart from my own?"[3] Despite the fact
that the three famous Gabor sisters racked up eighteen husbands
among them, Zsa Zsa was the only one to bear a child, a daughter she claims was the product of rape by her second husband.

The Vails and the Gabors are both outliers on the spectrum
of married life in the United States. There is no paradigmatic
marriage. Typically, couples marry in their mid- to late twenties,

produce two to three children, and run a decent risk of a divorce after about eight years.[4] We have discussed the formal law of marriage; and we will explore the property rights of husbands and wives in chapter 9. Marriage, however, is a crucial *social* institution as well. Many people bemoan the state of American marriage: opponents of same-sex marriage, supporters of the patriarchal family, anti-divorce moralists, advocates for children, and so on. Marriage may be weaker than before, it may have changed greatly; but it is still fundamental to society and to the lives of people in America. And its consequences reverberate throughout society and the law. In this chapter, we explore marriage in social and legal context. We look at *who* marries, and what marriage seems to mean to them. Then we will discuss what marriage means in *law*: rights and obligations of married couples, including economic rights; we look, too, at the darker side of marriage—domestic violence and marital rape.

Marriage in the United States: A Snapshot

If we compare the median age of first marriage at the beginning and end of the twentieth century, the results would be pretty unremarkable.[5] For women, the median age at first marriage increased by only three years from 1890 to 2009—from twenty-two to twenty-five; for men, the increase during the same period was only from twenty-six to twenty-eight. But in the 1950s, the age of first marriage dropped to its lowest points for both men and women—twenty-two and twenty, respectively. Beginning in the 1970s, the median ages increased by about a year every decade.[6] Delayed marriage can be attributed to a number of trends we have discussed and will discuss—cohabitation has increased dramatically, contraceptives are cheaper and easier to get, the demand for college education has gone up, and women have better economic opportunities.[7] As a *New York Times* article put it, the "Long Road to Adulthood is Growing Even Longer."[8] Young adults today are doing *everything* later than their parents did—finishing schooling, becoming financially independent, marrying, and having children. For many people, the twenties now serve as a decade-long transition from youth to adulthood, a transformation that used to occur much more abruptly.

Despite delays, Americans still, for the most part, eventually get married. The marriage "rate"—the number of marriages per 1,000 single women who are 15–44 years old—hit a low point in 1932; only 81 out of every 1,000 eligible women married that year. The marriage rate then rose steadily, through World War II, and peaked at 143/1000 between 1945 and 1947. From that point on, the marriage rate steadily declined, dropping to 1932 levels again in 1986, and then going even lower.[9] By 1990, the marriage rate was 54 per 1,000 unmarried women.[10] But even with this decline, the proportion of the population that *never* marries is still quite small. For example, the percentage of women "ever married" by age twenty-four dropped dramatically during those fifteen years (from 62 percent to 38 percent), while the percentage of women "ever married" by ages 50–54 stayed the same—and high—between 1975 and 1990 (95 percent).[11]

The divorce rate, of course, is part of the story of marriage. The divorce rate seems to alarm each generation. But everything is relative. The divorce rate tripled between 1870 and 1900, but even that rate—4 per 1,000 marriages—is dwarfed by 1980's 23 divorces per 1,000 marriages.[12] The divorce rate tended to alarm reformers, and led them to refuse in most instances to loosen up divorce laws, in the face of increasing demand.[13] The divorce rate rose steadily, but slowly, from the last quarter of the nineteenth century until the 1960s, when it began a more dramatic rise.

In the mid-1980s, social scientists studying marriage and divorce delivered the somewhat startling news that *half* of all marriages would end in divorce.[14] That rate has declined slightly since the 1980s; today, about four in ten marriages will ultimately end in divorce.[15] But not all marriages are created equal. Not every couple faces the same risk of divorce. People who marry very young run a much higher risk of divorce. Along other axes, though, the data are not as clear. For example, women who have less than or more than a college education are more likely to get divorced than women who have just a college degree.[16] Divorce rates are highest today in the Bible Belt, where people marry at a relatively young age (premarital sex is a sin).[17] Marriages are also most likely to dissolve in their first decade. A calculator available on a divorce website asks for only minimal information—gender, age at marriage, children, year the marriage began, educational level, and years already logged in marriage—before spitting out a prediction about the likelihood of a divorce for that person within the next five years.[18]

Most of those whose first marriage ends in divorce will remarry.[19] The median time between divorce and second marriage today is 3.5 years, and by ten years after a first divorce, 81 percent of those divorced before age twenty-five have remarried, as well as 68 percent of those who divorced at age twenty-five or older.[20] As many as half of the women who remarry will give birth to at least one child with a second or later spouse.[21] Different studies show the overall remarriage level to be two-thirds to three-fourths. But those unions, in turn, are more likely to end in divorce than first marriages.[22] As Andrew Cherlin has observed, "[b]oth marriage and divorce contribute to the larger picture of a country in which people partner, unpartner, and repartner faster than do people in any other Western nation."[23] But all these turnovers mean adults spend more time unmarried than they used to. The number of adults "currently" married declined from 72 percent in 1960 to 52 percent in 2008.[24]

Any depiction of marriage in the United States would be incomplete without at least some attention to racial variations, particularly between whites and blacks. During Reconstruction, African Americans quickly and enthusiastically demanded the right to marry; and so many actually did get married that the Union Army was almost overwhelmed.[25] By 1900, marriage "was nearly universal among African-Americans," as it was for most Americans; and remarriage was common among those who divorced.[26] As late as the 1940s, nearly 60 percent of black women and 40 percent of black men were married by age twenty-four—higher than the rates for whites.[27] But a stark "marriage gap" developed over the course of the second half of the century. (The gap is for African Americans; by most measures, Hispanic and Asian women follow marriage patterns similar to white women.)[28] The gap touched every marriage-related statistic and played a role in debates about the existence and causes of a black "underclass."[29]

Today, African Americans are significantly less likely ever to marry, more likely to divorce, and less likely to remarry.[30] The ongoing "Fragile Families and Child Wellbeing Study" found that African-American parents are also significantly less likely to marry one another within thirty months of a non-marital birth.[31]

An analysis of 1980 census data showed that the percentage of black women who never married had begun to rise by 1960; and has risen consistently since then.[32] For example, the percentage of black women who had never married by age twenty-nine rose from 13 percent in 1960 to 29 percent in 1980. For non-Hispanic white women, those numbers, respectively, were 8.3 percent and 13.2 percent. For black women with less than a high school diploma, the increase between 1960 and 1980 in those who had not married at age twenty-nine was even more dramatic, from 13.1 percent to 32.3 percent; and the gap relative to white women, whose rates were 6 percent and 9 percent for the same age group, was quite stark.[33]

The marriage gap only widened after 1980. Between 1980 and 2000, the percentage *ever* married in the 25–29 age group declined from 81 percent to 68 percent for white women, and from 63 percent to 38 percent for black women.[34] Data from the Current Population Survey 2009 show that 57 percent of white women aged 25–29, but only 31 percent of black women, have ever married.[35] In the 50–54 age group, the ever-married rate—a decent proxy for lifetime singlehood—stayed high, dropping only from 96 percent to 95 percent over that twenty-year period. The same rate for black women, however, fell from 93 percent to 85 percent between 1980 and 2000, and down further to 75 percent by 2009.

What explains the racial marriage gap? Attitudes toward marriage do not seem to explain it; indeed, black women are much more likely than white women "to believe their lives would be better if they were married."[36] Economics and marriage opportunity seem to be the driving forces instead. Black women face a more depressed marriage market than do white women.[37] Black men are much more likely to marry a nonblack woman than vice versa, and that gap seems to be growing.[38] According to a recent study, 22 percent of black men who got married in 2008 married someone of a different race, compared with only 7.9 percent who did so in 1980. For black women who married in 2008, only 9 percent married a nonblack man.[39] The pool of potential mates is also depleted by the staggering number of young black men who are in prison or suffer early deaths.[40] Finally, and perhaps most importantly, the relatively poor economic opportunities for black men make them less desirable as marriage partners;

the opportunities of black women are greater, so they have more incentive (than white women) to be independent.[41] And the evidence suggests that black men and women "seem to weigh economic considerations more heavily than white women and men in deciding when to marry—as might be expected, given their more precarious economic situation."[42] Other factors beyond the marriage market may also help explain the racial marriage gap, such as, for example, differences in the rate of nonmarital childbearing, which is inversely related to the likelihood of marriage.[43]

Race is not the only predictor of marriage practices. A recent report by the Pew Research Center, for example, notes a rising marriage gap by class. Adults with low socioeconomic status are "just as eager to marry" as other people, but they "place a higher premium on economic security as a prerequisite." This is a standard that is hard to meet in communities hit by hard times and at the bottom end of the rising income gap.[44] Educational level, too, is a significant predictor of marriage rates. The Pew study found that sixty-four percent of college graduates are married, but only forty-eight percent of those who did not go to college.

MARITAL EXPECTATIONS

The opening sentence of Leo Tolstoy's *Anna Karenina* is famous: all happy families are alike; but each unhappy family is unhappy in its own way. We think Tolstoy was only half right—happy families are all happy in their own way, too. And certainly, each *marriage*, whether happy or unhappy, is unique—and, to the outside world, largely unknowable. It is next to impossible to tell what went on in the minds of millions of men and women who married in the twentieth century. We get some hints—perhaps at times misleading—from advice books, magazine articles, and the like. Behavior—marriage and divorce rates, for example—also tells a story. Through these sources, we can at least say something about changing patterns and conceptions of marriage. And these changing conceptions and patterns have naturally had a profound impact on family law as well.

The master trend is clear: traditional marriage was—slowly, and only partially—giving way to what has been called *companionate* marriage.[45] Perhaps "giving way" is somewhat misleading.

Two things were changing: image and reality. The image of traditional marriage—the Norman Rockwell picture of marriage—was, to some extent, always an ideal, or perhaps more to the point, always a myth. The middle-class Victorian family, as Stephanie Coontz has pointed out, was hardly universal. Cozy and comfortable family life depended on the work and the help of other families, who were "too poor and powerless to retreat into their own little oases and who therefore had to provision the oases of others." For the middle-class family, there might be an "Irish or a German girl scrubbing floors," and a black girl doing the laundering; it might be a Welsh boy who mined coal for their furnace, and a young Jewish or Italian woman who worked in a sweatshop to make their clothes. Coontz's study of the family has the apt title, *The Way We Never Were*.[46] Moreover, death and disease broke into countless homes, like atom-smashers destroying tens of thousands of nuclear families. The good old days were also the days of millions of widows, widowers, and orphans.

It is hard—maybe impossible—to get a grip on the inner heart of families, to know what they were really like, what made them tick, how people felt inside these impregnable little kingdoms. Nonetheless, there seemed to be a real shift in the late nineteenth and early twentieth centuries—for middle-class families in particular—from traditional to companionate marriage. As the world turned, gender roles within marriage subtly altered. Companionate marriage rejects the old idea of "separate spheres" for men and women—at least to an extent. Rather, companionate marriage was based on "the importance of emotional ties between wife and husband—their companionship, friendship, romantic love," and (to be sure) a heightened emphasis on a "vigorous and harmonious sex life."[47] Changes in family structure, and the "mature liberalism of the nineteenth century," as William O'Neill has put it, "created a democratic, conjugal family ideal that appealed to the young, women, intellectuals, and the disadvantaged." The effect was, relatively speaking, to bring family members "closer together, to break down the status system based on sex and seniority, and to stress … individual uniqueness, warmth, emotionality, and character."[48]

But things did not always work out the way people expected. Probably men and women read the script of marriage differently. Companionate marriage did not really imply equality of gender roles. The strains and contradictions of companionate marriage often led to dashed hope and disappointments—and therefore to increased demand for divorce.[49]

In the late twentieth century, marriage appeared to evolve further to a kind of post-companionate marriage. In the age of cohabitation and the sexual revolution, the age of "expressive individualism,"[50] there emerged a new style of marriage, which one might call *expressive* marriage. Husband and wife were looking for personal fulfillment; they evaluated their marriage "in terms of self-development, as opposed to the satisfaction they gained through pleasing their spouse and raising their children."[51] Moreover, Americans tend to "to put all their emotional eggs in the basket of coupled love"; to "elevate marital affection and nuclear-family ties above commitments to neighbors, extended kin, civic duty and religion" in a way that previously would have been considered "dangerously antisocial, even pathologically self-absorbed."[52] This was of course a heavy burden for a marriage to bear, both for men and women. The way out, if marriage failed to live up to the ideal, was divorce. If the remedy for a failed companionate marriage was consensual divorce, the remedy for an expressive marriage was individualized—that is, unilateral, no-fault—divorce.

The Legal Consequences of Marriage

Law impacts married life at many points, at the beginning and the end, to be sure, but also, sometimes, during the marriage. The shift in *conceptions* of marriage is mirrored in shifts in family law.[53] The trend of family law thus has gone in the direction of dismantling the patriarchal family, toward making husbands and wives much more equal in the eyes of the law. The family is less of a unit, and more a collection of empowered individuals.

But not at first. Early treatises on marriage spoke of the "law of husband and wife" rather than of "family law" or "domestic relations." The law assumed and dictated certain specific gender roles for husbands and wives. Men had a duty to support wives and children. They were supposed to refrain from physical and mental abuse (past a certain point); and were also supposed to stay sober, faithful, and out of prison. So much for duties. Men also had strong rights—to choose a family religion and domicile, and, in most cases, to control the family finances. Women, on the other hand, were responsible for home and hearth. They had to give birth to, nurture, and educate children; they had to cook and clean, and submit to reasonable sexual demands. Wives also were supposed to be faithful, and the sexual standard for them was much higher than for husbands. Husbands could be forgiven, if they strayed; but never wives.

Men were thus, in every regard, "heads" of the family. They were preferred over wives in custody cases. Married women were in law little more than appendages to their husbands. Indeed, at one time, in criminal law, women were more or less excused from some forms of criminal liability, since they were assumed to be under the influence and domination of their husbands. Mr. Bumble, when told of this presumption in a famous passage in Charles Dickens' *Oliver Twist*, blurted out that if the law thinks so, then the law is "a ass—a idiot."

Men also owned or managed all of the marital property. The classic expression of these norms was set out in Blackstone's *Commentaries*, first published in 1765, summing up the existing (English) law of marriage.[54] The doctrines of "coverture" and the notion of "marital unity" buttressed traditional gender roles. Coverture was a "principle of the common law, by which the husband and wife are regarded as one person, and her legal existence and authority in a degree lost or suspended, during the continuance of the matrimonial union."[55] Husband and wife were, in Blackstone's phrase, "one flesh." But the husband owned the flesh. A married woman, during her marriage, had no legal capacity to enter into contracts, to own, sell, or exchange property, to keep any income she earned, to maintain her own domicile, or to sue and be sued on her own. A married woman took her husband's surname. This was often custom rather than law; but laws that did mandate or presume a name change were universally upheld into the 1970s.[56] The U.S. Supreme Court, in a famous nineteenth-century case (which rejected a woman's claim to the right to practice law in Illinois) commented that "a woman had no legal existence separate from her husband, who was regarded as her head and representative in the social state."[57]

The rules of coverture gave the husband full responsibility, during marriage, for managing property that had belonged to the wife; and he took title to all property acquired during marriage, including any wages she earned. There were, to be sure, ways to get around coverture. A father, for example, could set up a trust for his daughter, and transfer property into the trust before she got married. This put the property beyond the husband's control.[58] But these were complicated and expensive legal devices. They were most useful for wealthy families. For most couples, the husband gained both legal and financial control through marriage.

In short, in the nineteenth century, in general, when two people married, they opted into a status that was clearly defined for them by law. And though the marriage began by agreement, it could not (formally) end that way. (The reality was different, as we will see in chapter 8.) Marriage was a public institution; the state had a heavy stake in supporting it; and its terms were, in general, controlled by law, not individuals.

By the last quarter of the twentieth century, *legal* support for the traditional model of marriage had all but vanished. Two big nails in the coffin were the abolition of coverture (in the nineteenth century) and the legal enthronement of sexual equality (in the 1960s and 1970s). Beginning in the 1840s, states passed Married Women's Property Acts.[59] By 1850, "seventeen states had granted to married women some legal capacity to deal with their property."[60] The rest fell in line later in the century. These laws granted wives the right to hold and acquire property in their own names, and, eventually, to keep their own earnings. Gender relations were changing, but changes in the economy, and the need for a more modern and rational system of land titles and ownership, probably played a role as well. By 1900, women—married or not—were entitled to practice law (though the numbers were small). In the twentieth century, women (married or not) were treated as freestanding individuals: capable of running businesses, serving in the Senate or as Secretary of State, walking a beat, mining coal, piloting planes, and doing everything and anything that a man has historically done, and more. Marriage does not keep women off the job market or out of the hurly-burly of economic life—at least not formally.

Husband and wife, then, were no longer one flesh. Not all the traits of traditional marriage ended quickly, however; some persisted well into the twentieth century. The married woman's right to support from her husband continued. His failure to come through was a crime. Under an Indiana statute, well into the twentieth century, a husband who deserted his wife (unless it was for "adultery or other vicious or immoral conduct") and who left her "without reasonable means of support" could be imprisoned for as much as three years.[61] California law, as of 1907, also made it a crime for a husband not to support his wife, so long as he had "sufficient ability to provide." If he left her in a "destitute condition" or refused or neglected to provide her with food, clothing, shelter, and "medical attention," he too could be punished with a stiff prison sentence.[62] Sometimes, third parties could invoke the husband's duty of support. If a merchant provided a man's wife with "necessaries," on credit, the merchant could sue the husband for the cost. A wife, therefore, could enforce her husband's obligation indirectly, if she could persuade the merchant to let her have "necessaries"—food, clothing, medicine, and even furniture—on credit. The California support statute was not made unisex until 1976, when it was amended to substitute "individual" for "husband," and "spouse" for wife.[63] As late as 1980, a Wisconsin court, in *Sharpe Furniture, Inc. v. Buckstaff*, held a husband primarily liable for the sofa his wife had bought on credit; the wife was only liable if the husband could not pay.[64]

In a 1940 case, *Graham v. Graham*, Margrethe Graham agreed to pay her husband, Sidney, $300 a month, if he would quit his job and follow her in her "travels." This was a kind of reversal of gender roles.[65] After the couple split, Sidney sued for the unpaid amounts—over $25,000, he claimed. A federal court in Michigan turned him down. Two friends, or two strangers, could make such a contract; but not a married couple. Marriage, said the court, was "not merely a private contract between the parties," but a "status in which the state is vitally interested"; some of its rights and duties exist "irrespective of the wishes of the parties."[66] He could not, for money, give up his right to choose the couple's domicile; she could not contract away her right of support. A different rule "would open up an endless field for controversy and bickering ... in marital life." Margrethe was of course free to pay her husband $300 a month, and he was also free to follow her around like a puppy dog of his own free will. But they could not tie their hands through contract.

So, too, did a court in 1976 refuse to enforce a provision of a Louisiana couple's prenuptial agreement to limit sexual intercourse to "about once a week."[67] When the wife sought alimony during their divorce proceeding, the husband tried to raise, as a defense, that she had broken that agreement. (He alleged that she "sought coitus thrice daily"; she complained of not being "permitted" to "touch" her husband more than once a week.) But the court firmly rejected "the view that a premarital understanding can repeal or amend the nature of marital obligations as declared by [state marriage law]." The rights of "conjugal association" could not be modified by contract.[68]

Courts also were reluctant, in the name of marital or family privacy, to delve into the intimate heart of marriage. Lydia McGuire, in *McGuire v. McGuire* (1953), asked a Nebraska court to enforce her husband's duty of support.[69] They had married in 1919, and she did everything a wife of that period was supposed to do. She cooked, cleaned, raised chickens, sold eggs, and obeyed her husband and slept with him. But even though Charles owned 80 acres of land and had other assets, he forced her to live in poverty. In twelve years, he had not taken her to the movies. He denied her such essentials as indoor plumbing, for example; and furniture like her neighbors had. He was a miser, plain and simple. The court sympathized with Lydia. She was legally entitled to support. But the court refused to intervene in this case, in deference to family privacy. Living standards are for the household, and "not for the courts to determine." So long as he maintains a home, and they are living together, then "the purpose of the marriage relation is being carried out," despite his stinginess.[70] Ironically, she might have done better in court if they had separated, or if she had gotten a divorce.

As we will see in chapter 9, courts are rather willing today to enforce premarital, postnuptial, or separation agreements, for marriages that end in death or divorce. But contracts about conduct *during* marriage still give them trouble.[71] Of course, few couples enter into any such contracts, either before or during marriage. Sally Erickson and Renzie Davidson made headlines in 2006 with a weird prenuptial agreement, designed to "fix and determine various financial, emotional, and other" aspects of the marriage.[72] Sally promised to cook breakfast at least four times per week; he promised not to wake her up on the "off days." Sally obligated herself to pay the utility bills, but made clear that "Renzie does not get to complain about how cold Sally keeps the a/c temperature." Sally was supposed to be "mindful of Renzie's comfort level"; after all, "it is more socially acceptable to put on a sweater to warm up than to take off clothes to cool off." Other provisions included a mandatory schedule for backrubs, a $5 fee for nagging, and a penalty of seven days of yardwork for each utterance of "the F word." This agreement was never tested in court; Sally learned that Renzie had secretly divorced her two years before he left her. It is dubious if a court would have enforced this contract. Courts are still very reluctant to scrutinize "private" family matters. This hands-off attitude—coupled with the fact that husbands ordinarily owned or controlled more wealth than wives—created a zone of family privacy, which in practice favored husbands over wives.[73]

The Uniform Premarital Agreement Act of 1983 (UPAA), adopted by twenty-seven states, allows agreements regulating any aspect of marriage, including "personal rights and obligations."[74] But very few cases have tested this particular provision. Courts still fear that enforcing such provisions "would increase conflict between the parties, present severe enforcement problems, and frustrate judicial economy."[75] Such agreements are probably very, very rare in the first place. Passion and hope are what make people marry; only rich couples in second marriages are at all likely to put down financial and other terms on paper. Very few couples take advantage of the (limited) legal right to customize the incidents of an intact marriage.

Yet, despite this reluctance to let couples "customize" their marriages (at least in certain ways), the slow erosion of traditional marriage is leading in this direction. Individual choices about the terms and nature of a relationship gradually replace "standardized formulas imposed by the state."[76] As Hendrik Hartog has put it, today there are "as many types of marriages as there are married couples, each one the product of the distinctive choices and investments of its partners."[77] The development of no-fault divorce, discussed in chapter 8, also reflects a long-term shift to individual choice, as companionate and expressive marriage became increasingly common features of social life.[78]

OTHER INCIDENTS OF MARRIAGE

Besides the core rights and duties of marriage, other rules and doctrines, scattered throughout the legal order, deal with the consequences of marriage. These too, in general, show the impact of changing conceptions of marriage—though often in complex ways.

In the law of evidence, for example, there is the marital privilege—a doctrine that has survived all the ups and downs of family law and the changing roles of wives and husbands. In criminal proceedings, a spouse has the right to refuse to testify against the other spouse. In some states (not all), one spouse can *prevent* the other spouse from testifying. There is also a pillow talk privilege—the privilege of marital confidences. Either spouse can insist on the right to keep secret confidential statements made by the other spouse. And either spouse can refuse to allow the other to reveal such secrets.

These doctrines survive, perhaps, because they do not rest on any particular conception of marriage. They suit traditional marriage and the ideology of "one flesh"; but they also, arguably, fit companionate and expressive marriage as well. Husbands and wives may today stand more on a plane of equality; but since marriage is still seen as vital to society, an institution bloodied but unbowed, there is still reason to try to protect and encourage marriage. Sometimes this means insisting that man and wife still form a single unit, that their personalities and rights are not to be lightly severed.

Developments in tort law seem—but only seem—to be going in the opposite direction. At common law, a woman could not sue her husband in tort. It would undermine marriage, said the courts, to let wives sue their own husbands. In *Thompson v. Thompson* (1910),[79] a woman who lived in the District of Columbia tried to sue her husband for damages for assault and battery. The Supreme Court turned her down. District law had taken away most of the disabilities of married women. Did this mean the old tort rule was gone? The Court felt not. To "open the doors of the courts to accusations of all sorts of one spouse against the other" would hurt both "public welfare and domestic harmony."

One wonders how much "domestic harmony" was promoted in an Iowa case from 1936 in which the husband actually murdered his wife. The administrator of the wife's estate tried to sue him in tort, but the court stuck to the ancient rule and disallowed the claim.[80] Prosser's treatise on torts, published in 1941, reported that courts were willing to let wives sue husbands for property torts, but not for torts of personal injury.[81] That rule was, however, already then under attack. The master trend of the law, as we have seen, has gone to redefine marriage as the coming together of two distinct individuals. They keep their identities before, during, and after the marriage. Naturally, loving spouses are not in the habit of suing each other; but this was never the issue in the actual cases. It was certainly not the issue in *Waite v. Waite* (1993), the Florida case which overturned the doctrine; here the husband had attacked the wife with a machete.[82] And typically, the tort suit had nothing whatsoever to do with marital harmony. The real defendant was the spouse's insurance company. In *Beatie v. Beatie* (1993), the husband had been driving and caused an accident. His wife, a passenger in his car, was paralyzed as a result. She ran up massive medical bills. The husband was the nominal defendant; but of course she was really after his insurance company. The Delaware court overruled prior cases and allowed the lawsuit.[83] Most states have gone this route; but a surprising number still cling to the original doctrine.[84]

MARRIAGE AND CITIZENSHIP

Marriage affects citizenship, too. At one time, a woman who married an American citizen automatically became a citizen herself. She did not have to go through the usual procedures. She was more or less treated as an appendage to her husband. But this attitude had a darker side. Under the Expatriation Act of 1907, if an American woman married a foreigner, she *lost* her citizenship rights, and took on "the nationality of her husband."[85] A man who married a foreign woman, on the other hand, did not lose his birthright. The ideology of the Expatriation Act was obvious. A woman's first allegiance was to her husband. If he was a foreigner, she was no longer a real American; her husband's loyalty to a foreign state became her loyalty, too. Immigration was a major political issue in the early twentieth century. Many old-line Americans fretted about the future of the country, as millions of foreigners poured in from southern and Eastern Europe. Marriages of women to such foreigners seemed doubly undesirable.

The image of a wife under the Expatriation Act was a bit more complex than appears on the surface. An American woman who married a foreigner lost her citizenship. But not necessarily forever. If the marriage ended—through death or divorce—she was allowed to "resume" her citizenship, either by registering with a U.S. consul, or by coming back to the United States. Children of the marriage would be citizens if the mother "resumed" her citizenship, or if they actually lived in the country. This, according to Nancy Cott, reflected an "unarticulated national aim to enable American *mothers* to stay within the polity."[86]

But the nature of marriage, as we have seen, was changing. There were women who challenged the Expatriation Act. Ethel Mackenzie lived in California; she married an Englishman, Gordon Mackenzie, who was also living in California. Women already voted in California, and she applied to the Board of Election Commissioners of San Francisco to be registered. She was turned down, on the grounds that she was no longer a citizen. In 1915, the Supreme Court upheld the Expatriation Act. The "identity of husband and wife is an ancient principle" of law, said the Court; and it was "neither accidental nor arbitrary." The husband's legal and social dominance had real implications for "international policy."[87]

The Expatriation Act did not last very long. The Cable Act of 1922 undid most of the damage.[88] Under the Cable Act, a woman who married a foreigner did not lose her rights unless she formally renounced citizenship. (She did lose her rights, however, if she married an "alien ineligible to citizenship"—that is, essentially, if she married a Chinese man. In this period, of course, the Chinese were excluded from both immigration and naturalization.)[89]

Ethel Mackenzie was not the only woman who fought the rules. Another was Ruth Bryan Owen. Owen was a political animal by birth: her father was William Jennings Bryan. Owen married a British army officer. Later, she ran for Congress from the Fourth Congressional District of Florida, and was elected in 1928. The loser, Republican William C. Lawson, contested the election. The Cable Act had been passed in 1922; and, pursuant to its terms, Ruth Owen got herself naturalized in 1925. But Lawson argued that Ruth Owen was nonetheless not eligible to serve; she had not been a citizen of the United States for seven years running, which was a prerequisite for serving in Congress. The House of Representatives held hearings on the case. Owen, who testified, reminded the House that "no American man has ever been called before a committee of this sort to explain his marriage." She spoke up for the "dignity and individuality of the citizenship of the American woman," and the right of "an American woman" to "exactly the same treatment that is meted out to a man."[90] Whether her eloquence made a difference or not, the House in the end upheld her right to serve, probably for purely political reasons. The Cable Act was later amended to remove the remaining disabilities, and, by 1934, the issue had been resolved.

Immigration law, today, is essentially unisex. But family considerations—and gender roles—play a major role in the structure of that law. Citizens have a right to bring their spouses into the United States; and immigration law is shot through with family preferences. One anomaly in the law lasted into the twenty-first century. If a citizen brought his foreign spouse into the country, and the marriage ended within two years, the spouse could be deported. There were sad cases where an American was (say) killed in an auto accident and the grieving widow received, in the mail, instead of a letter of condolence, an order of deportation. Finally, in October 2009, this policy was reversed.[91]

I Was a Male War Bride

This is the title of a movie with Cary Grant and Ann Sheridan, which graced American screens in 1949. The War Bride Act of 1945 opened the gates to spouses of those who served in the armed forces. In 1946 and 1947, Congress passed two additional Soldier Brides acts. Of course, "war brides" were expected to be women, not men. In the movie, Grant plays a French army officer who marries a female officer in the American armed forces. All sorts of comic adventures follow; and at one point Grant disguises himself in women's clothing. Everything ends up alright, of course; but the humor depends on taking normal gender roles, and standing them on their heads.

In *Lutwak v. United States* (1953),[92] Marcel Lutwak, Munio Knoll, and Regina Treitler were indicted for violating the immigration laws. The offense? "[O]btaining the illegal entry into this country of three aliens as spouses of honorably discharged veterans." The defendants had arranged a real-life version of the Hollywood movie, but without the romance and the humor. Defendants had discovered, at the end of World War II, that other (male) relatives had survived the war in Europe. They were anxious to get these men into the United States, and they hit on the plan of marrying them off to women who had served in the armed forces. The marriages were to be "in form only." The women were paid "a substantial fee" for their services. The defendants were convicted; and the Supreme Court affirmed their convictions. Whether or not the marriages were technically valid under Illinois or French law was irrelevant. The parties engaged in a conspiracy to defraud the federal government by representing themselves as "married," though they "were never to live together as husband and wife." Three justices dissented: there was no fraud because the marriages, though "sordid," were technically valid in their opinion. "Marriages of convenience are not uncommon."

The defense in the *Lutwak* case leaned heavily on the old common-law rule that a spouse can prevent the other spouse from testifying against him or her. Yet the women—the "wives"—were star witnesses for the prosecution. Could the defendants keep them off the stand? No, the government argued; the marriages were fakes; hence the women could testify, despite what their "husbands" wanted. This was, in a way, the very point to be decided: whether these were real wives or not. But the defense failed on this point. The defendants ended up in prison.

The Married Couple as an Economic Unit

In modern law, in the age of companionate and expressive marriages, then, the husband no longer is legally in charge. Yet, tax-wise, husband and wife can elect to be precisely what Blackstone called them: one flesh. They can file a joint income tax return, and pool their income and deductions.

The income tax as we know it is a product of the twentieth century; the Sixteenth Amendment to the Constitution, which authorized Congress to pass such a tax, went into effect in 1913. In the early years, only very rich people paid income tax; and the marginal rates were quite low. This changed, but only gradually. During the 1930s, not even 5 percent of the population had a duty to file at all. The Second World War drastically altered this situation. The government needed money, and lots of it, to fight the war; and the income tax became a fact of life for millions of ordinary people—45 million, in fact, by 1945.

From 1918 on, married people were entitled to file a joint income tax return, pooling and aggregating their incomes. This put them more or less in the same position as couples in community property states. In these states, income of husband and wife was *community* income and taxed accordingly. This was a great advantage if the wife (for example) had no income; she was home, cooking and darning her husband's socks. Half the income was nonetheless hers, and the couple often paid less than if each had filed on their own. Extending this privilege to *all* states became a political necessity.

In many other ways, government and third parties treat married couples as an economic unit. For example, though husbands and wives need not promise to stay together "till death do us part," if they do stay together, and he or she leaves behind money payable to the survivor, that money is exempt from estate tax. In this sense, too, husband and wife are an (economic) community, taxed only when *both* are dead.[93]

Yet the idea that the husband is the breadwinner, and the wife an appendage, dies hard. In June 1932, in the midst of the Depression, Congress enacted a law which, in essence, got rid of married women in government service—if their husbands had federal jobs. In case of any "reduction in personnel," the first to go would be married people whose spouse was "also in the service of the United States or the District of Columbia." In hiring, preference would go to those who did not have a spouse already in government service.[94] Under the Social Security Act, any person married for at least ten years can collect on the basis of the other spouse's contribution.[95] This holds, even if the collecting spouse never engaged in paid labor or earned enough credits to get payment for herself. This is, of course, unisex in form, but not in result.

ERISA, a complicated federal law regulating private pensions, makes spouses the primary beneficiaries of pension rights.[96] The federal Family and Medical Leave Act allows spouses to take unpaid leave from work to care for one another during periods of serious illness.[97] States allow surviving spouses to sue for wrongful death.[98] Employers who provide insurance typically make it available to the spouses of employees, though often not to unmarried partners. There are also non-economic benefits that derive automatically from marriage—hospital visitation and rights to make medical decisions, to name just two. So, despite all the changes in the way the law treats married couples, they still stand apart from the unmarried in many ways, particularly economic ways; in some ways, they are still treated as a unit; and in other ways, decidedly not.

SEX DISCRIMINATION

Slightly more than a century after the Fourteenth Amendment was adopted, the Supreme Court abruptly decided the phrase "equal protection of the laws" meant that sex discrimination was unconstitutional. After 1971, the Court subjected laws or government actions that drew a gender line to "heightened scrutiny," which meant, in practice, that they were almost always invalid. The new line of cases dramatically changed the law of gender relations.[99]

Family law was deeply affected by this new line of cases, and by new civil rights laws which banned sex discrimination at work and in education.[100] Piece by piece, courts struck down rules that dictated different treatment of husbands and wives.[101] In *Orr v. Orr* (1979), the Supreme Court set aside an Alabama law that limited alimony to wives.[102] Many courts reinterpreted the doctrine of "necessaries" to mean that each spouse—not just the husband—was liable for such things as food and medical care, given on credit to the other.[103]

What of rules that sometimes required women to take their husband's name?[104] Rose Palermo, a lawyer in Nashville, married Denty Cheatham, also a Nashville lawyer, in 1973. Tennessee did not technically require women to take their husband's name, but its voter registration law purged women from the rolls unless they re-registered under their married names within ninety days. Rose refused to register as "Rose Cheatham" (perhaps she thought "Cheat 'em" was not a good name for a lawyer). She challenged the law, arguing that she should not be forced in this indirect way to change her name. The court agreed; a woman, when she marries, can choose to keep her own name, or adopt her husband's. "The choice is hers."[105]

Here, as elsewhere, however, older social norms about marriage and gender are deeply entrenched. As many as 90 percent of American women still take their husband's names when they marry, even though they could not constitutionally be required to do so by law.[106] Men still participate more in the labor force, and provide most of the family income—even though the (formal) duty of support is now mutual (see chapter 9). Women, in turn, still do most of the work around the house—cleaning, cooking, and caring for children. Many more women than men take a leave from work when a baby is born. Society is not quite ready to accept paternity leaves as easily as maternity leaves; *he* wasn't pregnant, *he* didn't give birth; he is incapable of breast-feeding, and child care is really her role, especially with newborn babies. Change in gender roles inside the family is very real—but has a long way to go.

SEX, MARRIAGE, AND VIOLENCE

The legal model of traditional marriage rested on four pillars: husband and wife as a unit, fixed gender roles, standard obligations set by the state, and marital privacy. The last has had the most staying power. Concern for marital privacy is one of the reasons courts give for refusing to support certain agreements between husband and wife. The leading case on the constitutional right of privacy (discussed at greater length in chapter 5), *Griswold v. Connecticut* (1965), explicitly referred to the "sacred precincts" of the bedroom and the "zone of privacy" that surrounded a married couple in their sexual life.[107]

Domestic Violence

A lot can go wrong, though, in these "sacred precincts"; and they can be violent places. Police and courts, it is said, hate to intervene in fights between husbands and wives, even when there is a safety issue. But legislatures and courts have begun to try to override this reluctance. Reva Siegel has argued that, before modern laws were adopted in the 1970s and 1980s, considerations of marital privacy shielded men from punishment for beating their wives. This was certainly true to a point, but it is

71

not clear how far the shield extended. Carolyn Ramsey, studying Denver and New York City in the period 1880 to 1920, found that men who killed their partners received very harsh sentences.[108] Women who killed abusers were treated much more leniently. It may be that *extreme* violence—violence that killed—was taken seriously; ordinary beatings much less so.

Wife-beating is epidemic in many societies. Men in these societies claim the right to "correct" their wives, if they fail to measure up to standards (and the husband is the sole judge of that). In Western countries, at least by the beginning of the twentieth century, no such norm was legally recognized. The language of the penal code, of course, did not end domestic violence. Wives or the neighbors often called the police when a drunken brute was beating his wife. (Once in a while, it was the wife who turned violent.) The police apparently hated these cases. They usually avoided making an arrest. A study of a county in Michigan, in the 1970s, found that police followed a "stitch rule." They arrested the husband only if he injured the wife badly enough to require a certain number of stitches. More commonly, the officer would come, give somebody a lecture or a walk around the block, suggest that he (and she) calm down and try to patch things up, and leave without further action. Or the family might be referred to some social service agency.[109]

In the late twentieth century, women's groups attacked this complacency. They demanded more protection against husbands and lovers who punched, kicked, and battered women. Women from the 1930s on seemed to become less tolerant of physical abuse. Before then, when women complained to authorities, it was mostly about non-support, according to Linda Gordon's research; after 1930, the focus was on wife-beating. When women were more dependent, she thinks, their foremost need was food and clothing and support, for themselves and the children. Women in the workplace had less of a sense of entitlement to support, but more of an insistence on "physical integrity."[110]

Whatever the reasons, by the 1970s, physical abuse had become recognized as a serious issue. Husbands or ex-husbands accounted for a quarter of all cases of violence against women, according to a victimization study covering 1972, 1973, and 1974. For women who were separated, the risk of assault by a husband or ex-husband was "as great as the risk of assault by all other persons."[111] In response to pressure from women's groups, many states enacted mandatory arrest laws. The police were *required* to make an arrest when they confronted a violent home situation. Prosecutors, too, were no longer quite so likely to drop charges. In 1976, Pennsylvania enacted a Protection from Abuse act.[112] Every state now has a law which gives abused wives or partners the right to get a protective order. These orders warn the abuser to stay away, on pain of punishment. Not all of these men, of course, obey.

Adultery

A marriage, whatever else it might be, is ordinarily a sexual union. At one time—but no longer—only married people were supposed to have sex. Adultery, as we will see in chapter 8, was almost uniformly allowed as grounds for divorce, in the days before no-fault.[113] It was also, quite commonly, a crime.[114] Not that this particular crime was often punished. Police arrest records show few signs that the police took much interest, or that many people complained to the police about adultery. Yet, it was hardly a rare event. According to the famous Kinsey report (1953), about a quarter of all married women "had had extra-marital coitus by age forty."[115] Men were even worse offenders; Kinsey estimated that about half of all married men had "intercourse with women other than their wives," at some point during the marriage.[116] Kinsey's statistics have been criticized, and it is likely that the numbers are at least somewhat off-base. But the key point remains: adultery was and is a fairly common occurrence.

In the last half of the twentieth century, most states decriminalized adultery. Those that kept laws against it on the books rarely used them. In one sense, however, law and society once took adultery quite seriously. A man who killed his wife's lover (or even his adulterous wife) was likely to have the sympathy of much of the (male) public. Sometimes the penal code either defined this crime as something short of first-degree murder, or actually excused it. If the code did not do the job, then the jury could step in. In 1918, Charles Hupp of Cleveland shot Charles Joyce. This was a "love triangle" situation. Hupp shot Joyce in a "red rage," ostensibly to preserve the sanctity of his home. The jury acquitted him.[117]

The laws themselves that excuse these murderous husbands have faded into oblivion; the facts of such cases might, however, still influence jury behavior. On the other side, women who kill abusive husbands or lovers are sometimes treated with indulgence. This, as we pointed out, may not be a new situation; but there are doctrinal and procedural innovations. Women who kill abusive partners can claim a kind of self-defense—even if (for example) the man was fast asleep when she killed him. Normally, "self-defense" requires imminent danger. But courts have been more and more receptive to psychological testimony about the "battered women's syndrome." This testimony lets a jury acquit a woman, or mitigate her offense, if she has acted against a man who was severely abusive.[118]

Marital Rape

It was—and still is—a common belief that men are always hungry for sex, and that nice women put up with sex from time to time, but could certainly live without it. Marriage gave a man the right to satisfy his sexual hunger. He was, in fact, encouraged to do so. The future of the human race depended on his sexual appetite. If a man refused to have sex, or was unable to perform, then his wife had solid grounds for annulment or divorce, as we will see in a later chapter. And if she refused to have sex, or couldn't, he too had solid grounds for divorce or annulment.

A wife was supposed to go along with her man, and gratify his sexual appetite. This notion lay behind the notorious doctrine that a man could not be guilty of raping his own wife.[119] This ancient doctrine was an obvious target for the feminist movement of the late twentieth century. The courts, to a degree, had nibbled away at the doctrine. In a 1922 New York case, *People v. Meli*, one Alfred Boehler, an eighteen-year-old, had raped Josie Meli. Her husband, John, was arrested; John, it was said, had "aided and abetted" the rape, and was "actually present and personally assisted in overcoming her resistance." His defense was the marital rape doctrine; but the court allowed his conviction to stand.[120] In a New Jersey case from 1981, the defendant, Albert Smith, "broke into the apartment of his estranged wife ... and repeatedly beat and raped her." They were still legally married. His conviction for rape was upheld.[121]

Still, as late as the 1980s, the marital rape exemption survived, in one form or other, in most of the states. Only a few of them—Oregon and Nebraska, for example—had done away with it completely; others had, however, modified the doctrine by statute. One of the more conservative states was New York. The rape statute defined rape as sexual intercourse "with a female ... by forcible compulsion"; and defined "female" for purposes of the statute as "any female person who is not married to the actor." In *People v. Liberta* (1984),[122] the Court of Appeals of New York finally struck down the marital exemption for rape.

The facts of the case are significant. Mario Liberta had a strong violent streak; his wife in 1980 got a "temporary order of protection" against him. Later, he forced his wife to have sex with him (in front of their two-and-a-half-year-old son). He was convicted of rape. As one might imagine, marital rape cases almost never came up in happy marriages; they arose out of ruined marriages, and separated couples, with bitterness on all sides. In many states, including New York, Liberta *could* have been found guilty, despite the marital rape doctrine, because he and his wife were living apart. But the court was anxious to go further, and get rid of the doctrine altogether.

The tide was running in this direction. By the end of the century, most states had modified the marital exemption for rape; and some had eliminated it entirely.[123] In California, the definition of rape is the same for spouses and non-spouses; and the law specifically says that a "marital relationship" is not "sufficient to constitute consent."[124] But the marital rape statute still treats marital rape a bit differently from other rapes. No prosecution is allowed, unless the victim reported the rape to "medical personnel, a member of the clergy, an attorney, a shelter representative, a counselor, a judicial officer, a rape crisis agency, a prosecuting agency, a law enforcement officer, or a firefighter," within one year of the commission of the offense.[125]

How common is marital rape? This depends, in part, on how "rape" is defined; and this too has been changing dramatically, under the pressure of women's groups and others. There are no decent records of marital rape. There has been one small study of *prosecution* for marital rape. A National Clearinghouse on Marital and Date Rape, using data from newspaper clipping services and from rape and counseling centers, found 210 cases between 1978 and 1985 in which a report was filed, and in which the police arrested the husband. Of these, 118 led to actual prosecutions; and 104 of these prosecutions ended in conviction—a very high rate. But, as Diana Russell has said, thousands of women "are raped by their husbands in … 'ordinary' ways"; but unless he used "tire irons, dogs, strangulation, or death threats," the women simply do not report their troubles to the police.[126]

Since marital rape cases almost always involve broken and miserable marriages, the usual arguments—about blackmail, or marital privacy, or undermining the institution of marriage—have very little force. Still, the new order got off to a bad start: the trial in 1978 of John Rideout, a twenty-one-year-old student in Oregon, accused of raping his wife, Greta. The case made headlines. Testimony was sensational (and sharply controverted). Did the Rideouts really chase each other "in and out of the bedroom before having sexual intercourse"? Did she start the trouble by kneeing him in the groin; or did he beat her viciously, without provocation, and force her to have sex? Faced with a barrage of conflicting testimony, the jury acquitted the defendant.[127]

Even more sensational was the sordid 1993 affair of the Bobbitts—John Wayne Bobbitt and his wife, Lorena—both in their twenties. He beat and raped her, she said. Lorena Bobbitt did not simply call the police; she took more drastic action, slicing off her husband's penis while he slept. (Surgeons reattached it.) Both of the Bobbitts had to stand trial; both were accused of violent acts.[128] The media had a field day. The Bobbitts and the Rideouts, subjects of jokes, headlines, and outraged denunciations, are surely not typical. More typical was William Rider, one of the first men to be convicted of raping his wife in Florida. Rider, forty-one years old, was a convicted murderer; on parole, he married Marion; later (she said) he raped her. This was in 1984, by which time there had been about fifty convictions for the crime, in twenty-two states.[129]

It is hard to know whether marital rape is rare or common, just as it is hard to know whether domestic violence is rare or common; and if common, *how* common. What is clear is this: inside the castle, millions of men mistreat and oppress their wives and lovers; and in some unknown number of these marriages, mistreatment takes violent or at least coercive forms. (A smaller number of women mistreat and abuse their husbands.) Has domestic violence increased, or decreased, since the nineteenth century? There is no way of knowing.

Marital violence may be, in a perverse sort of way, another symptom of modern marriage—companionate or expressive marriage. These are marriages in which men and women are supposed to be equal, supposed to be partners, supposed to fulfill each other's lives and realize each other's dreams. A thread that runs through all of (late) twentieth-century family law is the tendency to see marriage as a union of individuals, individuals who stubbornly retain their individuality. The woman is no longer drowning in the sea of masculine privilege; she can be (for example) a citizen in her own right. And marriage is socially, too, more intense, and more individual. Ironically, this form of marriage leads to an epidemic of divorce; it may, in some cases, spawn violence as well. But for families, as for society in general, there is no turning back.

Common-Law Marriage

T HE UNITED STATES entered the twentieth century with at least the remnants of a peculiar doctrine that had flourished in the prior century: the common-law marriage.[1] In this chapter, we describe the adventures—and the decline and fall—of the doctrine of common-law marriage in the twentieth century.

A common-law marriage was an informal, but perfectly legal, marriage. If a man and woman agreed with each other to be husband and wife, then, from that moment on, they *were* husband and wife, without a marriage license, a judge or clergyman, witnesses, or anything else. A series of court decisions, in the first half of the nineteenth century, established the doctrine in most of the states. The facts of the reported cases usually followed a pattern. In essence, two people had been living together in the community and acting as if they were, in fact, husband and wife. They shared a house and a life. Everybody in the community *assumed* they were married. The law would then make the same assumption—that, at some point, they had spoken the magic words "we are married now" to each other. If so, then they were legally married; and their relationship was not sinful, but pure. Of course, in the usual case, there was not a shred of evidence that they had, in fact, said the magic words. Most likely they had not.

What lay behind this rather odd doctrine? The reported cases give us the answer. In all of them, there was some sort of dispute— over land or money. A woman claims she is a widow, and has a widow's rights; but other family members deny this, and claim the property for themselves. In this period, record keeping was poor. Why not adopt a rule that protected a woman who everybody *thought* was married. It kept the children from the stigma of bastardy, and kept land and money in the family.

Judges, too, were certainly aware that the issue was land and money. But not only land and money. Religious and moral codes regulate sexual behavior; in this period, in theory at least, sex outside of marriage was a terrible sin. Morality was never far beneath the surface of the cases. A common-law marriage is a real marriage, a holy relationship, as valid and binding as if ten bishops had presided over a formal ceremony. But if there is no common-law marriage, then the man and the woman are sinners, living together in a state of deepest, darkest sin. In many of the reported cases, the so-called marriage probably started out as mere cohabitation—a "meretricious" relationship, as the courts put it ("meretricious" is legalese for illicit). Since some "meretricious" relationships grow "insensibly into permanent unions," as one commentator solemnly pointed out, it would be "sound public policy to accept the final compliance" and ignore the "initial disregard of law."[2]

Legal sources, over and over again, described marriage as a "civil contract." Not a sacrament, not something which the state in its infinite wisdom and mercy chooses to confer, but an agreement, a set of mutual promises. And the common-law marriage was just that: a civil contract. It was, to be sure, a most peculiar contract. If two people enter into an ordinary civil contract— to buy or sell a horse, for example—they can call it off if they choose. A common-law marriage, however, could not be called off in this way. There is not—and never was—such a thing as a common-law divorce.[3] Still, the notion of a "contract" did mean something here. It represented, among other things, a real ideology. Marriage was the choice, the decision of two people. The state was an outsider. So was the church. The basis of marriage was love, or at least commitment. Not family, not property, not the state, but personal choice.

The factual assumption behind the common-law marriage was, as we said, probably a fantasy. The idea that at some point these two people looked at each other, sighed, and made a solemn promise, was no doubt in most cases unreal. And there was rarely evidence of any such thing. The proof almost always rested on external circumstances—on behavior. This was, as we said, a kind of legal fiction. It was not a fiction, of course, to assume that marriage was a matter of free choice, of will, an actual agreement between a man and a woman, or that it reflected, ideally, a strong attraction and romantic love. But an actual set of promises? No matter: the doctrine papered over this problem. If the community felt that you were married, if the couple behaved the way married people behaved, that was enough. Bourgeois behavior, then, cast a kind of warm, moral glow over the relationship. If the behavior looked like a conventional marriage, if it acted like a conventional marriage, if it felt like a conventional marriage, then legally it *was* a marriage. Perhaps ironically, our understanding of the expectations for marriage comes in part from common-law marriage cases in which judges sometimes went on and on about how *real* husbands and wives behaved.[4]

The doctrine was useful in many ways. It was useful, for example, as we said, when record keeping was very poor and clergy were in short supply. It also helped in the occasional case when a ceremonial marriage failed for some reason or other (as in one case where the "clergyman" who performed the ceremony was an imposter).[5] But, most importantly, it was a way to clean up the mess made by illicit sex. The marriage was real, and valid, rather than something else, some halfway status, something between "criminal intimacy" and full marriage. In a way, this undergirded the traditional norm: sex was legitimate only in marriage. Of course, common-law marriage bent the definition of "marriage" somewhat out of shape, in fact if not in theory; apparently this was worth the price. But as law and society changed, institutionally and in terms of social norms, the common-law marriage was bound to be affected.

Most states, by the middle of the nineteenth century, had come to accept the idea of the common-law marriage. After that, the doctrine had its ups and downs. Mostly downs. In 1900, about half the states recognized the common-law marriage as valid. By the end of the twentieth century, only ten or so did.[6] One by one, the states got rid of the doctrine. California abolished it in 1895. Early in the twentieth century (1905), Illinois did the same; in each decade more states joined the parade. Minnesota acted in 1941. Florida's move came in 1967, Ohio's in 1991, Idaho and Pennsylvania not until 1995.[7] In all of these states, a formal, ceremonial marriage is now required: to marry, the couple needs a license, and a clergyman or judge must perform the ceremony.

While it lasted, the common-law marriage produced its share of sensational trials. Charlotte Fixel succeeded in her 1932 claim to be the common-law widow of Abraham Erlanger, entitled to half of his vast estate. They had lived together for ten years before his death in New York, which abolished common-law marriage the following year. The trial lasted three months—a record—and produced a 500-page opinion by the probate judge. The nail in the coffin for Erlanger's next of kin, who hotly contested Fixel's claim, was an incident recounted by a witness who ran into Fixel and Erlanger on the Atlantic City boardwalk. Fixel showed off a second new ring, and Erlanger exclaimed, "Yes, and now we are doubly married."[8] Erlanger also introduced Fixel to acquaintances as "my wife," and referred to her as "Mrs. Erlanger." The ring, the judge felt, was a clear symbol of marriage; the judge was also swayed by "a decade of mutual fidelity unstained by even a suggestion of indifference or inconsistency; a blending of two lives, which both, in a seclusion of the domestic circle, and in all the other external and public aspects, were such as are lived by the average husband and wife faithfully devoted to each other." The judge also made clear his desire to save their reputations. He drew support from the presumptions "in favor of innocence as against the commission of crime and immorality," and "as against concubinage, of honor as against dishonor, of decency as against indecency"—presumptions he claimed were "recognized throughout the whole domain of common-law marriage law." Although Fixel won, publicity about this case was a factor that helped lead to the abolition of common-law marriage in New York.

In the ten jurisdictions that continue to permit common-law marriage today, the traditional requirements basically hold.[9] In Texas, for example, an "informal marriage," as it is called there, can arise from a signed declaration of marriage, or evidence of an agreement to marry, if the couple acts as if married and represents themselves as married to other people.[10] A handful of states have statutes that preserve common-law marriage, but impose a minimum age of eighteen.[11] Several states simply have statutes which make clear that the requirements for ceremonial marriage do not preclude the establishment of common-law marriages, without specifying any special rituals or magic words necessary to create one.[12] Most states, too, will give effect to a common-law marriage that was validly celebrated elsewhere, under the marriage recognition rules we discussed in the previous chapter.[13] The South Dakota Supreme Court—South Dakota has no common-law marriage—recently held it would recognize such a marriage.[14]

Few people today claim common-law marital status. Cases successfully proving such a marriage are fewer still. A high-profile trial involving an alleged common-law marriage between ballet dancer Sandra Jennings and actor William Hurt sparked a brief flurry of attention in 1989.[15] Hurt and Jennings met doing summer theater in upstate New York in 1981. Eighteen months later, he was famous and they had become parents to a son, Alexander. The question for the court in New York was whether the couple had established a common-law marriage in South Carolina during the ten weeks they lived there while Hurt filmed the Oscar-nominated movie *The Big Chill* (1983). New York would give effect to the marriage if it met the requirements of South Carolina law. Jennings already had an agreement from Hurt to pay $65,000 a year in child support, but she wanted a share of his earnings for herself. The evidence she mustered, however, fell short of the standard for proving common-law marriage. While he may well have told her they had a "spiritual marriage in the eyes of God" and that they "were more married than married people," the judge found insufficient evidence that, under South Carolina law, they had a "present intention and agreement" to *be* married. The star-studded movie cast testified that they knew Jennings and Hurt were not married—the kiss of death for a cause of action that turns on how a couple holds itself out to the public.[16] It was more than enough to counterbalance testimony about an isolated incident in which he accepted a phone call for his "wife." The case ended with a whimper: Jennings was left to rely on her child support agreement. Her lawyer told the *New York Times* that the judge in the case ruled against Jennings because she, the judge, was "in love with Bill Hurt." He claimed that the judge's first words in the trial had been that *The Big Chill* was her "favorite movie" and Hurt was her "favorite actor."[17]

Aside from the occasional celebrity who films and fornicates in South Carolina, how important is common-law marriage in the few states in which it survives? As a social phenomenon, it probably has little or no importance. Do people even know it exists? That is hard to say. Probably most people who live together know nothing about the doctrine, and have no idea whether their state does or does not recognize it. (Much of the 2009–10 season of the popular television show, *Grey's Anatomy*, revolved around its leading couple getting married "by post-it note"; but

the show takes place in Washington, a state that does not recognize common-law marriage.) A marriage, to most people, is
a license, a ceremony; and usually, too, flowers, a party, a white
dress and a veil, and lots of dancing and drink. Or a procedure,
more or less dignified, in front of a local judge or justice of the
peace; at home, or in one of the flossier "marriage chapels" of
Las Vegas. On the other hand, apparently quite a few people
think a man and a woman who live together for seven years
have become common-law spouses. A law professor took an "informal survey" of entering law students, in 1997 at UCLA, and
found that this myth was very much alive in California.[18] In fact,
common-law marriage had been gone in California for over a
century. (An English survey found that more than half of respondents believed common-law marriage was alive and well there
in the twenty-first century, but it was abolished in 1753.)[19] And
seven years has no particular meaning in *any* state, even those
that recognize common-law marriage. The number seven seems
to have some sort of magical significance in people's minds. Legally it is totally meaningless—a common-law marriage can be
established in a matter of minutes.

More typically, people use the term "common-law marriage,"
or "common-law wife," simply to mean two people living together who are not actually married. A woman wrote in to the advice columnist, Abigail Van Buren, in 1972, describing herself as
an "attractive, intelligent, affectionate woman of twenty-three."
She wanted to marry and settle down, but her twenty-six-year-
old boyfriend was not ready. He said (according to her) that "all
the males in his family (his father included) take common-law
wives. They don't marry! Nobody outside the family knows this,
so there is no scandal." She asks: what she should do? Abby basically tells her to insist on marriage. Clearly, the "common-law
marriages" the woman referred to were simply cohabitation. In
many newspaper stories, the phrase is used in this way.[20]

In a sense, a common-law marriage, where it is still recognized,
only comes into being when somebody challenges it. Otherwise,
all we have is a couple living together, acting as if they are married, and considered married by their neighbors. If nobody questions the arrangements they make as to their property, we will
never know if they were married or not. Their "marriage" is a
tree falling in a forest, with nobody around to hear the sound.

What social factors led to the decline of the common-law marriage? In a way, the trend away from common-law marriage seems to contradict a powerful line of development in family law. It seems to deny the whole notion of marriage as a civil contract, which depends upon nothing but the wishes and desires of a man and a woman. The common-law marriage seems to fit well with modernity, with its stress on the individual and its downgrading of status and ritual. In the law of divorce, for example, the state has less and less control; the decision to get a divorce is solely up to the married partners. Why then is the state still involved in marriage? Why is the common-law marriage in steep decline?

To begin with, the modern world is a bureaucratic world. It is a world of records and documents. The common-law marriage is anomalous. It leaves no record behind. It shows up nowhere in the great registries of the state. In the early nineteenth century, in a period of very bad record keeping, the common-law marriage helped to solve some puzzles about ownership of property. By 1900, this was no longer useful. The states gathered statistics routinely. The common-law marriage had become a nuisance. It hindered rather than helped the orderly disposition of wealth and was a fertile source of legal uncertainty. During the First World War, more than a hundred thousand soldiers in the American army claimed common-law wives and children. This was a gigantic headache for the Bureau of War Risk Insurance. One official of the United States Veterans Bureau stated that the Bureau, in effect, was "the largest court of domestic relations in the world."[21] The official, Otto E. Koegel—author of a treatise on the subject of common-law marriage—was skeptical about these supposed marriages; most, he said, were nothing but couples living in sin. As Mary Richmond and Fred Hall put it, in 1929, common-law marriage (even though many states still recognized it) had become an "anachronism." It lacked any "permanent, official record"; it was "nebulous ... confused and undocumented." It made trouble in inheritance situations; and for claims to pensions and other benefits, under Workers Compensation laws, or the Social Security Act. Social Security left to state law the question of who was, and who was not, a widow entitled to benefits. The doctrine was also a nuisance in divorce proceedings, in prosecutions for bigamy, and in many other situations.[22]

There was a second strong reason why common-law marriage fell into disrepute. The state could not get a grip on who married, and who did not. And the state, more and more, desperately wanted to control this subject. Marriage, after all, was the gateway to reproduction. Married people had children and unmarried people (generally) did not. At least they were not supposed to. From the late nineteenth century on, states worried and worried about the issue: who was fit to be married and, more importantly, who was not. Or, rather, who was fit to have babies; and who was not.

Why this sudden concern? It ties in with a number of other developments of the period. In the late nineteenth century, for example, many states passed stringent abortion laws. Essentially, abortion was criminalized.[23] One reason for this eruption of harsh legislation was the widespread belief that the country faced a demographic crisis. Good middle-class Americans, Americans of fine old stock, solid and respectable married women, were not doing their duty as wives and mothers. Most of the babies were coming, instead, from immigrants. These were from southern and Eastern Europe. They were immigrants of "less desirable" stock, but incredibly fertile. Even worse was the danger of babies born to people thought truly inferior, the dregs of society—paupers, sick people, criminals, and the feeble-minded. (We discussed the effects of these fears on marriage law in chapter 1.) The nation might lose its soul, its energy, its moral fiber. There were people who feared that the Anglo middle class seemed to be committing "race suicide," as Theodore Roosevelt put it in 1903.[24]

Hence, marriage and reproduction became important issues of state policies. The state had a right and a duty to regulate how people got married. Common-law marriage obviously would not do. It was an open invitation to just about anybody to marry—even the genetically unfit. This was the age of eugenic theory, and of scientific racism. It was widely believed that pathology was inherited; that tendencies to crime, vice, and prostitution were handed down from generation to generation; bad people reproduced in kind. This was the subject of a big literature, beginning in the 1870s when Richard Dugdale published his research about the family he called "The Jukes." Dugdale argued that a whole line of misfits and criminals could be traced to a single wretched man, an illegitimate child of the first Mr.

Jukes. Dugdale felt that these misfits and criminals multiplied like "rats in their alleys" and threatened "to overwhelm the well-bred classes of society."[25]

Later studies painted the same dismal mural. In 1912, Henry Herbert Goddard, Director of Research at a New Jersey institution for "feeble-minded" people, made what he considered a similar discovery. He called his miserable family the Kallikaks. The Kallikaks descended from the bastard child of a soldier, at the time of the Revolutionary War. The mother was a feeble-minded woman. They produced a long line of prostitutes, alcoholics, criminals, and other degenerates.[26]

Goddard recommended sterilization for people of this type and, in fact, in the heyday of the eugenics movement, states did begin to pass sterilization laws. Indiana was the first of these, in 1907.[27] California followed in 1909. Under the California law, an inmate of the state prison could be sterilized if his behavior and record showed that he was a "moral and sexual pervert." California led the way in sheer numbers of sterilization.[28] Sterilization never really made a dent in the number of "misfits" who might have reproduced; and certainly could not accomplish the purposes behind it; nonetheless, by 1921, more than two thousand people had been sterilized.[29] Under these conditions, getting rid of common-law marriage might close one loophole in the fabric of demographic control.

Another factor helped kill common-law marriage. The validity of these marriages came up in cases involving property rights and inheritance. As we saw, there was a feeling that many of these marriages were fraudulent; that many "wives" were mistresses trying to get money out of an estate. In 1935, a woman named Geraldine Ott claimed she was the widow of Bertrand Taylor. She claimed she and Taylor had entered into a common-law marriage when she was twenty-seven years old and Taylor was sixty-five. The "marriage" took place at her home in Pittsburg, Kansas, in 1928. According to Geraldine, Taylor wanted the marriage to be kept secret. He wanted to "avoid publicity." He thought that the great "disparity in age between him and Geraldine" could cause "considerable notoriety." His lawyers, she said, had explained to him that a common-law marriage was perfectly valid. Taylor asked her if she would consent to be his wife; and she said yes. Seven years later he died. He left a big estate, more than a million dollars. In his will, he bequeathed $10,000 to his "friend," Geraldine Ott. She, of course, insisted on more—on the share a widow would receive.[30]

The trial took place in New York, where Taylor had one of his homes. Evidence was produced for both sides. Lawyers for the estate introduced "several applications for automobile driver's licenses," in which Geraldine claimed she was unmarried.[31] Geraldine, however, had witnesses, including two doormen and a jewelry salesman, who testified she was sometimes referred to as Mrs. Taylor. A Los Angeles doctor told of going to dinner with the couple. When Miss Ott was late, Taylor said, "These are some of the penalties of being married."[32] A surgeon, Dr. H. H. Blodgett, had treated Geraldine for appendicitis. In his deposition, he said that "Mr. Taylor remained in the room while he examined Miss Ott for the operation." Taylor also paid the bill.[33] The obvious implication is that the couple were married. Why else would a doctor let the man stay in the room, while he examined a woman who undressed? The court, however, ruled against Geraldine; Geraldine was, naturally, disappointed; not only because of the money (she said), but because of "the position this puts me in."[34] Her disappointment was no doubt real; yet it was precisely cases of this kind that helped kill common-law marriage: a rich, dead man; and a live young woman.[35] The fate of common-law marriage, then, was not unlike the fate of breach of promise, alienation of affections, and criminal conversation, which we will discuss in the next chapter.

In Illinois, one heard yet another critique of common-law marriage. An article in the *Chicago Tribune*, in 1904, pointed out, in horror, that the doctrine allowed boys age seventeen and girls age fourteen "to enter upon a common-law marriage without the knowledge or consent of father, mother, or friends," an "evil and dangerous" system. Also, the article alleged, every year "dozens of girls from 14 to 17 years old, mere children," are given away "to boys and men of various ages by ignorant parents, and in some cases by subsidized guardians," sometimes just to be "rid of an unprofitable dependant." Foreigners were particularly responsible for these noxious practices. The state was urged to get rid of this abuse.[36] Indeed, Illinois' legislature abolished common-law marriage in 1909.[37]

In the course of the century, then, common-law marriage died in the majority of the states.[38] Most states did not feel an occasional just result was worth the cost of keeping common-law marriage alive. They have, instead, found other ways to reach this "sound public policy" result. Courts increasingly recognize rights between cohabitants, as we discuss in chapter 6, but courts have also drawn on equitable powers to provide remedies when justice requires. These doctrines, called variously de facto marriage, putative marriage, or good-faith marriage, permit courts to overlook the technical flaws in a marriage and focus instead on the marriage-like relationship in front of them. In a New Jersey case, for example, Ruth and Richard Parkinson were devout Roman Catholics.[39] In 1927, a Roman Catholic priest performed the marriage. They had two children. In 1939, Ruth divorced her husband, the same year that New Jersey abolished common-law marriage.[40] In 1950, Ruth and Richard decided to live together again. They visited the local priest, told him of the divorce, and asked him to remarry them. But the priest explained that they "were already married in the eyes of God." Ruth and Richard apparently accepted this view, assumed they were married, and kept on living together, without further ceremony. (The appellate court described Ruth, the holder of a "sixth-grade parochial school education," as "somewhat unsophisticated" in understanding what had happened.) Later, when Richard died in an accident, Ruth claimed dependency benefits under Workers' Compensation. She lost the case at the administrative level, on the grounds that whatever their status in the eyes of God, in the eyes of the state of New Jersey, they were not married. The Appeals Court disagreed. Ruth was a "de facto" or "putative" wife. She and Richard thought they were married; they behaved in good faith as if they were married; and the state of New Jersey would treat them accordingly.

CONCLUSION

The common-law marriage, even in states that still have it, is not popular; and is under constant pressure. It is not surprising that old doctrines, in the light of modern circumstances, are falling like tenpins. Yet, curiously enough, there is constant talk in the literature about the revival of the common-law marriage.[41] Not literally, to be sure. But functionally, perhaps. The social fact underlying this idea is the rise of cohabitation. Thousands of couples live together in "committed intimate relationships," without bothering to get married. The so-called sexual revolution is largely to blame. A massive social phenomenon must necessarily leave its mark on the legal system. Does the death of common-law marriage mean that unmarried partners in committed relationships have no rights? Courts find this idea uncomfortable. In a later chapter, we take up cohabitation and its legal consequences: consequences which hearken back to the days of common-law marriage, the rights it protected, and the problems that bedeviled it.

The End of Heart Balm

O NE STRIKING ASPECT of family law in the twentieth century was the decline and fall of a group of closely related causes of action: breach of promise of marriage, alienation of affections, and criminal conversation. One might add here, too, civil and criminal actions for "seduction."

The story is tangled and complex; no one factor explains why these causes of action lost ground. But they are obviously connected with the social meaning of marriage, and very notably, with one striking twentieth-century development: the sexual revolution—specifically, the end of the idea that only married people were entitled, legitimately, to have sexual intercourse. These causes of action lived in the shadow of traditional marriage, and depended for their validity on traditional marriage. As it declined, they too receded into history, although not entirely.

BREACH OF PROMISE TO MARRY

The most significant of the group was the action for breach of promise to marry. An engagement, in the eyes of the law, was a kind of contract. A person who broke this contract by calling off the wedding could be sued for breach of promise. In theory, this could be either the man or the woman. In practice, this action was for women alone. It was a remedy for respectable, mostly middle-class women—women (above all) who had been seduced and abandoned. Male plaintiffs were exceedingly rare. In one bizarre case, *Olson v. Saxton* (1917),[1] Arthur P. Olson, a married man, had an affair with Mollie Patton, the defendant. Later, Olson and his wife were divorced. Olson gave Patton money, and built a house for her. She promised to marry him; but instead she married another man. Olson then demanded $1,700; she in turn asked him to reduce the claim, by deducting $5 for "each act of sexual intercourse." Apparently there were quite a few such "acts," because even at the low price of $5, they reduced the claim a full $200. In any event, Olson lost his case.[2] Social norms did not permit men to sue for breach of promise. No gentleman, apparently, should ask money from a woman who broke off an engagement. He might have a broken heart, but he could recover no further damages. A woman was different.

Or so the world thought. First of all, it was commonly believed that women had more delicate feelings than men, and that they suffered more emotional damage. But the main point of the cases was not humiliation, embarrassment, and mental trauma. If a man promised to marry a woman, then kept postponing it—for years, perhaps—and finally broke off the engagement, the damage was severe. She had been off the marriage market during what were probably her prime years. And the very fact that somebody had courted her, only to jilt her later, could scare off possible suitors. This was bad enough if all she had done was wait patiently, with some kisses, hand-holding, and walks in the moonlight. But often there had been sex, meaning of course that the woman had lost her virginity—she was "ruined," she was used goods. For a respectable woman, this was an almost fatal blow to prospects for marriage. The worst case was if she had gotten pregnant and given birth to a child outside of marriage. Thus the man was a cad, and often worse: he was a villain who had seduced, debauched, and "ruined" a poor helpless woman who was otherwise as pure as the driven snow.

How often was sex in the background of the cases? In twenty-three of fifty-four reported cases decided between 1880 and 1890, there was evidence of sexual intercourse, and in ten of these cases, the plaintiff had had a child. In a few cases (six), no sex had taken place; the facts in the rest of the cases are simply unclear.[3] For the twentieth century, we have no comparable figures. Reported cases, too, may be an unreliable guide to cases at the level of the trial court; and even less of a guide to cases settled out of court. But sex and illegitimate births were surely a factor in many, if not most, of the instances.

In theory, of course, virginity was not essential. A widow, or a divorcee, or a woman who was not exactly pure, had a perfect right to sue a man who did her wrong. In practice, lost virginity helped the plaintiff's case enormously. Logically, too, if the sex was consensual, the woman's case should have been a weak one. These were not, after all, cases of rape. If she said yes, then she was party to an immoral agreement, and why should she benefit from her own wickedness and folly? But the life of the law, as we all know, is not logic; the life of the law is congruence with social norms. Sex made the plaintiff's case stronger, not weaker.[4] As Frank Keezer put it in his treatise on family law, "The courts are not disposed to make smooth the path of a seducer."[5] "Nice" women were, after all, weak, fragile, innocent creatures; a woman's "consent" must have been the product of lies, fraud, or seductive sweet-talk. But for all the talk about "seduction," whatever that might mean, seduction was not an element that the plaintiff had to prove, in her claim for breach of promise. (Wrongful seduction was an independent civil cause of action, as well as a crime, in many jurisdictions.) Often, the court simply assumed "seduction." The woman was, by definition, a victim. The plaintiff, at any rate, had to *present* herself as a victim—victim of a heartless man. In a Tennessee case, *Spellings v. Parks* (1900), the plaintiff was described as a "timid, reserved, and modest girl," a girl who, at first, would not let him even touch her. But "it was not long before she got tame, and when she did it was all at once." A child was born; and a jury awarded the plaintiff $1,500. Was the plaintiff really so timid and modest? Defendant tried to show that plaintiff's mother was a prostitute; but the court refused to allow this.[6]

Engagements, one imagines, were and are broken off every day. Most women simply swallow disappointment. Only a few feel inclined to file suit. After all, a lawsuit was and is humiliating, a kind of public ordeal. Who would want to go through with it? If a woman had given birth, of course, she was already severely damaged. In those cases, the law, and often enough juries, naturally sympathized with her. In theory, too, breach of promise had nothing to do with race or class. Some working-class women did make use of this cause of action. But in practice it was a cause of action for respectable middle-class women.

Some cases suggest very sympathetic juries, producing extremely large damage awards. A Maine jury, in *Garmong v. Henderson* (1915),[7] brought in a verdict for $116,000, which was, for the times, a gigantic recovery. In a Michigan case from 1931, with a rich defendant, the jury verdict came to $450,000—which today would be equivalent to millions. The judge reduced this award to $150,000.[8] These big verdicts were larger than recoveries in personal injury cases; but they were perhaps not typical. There were plenty of examples on the other side: where defendants won their case, or had to pay only trivial amounts of damages. This was true of the related causes as well: thus, when Chester B. Knapp, of Queens, sued a boarder in his house for alienating his wife's affections (1925), he asked for $100,000, but got the princely sum of six cents in damages from the jury.[9]

Often, in breach of promise cases, man and woman were socially on a par—members of the middle class or above. But not always. When there was a disparity, it was usually tilted in one direction: a woman of lower status, suing a man of higher status. And this, indeed, was the Achilles' heel of the action. It is why breach of promise was controversial, even in the nineteenth century. What kind of woman would bring such an action? Wounded doves, yes, from time to time; but perhaps another sort of woman too, possibly gold-diggers or blackmailers. This is the image that Gilbert and Sullivan made fun of in *Trial by Jury*.[10] In literature, the plaintiff is often pictured as a shrewd young vixen, as bold as brass; and the defendant as an old, rich fool. The plaintiff's motive is almost always "purely mercenary," as one scholar put it. Money cannot fix a broken heart. The lawsuit is "generally ... blackmail." And it leads to "a scandalous publicity which is intolerable to a woman of modesty and good breeding."[11]

Into the twentieth century, breach of promise held its own, despite all the criticism. Juries handed out decent awards; and courts generally upheld them. But image was everything: in a case in 1928, the plaintiff, Cordelia P. Carney, was fifty-nine years old; her suitor, Duncan McGilvray, was sixty-nine. Cordelia did not seem to be in love: she said that Duncan "smelled like a wet horse"; she was probably after his money. The jury felt she deserved not a penny.[12] In general, too, when the defendant was older and richer than the plaintiff, a certain flavor of dishonesty, greed, or blackmail often influenced the outcome.

CRIMINAL CONVERSATION AND ALIENATION OF AFFECTIONS

Another cause of action on the margin of marriage went by the odd and deceptive name of criminal conversation. But these were civil, not criminal, suits, and the complaint was hardly about "conversation." The gist of it was sex, not words. If a married woman had sex with somebody other than her husband, the husband could sue the adulterer. "Crim con" was an old cause of action. In England, it dated at least to the seventeenth century.[13]

In a lawsuit for alienation of affections, another type of heart balm lawsuit, plaintiff could sue anyone who destroyed the relationship between plaintiff and the plaintiff's spouse. A man could bring this kind of lawsuit, for example, against a meddling mother-in-law, who poisoned his wife's mind against him. In one case, in the late nineteenth century, Jacob Vanderbilt married beneath himself; his family objected, and refused to admit the wife, Violet Ward, to the Vanderbilt home. When Jacob left Violet, she sued her father-in-law for alienation of affections.[14] The roots of these causes of action probably lay in the ancient right of a man to his wife's "consortium." This meant his right to custody, affection, and services. Sex was, of course, a prominent "service." A woman also had a right of "consortium," but it was worth less than her husband's right.

Alienation of affection was, in a way, the opposite of breach of promise. That was a complaint exclusively for women; and this was a complaint almost exclusively for men. The Supreme Court of Maine made this point, in an 1890 case. The plaintiff, a wife, complained that the defendant "debauched and carnally knew" her husband, thus "alienating his affection." An unfaithful wife, said the court, might cast doubt on the legitimacy of the husband's children. But a husband's infidelity had "no such consequences." A woman's suit for alienation of affection could inflict "untold misery upon others with little hope of redress for themselves."[15]

The doctrine, in short, reeked of the double standard. Seduction was something men did (or tried to do); women did not (as a rule) seduce men; and men could not be "ruined" the way a woman could be. When a husband strayed from the straight and narrow, the wife was supposed to forgive and forget (up to a point, of course). Casual adultery on his part was excusable. *Her* adultery was not. In cases of alienation of affection, or criminal conversation, the wife's consent to sex was, in a way, irrelevant. She was presumptively a victim. The villain was always the man.

A few cases, even in the late nineteenth century, began to open these causes of action to women; more did so in the early twentieth century. A New Jersey court, in 1910, allowed a woman to sue her rival for "maliciously enticing away" her husband.[16] Statutory law, said the court, gave married women the right to sue under their own names in tort; so why not for this tort as well? In 1930, according to the *New York Times*, Cecilia Bairnsfather, "wife of Bruce Bairnsfather, cartoonist and playwright," asked for $100,000 in damages from an actress named Constance Collier. Constance, she said, had "maliciously enticed" Cecilia's husband, and induced him to leave her, to her "great distress of mind and body." Bruce insisted that the marriage was essentially over, and moved in with Constance.[17] The case was probably settled out of court.

In New York, reported cases between 1888 and 1920 suggest how the action had evolved, and rather dramatically. In this period, out of twenty-nine reported cases, women were the plaintiffs in seventeen, men in twelve. In nine of the cases, the woman sued her husband's lover; in eight, some other party, usually a relative. The men sued the wife's lover in ten cases, a relative in only two.[18] Clearly, these cases had shucked the archaic clothing of the action; they were based on emotional damage, rather than on some right that smelled suspiciously like a patriarchal property right. And the action had become definitely gender neutral.

Alienation of affections and criminal conversation were very often joined together in one complaint, for obvious reasons. In a 1927 case in New Jersey, Ward Brougham, a retired naval lieutenant, filed a lawsuit for criminal conversation and alienation of affections against John A. Frech, a judge of the Somerset County Court, a man in his seventies. Mrs. Brougham was thirty-eight years old. At the trial, in 1928, the plaintiff alleged that the judge came calling at his house in the morning, after Ward had left; the judge took Ward's wife "on motor trips to New York and Atlantic Highlands, and on picnics in the woods"; he showered her with "money, clothing, and jewelry." There were also love letters sent to the judge; his nickname in the letters was "Big Boy." Witnesses had seen the two embracing. The judge, for his part, insisted he was being framed. After the close of testimony, the court dismissed the action for criminal conversation, but sent the issue of alienation of affections to the jury. The jury deliberated for twelve hours, and decided for the judge. Brougham ended up with nothing.[19]

BREACH OF PROMISE AND ITS RELATIVES:
DECLINE AND FALL

The three causes of action, as we have seen, gave off mixed messages. They were supposed to protect middle-class honor and respectability, especially for women. They also promoted a traditional image of women as weak, delicate, and innocent. Yet as time went on, the other images got stronger: women as gold-diggers, Jezebels, temptresses—grasping and greedy; and men as dupes and fools, attracted to a dangerous sexuality like moths to a flame. Gradually this image grew strong enough to threaten the very life of the three kinds of "heart balm" suit.

The media played an important role in strengthening negative images. They reported, of course, the scandalous and outrageous cases. In 1909, in Chicago, a man named James H. La Pearl, a "novelty seller and former circus proprietor," sued Adrian C. Honore for alienation of the affections of his wife. Honore was the "brother of Mrs. Potter Palmer," one of the most glittering names in Chicago society. Mrs. La Pearl was "a conspicuous blonde, and has a diamond set in one of her front teeth." Until she had an accident, "she was a bareback rider in the circus." La Pearl himself, in his circus days, had been "shot out of a cannon."[20] Now Mr. and Mrs. La Pearl were in business together. Plaintiffs of this type and their wives were not exactly good advertisements for these lawsuits.

In 1922, a dancer, Evan Burrows Fontaine, accused Cornelius Vanderbilt Whitney of fathering her baby. She filed suit for breach of promise and asked for $1 million in damages. Whitney's lawyer called the lawsuit a "blackmail plot."[21] A kind of legal soap opera followed. Whitney's lawyers discovered that Fontaine had been married before, to a sailor. The marriage was annulled; but only on the basis of perjured testimony (so they claimed); arguably, the annulment was invalid. Of course, if Fontaine was still legally married, she could hardly sue Whitney for breach of promise. At least one judge bought this argument. Fontaine, he felt, had perjured herself. On appeal, this ruling was reversed. But in the end, Fontaine's lawsuit came up empty.[22] Her dreams of riches disappeared. Later, she appeared at a "beach front cabaret" in Atlantic City; she put some of her goods in storage, but then seemed to vanish into the black hole of American obscurity. Her goods were auctioned off in 1931; the storage fees were unpaid. An "unidentified woman" bid $6 to buy a poem, "apparently inspired" by Evan's "blighted romance."[23]

Young women were not always successful in their efforts to seek legal recourse. In 1917, Honora O'Brien, age twenty-nine, sued John Bernard Manning in New York. He was eighty-four.[24] Manning, it was said, was "partially palsied," but still a person of "considerable vigor." He was also filthy rich—his fortune was worth approximately $15–20 million, an enormous amount. They enjoyed a whirlwind courtship, but then the old man got cold feet. The jury, which found Manning quite unsympathetic (supposedly, he "strangled his daughter's pet dog," and was "expelled from the stock exchange for altering some certificates"; and he also told "inexcusable" and "vicious" lies on the stand), came out with a huge award: $200,000. The appeals court thought this was excessive. O'Brien had suffered "no loss of social position, no loss of a chance to marry some one else." Was she just after Manning's money? No matter; a woman could marry for "mercenary motives," without losing her rights. The court ordered the damages reduced to $125,000 but otherwise, perhaps reluctantly, affirmed the decision.

Evan Fontaine and Honora O'Brien were young women who sued older, richer men. But, at least occasionally, it went the other way around, as when a young gigolo became involved with a wealthy woman. Thus Max Frederick Kleist, a gardener, married Juliet Breitung, daughter of a "multi-millionaire"; when the marriage went sour, he sued her father for alienation of affections (and for a quarter of a million dollars). But the case was thrown out of court.[25]

In still other cases, the press was entranced by the celebrity of the litigants. In 1936, a jury awarded a quarter of a million dollars to Lilian Mandel, who sued a department store heir, Frederick Gimbel. She met Frederick in 1917 when she was twenty-two years old (he was twenty-five); she was working as an assistant buyer in a gown shop.[26] In 1930, Miss Madge Mitchell, an actress, sued William N. Fleischmann, fifty-seven ("director of the Fleischmann Corporation and a cousin of Major Max Fleischmann, yeast magnate") for breach of promise. Miss Mitchell was a beauty contest winner, who met him "while working as a manicurist in a Hollywood hotel."[27]

Readers who followed these cases in the press were likely to buy into the negative images. Newspapers covered only the most lurid and infamous cases, which did give off a rather rancid smell. More typical cases were no doubt less flamboyant than the ones covered by the press.[28] But they were more obscure. In any event, legislators began to listen to elite men outraged by "heart balm" lawsuits. Plaintiffs were said to be heartless parasites, and blackmailers, sucking the blood of rich and famous men. Clarence Funk, for example, "General Manager of the International Harvester Company," was sued in 1911; he had been paying (it was claimed) "undue attentions to Mrs. Josephine Henning." He insisted he had never heard of the woman; it was all a "frame-up," an attempt to "besmirch" his character.[29]

The criticism grew over the years. By the 1930s, the noise was deafening. Robert C. Brown, writing in 1929, said that breach of promise did "nothing but harm," and could and did "function as an instrument of blackmail."[30] In 1935, it was, according to Harriet Spiller Daggett, a "dishonorable sword for a class of women who are trading on their sex"; the plaintiffs, she felt, were on the whole "unscrupulous women fortune hunters."[31] Love was the true basis of marriage. If love vanished like the winter snows, so did the right to complain of a broken engagement. By the 1930s, these cases had become quite uncommon—if they had ever been common. In the 1923–24 fiscal year, there were 22,297 civil lawsuits filed in Los Angeles Superior Court. Forty-five were for alienation of affections; and fifteen for breach of promise of marriage. In the thirteen years ending in 1935, there were only four criminal conversation claims in the whole state of New York.[32] Of course, cases could be settled out of court; and no doubt some were. Media reporting, however, gave the impression of a kind of heart balm crisis. Surveys of the *New York Times* and other prominent newspapers, in the first half of the twentieth century, show dozens of stories about breach of promise, alienation of affections, and the like. Between 1934 and 1935, the *New York Times* ran many stories—more than eighty—about breach of promise and alienation of affections; in the *Chicago Tribune* there was "a six-fold increase in coverage in less than two decades."[33] There is little wonder, then, that a serious and successful campaign against breach of promise began.[34] Some states, including Indiana and Michigan, flatly abolished the cause of action. In the process, they often also got rid of actions for seduction, alienation of affections, and "criminal conversation."[35] The bill introduced in Michigan, in 1935, began by calling the group of causes a source of "grave abuses," harming "persons wholly innocent and free of any wrongdoing," and brought by "unscrupulous persons" seeking "unjust enrichment."[36] In Indiana, Mrs. Roberta West Nicholson, "a soft-voiced woman," the only woman in the Indiana house, wearing a "plain black dress offset by wide, ruffled collar and cuffs," led the campaign to get rid of these lawsuits. She spoke of "itching palms in the guise of aching hearts." Marriage was "a divine sacrament, not a commercial agreement." Very few of these lawsuits, she said, ever reached court: they were nothing but attempts at blackmail.[37]

The situation in Illinois was more complex. Here, too, there was a campaign against "heart balm." The *Chicago Tribune* voiced the usual complaint about "extortion, blackmail, and scandal," and the "abuse of justice." The newspaper called for abolition.[38] Illinois's legislature dutifully abolished breach of promise, alienation of affections, and criminal conversation in 1935—the Senate vote was 37 to 0; and the bill was "hailed as 'farewell to the gold digger.'"[39] The Illinois Supreme Court, however, took the gold-digger's side, and declared the statute unconstitutional in 1946, restoring, as one newspaper put it, to "[b]attered and bleeding hearts" the right to receive "soothing applications of cold cash."[40]

The legislature passed a new law in 1947. It recited the claim that breach of promise served "as an instrument for blackmail." Under the new statute, a plaintiff could recover only "actual" damages, but not "punitive, exemplary, vindictive or aggravated damages."[41] The statute also required the victim to give notice, in writing, within three months of the time the promise was breached, setting out the date the marriage was supposed to be performed, the damages incurred, and whether the defendant was or was not "still willing to marry." In 1949, Tennessee passed a statute limiting breach of promise suits. That law, still on the books today, prohibits punitive damages when the defendant is older than sixty years of age at the time of trial. The law also requires corroboration of the plaintiff's testimony—either in writing or by the testimony of two disinterested witnesses; and if the plaintiff had been married before, this fact could be used to reduce any damages.[42]

By the time of the Mandel-Gimbel trial, discussed earlier, New York was in the process of getting rid of breach of promise. The New York Court of Appeals sustained the 1935 law that abolished it, as well as all other heart balm causes of action.[43] "Thoughtful people," said the court, had "long realized" that "scandals growing out of actions to recover damages for breach of promise ... constitute a reflection upon the courts and a menace to ... marriage."[44] This cause of action, as one commentator put it, was out of step with "changed *mores* concerning sex morality, the status of women, and the functions of the family."[45]

The attack on "heart balm" included alienation of affections as well, as we have seen. This was also supposed to be a prime vehicle for blackmail against rich and respectable people. Usually, one supposes, these "respectable" people had something to hide. One Edward McFarlin sued Senator Ralph Cameron of Arizona, in 1921, for alienating the affections of McFarlin's wife. McFarlin claimed that Cameron had "detained and harbored" Marjorie McFarlin; and had been "guilty of misconduct" with her, on a New Haven railroad train, among other places. He wanted $100,000 in damages. The senator had just been elected in 1920; he angrily denied the charges, and labeled them as blackmail. He won his case: the claim was barred by the statute of limitations.[46] It is certainly possible that the McFarlins were indulging in a little bit of blackmail. But it is also quite possible that the senator was not as innocent as he claimed. Still, it would be hard to label the McFarlins as poor, suffering victims. It was this sort of case that strengthened the case against alienation of affections. It ended up in the rubbish heap of history, along with breach of promise.[47]

Criminal conversation suffered a similar fate. In these cases, the gold-diggers were men instead of women; but the odor and the bad publicity were the same. The Indiana law of 1935, "An Act to Promote Public Morals," made a clean sweep: it abolished breach of promise, alienation of affections, criminal conversation, and actions "for the seduction of any female person of the age of twenty-one years or more."[48] In 1939, California, like Indiana, made the same move: it abolished alienation of affections, criminal conversation, "seduction of a person over the age of legal consent," and breach of promise of marriage.[49] By the end of the 1930s, nine states had abolished the whole cluster of causes; other states followed somewhat later.

In the remaining states, "heart balm" suits remained; but it seemed, for many years, that they were moribund, fossilized. After all, in the age of the sexual revolution, what was the point of these laws? Chastity was not what it used to be. It was harder to "ruin" a woman in the 1930s than it had been in the nineteenth century.[50] And it got steadily harder. In the age of cohabitation, in many parts of the country, it was downright impossible. When, in 1992, a (male) lawyer sued his ex-fiancé, asking for some $40,000—the "costs of the fur coat, the car, the typewriter, the engagement ring," and "even the champagne with which he toasted his bride-to-be," it was startling enough to make the *New York Times*.[51]

Another wave of abolitions occurred in the 1970s and 1980s.[52] In a few states, the courts, rather than the legislatures, "repealed" the action of criminal conversation.[53] In Idaho, one Thomas Neal sued his wife Mary Neal for divorce; she counter-claimed, and asked for damages from her husband, who was having an affair with one Jill LaGasse. No case of criminal conversation had been reported in Idaho since 1918; and the court simply abolished the cause of action.[54] Men no longer owned women, said the court. This kind of lawsuit might expose a person to "extortionate schemes"; it might "ruin" a person's reputation.[55] In an earlier case, the Idaho court had similarly gotten rid of the action of alienation of affections.[56] In 1976, a court in Washington State ended the action for alienation of affections, saying it was archaic, dysfunctional, and harmful: even a "successful plaintiff is the loser.... He or she has engaged in self-degradation for money."[57]

By the late twentieth century, alienation of affections had been done away with in about half the states, either because the legislature said so, or because a court had so decided. Other states had imposed procedural or other restrictions on these lawsuits, which were, in any event, fairly rare (as far as we can tell).[58] By 2000, these ancient causes of action survived only in a handful of states. One of these, egregiously, was North Carolina. There, alienation of affections still seems to appeal to juries; and apparently, also, to courts.[59] In 1997, a jury in North Carolina ordered the "other woman" to pay Dorothy Hutelmyer more than $1 million after Dorothy's husband, Joe, told her he was leaving her, and replacing her with his secretary.[60] In a later case, a wrestling coach sued a man who had "engaged in sexual intercourse at a hotel" with the coach's wife. The jury awarded $910,000 in "compensatory damages" and $500,000 in punitive damages.[61] In 2006, George Berg, tipped off about his wife's affair by a comment from his five-year-old son, sued his wife's lover; the man settled out of court for more than $150,000.[62] About two hundred alienation actions are filed each year in North Carolina, according to one law firm; in many of them, criminal conversation is added on.[63]

The highest verdict ever recorded in an alienation of affections case came in 2010—an award of $9 million to Cynthia Shackelford against Anne Lundquist, the woman she sued for breaking up her thirty-three-year marriage. She told reporters that she hoped the verdict would send a simple message to "would-be homewreckers": "lay off."[64] Elizabeth Edwards, ex-wife of former senator and presidential candidate, John Edwards, threatened to file an alienation of affections lawsuit over John's affair with his campaign videographer, Rielle Hunter, a relationship that produced a child. But instead of suing Hunter, she threatened to sue Andrew Young, a campaign aide who allegedly facilitated the affair and the cover-up, and thus caused the "alienation" of John's affections for Elizabeth.[65]

Utah is another holdout;[66] so is South Dakota;[67] and so, quite notably, is Mississippi. This despite the fact that in 1992, the Supreme Court of Mississippi abolished criminal conversation.[68] Patricia Alford, married to a farmer, Jeffy Alford, had an affair with her boss at the Billups Petroleum Company. He was "forty-years old and wealthy" (she was "twenty-four years old and unhappy"). Divorce followed, as did a lawsuit against the boss. The jury, for some reason, said no to the claim for alienation of affections, but awarded damages for criminal conversation. The Supreme Court reversed and put an end to this action in Mississippi.

But the court specifically withheld judgment on alienation of affections. Criminal conversation was, the court felt, too extreme. Any act of adultery, even consensual, laid a person open to this lawsuit. Alienation of affections was different. In 2007, the

Supreme Court of Mississippi upheld a jury verdict of $642,000 (plus punitive damages of $112,000) for alienation of affections.[69] This was another instance where a woman slept with her boss. The plaintiff, Johnny Valentine, despite his name, was unlucky in marriage, if not in love. His wife Sandra had an affair with her boss, Jerry Fitch, and bore him a child. Fitch argued that alienation of affections was an outmoded cause of action; and he invited the court to do away with it. But the court declined, preferring to protect "the marriage relationship and its sanctity" against someone who "through persuasion, enticement, or inducement" had brought about the end of a marriage, and the loss of a spouse's affection.[70]

Thus, at the beginning of the twenty-first century, these causes of action are endangered species; they hang on here and there, like rare reptiles that have lost most of their habitat, and survive in a handful of swamps. A few plaintiffs win big, but the rest are unsuccessful. In a Georgia case, *Finch v. Dasgupta* (2001), Billie Ann Finch began "dating" Gautam Dasgupta in 1988 ("dating" is probably a euphemism here). He asked her to marry him; she said she wasn't ready. Big mistake. A few years later, she felt ready; and "she left a note in one of Dasgupta's shoes asking him to marry her." No promise was forthcoming. In 1992, she asked him for an engagement ring, but he gave her a ring box instead (with a check inside, to be sure). He said he needed to get his "priorities straight" before he could get married. The relationship dragged on in some form for ten years. The courts rejected her claim for breach of promise and of common-law marriage. Dasgupta (the sly dog) never made any promises, and never signed anything; and in fact refused to make promises. How, then, could there be *breach* of promise?[71]

But another woman, RoseMary Shell, was awarded $150,000 by a jury in 2008.[72] The defendant was her ex-fiancé, Wayne Gibbs. RoseMary testified that she left a high-paying job in Pensacola, after he proposed in 2006; she moved back to Gainesville, Georgia and moved in with Gibbs. But in December of that year, he left a note in their bathroom, "expressing second thoughts." And a few months later, he broke off the engagement entirely. RoseMary was then holding down a job, which paid less than half of what she had been earning before she moved to Georgia. This apparently had a strong influence on the jury.

The fact that Shell and Gibbs were "living in sin" seemed to count for nothing with the jury. Even in the depths of the Bible Belt, sin is not what it used to be. The case was unusual enough to make the newspapers. A Georgia jury was willing to punish Gibbs for his behavior; and a Georgia judge went along. In 2009, the wife of Chip Pickering, a Republican Congressman who was part of a delegation that urged President George W. Bush to declare 2008 the "National Year of the Bible," filed an alienation-of-affections lawsuit against a woman with whom the Congressman, she claimed, had had an affair.[73]

Traditional *sexual* mores are in deep decline. But other norms are not. Chastity is no longer the issue. But fairness is. Some who defend these ancient causes of action talk about "family values." Dorothy Hutelmyer, who sued her cheating husband's lover, put it this way: "America is speaking out and saying that family is important and ... marriage is a gift from God."[74] Yes; but even in the deep South, the issue is the *institution* of marriage, not sexual purity. Or perhaps commitment and long-term relationships impose duties; and breaking the bonds may carry a price tag. This might well be the lesson of these recent events.

Modern Heart Balm?

Today, the real cost of a broken engagement is not the loss of a chaste reputation or the opportunity cost on the marriage market. There are often hurt feelings, to be sure, but also the loss of cold, hard cash. For him, it may be the expensive engagement ring. For her, it may be preliminary wedding expenses. Courts have entertained a surprising number of engagement ring lawsuits, and at least a handful over wedding expenses. Outside of the few jurisdictions that continue to recognize heart balm actions, these are the only losses flowing from a broken engagement that a court might deign to recognize.

Etiquette experts insist that an engagement ring—the average cost in 2009 was $6,348—should be returned in most instances, and the law in most states agrees with this rule. The engagement ring is typically viewed as a "conditional gift." This approach means the gift of the ring "vests" with the would-be bride only when the condition—the marriage—occurs. Under a strict no-fault rule, which many courts follow, the donor is entitled to a return of the ring—or its value—if the marriage never takes place. No questions asked. By statute, New York grants courts the discretion to order return of property or money transferred in contemplation of marriage.[75] Soon after this statute was passed in 1965, courts began to apply it to engagement ring cases, ordering the ring returned in case of a broken engagement, regardless of whose fault it was that the wedding did not occur. As the state's highest court wrote in *Gaden v. Gaden* (1971): "In truth, in most broken engagements there is no real fault as such—one or both of the parties merely changes his mind about the desirability of the other as a marriage partner."[76] Most recent engagement ring cases adopt this approach.[77]

Some wedding preparation expenses can never be legally recouped. Bad news for the forty-six percent of all brides-to-be who have their teeth whitened in anticipation of the big day. Expenses of caterers, florists, dress designers, and reception halls are still disproportionately borne by the bride or her family. According to the 2008 American Wedding Survey, the bride's parents contribute money for the wedding 58 percent of the time, while the groom's parents do so only 32 percent of the time. Couples, however, are marrying later; and the couple pays for at least part of their wedding 77 percent of the time.[78] Although couples can buy wedding insurance, typical policies tend to cover cancellations caused by "acts of god" or family illness; most do not cover "change of heart" cancellations, and if they do, they require proof that the one seeking repayment of expenses was "stranded."[79]

Virginia DeFina sued her ex-fiancé, Stephen Scott, in New York in 2001 for wedding preparation expenses after their engagement was called off "in a flurry of heated actions." Both "strong-willed, strong-minded, highly educated, and sophisticated adults," Virginia and Stephen planned to pay for the entire wedding themselves. They agreed that she would pay the wedding expenses and he, in return, would give her a one-half interest in his condo. She laid out $16,000 on the wedding before it was cancelled. He argued that he should get back the interest in the condo and the ring he purchased at Tiffany's; she should be left unreimbursed for the wedding outlays.

As we saw, New York had abolished breach of promise to marry in 1935, and wedding expenses were one element of damages under that cause of action. But the 1965 statute mentioned earlier made it clear that property, money, or real estate "transferred in contemplation of marriage" could still be recovered.[80] This provision has been interpreted to allow courts to order the return of premarital gifts, and the court in Virginia's case ruled that it could also permit enforcement of a genuine contract regarding payment of wedding expenses. The court could do this, it thought, without considering "tales of broken hearts and frustrated dreams," as in breach of promise cases.[81] The goal, instead, was to return the parties, economically speaking, to the position they were in before the engagement "without rewarding or punishing either party for the fact that the marriage failed to materialize."[82] The court ordered the interest in the condo returned to Stephen, subject to a lien in the amount of the wedding expenses.

But New York is an outlier in permitting suits to recover wedding expenses. Most courts have held that such a lawsuit is "prohibited by anti-heartbalm laws."[83] This is true even though the type of expense is tangible and easy to document. In light of the tradition that brides pay for weddings, this means that women "are necessarily the economic losers in broken engagements."[84] And while the majority rule on engagement rings treats men's sense of loss as "real and deserving of compensation," the rule on wedding expenses does the opposite for women. As Rachel Moran notes, the "disappointed bride to be who spends money on wedding preparations or makes herself sexually available because she has been promised marriage cannot seek compensation of any kind."[85]

·　·　·　·　·

Social change in the twentieth century had by and large doomed these causes of action, which came to seem at least quaint if not positively harmful. In the age of the sexual revolution, the age of expressive individualism, the age of the modern woman, these were fossils, vestiges, left over from an earlier time. By the beginning of the twenty-first century, the vast majority of heart balm laws had joined the ranks of lost and discarded doctrine.

PART TWO

ANYTHING GOES:

LOVE AND ROMANCE IN

A PERMISSIVE AGE

*

The Rise of Sexual Freedom

IN THE FIRST DECADE of the twenty-first century, a flurry of cases asked the same curious question: does the U.S. Constitution protect an individual's right to purchase, promote, or use sex toys? That this question was even asked in a court of law is a remarkable sign of the times. After all, there is a long history in the United States of regulating, and prohibiting, a whole range of sexual practices. But at least one federal appellate court answered the question in the affirmative: yes, friends, the right of sexual privacy may well be broad enough to include buying and using sexual aids. This might be, in a way, the final triumph of a right of sexual freedom that challenges and undermines assumptions about the role of the state in regulating sex and the family. And the development of a right of sexual freedom is of course central to the growth of modern family law.

In this chapter, we discuss some of the dramatic changes in the law relating to sexual behavior since the middle of the twentieth century. The ultimate cause, of course, was changing sexual mores. But at several points, the Supreme Court, by recognizing a constitutional right to privacy, acted in ways that gave these changing mores a solid foundation in law. This right of privacy was expanded over time to include contraception, abortion, and even same-sex behavior. Through these cases, the Court authorized marriage without sex (by prisoners, for example) and sex without marriage (between gay people, who were forbidden to marry). It also authorized marital sex without reproduction (through contraception and abortion) and reproduction without marriage (through rights of illegitimate children and unwed fathers). These new rights dramatically limit the power of states to confine sex to marriage, as they had long attempted to do, or to enforce a fixed, traditional moral code. Some state high courts, too, went even further than the federal courts in recognizing the new sexual order.

CRIMES AGAINST MORALS: REGULATING
SEX OUTSIDE OF MARRIAGE

The beginning of the twentieth century was, in some ways, the high point of state concern with sexual morality.[1] Many states raised the age of consent (consent to sex, that is). By 1913, the age of consent in California was eighteen; in Tennessee the age of consent was twenty-one. It was a serious crime—for the male at least—to have sexual intercourse with a teenager. This was statutory rape. Legally, the female was always deemed the victim, even when she had been willing or even eager to have sex. Sodomy of course remained a serious crime. In 1910, Congress passed the Mann Act, the notorious "White Slave Traffic Act." This law made it a crime to transport a woman across state lines, for the "purpose of prostitution or debauchery, or for any other immoral purpose."[2] The "red light abatement" movement was a war on organized prostitution, in the period from 1910 on. With great hoopla and passion, crusaders paraded, orated, and legislated, in an (ultimately vain) attempt to close down the brothels and drive prostitutes out of business. All this was part and parcel of a war on vice that included, in addition, a war on drugs, and, notoriously, a war on drunkenness that climaxed in national Prohibition.

Thus, in the Progressive Era, the early twentieth century, the anti-vice movement was in full swing. State statute books were full of laws reflecting traditional morality and reinforcing the traditional family. Adultery was a crime. Bastardy (fathering a child out of wedlock), prostitution, and seduction were crimes as well. Fornication—sexual intercourse by unmarried people— was criminalized in most states. Cohabitation, which we discuss in chapter 6, was therefore also a crime.[3]

The vice warriors were not against sex as such—the human race after all cannot go on without it. (Ironically, only in the new world of permissive sex, later on, was it possible, thanks to technology, to reproduce without sexual intercourse, though most people naturally prefer the old-fashioned way.)[4] It was sex outside of marriage that the moralists objected to. Lust and lascivious impulses were reserved for the marital bedroom. Sex within marriage was more than simply allowed; it was a sacred duty.

Law also regulated sex at the margins of marriage. Breach of promise lawsuits, as we saw, concerned engaged people whose wedding day never came. Sex and cohabitation between people who "acted" married sometimes was enough to create a claim of common-law marriage. But sex with no plausible connection to marriage was simply prohibited.[5]

These criminal bans were not just phantom limits on immoral conduct. True, they were hardly rigorously enforced for the most part—how could they be?—but criminal dockets did show fair numbers of people charged with "crimes against morality."[6] Where these laws were enforced, they did sometimes serve a purpose. Abandoners were forced to return home upon threat of imprisonment; unwed fathers convicted of "bastardy" were forced into the law's only slightly more civilized version of the "shotgun" marriage; and adulterers and fornicators were punished for their sins. But change was soon to come.

By the time of the New Deal, Prohibition had ended in disgrace, and over time the whole moralistic structure was dismantled—with the notable exception of the war on drugs. By the end of the twentieth century, criminal courts had ceased playing an active role in regulating sexual relations, and family relations in general, except where there was domestic violence. (The role for civil courts in regulating family formation and dissolution only increased through the century, as we discuss in later chapters.) Most states quietly repealed laws against fornication and adultery.[7] A few relics survived into the twenty-first century—largely ignored by prosecutors. Instead of a heightened war on vice, vice seemed to triumph over what used to be considered virtue. The strict sex rules—strict on paper at least—disappeared. This was the age of the so-called sexual revolution.

There was a legal revolution as well; and also a revolution in public attitudes. Cohabitation came out of the closet. Gay people came out of the closet. Was there also a revolution in actual behavior? That is harder to measure; but probably this too occurred. Of course, a lot had been going on beneath the surface. Reality was sharply different from theory. This was the message of the famous Kinsey reports; the first report, on male sexual behavior, appeared in 1948; the companion volume, on women, appeared in 1953. One of Kinsey's main points was that illegal sexual behavior was an ordinary part of life for many people.

This included adultery. The Kinsey reports surely did not *cause* the sexual revolution; but they were a sign of the times—a sign of changing attitudes. And, presumably, changing attitudes led to changes in behavior.

But what brought about the sexual revolution? Many factors vie for attention: the birth control pill;[8] the civil rights revolution; the decline of traditional religious beliefs in some sectors of the population; the emancipation of women and the young; the influence of movies, television, and the mass media; the rise of expressive individualism. Perhaps all of these played a part. Whatever the cause, the changes in attitudes and behavior had a profound effect on family law, as was only to be expected.

THE CONSTITUTIONAL RIGHT TO PRIVACY

Family law in the United States is almost entirely a matter for the individual states. There are notable exceptions, but the federal government stays mostly offstage, and plays only a minor role in shaping this field of law. Family law, however, has been strongly affected by the development of a federal constitutional right of privacy.

This right was dimly foreshadowed in *Skinner v. Oklahoma* (1942).[9] At issue in the case was an Oklahoma statute that allowed sterilization of habitual criminals and the "feeble-minded." The Oklahoma statute was one of many, beginning with an Indiana law of 1907, and a California law of 1909.[10] In the background was the eugenics movement, and the idea that crime, immorality, perversion, and mental defects were hereditary, passed down from generation to generation. The sterilization statutes were supposed to be at least a partial solution to this problem. As we have seen, there were laws restricting or regulating the right to marry that came from the same impulse. Marriage was the key to reproduction; and reproduction was only for the fit.

A few years before *Skinner*, in 1927, sterilization won its biggest honor: endorsement by the United States Supreme Court. This came in the case of *Buck v. Bell*.[11] Carrie Buck, who was supposed to be "feeble minded," had been the child (it was said) of a "feeble-minded mother"; and had given birth also to "an illegitimate feeble-minded child." She was to be sterilized, under Virginia law. Oliver Wendell Holmes, Jr., wrote the notorious opinion upholding the Virginia law, with the famous line, "three generations of imbeciles are enough."[12]

By the time of the *Skinner* case, however, the eugenics movement had just about run its course. It was associated—not totally unfairly—with Nazi theories of race, and the United States was at war with the Nazi regime. By 1942, too, many scientists had argued, persuasively, that the eugenics movement was based on junk science. *Skinner* struck down the Oklahoma statute on sterilization. Skinner, who had been convicted of stealing chickens and armed robbery (of people), faced a vasectomy. The Supreme Court made a number of arguments against the statute; but in the course of the decision, it also made noises to the effect that having children was a fundamental right.[13]

The true leading case on the right to privacy was *Griswold v. Connecticut* (1965).[14] A Connecticut statute essentially made the sale of contraceptives, and advice on how to use them, criminal acts. The Court voided the statute. The main opinion, by Justice William O. Douglas, claimed to find a right of privacy hidden somewhere in the Constitution, or at least implied in "emanations" from the Bill of Rights. Douglas wrote of the "intimate relation of husband and wife" and of the marital bed as a "sacred precinct." Would we allow the police to search these "sacred precincts," for "telltale signs of the use of contraceptives?" "The very idea is repulsive to the notions of privacy surrounding the marriage relationship."[15]

In *Eisenstadt v. Baird* (1972),[16] the Court went a step further. Massachusetts allowed contraceptives to be distributed, but only to *married* couples. The "right of privacy," however, according to Justice Brennan, was a right of *individuals*, whether married or single. They must remain free to make the delicate decision about having or not having babies, without "unwarranted governmental intrusion." The climax of this line of cases was *Roe v. Wade* (1973),[17] which declared unconstitutional all existing abortion laws, and insisted that the right to have an abortion, at least in the early months of pregnancy, was a fundamental right, and constitutionally protected. *Roe* was and still is controversial; later cases backtracked somewhat, at least at the margins. But the core right to choose abortion without undue burden from the government, until a certain point in pregnancy, remains constitutionally protected.[18]

From *Bowers* to *Lawrence*

By the 1970s, then, the Supreme Court had read into the Constitution a somewhat nebulous "right of privacy," which gave federal constitutional protection to certain major life decisions—decisions about reproduction, and, presumably, about most forms of sexual activity. It was never entirely clear what the Supreme Court was up to in these cases; and they can be analyzed as an endorsement of rational family planning, through contraception and, in extreme cases, even abortion, rather than as a license to have sex and more sex.[19] But rights to abortion and contraception are critically important for family life. Anchoring these rights in constitutional law was both symbolically and practically significant. It is important, to be sure, not to overemphasize the role of the Supreme Court. The Connecticut statute struck down in the *Griswold* case was uniquely harsh—and only fitfully enforced, if at all. Contraception was, in general, freely available in most parts of the country, although contraceptives were often hidden behind the pharmacist's counter in the drug store, forcing the customer to ask for them in a whisper. Perhaps it took *Griswold* to put condoms boldly on the shelves in plain view; though this was probably inevitable. Abortion was a more complex issue; but it too was widely accepted, at least in some parts of the country.

In any event, a Georgia law, which made consensual sodomy a crime, tested the limits of this right to privacy in 1986. In *Bowers v. Hardwick*,[20] the Court upheld the sodomy law. The majority read the Due Process Clause to protect only rights that were fundamental—"implicit in the concept of ordered liberty," in constitutional jargon. Laws that made homosexual behavior criminal had a long history; and this behavior was also socially stigmatized. Same-sex sodomy was therefore not a fundamental right. *Bowers* was a narrow, 5 to 4 decision; and, indeed, one of the justices in the majority, Lewis Powell, said publicly a few years after the ruling that he "probably made a mistake in that one."[21] Still, *Bowers* had the effect of blocking further attempts to expand the constitutional right to privacy. The very same sodomy law upheld in *Bowers* was eventually struck down, but by the Georgia Supreme Court, rather than by a federal court. The Georgia court construed its own state constitution to afford broader privacy rights than the federal counterpart.[22]

On the federal level, *Bowers* lasted less than twenty years. The U.S. Supreme Court sharply reversed course in *Lawrence v. Texas* (2003).[23] This case struck down a Texas criminal law that outlawed sodomy. The case began when police responded to a call about a disturbance at a private residence. At the house, the police discovered, instead, two gay men engaged in anal sex. The Texas Penal Code prohibited "deviate sexual intercourse with another person of the same sex."[24] This statute, said the Court, violated the Due Process Clause of the Fourteenth Amendment. The Court specifically overruled *Bowers v. Hardwick. Lawrence* had reached the Court at a different moment in time—after significant developments in the gay rights movement, a good deal of state and local legislation, and broader societal acceptance of homosexuality. *Bowers*, said the Court, had been wrong when decided, and was still wrong. The opinion breathed a different air than the narrow, cramped analysis in *Bowers*. But the difference between the two cases was in fact also the result of a slight shift in court personnel—as well as a broader shift in public opinion.

Even in *Lawrence*, the Supreme Court did not explicitly extend constitutional protection to *sex* per se. It found protection, instead, for the liberty interest of adults to conduct consensual personal relationships "in the confines of their homes and their own private lives."[25] The right it recognized was said to include the "overt expression" of the relationship in "intimate conduct"; the right of individuals, whether married or not, to make decisions about "intimacies of their physical relationship, even when not intended to produce offspring."[26]

Significantly, the Court in *Lawrence* rejected the long-accepted view that states could use their police power to insist on adherence to the traditional moral code, at least in matters of intimate relations. But the Court did suggest limits to the "private relationships" protected by the Fourteenth Amendment. The case "does not involve minors. It does not involve persons who might be injured or coerced or who are situated in relationships where consent might not easily be refused. It does not involve public conduct or prostitution." [27] Sex in those contexts is presumably still fair game for state regulation. The Court also tried to anticipate (and blunt) later cases challenging bans on same-sex marriage: "It does not involve whether the government must give formal recognition to any relationship that homosexual persons seek to enter."

The direct impact of *Lawrence* was to put an end to sodomy laws, which still existed in some thirteen states. But the opinion potentially had broader implications for other aspects of criminal law and family law. Laws that regulated consensual sexual conduct between adults were all in jeopardy after *Lawrence*. And the decision, as we said, cast doubt on the right of states to impose a particular moral code on society. Of course, this is not to be taken literally. Laws against stealing and against perjury and forgery are also most definitely laws that rest on a moral code. But laws touching on fundamental or important rights—for no reason other than to dictate adherence to a traditional code of morality, especially sexual morality—were now constitutionally suspect. As a result, the state's right to regulate sexual behavior has been sharply curtailed.

The sodomy laws followed other laws about sexual behavior into extinction. Most states had already repealed their laws against adultery and fornication. "Statutory rape" had been replaced by "unlawful sexual intercourse," which was gender neutral, and which restricted the crime to sexual predation by older men or women on minors. The federal Mann Act had been amended to the point where it meant almost nothing. But not all states had climbed on the bandwagon. At the time *Lawrence* was decided, about a fifth of the states still had criminal laws prohibiting non-marital sexual behavior for adults.[28] In the wake of the decision, the District of Columbia passed a law to get rid of "outdated crimes" like adultery.[29] But some states kept the old laws. There were cases challenging every conceivable sex law—bans on polygamy and adultery or the promotion or sale of sex toys; and statutory rape laws, to give just a few examples.

These so-called *Lawrence* challenges met with mixed results. Statutes that restricted or criminalized consensual, private, sexual conduct between adults did not survive. Fornication and cohabitation laws seemed clearly invalid after *Lawrence*. Virginia's fornication law, for example, was invalidated in 2005. Muguet

Martin had sued her ex-lover, Kristopher Ziherl, for negligent transmission of genital herpes, a recognized tort. He tried a technical defense: she had no right to recover for any injury incurred while engaging in an illegal activity—fornication.[30] Martin countered by challenging the fornication law on the basis of *Lawrence*, and the Supreme Court of Virginia agreed.[31] This cleared the way for Martin to hold Ziherl accountable for her loathesome disease. As we will see in the next chapter, North Carolina's criminal ban on cohabitation was struck down on similar grounds.

The fate of other laws regulating sexual conduct was less clear. Could the state of Texas still prosecute a Texas mother of three who worked out of her home selling sex toys? Joanne Webb sold sex toys at home parties, the way some stay-at-home mothers sell Tupperware. (Passion Parties, the leading sex toy party company, uses the phrase "The Ultimate Girls' Night In." The company's stated mission is to promote business ownership by women, while "enhancing the sexual relationships of our clients with sensual products designed to promote intimacy and communication between couples.")[32] She was arrested in 2004 after selling sex toys to what she thought was a young married couple searching for sexual fulfillment; they were actually undercover police officers. Texas' obscenity law made it a crime to promote a device "designed or marketed as useful primarily for the stimulation of human genital organs."[33] Apparently, the sale itself was not prohibited; the crime was advising the couple about different products and how they work; this allegedly constituted unlawful "promotion" of sex toys.

Eight states criminalize the distribution of sexual devices.[34] But sexual aids have come out of the closet as part of the broader sexual revolution. In one episode of HBO's popular television show *Sex and the City*, featuring the sex lives of four single women in Manhattan, the most reserved character, Charlotte, becomes obsessed with "The Rabbit," to the point that her friends have to "stage an intervention, as Charlotte is repeatedly cancelling her social engagements to stay home with her new friend." [35] The day after the episode aired, "sex shops across North America reportedly sold out of the model."[36]

Federal courts have split over whether *Lawrence* gives constitutional protection to the purchase or use of sex toys. The charges against Webb were dropped, but the Texas law under which she was charged was invoked against others. It was challenged and ultimately invalidated by the U.S. Court of Appeals for the Fifth Circuit in 2008, in *Reliable Consultants, Inc. v. Earle.*[37] The Texas law meant that an "individual who wants to legally use a safe sexual device during private intimate moments alone or with another is unable to legally purchase a device in Texas, which heavily burdens a constitutional right." Alabama too had a ban on the sale of sex toys. But only the actual sale of the toys was a criminal offense. In *Williams v. Morgan* (2007), the U.S. Court of Appeals for the Eleventh Circuit upheld the Alabama law. Even after *Lawrence*, the court held, the state had a "legitimate interest" in "public morality."[38]

The Alabama Supreme Court upheld the same law in a separate challenge brought by a company doing business as "Love Stuff," which sold books about sex toys (one of these books was called "The Little Bit Naughty Book of Sex Toys") along with the toys themselves.[39] The court in the "Love Stuff" case cited, as it had to, *Lawrence*, but pointed out that there were broad and narrow ways of reading the case. The court opted for the narrow way. *Lawrence* had concerned a statute that "criminalized private sexual activity"; the Alabama statute prohibited "public, commercial activity" (the sale of the toys). The court concluded that the statute passed the constitutional tests.

Lawrence was indeed ambiguous, and it is not yet clear how far courts will take it. In Kansas, Matthew Limon, a developmentally disabled eighteen-year-old, had oral sex with a fourteen-year-old male classmate. The act was mutually consensual; but Limon was sentenced to seventeen years in prison. If Matthew's partner had been a girl, he would have been charged under the less sinister-sounding "Romeo and Juliet" law,[40] expressly limited to heterosexual statutory rape. The maximum sentence Limon could have received under that law was fifteen months. Limon lost his initial round of appeals, but after *Lawrence* was decided, the U.S. Supreme Court vacated his conviction and sent it back to the Kansas courts for reconsideration.[41] The Kansas Supreme Court then ruled in his favor; *Lawrence* did not permit the state to penalize homosexual conduct more severely than heterosexual conduct in the statute on statutory rape.[42]

On the other hand, Utah (for example) upheld its law banning polygamy.[43] The state's highest court held that *Lawrence* did not apply, even though the statute criminalizes not only a second, civil marriage, but also a religious marriage or cohabitation with another person while already married.[44] The court refused to see a privacy right to pursue multiple relationships simultaneously. Chief Justice Christine Durham filed a strong dissent on this point, arguing that the state had exceeded its constitutional power by giving bigamy such an expansive definition; *Lawrence* means that the state cannot "criminalize behavior merely because the majority of its citizens prefers a different form of personal relationship."[45] A federal appellate court also upheld Wisconsin's law barring sibling incest. *Lawrence*, said the court, "did not announce a fundamental right of adults to engage in all forms of private consensual sexual conduct."[46]

Adultery is still a crime in about thirteen states, and none of these laws has been invalidated yet on the strength of *Lawrence*. These relics are rarely enforced. People thus took notice when a man in Virginia was accused of criminal adultery in 2003. After his affair, the defendant and his wife were reconciled. But his ex-lover lodged against him a vengeful criminal complaint of adultery, which carried a maximum penalty of $250. He initially pled guilty to the charge and resigned from his post as town attorney after thirty-two years in the position.[47] He later withdrew the plea and filed a challenge to the state's law. But the prosecution decided to drop the charges, leaving the law untested.[48]

Adultery in most states has purely private consequences, so much so that a governor of New York, David Paterson, admitted in a press conference on his first day in office that both he and his wife had committed adultery. The governor had inherited the office after his predecessor, Eliot Spitzer, who was caught using a high-priced call girl service, resigned in disgrace.[49] No legal or even political consequences followed Paterson's confession, even though adultery is, at least technically, still a crime in New York.[50] Another recent scandal involved the governor of South Carolina, Mark Sanford. Sanford disappeared for several days, leaving no way to reach him and no one else in charge. Sanford, a married man, had flown off to rendezvous with his South American lover. Many people considered this a purely private affair.[51] There were moves to impeach Sanford, but more for the use of taxpayer money and dereliction in office, than for any moral lapse. In the end, his governorship outlasted his marriage.[52]

Eliot Spitzer, David Paterson, and Mark Sanford all illustrate the point that sex can still scandalize; it can still jeopardize or even end a political career. But behavior that would have shocked and appalled the Victorians often barely registers on the screen of modern life. The sexual revolution may not have overthrown the old regime absolutely; but, as we have seen, it has turned inside out a tradition that once dominated the legal order of the United States.

Cohabitation

No trend has so impacted family life in the twentieth century as the meteoric rise of cohabitation, both as a prelude to marriage, or as an outright substitute. This trend is one outcome of the sexual revolution, the new sexual freedom, which we talked about in the last chapter. Courts and legislatures have had to grapple with a new social fact. In this chapter, we consider how cohabitation has come to lose its criminal stigma; along with the growing ability of couples who live together to make claims against each other, or to demand some sort of family-like status. The trend, in short, has gone from legal and social disapproval to piecemeal civil protection. Legally speaking, cohabitation has become an accepted part of life. This has implications we will discuss in chapters on marriage and on parentage.

The "Crime" of Cohabitation

Historically, the law was either indifferent or positively hostile toward cohabitation. In some states, especially those in the South, cohabitation was a criminal offense. A North Carolina statute, passed in 1805, provided that "If any man and woman, not being married to each other, shall lewdly and lasciviously associate, bed and cohabit together, they shall be guilty of a Class 2 misdemeanor."[1] Many states had similar laws, which subjected couples to criminal penalties for living together outside the bounds of marriage—"lewd and lascivious cohabitation" in legalese, "living in sin" in more colloquial terms. C. H. Hamilton, for example, served a year in the county jail after his 1912 conviction for living "in a state of cohabitation and adultery with one Mary Doe." Hamilton was married, Doe was single, and their living together was a crime under California law.[2] Henry Thomas and Mary Long were convicted in 1897 of lewd cohabitation and sentenced to eighteen months in prison after the sheriff broke down her door and struck a match to shed light on the two of them in a room with only one bed. But the convictions were reversed by the Florida Supreme Court.[3] The evidence tended to "show one act of secret lewdness," but not "open dwelling or cohabiting together, as though the marriage relation existed between the parties." This particular statute was focused not just on illicit sex, but on the "public scandal and disgrace of such living together by persons of opposite sexes, and unmarried to each other"; cohabitation was criminalized in order "to prevent such evil and indecent examples, with their tendency to corrupt public morals."[4]

The world of the late twentieth century was light-years away from the world of that Florida case. The Model Penal Code (1962) did not treat unmarried sex as any kind of crime. There was widespread criticism, by then, of the use of criminal laws to enforce an old moral code.[5] At that time, nearly all states still criminalized cohabitation, but many of the bans were repealed during the 1970s and 1980s, or narrowed to target sexual behavior in public rather than in the privacy of homes. Massachusetts, for example, amended its law in 1987 to delete the criminal penalty for a "man and woman who, not being married to each other, lewdly and lasciviously cohabit together," but retained the misdemeanor status for "a man or woman, married or unmarried, who is guilty of open and gross lewdness and lascivious behavior."[6] Sex, masturbation, and flashing are still off limits in public places, but merely cohabiting with a non-marital partner is now permissible in virtually every state.

The criminal cohabitation laws that remained—in Florida, for example, and Michigan, were and are seldom enforced.[7] An empirical study of cohabitation prosecutions in Wisconsin in 1978 showed that most counties did not prosecute cohabitation at all, in some cases because the district attorney had this as express policy.[8] In other counties, district attorneys reported that they only invoked the cohabitation law when other illegal conduct, such as welfare fraud, was suspected. Non-enforcement was quietly the rule everywhere. An appellate court in Massachusetts took judicial notice, in 1981, of the fact that the crimes of fornication, adultery, and cohabitation "are never, or substantially never, made the subject of prosecution.... Despite widespread official knowledge of such violations, prosecutions by law enforcement officials are essentially nonexistent.... [These] statutes ... have fallen into a very comprehensive desuetude."[9]

Few modern-day couples have faced a sheriff's pounding on their door in the middle of the night demanding to see a marriage license. Yet, anti-cohabitation statutes do sometimes wreak havoc. The *fact* of unlawful cohabitation was sometimes used against people in custody disputes, for example. Jacqueline Jarrett was granted a divorce, on grounds of extreme cruelty, in 1977, and won custody of her three children. But seven months later, her ex-husband, Walter, petitioned for an order to make him the primary custodian, because Jacqueline had begun "shacking up" with a man.[10] Walter conceded that Jacqueline took good care of the children, but claimed that her conduct jeopardized their moral well-being. The Supreme Court of Illinois agreed; "open and notorious" cohabitation was still a crime under Illinois law. Jacqueline defended her lifestyle. She argued that the children understood why she chose not to marry her lover and were not harmed by her conduct. She also objected that the law banned commonplace behavior, and was almost never enforced. But the Court was not convinced on either point. The criminal code, it held, reflects the "moral standards" of the state, which *can* be enforced at will. Because she planned to continue violating the law—thereby demonstrating lax moral standards to her children—the trial court had been right to give the children "to an equally caring and affectionate parent whose conduct did not contravene the standards established by the General Assembly."[11] Had Jacqueline been more discreet about her sex life, it might not have met the statutory definition of "open and notorious" cohabitation. But she chose to discuss her "relationship and her rationalization of it with at least her children, her former husband and her neighbors," making it fair game for consideration in a custody proceeding.

Susan Burns entered into a consent decree following her divorce from Darian, which specified that Susan, who was not the custodial parent, would refrain from "overnight stays with any adult to [whom] she is not legally married or to whom [she] is not related within the second degree" during periods of visitation with her three children. When Susan began a live-in relationship with another woman, her ex-husband sought to deny her further visitation. Her relationship was with someone of the same sex, but the agreement would have precluded the cohabitation even if Susan had been living with a man.[12] Restrictions like this—by consent or by order—are not unusual in custody decisions, even when cohabitation is perfectly legal. (Courts are hesitant to impose significant lifestyle restrictions on *custodial* parents, but non-custodial parents often suffer greater interference during periods of visitation.)

Likewise, alimony agreements or orders may provide that the paying spouse can end payments when the ex-wife marries *or* cohabits. Traditionally, non-marital cohabitation had no effect on a support obligation, because the law did not recognize it. But now, at least to a limited extent, courts are more likely to consider it when fixing or modifying alimony. Divorcing spouses can certainly agree as to what effect subsequent cohabitation with a third party will have on the alimony obligation, but, even in the absence of such an agreement, courts may take it into account. The most recent trend is to limit alimony only if the ex-spouse receives financial support from her unmarried partner.[13] The more he acts like a husband, in other words, the less her ex-husband must continue to act as one.

Criminal bans on cohabitation (like other laws regulating non-marital sexuality) can also interfere with employment. North Carolina's 1805 cohabitation law, for example, was invoked indirectly in 2004 against a sheriff's dispatcher, Debora Hobbs. Like 144,000 other North Carolina couples at the time, Hobbs and her boyfriend were living together, and had been doing so for three years. Her boss tried to insist that she either get married or quit—rather than enforcing the law by day and breaking it by night. An earlier, high-profile case, *Shahar v. Bowers* (1997), had involved a similar issue. The attorney general of Georgia revoked an offer of employment to lawyer Robin Shahar, after learning that she had undergone a "marriage" ceremony with her lesbian partner. Although the marriage was not legally valid—no state at the time authorized same-sex marriage—the state argued that it would be unseemly to hire her into a law enforcement position while she openly violated the state's criminal ban on sodomy. A federal appellate court upheld Georgia's revocation of the offer of employment. At the time her case was heard, the court concluded that the state's interest in avoiding public confusion and enforcing its sodomy ban outweighed whatever associational interest she had in living in a marriage-like relationship with another woman.[14] Her "participation in a same-sex 'wedding' and 'marriage' could undermine confidence about the Attorney General's commitment to enforce the state's law against homosexual sodomy (or laws limiting marriage and marriage benefits to traditional marriages)."[15]

By the time Debora Hobbs's situation arose, however, the landscape had changed. As have seen, *Bowers v. Hardwick* had been overturned by *Lawrence v. Texas*.[16] The American Civil Liberties Union successfully challenged North Carolina's cohabitation law under *Lawrence* in Hobbs's case. A superior court judge agreed with Hobbs, issuing a short opinion declaring the cohabitation law unconstitutional on its face under *Lawrence* and permanently enjoining its enforcement.[17] The state did not even bother to appeal. Criminal cohabitation bans are effectively dead.

The Rise of Non-marital Cohabitation

A dramatic increase in cohabitation began in earnest in the 1970s.[18] In 1970, only 523,000 couples were cohabiting; by 2000, there had been a tenfold increase, to 5.5 million.[19] These cohabiting couples comprise 9 percent of all "coupled" households, and one out of nine of these are same-sex couples.[20] Cohabitation "has grown from a rare and deviant behaviour to the majority experience among cohorts of marriageable age."[21] Cohabiters are not evenly spread across the country; they are more concentrated in metropolitan areas, and found least frequently in rural areas and deeply religious enclaves.[22] One out of every eight unmarried couples is found in California. Individuals of lower socioeconomic status are slightly more likely to cohabit, and cohabitation "tends to be selective of people who are slightly more liberal, less religious, and more supportive of egalitarian gender roles and nontraditional family roles."[23]

For many of these couples, cohabitation is a precursor to marriage. While only 10 percent of marriages contracted between 1965 and 1974 were preceded by cohabitation, by the 1990s, that number had increased to 50 percent.[24] Nowadays, cohabitation precedes remarriage even more often than that. Seventy-five percent of cohabitating couples say they plan to marry eventually, and 60 percent of them actually make it to the altar. But a trial run can do more harm than good. Research suggests, perhaps counter-intuitively, that couples who cohabit before marriage experience worse marital quality and a higher rate of divorce.[25] Marriages that start as cohabitations are twice as likely to end in divorce in the first decade as compared with all first marriages.[26] Much of this effect can be explained by selection—characteristics of the people who cohabit, such as lower socioeconomic status, are associated with worse marital outcomes—rather than cause and effect.[27]

Much of the decline in marriage rates, which we discuss in chapter 2, is offset by the increase in cohabitation rates; the number of joint households has not significantly changed. That data and the average age of cohabiters—they tend to be twelve years younger than married couples—suggest that cohabitation is increasingly a definite stage in life. Among women in their thirties in 1995, half had lived at some point in a cohabiting relationship.[28] Though cohabitation has become a common phase in life, it is often a short one. Almost all cohabiting couples either marry or split up within five years;[29] the median duration is barely more than one year.[30] As many as four in ten unmarried-partner households include children, almost as many as in married-couple households.[31] Many of the children reportedly born to "single" mothers in fact begin life in unmarried, co-parenting households.

Why do people cohabit? Clearly, the taboo on sex outside of marriage has gone, and with it the stigma associated with cohabitation.[32] By the 1970s, young people were already showing signs of acceptance—more than half of high school seniors in one study responded that an unmarried man and woman living together "were doing their own thing and not affecting anyone else."[33] Not surprisingly, the trend toward acceptance continued in later decades. The disapproval rate for living together has steadily declined, and the percentage of people who describe cohabitation as not just acceptable, but a "good idea," doubled between 1976 and 1997.[34] A 2010 Pew Research Center survey found that nearly four in ten Americans agreed that marriage is "becoming obsolete," and less than half view non-marital cohabitation as "a bad thing."[35]

Greater control over reproduction has also played a role in the expansion of these relationships. Cohabitation is also consistent with long-term trends against strict adherence to traditional religious dogmas, and toward an ethos of individualism—of doing your own thing.[36] The economic landscape for women and a decline in fixed ideas about gender roles have also played a role.[37] For many, however, cohabiting simply permits them to delay the obligations of marriage, for which they feel unready, economically or otherwise.

FULL CIRCLE: A RIGHT TO COHABIT?

Cohabitation has become so entrenched in the United States that it seems almost as if there is some kind of right to cohabit. Many states now prohibit "marital status" discrimination, which is sometimes interpreted to protect cohabitants.[38] In other states, cohabitants have met with mixed success challenging discrimination against them. A federal appellate court, for example, upheld the firing of two cohabiting library employees in *Hollenbaugh v. Carnegie Free Library* (1978), in large part because the relationship was offensive to library customers.[39] This was over thirty years ago—perhaps it would be decided differently today.

In zoning issues, too, cohabitants often face the challenge of proving they should count as a "family." A Missouri court upheld the application of a single-family zoning ordinance against an unmarried couple, who lived together with her two children and his one child. The zoning law defined a single family as "one or more persons related by blood, marriage or adoption, occupying a dwelling unit as an individual housekeeping organization." Joan Horn and Terrence Jones clearly constituted an "individual housekeeping" entity, as the ordinance required, but their legal relationship to one another was not sufficient.[40] The court noted that the household functioned like a family, but said that a "man and a woman living together, sharing pleasures and certain responsibilities, does not *per se* constitute a family even in the conceptual sense."

Horn and Jones challenged the ordinance as unconstitutional, but did not succeed. Prior Supreme Court rulings had carved out a protective sphere for choices about living arrangements, but only those involving family. In *Moore v. City of East Cleveland* (1977), the Court held that the constitutional right to privacy, which we discussed in the previous chapter, was broad enough to include the right to live with relatives, whether or not they were part of a traditional nuclear family.[41] There, a grandmother lived with her two grandsons, who were cousins, not brothers. The City of East Cleveland's zoning ordinances prohibited this particular combination of relatives under its single-family provision. The Court held, however, that the city could not tell residents *which* relatives they could live with. Such a regulation of occupancy was invalid for "slicing deeply into the family itself." But three years earlier, in *Village of Belle Terre v. Boraas* (1974),[42] the Court had upheld the restrictive zoning ordinance of an exclusive Long Island enclave that prevented six college students from living together in a house. There is no constitutional right, the Court held, to choose to live with non-relatives. The precedent in *Boraas* was fatal to Horn's and Jones's claim, for they were as unrelated in the eyes of the law as the six college students. They looked and acted much more like a traditional family, but without a recognized legal tie, their hometown was free to exclude them from a neighborhood zoned for families.

CIVIL REGULATION OF COHABITATION: PARTNER V. PARTNER

Some cohabiting couples have also tried to invoke the law in disputes with each other. The more unmarried couples begin to act like married couples—intermingling their finances, dividing labor between wage-earning and domestic work, co-parenting children—the more likely they are to need or seek marriage-like rights when their relationships dissolve.

When married couples combine their lives, one of the two is often financially dependent on the other. As we discuss in chapters 9 and 11, family law (including inheritance law) gives a dependent or non-wage-earning spouse a share in the other spouse's assets or in community property, which is some protection against destitution, if divorce or death ends the marriage. This compensates, at least partially, for the economic dependency that occurs in so many marriages. But these rights are limited to married partners.

What rights do unmarried partners have? Does it matter whether they acted very much like husband and wife while they were together? Could they make an enforceable agreement before or while cohabiting about how they wanted to be treated at dissolution? Historically, there were easy answers to these questions. Unmarried cohabitants did not have any legal status as such. If the relationship was similar *enough* to marriage, state law might have used such doctrines as common-law marriage or putative marriage, which are described in chapter 3 to validate it. Most cohabiting couples, though, do not qualify for these protections because they lack the intent to marry—they may even be specifically trying to avoid marriage, rather than claim its benefits. If a woman took care of home and hearth, while her cohabiting boyfriend devoted himself to wage-earning work, she might well end up with nothing if their relationship ended. If he died, she was entitled to no inheritance or support. The rules, by and large, turned entirely on formal legal status, without regard for individual need, or the nature of the couple's relationship. And if the couple parted ways before one of them died, a simple breakup, the law would treat them as if they had been merely roommates. The couple could of course agree to split possessions, but, ultimately, neither would have the right to insist on the sharing of property.

But suppose this couple had promised one another up front that they would share property at the end, that she would iron his shirts and put dinner on the table every night in exchange for the right to share his paycheck, or vice versa. In the old days, virtually no court would have enforced such an agreement. The agreement, no matter how it was described by the parties, was against public policy—predicated on "meretricious" consideration, that is, sex. A woman who planned to play the role of a traditional wife could not protect herself even by contract.

A New Era: Enforceable Cohabitation Agreements

The upsurge in cohabitation forced courts and legislatures to revisit the law's traditional hostility toward, or at least its benign neglect of, cohabitants. Today, the rights of unmarried partners are still very much in flux. But they have evolved a good deal in recent decades. There are two possible sources of their rights and obligations—status and contract. For married couples, both concepts play a role. On the one hand, the state sets out the basic rights and obligations of marriage. Each spouse, for example, must support the other during marriage. Upon divorce, courts in most states have the authority to order one spouse to transfer assets or pay alimony. But contract also plays a role: before marrying, a couple can enter into a prenuptial agreement that sets out the financial consequences of divorce or death. And in anticipation of divorce, a couple can enter into a separation agreement, resolving their financial and other entanglements; such an agreement is very likely to be enforced.

In some jurisdictions, however, unmarried couples cannot look to status or contract for similar rights. Victoria and Robert Hewitt lived together for fifteen years in, as she described it, "an unmarried, family-like relationship to which three children have been born."[43] Robert was a successful dentist who had relied on her support, including money she borrowed from her parents, while he went to school and set up his practice. She made other contributions to his success and happiness, including services as a "wife" and mother. In some ways, Victoria made a very traditional claim—that she should share in the "profits and properties accumulated by the parties" during their long relationship. Had they been married, Victoria would certainly have been entitled to some of the property, perhaps even more than half of it. Indeed, she had initially come to court requesting a divorce, but her complaint was dismissed when she admitted that there was never a marriage ceremony. She amended her complaint, this time relying on theories of contract and equity—that he had agreed to share his earnings with her in exchange for her contributions and that, even in the absence of such an agreement, it would be inequitable to let him keep all the earnings. The essence of her claim was that she had devoted "her entire life to him," and that he had been unjustly enriched.

The Illinois Supreme Court rejected her claim altogether in a 1979 ruling. It refused to see the problem before it as a simple question of contract law or a question of fairness. Instead, the question was whether granting Victoria Hewitt rights against Robert would "weaken marriage as the foundation of our family-based society" by encouraging cohabitation.[44] Even though the court did *not* find Victoria's claims "totally devoid of merit," they were against public policy, and thus could not validated.[45]

The *Hewitt* case came just three years *after* the California Supreme Court had shaken up this terrain by recognizing, for the first time, a claim of "palimony." The case was widely publicized, mostly because one of the parties was a famous Hollywood actor—Lee Marvin. But the case was legally noteworthy as well. Michelle Triola, a singer, had lived with Marvin for seven years. They had, she alleged, an oral agreement that as long as they lived together, "they would combine their efforts and earnings and would share equally any and all property accumulated as a result of their efforts whether individual or combined."[46] Triola alleged that she had given up a lucrative career as a singer in order to devote herself full-time to Marvin "as a companion, homemaker, housekeeper and cook"; the bargain, she claimed, was that he would support her for life. Every penny they acquired during the relationship was taken in his name. In court, she asked for half of the $3.6 million he had accumulated, as well as support payments (thus the popular reference to *Marvin* as a "palimony" case).

Was such an agreement enforceable? The first two sentences of the opinion in *Marvin* show the court grappling with the new social order: "During the past 15 years, there has been a substantial increase in the number of couples living together without marrying. Such nonmarital relationships lead to legal controversy when one partner dies or the couple separates."[47] The court went on to make new law. Yes, the two could, indeed, make contracts about property acquired during the relationship. The "mores of the society" have "radically" changed; a "standard based on alleged moral considerations that have apparently been so widely abandoned by so many" is no longer appropriate. Express contracts could be enforced as long as they were not "explicitly founded on the consideration of meretricious sexual services."[48] Indeed, the court wrote, the "fact that a man and woman live together without marriage, and engage in a sexual relationship, does not in itself invalidate agreements between them relating to their earnings, property, or expenses." Implied contracts could also be enforced if there was a "tacit understanding" by the parties that their relationship constituted some kind of joint venture or partnership. And even with no evidence of an agreement, courts could resort to equitable remedies to avoid the injustice of enriching one party at the expense of the other.

While the *Marvin* case put fear in the hearts of men, who worried that any sign of commitment to a woman would cost them in the long run, it was a hollow victory for Triola. On remand, after a three-month trial, the court found that she had not provided sufficient evidence of a palimony agreement, nor of harm suffered because of the relationship.[49] She was awarded only a fraction of the $1.8 million she sought—$104,000 for expenses while she "rehabilitated" her job skills, and even that award was vacated on appeal. An appellate court concluded that the circumstances did not justify an award "in equity" given the economic and social benefits she experienced from the relationship. Lee Marvin had not, the court concluded, been unjustly enriched by Michele's services.[50] She may have contributed to his success, but she benefited from it, too; she got to be the wife-like partner of a famous movie star. (Triola went on to a second non-marital relationship—she lived with Dick Van Dyke for thirty years until her death in 2009.)[51]

In the decades that followed *Marvin*, courts in most states ruled that agreements between cohabiting partners with respect to property or finances were enforceable.[52] This was true even in some states that still criminalized cohabitation. The Wisconsin Supreme Court, for example, enforced a cohabitation contract in a 1980 case, even though the underlying relationship was adulterous.[53] Mary Lou Brooks moved in to Virgil Steffes' farm to provide nursing care to him, as well as a wide variety of other household services—everything from the laundry to chasing down escaped farm animals; and including sex. Mary Lou and Virgil were both married to other people. (Indeed, Virgil's wife also lived at the farm until she died, five years after Mary Lou moved in.) When Virgil died, Mary Lou sued his estate for compensation, a claim the court allowed despite their intimate relationship.[54]

A few states only permit recovery on express agreements. Some states provide by statute that cohabitation agreements are enforceable, but require some level of formality—a written agreement, for example.[55] Other states permit proof of implied contracts. Courts in those jurisdictions look at the relationship, and what the parties expected, with regard to the sharing of property. Sharon Wallender cohabited with her *ex*-husband in Oregon. When she claimed a share in property acquired during this period, the court looked to see whether an "implied-in-fact" contract could be found—whether the court could infer that "the parties implicitly agreed to share assets equally."[56] The court decided that the couple had implicitly agreed to share one piece of real property, though not the rest of the assets.

Inferring intent to share property, based on the fact that one spouse provides homemaking service and the other accepts it, is indeed an uncertain business.[57] In theory, one could find a tacit understanding to share assets anytime one partner commits her efforts more to the running of the household than to paid labor. But is it fair to say that every couple of this kind understands that a court may force them to share assets when they break up? Should their intent be dispositive? Another approach is to bypass the search for the parties' "true" intent and simply look directly at what happened—did one party perform valuable services for the other that deserve to be paid for? Legally speaking, this approach recognizes an "implied-in-law" contract or "quantum meruit" recovery—legal jargon that means, there's no real contract here, but one party deserved money for services rendered, or one party benefited more from the relationship than the other.

In *Maglica v. Maglica* (1998),[58] the defendant, Anthony Maglica, was in many ways the embodiment of the American dream, or myth, whichever you choose. Maglica was born in New York but grew up in Croatia. During the Second World War, his family was so poor that his mother, according to one tale, had to have a gold tooth pulled to get money for food. Maglica returned to the United States in 1950. He began making machine parts in Los Angeles; he later developed a flashlight called the Maglite, an extremely successful product that eventually became standard equipment for police forces. By then, Maglica was a rich man. His marriage broke up, and he set up housekeeping with a woman named Claire. They lived together for some time, but then split up in a rather spectacular fashion. Claire filed a palimony suit against Anthony Maglica asking for $200 million. At trial, a jury awarded her $84 million. Anthony, unsurprisingly, appealed.

The appeals court reversed the judgment, partly on the basis of faulty instructions to the jury. Claire, unlike Michele Marvin, did not base her claim on some sort of agreement or contract. The court therefore had to discuss an alternative theory of recovery, *quantum meruit*, which, as we explained, allows recovery for services provided whether or not the other party agreed up front to pay for them. In the eyes of the Appeals Court, it was ridiculous to imagine that Claire's services were worth $84 million. "People who work for businesses for a period of years and then walk away with 84 million, do so because they have acquired some *equity* in the business, not because 84 million dollars is the going rate for the services of even the most workaholic manager." The trial court had, in effect, allowed the jury to value the plaintiff's services "as if she had made a sweetheart stock option deal." Because (in the opinion of the appeal court), the trial court had not correctly understood the law, the case had to be sent back down for retrial. In the end, Claire and Anthony settled out of court for $29 million. This, of course, is still a lot of money.

Only a handful of states still refuse to recognize any contractual rights of cohabiters.[59] But even those that do recognize such rights often limit remedies to "untangling shared property interests and reimbursing extraordinary contributions made by one partner to the other's business or property interests." Ann Estin argues that *Marvin* ultimately "stands more as a cultural icon than as a legal watershed." Under the rules developed in its wake, "most cohabitants have no rights or obligations that arise by virtue of their shared life."[60] The courts also have not given up on the idea that a strong public policy favors marriage. Most courts pay at least lip service to this idea. To enforce cohabitation contracts may mean only that the policy in favor of legal marriage is not "well served by allowing one participant in a meretricious relationship to abscond with the bulk of the couple's acquisitions."[61]

Some courts are still leery about so-called meretricious relationships. The use of the word "meretricious"—variously defined as "relating to or resembling a prostitute" or "attractive in a tawdry manner"—tells us that some courts are struggling to draw the line between a palimony agreement and prostitution. Of course, Lee Marvin would never have agreed to pay half his earnings to a cook, maid, or housekeeper; nor would he have let a domestic servant call herself "Mrs. Marvin," as Triola often did. If Marvin and Triola did have an agreement to share property, it was because of their intimate relationship, not because she was good at ironing. What differentiated Triola from any other woman who provided services to Marvin was that she was his lover, plain and simple.

Attitudes today are becoming more realistic. In a 2002 case, *In re Estate of Roccamonte*,[62] the New Jersey Supreme Court enforced a man's promise to support his live-in girlfriend for life. The man had died, and his estate defended against her claim, arguing that the contract was based solely on sexual services, since she had not performed much in the way of domestic chores. But the court insisted this argument "misperceives the fundamental point of our palimony cases." A "marital-type relationship is no more exclusively dependent upon one partner's providing maid service than it is upon the sexual accommodation. It is, rather, the undertaking of a way of life in which two people commit to each other, forgoing other liaisons and opportunities, doing for each other whatever each is capable of doing, providing companionship, and fulfilling each other's needs, financial, emotional, physical, and social, as best as they are able." Thus, a woman who entered such a relationship and conducted herself "in accordance with its unique character" could enforce her partner's promise of support.

Marvin rights may still be in flux. In a 2008 case, *Devaney v. L'Esperance*, the New Jersey Supreme Court held that actual cohabitation is not necessarily essential to a palimony claim and that adultery is not an absolute bar.[63] Helen Devaney worked as a receptionist in Francis L'Esperance's ophthalmology office. Though he was married to another woman, and she was less than half his age, Helen and Francis conducted a twenty-year-long intimate relationship. He paid many of her expenses during those two decades, and she at least occasionally helped around the office, even after leaving her paid position there. He repeatedly promised to divorce his wife, and enticed her to return to New Jersey to carry on this relationship. They spent some time near the end of the relationship trying to conceive a child, but gave up when she learned she was infertile and he, now in his seventies, was not interested in pursuing in vitro fertilization. Here, the court adopted a "more flexible approach that seeks to achieve substantial justice in light of the realities of the relationship." As long as a couple participated in a marriage-*like* relationship, a cause of action for palimony could succeed even without cohabitation—and even with adultery.[64] But the court here may have gone too far. Almost immediately, the legislature began to consider bills to require that palimony agreements be in writing—a requirement that would almost never be met. On the governor's last night in office in 2010, he signed one of these bills into law.[65]

Cohabitation: From Contract to Status

No matter how broadly interpreted, *Marvin*-type rights are flimsy protection for most cohabiting couples. *Marvin* basically only means that two individuals do not *lose* their rights to enter into binding contracts simply because they are involved in an intimate, personal relationship. Having the right and exercising it are two different things—and proving it has been exercised is another thing altogether. Cohabiting couples very rarely make explicit the terms of the relationship, and what would follow if the relationship ended; usually there is no reliable evidence of what, if anything, they intended. This may change, as cohabitation becomes a more fully accepted substitute for marriage, but formal agreements are still uncommon.[66] Yet, without agreements, cohabiting couples often do order their lives very much the way husbands and wives do: one provides and the other is dependent. Without marriage, the dependent partner is quite vulnerable, economically speaking. Status-based rights might work better than contractual rights. Indeed, the court in *Marvin* was initially asked to recognize Michelle and Lee as something like a married couple, and to apply the rules of property division upon divorce. But the court expressly held that those rules did not apply to an unmarried couple. Only a contractual agreement or an equitable remedy could be used to protect a woman in Michelle's position.

Status-based rights, unlike *Marvin* rights, exist because of the relationship rather than in spite of it. A status theory would mean that unmarried partners who live in marriage-like relationships would automatically gain some of the protections of marriage, with or without an agreement. Status-based rights for unmarried partners is still a distant goal; but it has gained some traction in the last decade or two.

The Supreme Court of Washington, for example, has treated cohabitation as a legal status since 1984.[67] In one case, *Connell v. Francisco* (1995), Shannon Connell made a claim against her ex-lover, Richard Francisco.[68] She had left a job dancing in Toronto to live with him in Las Vegas, where he produced stage shows for hotels. She worked as a paid dancer, but also helped out in his business. After several years, he bought a bed and breakfast in Washington, and she moved there with him. For more than two years, Shannon worked at the inn without pay. She cleaned rooms, made breakfast for the guests, washed linens, and so on. They broke up after seven years. She had acquired about $20,000 in savings or property, plus a leasehold interest in an apartment; but his net worth had increased by $1.4 million. In her lawsuit, she asked for equitable distribution of the property acquired during their relationship—a right that wives or husbands had by law upon divorce.

The Washington court deemed Shannon and Richard's relationship a legal *status*, turning the demeaning phrase "meretricious relationship" on its head. Instead of something akin to prostitution, the court defined a "meretricious relationship" as "a stable, marital-like relationship where both parties cohabit with knowledge that a lawful marriage between them does not exist." The court listed factors that might show or disprove this relationship—cohabitation, duration, and the pooling of resources and services. If a court finds that such a relationship existed, it could apply, purely by analogy, the statutory rules for the sharing of property after a divorce. But the court in *Connell* stopped short of granting the same rights to unmarried partners. A divorcing wife could ask for equitable distribution of any property—whether separate or community property.[69] "Meretricious" partners, the court said, could only ask to share in the community property—the assets either partner had earned during the relationship. Cohabitants also could not receive spousal maintenance awards. (In a later case, the Washington Supreme Court affirmed the "meretricious relationship doctrine," but renamed it "Washington's law of committed intimate relationships.")[70] For Shannon, even quasi-marital status was significant, since the bulk of Richard's real property had been acquired during their seven years together and was presumptively community property. Nevada has also applied its community property laws by analogy to cohabiting couples.[71]

How do we know when a relationship is sufficiently committed? Relationships go all the way from one-night stands to "domestic partnerships." In some cases, the rights depend on a delicate weighing of facts. The criteria for judges have a certain familiar ring; they seem to hearken back to the old cases on common-law marriage. In a Washington State case from 2006, for example, Cung Ho and Thuy Ho had lived together for sixteen years.[72] They had gone through some sort of religious ceremony, but apparently not of a kind that would make them legally married in Washington State. They certainly behaved like married people. They "built a business together, raised their children together, and were jointly listed on their automobile insurance policy." Under these facts, the court came to the conclusion that they had a committed relationship, with important consequences for property rights.

In 2002, the American Law Institute published Principles of the Law of Family Dissolution (ALI Principles), a comprehensive set of rules and principles on property rights in family breakups that it urges states to import into law.[73] With respect to unmarried partners, whether of the same or opposite sex, the ALI Principles adopt and extend the approach seen in Washington and Oregon. The Principles make property rights at dissolution available to domestic partners on the same basis as married couples. Two persons "not married to one another, who for a significant period of time share a primary residence and a life together as a couple" are entitled to property division and spousal support, unless they have waived this right. The ALI Principles in essence turn the *Marvin* rule on its head: cohabiting couples are treated for many purposes like husband and wife unless they opt *out* of that status.

There is surprisingly little research to tell us what cohabiters actually think or expect about the sharing of property when the relationship ends. The ALI may impose obligations on couples that many would not choose for themselves—the price perhaps for trying to allocate fairly the economic losses of a relationship. Cohabiting couples seem to mimic married couples to at least some degree in terms of economic dependency and financial entanglement, and thus women often suffer worse economic effects upon dissolution.[74] In any event, a status-based standard puts the burden on people who might want to avoid financial commitments not only to avoid marriage, but also to avoid marriage-like relationships; or else to enter into cohabitation agreements that settle the rights of the parties explicitly.

But even the ALI Principles do not completely equate unmarried and married couples. The unmarried couple would still lack many benefits of marriage—like the right to sue for wrongful death, or Social Security benefits. An unmarried partner has no protection against accidental or intentional disinheritance; he or she takes nothing if one member dies without a will.[75] Rules of inheritance are rigid; and reward only *formal* relationships of blood, marriage, or adoption.[76] The unmarried partner is left out in the cold, unless a state changes its law, as California has done (see chapter 11).

Surprisingly, there are very few statutes that spell out the rights and obligations of cohabiting couples. The law has developed piecemeal, primarily by judges, borrowing legal concepts and tools from other contexts. Despite the dramatic increase in the number of cohabiting couples in the United States, few legislatures have accepted the invitation to craft standard rights and obligations. This may simply reflect a lack of consensus on the basic question: to what extent should law and society support cohabitation as a valid alternative to marriage? Because the question is perhaps still controversial, legislatures may be only too happy to leave it, in general, to courts. As Steven Nock has observed, "[c]ohabitation is an incomplete institution. No matter how widespread the practice, nonmarital unions are not yet governed by strong consensual norms or formal laws."[77] There is little disagreement that cohabiting relationships differ a good deal from marital ones—they tend to be "shorter, less stable, more violent, perhaps less mentally healthy for the partners and typically not as good a setting for children."[78] The disagreement is about whether to shore them up by extending the benefits of marriage, or whether to draw legal distinctions designed to discourage this form of family. The only real consensus is that it should probably not be illegal to do something that more than half the population has done.

The Worm Turns: The New Common-Law Marriage?

The cases and theories that aim to protect parties in non-marital relationships show a tendency, even in states that have abolished common-law marriage, to create something that is the same, only different; a kind of substitute for common-law marriage. In

Marvin, the substitute was a doctrine of implied contract. Other courts have used status-based theories, as we saw. The Washington State approach endorsed in *Connell* reaches results rather close to those that a common-law marriage regime would reach. People who act married are treated more or less like spouses. Yet common-law marriage had long since been abolished in that state.

There are, to be sure, significant differences between old and new. Nobody claims that a "committed intimate relationship" is an actual marriage for *all* purposes. In many cases, the court divides property or awards damages in ways that differ from the divisions that would be made in "real" marriages (or divorces). In states that follow *Marvin* rather strictly, the court will search for something they can call a contract; courts, to be sure, are clever about implying such contracts. In other states, as we saw, they have used other devices, or some vague notions of fairness, equity, or "quantum meruit" (reasonable value of services).

Socially, too, there is a great deal of difference between the world of the common-law marriage and the world of "committed intimate relationships." The world of the common-law marriage, on the whole, was the world of Victorian notions of sex, marriage, and propriety; and the doctrine reflected those norms. It stepped in to protect economic rights of spouses and children, but also to validate "marriages" to save reputations and prevent bastardization of children. The world of today is the world of the sexual revolution, a world in which cohabitation before marriage, or instead of marriage, is almost the norm. The main focus of concern is not the damaged reputation of a woman who has had sex without formal marriage. As we discussed in chapter 4, we saw this same shift in focus in heart balm laws, from protecting reputation to merely protecting financial investment.

By the beginning of the twenty-first century, "marriage" had clearly lost its monopoly over legitimate sexual relations. Various kinds of "committed relationships" shared in the consequences of marriage. *Factual* commitment shared legitimacy with *legal* or *ceremonial* commitment. In the contemporary world, it is easy to get married; and also easy to get out of marriage. Marriage in most states is a formal procedure, but the formalities are easy to comply with, and not terribly restrictive. No-fault divorce means that it is quick and cheap to get out of marriage as well. Getting out of the *consequences* of marriage (property rights, very notably) is, however, not quite so easy. The same is more or less true for other forms of commitment.

The law here mirrors what is happening in the family as a whole. There is less stability, more fluidity. The divorce rate is high. The breakup rate of couples is, of course, even higher. Throughout the twentieth century, the search for fulfillment, for individual happiness, became more tense, and for many people, more desperate, more elusive as a goal. Relationships are still central to the lives of almost everyone. But these relationships can be incredibly brittle. To be sure, millions of people resist the trends, and millions more deplore them. The trends, though, are stubborn; and they seem to be quite irreversible. They rest on the larger culture, and the larger culture is, in the short run, itself quite stubborn and immoveable.

Same-Sex Relationships

THERE HAVE BEEN two big marriage stories in the twentieth century—the decline of anti-miscegenation laws and the emergence of gay marriage. But the second story is incomplete. Here, we describe the social and legal revolution that brought us from an era in which same-sex marriage was never contemplated to one in which, depending on the state, it is either expressly authorized or expressly prohibited. This may be the last battleground over "traditional" marriage, whatever that may entail.

THE FIRST WAVE: TESTING THE WATERS

Richard Baker and James McConnell applied for a marriage license in the Hennepin County clerk's office in Minnesota on May 18, 1970. Observing that both applicants were male, the clerk sought an advisory opinion from the County attorney and later, opinion in hand, declined to issue the license. The couple sued, asking a state court to order the clerk to issue the license since Minnesota's marriage code contained no express ban on a same-sex union. Minnesota, like most every state at the time, did not expressly restrict marriage to opposite-sex couples, though the state code did use gendered terms like "husband and wife" and "bride and groom" in describing the many technical requirements of ceremonial marriage.[1]

Marriage laws in most states date back to codes adopted at the time of, or even before, statehood. These provisions have undergone many changes over time. States have repealed bans on miscegenation; restrictions on marriages by "idiots and imbeciles" were softened with the decline of the eugenics movement; common-law marriage rose and fell. The story of same-sex marriage may ultimately conform to the usual pattern—but the story, and the fierce controversy it comprises, is still unfolding.

Before 1970, the story of same-sex marriage was that there was no story. Marriage laws in most states, as noted, made no mention of same-sex marriage or the requirement that couples consist of one man and one woman. Marriage was simply assumed to be so limited, as the casual use of gendered terms suggests. The burgeoning gay rights movement in the 1950s and 1960s was focused on fighting police brutality or hate crime, or staving off the efforts of Anita Bryant—spokeswoman for orange juice and morality—to overturn or block passage of local ordinances banning discrimination on the basis of sexual orientation. "Job discrimination and police harassment" were key issues to "the lives of the gay men who set that agenda."[2] Legitimation of gay relations—and gay marriage—was not a plausible goal at that time. The Stonewall Riots of 1969, touched off when police shut down a gay bar, "inspired thousands of lesbians, gay men, and bisexuals to come out of their closets and openly proclaim erotic love for persons of the same sex."[3] The first wave of efforts to gain public recognition of gay rights followed in the 1970s.

The assumption that marriage was not open to gay couples held until the 1970s—when, in a rash of cases, same-sex couples, like Baker and McConnell, sought marriage licenses in a number of jurisdictions. They pointed out, correctly, to county clerks that the applicable law did not expressly forbid them to marry. Yet, clerks uniformly refused to issue such licenses. In a handful of cases, litigation followed. The first line of argument in these cases was always the same: the law's silence meant, as a matter of statutory interpretation, that the clerks could not refuse the couple a license, as long as they satisfied the other requirements for marriage. That argument never prevailed (not even in the very recent cases that ultimately ruled in favor of same-sex marriage). In those early cases, the argument was dismissed out of hand, often with a footnote to Webster's definition of "marriage."[4] When two women filed such a claim in Kentucky in 1973, the court dismissed their appeal, noting: "It appears to us that appellants are prevented from marrying, not by the statutes of Kentucky or the refusal of the County Court Clerk of Jefferson County to issue them a license, but rather by their own incapability of entering into a marriage as that term is defined."[5]

The second line of argument in those early cases was based on the constitutional right of privacy. In the early 1970s, this was still somewhat nebulous, but the plaintiffs could cite *Griswold v. Connecticut*, *Skinner v. Oklahoma*, and *Loving v. Virginia*—cases on constitutional protection for marriage and intimate relations that we discussed in chapters 1 and 5. Yet, despite these precedents, the Minnesota Supreme Court rejected Baker and McConnell's argument without much analysis. The court distinguished *Loving* by simply noting that, "in commonsense and in a constitutional sense, there is a clear distinction between a marital restriction based merely upon race and one based upon the fundamental difference in sex."[6] The case was appealed to the U.S. Supreme Court, which gave it even less consideration. After the Court agreed to review the case, the county clerk filed a motion to dismiss the appeal on the grounds that the regulation of marriage was exclusively reserved to the states.[7] The Court dismissed Baker's appeal for "want of a substantial federal question."[8]

Litigants like Baker and McConnell were wading into untested waters. Same-sex marriage was not yet a critical issue. Indeed, they conceded that "the question and the proposed [marital] relationship may well appear *bizarre*—especially to heterosexuals."[9] Their brief asked for legal and social acceptance of gay people, who are "neither grotesque nor uncommon." Only with "the full protection and recognition of the law ... will the public perceive that homosexuals are not freaks or unfortunate aberrations, to be swept under the carpet or to be reserved for anxious phantasies about one's identity or child rearing techniques."[10] But, as William Eskridge has observed, "[t]heirs was an idea whose time had not come."[11]

Homosexuality was certainly not new. The Kinsey reports, published in 1948 and 1953, had suggested it was quite common. But the idea that same-sex couples could seek or get the same kind of formal recognition as heterosexual couples was not yet a mainstream idea. The fight over legal recognition for same-sex relationships and social acceptance of same-sex partners and parents would come in the decades that followed—an important part of a larger debate about the legal and social definition of "family," as well as the scope of the right to privacy.

The litigants in these early cases did not win—indeed, they did not even gain the attention of courts; but they did have some impact. At least a few states woke up to the potential implications of a marriage law that did not mention gender; they passed amendments to make clear that silence meant exclusion, not inclusion. In 1977, for example, the California legislature added the phrase "between a man and a woman" to its definition of marriage; previously it had defined marriage only as a "personal relation arising out of a civil contract."[12]

In the 1980s, a few municipalities passed ordinances granting limited, though sometimes important, rights to same-sex couples who registered their unions. Over time, those ordinances spread to most big cities with any sizable gay and lesbian population, and ultimately to a host of smaller cities as well. In hindsight, it appears that these ordinances were the beginning of something new in family law—a sliding scale of statuses, with different rights based on the identity, gender, and intent of the parties. When San Francisco was poised to adopt domestic partner benefits for city employees in 1982, the city supervisor who drafted the proposal predicted that it would be "a step towards redefining the family less in terms of a marriage license and more in terms of the facts of dependency between partners."[13] It was a dent in the traditional notion that defined "family" solely by the legal ties of blood, marriage, or adoption. The fight for full marriage rights had taken a back seat to more pragmatic parts of the gay rights agenda, but the rising number of people living openly as homosexuals continued to exert pressure on the traditional family form.

The Second Wave: The Mobilized Fight for Legal Recognition

Beginning in the early 1990s, gay advocacy groups began to push again the idea that same-sex couples should be granted the same kind of formal recognition as other couples. A *USA Today* poll in 1987 surveyed adults to determine how flexible their definition of "true families" had become. Ninety-one percent of respondents said that a single parent living with a child was a "true family," while only 33 percent said the same of a homosexual couple raising children, and only 20 percent, of homosexual cohabitants without children.[14] But the very fact that surveys were asking such questions shows that times were beginning to change. In the decades that followed this survey, these numbers would change dramatically. A 2010 Pew Research Center poll found, for example, that 63 percent of respondents would define a same-sex couple with children as a "family," 45 percent for a same-sex couple without children.[15]

Many more gays and lesbians came out, and the level of cultural tolerance increased dramatically. At the same time, courts had developed a robust jurisprudence on sex discrimination, which made it easier to argue by analogy that bans on same-sex marriage were unacceptable. In the wake of these legal and societal changes and the Stonewall Riots, same-sex marriage advocates began a formal campaign to earn marriage rights (an agenda not supported by all gay rights advocates). The litigation strategy was central to the campaign; lawsuits were filed in a number of jurisdictions challenging the constitutionality of traditional marriage laws.

The Constitution and the Right to Marry

Courts in the early cases did not take these constitutional arguments seriously. But *Loving v. Virginia* put an end to anti-miscegenation laws, and was important beyond its effect on interracial marriage. It represented a shift toward greater constitutionalization of family law generally, and of marriage law in particular. Whether the constitutional right to marry extended to same-sex couples was at the heart of a second wave of gay marriage cases.

The first second-wave lawsuit to capture national attention came from Hawaii. A decision of the Hawaii Supreme Court in *Baehr v. Lewin* (1993) seemed to imply that same-sex marriage might be legally required.[16] Lawsuits in the second wave were carefully aimed at *state* constitutions, to prevent an adverse ruling from the U.S. Supreme Court that would be binding on the whole country.

But federal precedents were still relevant, since many state constitutions have language modeled on the federal one. The Hawaii Supreme Court cited *Loving* as implying a fundamental right to marry and rejecting the idea that a state could ban a marriage because the "Deity had deemed such a union intrinsically unnatural."[17] The Virginia trial court had relied on "Almighty God['s]" separation of the races to uphold the miscegenation ban,[18] a line of reasoning that, in the Hawaii court's view, had been clearly repudiated by the U.S. Supreme Court.[19]

The plaintiffs in *Baehr* also made the so-called *Loving* analogy, claiming that the ban on same-sex marriage discriminated on the basis of sex, just as the anti-miscegenation laws discriminated on the basis of race. Men are denied the right to marry men solely because of gender.[20] The *Baehr* majority refused to accept the argument made by one of the dissenting judges that the ban on same-sex marriage was valid because it "treats everyone alike and applies equally to both sexes."[21] The court concluded instead that the ban on same-sex marriage constituted a sex-based classification.[22] This almost certainly doomed it to invalidation under the Hawaii Constitution, which calls for "strict scrutiny" of such classifications.[23] *Baehr* was closely watched as it wound its way through the Hawaii court system.

Hawaii never did recognize same-sex marriage, however. Although the state never provided a compelling justification for banning gay marriage,[24] the ruling in *Baehr* was mooted by an amendment to the state constitution giving the Hawaii legislature the power to ban same-sex marriage, which it did.[25] A legislative compromise in 1997 resulted in the creation of a "reciprocal beneficiary" status, which allowed gay couples the opportunity to register for some of the rights and benefits enjoyed by married couples. In 2011, the legislature passed a law to allow civil unions, a status equivalent to marriage.[26]

THE ANTI-SAME-SEX MARRIAGE MOVEMENT

Hawaii's near-miss with same-sex marriage changed the national landscape. It was widely assumed (and feared) that other states would be compelled to give effect to same-sex marriages celebrated in Hawaii under principles of Full Faith and Credit.[27] As a memo written by Evan Wolfson, director of the Marriage Project of the Lambda Legal Defense and Education Fund, put it:

> Many same-sex couples in and out of Hawaii are likely to take advantage of what would be a landmark victory. The great majority of those who travel to Hawaii to marry will return to their homes in the rest of the country expecting full legal nationwide recognition of their marriage unions.[28]

This "plan" was cited frequently in congressional debates to whip up fears that same-sex marriages in Hawaii would be immediately and relentlessly thrust upon other states, and that the

Full Faith and Credit Clause would leave states defenseless to resist.[29] The same argument was made about the impact on federal law, only there the point was better taken since many federal statutes and regulations defer to state definitions of "marriage" and "spouse" in assigning federal burdens and benefits. Gay marriages from Hawaii would, presumably, be given recognition under federal law. The panic about the spread of gay marriage led to rhetorical outbursts in legislatures across the country. Same-sex marriage was front and center in a legal and cultural war. The issue figured prominently in state and federal politics, including presidential campaigns. Then-President George W. Bush warned in a radio address that same-sex marriages threaten "the most fundamental institution of civilization."[30] There were strong reactions from social conservatives and religious moralists. The leader of Concerned Women of America warned that: "The time is now"; it would be too late once "you see the American public disintegrating and you see our enemies overtaking us because we have no moral will."[31] On the other side, mayors in several American cities issued marriage licenses to same-sex couples, in an act of civil disobedience.[32]

The federal Defense of Marriage Act (DOMA) (1996), a direct response to developments in Hawaii, was designed to "protect" states from forcible recognition of same-sex marriages validly celebrated in another state.[33] Senator Trent Lott, for example, argued that if "such a decision affected only Hawaii, we could leave it to the residents of Hawaii to either live with the consequences or exercise their political rights to change things. But a court decision ... would raise threatening possibilities in other States."[34]

DOMA defined marriage, for federal purposes, as a union between a man and a woman.[35] It also amended the Full Faith and Credit Act to grant states the explicit power to refuse recognition of same-sex marriages.[36] DOMA passed the House by a margin of 342–67 and the Senate by 85–14. The federal definition of marriage had teeth, since it meant that same-sex marriage was irrelevant for immigration, tax, or other important federal purposes, even if a state or foreign country legally solemnized it.[37] The second clause of DOMA, though, was essentially unnecessary, based on a misunderstanding about what full faith and credit meant for marriages. Full faith and credit has never been understood to compel one state to recognize another's marriages, as we discussed in chapter 1. The Supreme Court has reserved the "exacting" obligations of full faith and credit for final judgments in judicial proceedings.[38] To be sure, in *Williams v. North Carolina* (1942),[39] the Court said that states were compelled to recognize divorce decrees issued in other states, so long as they met certain procedural standards.[40] But marriage, unlike divorce, is neither a judgment nor the product of a judicial proceeding. For state law *not* embodied in judgments, states need only comply with "certain minimum requirements" of full faith and credit.[41] A state may choose not to defer to the law of another state, and prefer its own law, so long as its choice is "neither arbitrary nor fundamentally unfair."[42] In other words, if a state has a sufficient stake in the dispute, it can ignore an inconsistent law from elsewhere. Marriages may not be subject even to these minimal protections if they do not qualify as an "act" within the meaning of the Full Faith and Credit Clause.[43] It is this discretion that gives rise to the marriage recognition rules we discussed in chapter 1.

Even though DOMA was premised on a misunderstanding of the law on full faith and credit, within a decade four-fifths of the states had accepted Congress's "invitation" to refuse recognition to same-sex marriages from other states. In rapid succession, states passed so-called mini-DOMAs, which banned the celebration of same-sex marriage and, in most cases, categorically refused recognition to such unions, even if valid where celebrated. A majority of states also put non-recognition into their constitutions. Only in New York and Maryland do the traditional recognition principles seem to apply to gay marriages.[44]

The First Signs of Success in the Same-Sex Marriage Movement: Civil Unions

On the one hand, most states rushed to take steps to hold off same-sex marriage; on the other hand, same-sex marriage made progress in a few other states. In 1999, in *Baker v. State*, the Vermont Supreme Court did the unthinkable. It held that denying same-sex couples the right to marry *or* to enter into a substantially comparable, and legally recognized, relationship, violated the state constitution.[45] The Common Benefits Clause of the

Vermont Constitution was read to ensure that "any exclusion from the general benefit and protection of the law" had to "bear a just and reasonable relation to the legislative goals." The right being withheld *was* very significant, and there was no decent justification for withholding it. Accordingly, the Court found no basis for "the continued exclusion of same-sex couples from the benefits incident to a civil marriage license under Vermont law." The court gave the legislature a "reasonable" period of time to "craft an appropriate means of addressing this constitutional mandate."[46] The legislature crafted an entirely new legal status—the civil union—that gave same-sex couples formal recognition, as well as entitlement to all the benefits, rights, and burdens of marriage, which numbered at least a thousand. It withheld only the name of "marriage."

The civil union proved popular among same-sex couples (hundreds flocked to Vermont to enter one), and it was surprisingly acceptable to many opponents of same-sex marriage. The spread of civil unions and the increasing public support for them are important parts of the same-sex marriage story. A 2006 poll by the Pew Forum on Religion and Public Life found that 54 percent of Americans approve of civil unions as a legal alternative for same-sex couples. Civil unions were eventually adopted in Connecticut, New Jersey (to comply with a court ruling similar to the one in Vermont), New Hampshire, Illinois, and Hawaii. And California offers a domestic partnership status that is virtually identical to a civil union (and thus to marriage), as do Nevada, Oregon, and Washington.

The civil union may be an ingenious way to appease opponents *and* proponents of same-sex marriage, but it is still relatively new and untested. Civil unions provide meaningful rights to couples who enter them, but fall short of the substantive and symbolic advantages of marriage. Withholding the name "marriage" reinforces a kind of second-class citizenship, which the gay rights movement has struggled against. Substantively, the civil union is a source of confusion for couples who want to enjoy certain benefits, in their home state or elsewhere. Both Vermont and New Jersey appointed commissions to study civil unions, and each concluded that the status poses many practical problems for couples and inflicts symbolic harm.[47]

Dissolution has posed a particular problem for civil union partners. Because states grant divorce only to their own residents, dissolution of civil unions has proven nearly impossible for couples who do not live in Vermont or in one of the few other states that offer civil unions. A Connecticut couple who tried to dissolve their civil union in their home state met with a real legal puzzle. An appellate court in *Rosengarten v. Downes* (2002) held that the civil union could not be dissolved in Connecticut because the state's divorce code only gave courts jurisdiction to dissolve a "marriage."[48] A few couples have been able to convince judges to dissolve their unions on some more or less equitable principles, but the legal situation is still confused. Thus, Susan Burns, whose case we mentioned in chapter 6, found herself unexpectedly in violation of a custody order when her civil union partner, another woman, moved in. According to a Georgia court, because the civil union was not a "marriage," her overnight visitor was "non-marital" and thus prohibited. Even though the relationship had been formally sanctioned by the state of Vermont, it was legally irrelevant in Georgia.[49] So, too, was the Vermont civil union of John Langan and Neal Spicehandler irrelevant in New York. After the couple entered into the civil union, Spicehandler was killed through the combination of a car accident and alleged medical malpractice at a New York hospital. An appellate court ruled that Langan did not have standing to bring a wrongful death claim against the hospital, a legal right reserved under New York law for a "spouse" or other next-of-kin.[50]

The Third Wave: Same-Sex Marriage Begins in the United States

More than ten years after the Hawaii "scare," one state finally *did* legalize same-sex marriage. In 2003, the Supreme Judicial Court of Massachusetts ruled in *Goodridge v. Department of Public Health* that the ban on same-sex marriage violated the state constitution, which guarantees due process and equal protection.[51] Denial of the right to marry, the Court explained, "works a deep and scarring hardship on a very real segment of the community for no rational reason." Moreover, the harm to gays and lesbians, the Court said, is not only the harm that comes from denying them

151

the benefits of marriage. It is also the harm of being deemed "second-class citizens" in the process.

The court in *Goodridge* gave the legislature 180 days to "take such action as it may deem appropriate in light of this opinion." Though it was obvious that the only action contemplated by the court was opening up the laws of civil marriage to same-sex couples, the state legislature acted quickly to pass a bill allowing same-sex couples to enter civil unions with all the benefits and rights of marriage, but not "marriage" itself. But in an advisory opinion, the court rebuked the legislature's effort to circumvent the ruling in *Goodridge*.[52] Then, after a 180-day delay, same-sex couples began to marry legally in Massachusetts, on the fiftieth anniversary of the Supreme Court's historic ruling in *Brown v. Board of Education* (1954), which ordered desegregation of public schools. Initially, only couples residing in Massachusetts could marry there, under the terms of a 1913 marriage evasion law that Governor Mitt Romney ordered enforced.[53] The law, adopted at a time when states had greater variations in marriage law, prohibited out-of-state couples from marrying in Massachusetts unless they would have been permitted to marry in their home states. Since no other state then authorized same-sex marriage, and almost all of them had laws expressly prohibiting it, this effectively restricted the reach of same-sex marriage to locals. Through litigation, however, couples from Rhode Island and New Mexico eventually earned the right to marry in Massachusetts, since there was no clear indication that those states considered same-sex unions void.[54]

THE CURRENT LANDSCAPE

Around the time of *Goodridge*, same-sex marriage became legal in a number of foreign countries, including Canada, Spain, Norway, the Netherlands, Belgium, and South Africa. In 2010, Argentina became the first South American country to legalize same-sex marriage. And although Massachusetts initially restricted same-sex marriage to resident couples under its marriage evasion law, it eventually opened the doors to non-resident same-sex couples in 2008.[55] That same year, the highest courts in California and Connecticut invalidated the state bans on same-sex marriage.[56]

The gay marriage window in California was opened only briefly; it was closed by referendum less than six months later in November 2008, after the passage of Proposition 8, though not before more than 14,000 same-sex couples had been married in California. The California Supreme Court upheld Proposition 8 against a subsequent legal challenge, but grandfathered in the marriages that had already taken place.[57] (In 2010, a federal district court ruled that Proposition 8 violated the federal constitution, but the ruling has been stayed pending appeal.)[58] Iowa joined Connecticut and Massachusetts with a 2009 court ruling that declared the ban on same-sex marriage unconstitutional.[59] (Three of the Iowa judges who voted for this were recalled from their seats in the November 2010 election.) Finally, in a somewhat surprising cascade, the legislatures of Vermont, New Hampshire, and Maine each adopted a law to permit same-sex marriage, while expressly allowing religious institutions to refuse to perform same-sex marriages or host same-sex weddings.[60] (Maine's law was short-lived; voters amended the state constitution by referendum in the November 2009 election to ban same-sex marriage.)[61] Most recently, the District of Columbia passed a law to permit same-sex marriage.[62] Same-sex couples can thus now marry in five American states plus the District of Columbia. As we have seen, several additional states offer robust marriage alternatives like civil union or domestic partnership, which, depending on the jurisdiction, offer many or all of the benefits of marriage.[63] In 2010, Illinois enacted a bill to allow both gay and straight couples to enter into civil unions.[64]

Social support for same-sex marriage is clearly growing. According to a 2008 poll by the Pew Research Center for the People and the Press, the percentage of individuals who oppose same-sex marriage has declined from 54 percent to 49 percent since 2004.[65] Even the dictionaries are changing—several major ones have, in the last five years, added a secondary definition of marriage that includes same-sex unions.[66] Still, more than forty states have passed an anti-same-sex-marriage statute or constitutional amendment, some of which are broad enough to prohibit contracts or other mechanisms designed to mimic the status of marriage. In the twenty-nine states that have written a prohibition of same-sex marriage into the state constitution, the issue is dead, at least for now. Current and future challenges will focus on the small number of states with no express ban on same-sex marriage, or those with only a statutory, as opposed to a constitutional, ban. The results have so far been mixed—the high courts in Maryland, New York, and Washington have held that their constitution does not require recognition of same-sex marriage, and the high court in New Jersey has held that an alternative, equivalent status will constitutionally suffice.[67] Chances for change in states such as Utah or Mississippi are close to zero.

Though the battle for same-sex marriage has been hard-fought, the gay rights movement is not of one mind on whether marriage rights are central to their agenda, or even whether they should fight hard for the right of gays to marry. A 1989 exchange between two senior lawyers at the Lambda Legal Defense and Education Fund, Paula Ettelbrick and Thomas Stoddard, exemplifies the split in the movement, which continues today.[68] Some urge moving beyond an inherently patriarchal and perhaps outdated institution. (Even beyond the gay rights community, there have been calls for the elimination of civil marriage altogether.)[69] But many want marriage equality not only because of its tangible benefits, but precisely because of the tradition it represents. And, regardless of any split within the gay rights community, access to marriage has become, in the public's eye, the "true test of LGBT equality."[70]

A handful of cases have addressed the marriage rights of transsexuals, a small but increasingly vocal group of people who suffer from gender dysphoric disorder and have begun to demand legal recognition and civil rights. J'Noel Ball is a male-to-female transsexual who underwent sexual reassignment surgery to align her anatomical gender with her self-perceived gender. Living as a woman, J'Noel married a rich and much older man, Marshall Gardiner. When Marshall died, his angry son filed suit to challenge J'Noel's right to a widow's share of his estate. Under Kansas law, J'Noel, as a widow, would have been entitled to half of the $1.5 million estate. The Kansas Supreme Court ruled that a person's birth sex cannot be changed; once a man, always a man.[71] This means that in Kansas, which amended its marriage law in 1975 to make explicit a ban on same-sex marriage,[72] a male-to-female transsexual can only marry another woman since legally she remains a man. Ironically, these rulings imply that a kind of same-sex marriage would be legal, since J'Noel, now an anatomical female, could presumably marry another woman. It is doubtful, of course, that the Kansas court would so hold. Logic rarely stands in the way of emotion.

Conclusion

Same-sex marriage has posed—and continues to pose—a challenge to traditional definitions of marriage and family. But, more importantly, the issue implies broader changes in family law— the increasing role of constitutional analysis; limits on the right of government to regulate the family; and the clash between the traditional family form and a new and wider menu of intimate and household arrangements, and all this against the background of the rise of a stronger form of individualism.

Same-sex marriage continues to be a central player in a stormy political drama. There is a strong current flowing in the direction of legalization. But the opposition is also powerful, and powerfully determined: it would be foolish to predict either that the movement will certainly win, in the long run at least; or that the opposition will succeed in stopping it cold, except for a handful of liberal states and liberal courts. Only the passage of time can provide an answer.

PART THREE

WHEN THE MUSIC STOPS: DISSOLVING A

MARRIAGE AND THE AFTERMATH

*

Untying the Knot: Divorce and Annulment

IN THE TWENTIETH CENTURY, one frequently hears that marriage and the nuclear family are under siege. Divorce—and especially the rise of no-fault divorce—contributes centrally to that image. This chapter tracks the divorce story, from the traditional system of fault-based divorce to the new system of divorce on demand, and takes a look, too, at annulment; and the recent backlash that tries, mostly without success, to use the law to try to stem the tide of family breakdown.

There are, basically, two legal ways to end a marriage: divorce and annulment. Of course, there are also informal ways of ending a marriage. A man (less often a woman) can simply walk out into the night and never come back. This happens often enough; and it has a real impact on families. A couple that does not want to keep on living together can also decide, for whatever reason, to ask a court for a legal *separation*. In older sources, separation was often called "divorce from bed and board" (*a mensa et thoro*); and absolute divorce was called divorce "from the bonds of marriage" (*a vinculis matrimonii*). "Separation" is a better and less confusing term. A legally separated couple will live apart, still officially married, but often with the same kinds of arrangements a divorced couple might have, about custody, property division, and support for the dependent spouse.

Not every state provided for legal separation. In 1931, separation was available in twenty-seven states; one state, Florida, expressly forbade it; and in the rest, the laws were silent, which presumably meant no legal separation was allowed.[1] Chester Vernier, who compiled these and virtually all other laws related to the family in a massive five-volume treatise, disliked "limited divorce" (his name for separation). Separated people could not legally marry. Thus, separation deprived people "of the pleasures ... incident upon cohabitation"; it required, in other words, "a degree of chastity scarcely to be expected in an ordinary mortal."[2] Whether "ordinary mortals" in fact stayed chaste is another question. And the world has changed dramatically since Vernier's day. Nobody today expects much chastity, whether from separated couples or anybody else.

Some couples separate, as a kind of prelude to divorce. They execute a separation agreement, to be incorporated into later divorce proceedings. How many couples enter into these contracts, *without* the looming shadow of divorce, is hard to say—probably not very many. Legal separations likely were never very common. A study of matrimonial actions in Maryland, for 1929, showed 120 actions for legal separation, as compared to 1,973 actions for divorce.[3] Why would a couple choose legal separation, rather than divorce? They might, for example, be Roman Catholics, opposed to divorce on religious grounds. There might be financial reasons—tax or pension problems. In New York, for most of the century, adultery was the only legal grounds for divorce. But cruel and inhuman treatment was grounds for separation. In separation cases, as in divorce, one party could resist. In 1924, Margaret Straub asked for a legal separation from her husband Walter; she also wanted custody of their son, and support payments.[4] Walter resisted and appealed. The Straubs clearly had a miserable marriage; and in court they flung mud at each other. Margaret claimed her husband was a "habitual drunkard," drunk every weekend (he denied this). His behavior caused her "great mental anguish." She claimed he called her "vile and filthy names"; and that he once locked her out of the house. The court thought they were both responsible for their quarrels, their "petty bickerings and fancied grievances, endeavored to irritate and annoy each other." The legal separation was denied. As far as the court was concerned, these two were condemned to live together for the rest of their lives.

Legal separation and annulment are substitutes for divorce— one quite feeble, the other quite powerful. Legal separations keep a thin version of a marriage alive. Annulments are hard to get (in theory). But if a marriage is annulled, both parties can remarry; indeed, this is usually the point of an annulment. Both annulments and legal separations appeal mostly to people with religious scruples against divorce—devout Catholics, very notably. We will deal with annulments in a bit more detail later in this chapter.

Divorce

At the beginning of the twentieth century, every state in the union, with one exception (South Carolina), had some provision for absolute divorce.[5] South Carolina had no divorce law in the nineteenth century, and, indeed, the South Carolina Constitution of 1895 provided that "Divorces from the bonds of matrimony shall not be allowed in this State" (Art XVII, section 3). Divorce did not arrive there until 1948.[6]

During the century, the divorce laws of the various states differed considerably. There were "easy" states and "hard" states. The general shape of divorce law, at least officially, was much the same everywhere. To get a divorce, a person had to file a lawsuit in court. A good spouse filed suit against an (alleged) bad spouse. The plaintiff would claim that the defendant, the bad spouse, had done something wrong—something which gave plaintiff, the good spouse, valid "grounds" for divorce. In the tough states, the statutory list of "grounds" was short. In the easy states, the list was longer. The defendant was supposed to file an answer to the petition. At the trial, both sides could present evidence. In the end, the judge would decide whether or not the plaintiff had made her case. Or his case; though, in fact, most of the plaintiffs were women.

As of the 1930s, every state that recognized divorce at all listed adultery as one of the available grounds.[7] Almost all of them added desertion and cruelty; and imprisonment or conviction of a crime; and some forty jurisdictions added drunkenness. Nonsupport was grounds in some fifteen states, drug addiction in six. Other grounds were more idiosyncratic; in Florida, "habitual indulgence by defendant in violent and ungovernable temper";[8] in Louisiana, public defamation of a spouse; in Illinois, infecting a wife with venereal disease; in New Hampshire, refusal to cohabit for three years. In Alabama, one grounds for divorce was "commission of the crime against nature, whether with mankind or beast, either before or after marriage."[9] In Tennessee in the 1930s, it was grounds for divorce, quite reasonably, if "either party has attempted the life of the other, by poison or any other means showing malice."[10] In New Hampshire, a divorce was available when either spouse "has joined any religious sect or society which professes to find the relation of husband and wife unlawful, and has refused to cohabit with the other for six months together."[11] This statute, which went back to the early nineteenth century, was aimed at the Shakers, an (obviously) small religious group, which did not believe in sexual intercourse.

Divorce laws and practices of course also bore the imprint of conventional gender roles. Wives were supposed to be chaste, loyal homemakers. Men were breadwinners, with stronger sexual appetites. In Kansas, and a number of other states, as of 1935, a husband was entitled to a divorce "when the wife at the time of marriage was pregnant by another than her husband."[12] Nothing was said about a woman's right to divorce, if her groom had made some other woman pregnant. Under the Maryland Code, the husband was entitled to a divorce if, unknown to him, the woman, before the marriage, had committed "illicit carnal intercourse with another man." There was no comparable stricture about men.[13] Many statutes gave the wife, on the other hand, the right to a divorce if the husband, for no good reason, refused to support her; in New Mexico, for example, "Neglect on the part of the husband to support the wife, according to his means, station in life and ability" was grounds for divorce.[14] Women, on the other hand, were not required to support their husbands.

Traditional morality peeps out of the pages of the statute books. In Texas, if a man seduced a woman, and then married her to escape prosecution for seduction or fornication, he had to stay married for three years before he could sue for divorce.[15] An old Pennsylvania law, which lasted into the twentieth century, provided that an adulterer (male or female) could not marry "the person with whom the crime was committed during the life of the former wife or husband."[16] Everywhere, to get a divorce, the plaintiff herself had to be innocent, blameless, pure. This doctrine, called "recrimination," meant that a woman who committed adultery could not divorce an adulterous husband if she had committed adultery herself, or vice versa. Under the doctrine called "condonation," a plaintiff also lost her case if she forgave her husband, and slept with him after he confessed his adultery. Moreover, she had no case if he had *colluded* with her, agreed to "give" her a divorce, and agreed not to contest; in short, if the divorce case was a fraud. As we will see, none of this reflected the real, working law of divorce.

Cruelty was the grounds of choice in many states. In Ohio, in 1930, between July 1 and December 30, almost all of some 6,500 petitions for divorce alleged gross neglect of duty, or cruelty, or both. In San Mateo County, California, in the 1950s, an astonishing 95.1 percent of all petitions alleged "extreme cruelty."[17] The statutes defined cruelty in various ways. For example, the Oregon Code of 1930 spoke of "cruel and inhuman treatment, or personal indignities rendering life burdensome."[18] In California, cruelty was defined as "the wrongful infliction of grievous bodily injury or grievous mental suffering."[19] Over time, regardless of statutory language, courts expanded the definition to include mental or emotional cruelty. In many states, adultery was distinctly unpopular as a ground for divorce. Of course, this tells us nothing about the incidence of adultery in real life.

So much for the theory—the official law of divorce. What was the actual practice? The vast majority of divorces—perhaps 90 percent or more—were collusive and fraudulent, based on a kind of semi-legitimate perjury. In the typical case, the wife filed for divorce. The husband simply failed to respond; or in any case failed to contest. The formal official law, the law in the treatises, the law mouthed by high court judges, had absolutely no relationship to what was happening on the ground. At the level of trial courts, divorce was a matter of routine—courts simply acted as rubber stamps; couples by the thousands got their divorces; a messy system of lies and collusion was in effect; and judges, for the most part, buried their heads in the sand. In the rare contested cases, the formal law had some bite. The reported cases are all, of course, solely *appellate* cases. No one was likely to appeal from a consensual divorce, a collusive divorce, a divorce both parties wanted, or were at least willing to have.

The Age of Collusion

Changing ideology, changing culture, and changing gender roles increased the *demand* for divorce. The divorce rate kept increasing in the United States—faster, indeed, than population. In 1929, there were 201,468 divorces, or, as one writer put it, about one every two minutes.[20] From 1867 to that date, the population increased 300 percent, but the divorce rate rose by 2,000 percent.[21] The divorce rate kept increasing in the twentieth century; there were, to be sure, ups and downs, but mostly ups. There was a bulge in divorces right after the Second World War; and a rapid rise again from the 1960s to the 1980s. In that decade, there were more than 5 divorces per 1,000 total population. After 1986, the divorce rate declined; in 2007, the rate was 3.6 per 1,000 total population.[22] The marriage rate has also declined; and this decline, of course, has an impact on the rate of divorce. Couples who cohabit can end their relationship by packing a suitcase; no need to go to court.

Historically, many people—especially people in authority—tended to deplore divorce, and easy divorce in particular. But in the twentieth century, attitudes began to change. There were voices speaking out against the system. William N. Gemmill, a Municipal Court Judge in Chicago, in 1914 compared the "repeated assaults against divorce" to Don Quixote tilting against windmills.[23] Some feminists, sociologists, and free thinkers agreed. It was useless to try to stem the flow of divorce suits. But the law on the books blocked the way to genuine reform. The law was stalemated. Catholic dogma refused to countenance divorce; Catholics were a powerful minority, and, in some states, close to a majority. Protestant churches accepted divorce, but only as a last resort and a necessary evil. An irresistible force (the demand for divorce) ran up against an immoveable object.

The living law, however, made nonsense of the official law. Divorce law, in practice, was a fraud, a charade, a lie. Official doctrines had no impact (or very little) on living law. Consider, for example, the doctrine of "recrimination," which we mentioned before—the rule that when the pot calls the kettle black, the court should not grant a divorce. A wife who commits adultery cannot divorce an adulterous husband.[24] But a study of recrimination in Dane County, Wisconsin, for the years 1927– 1931 showed that the doctrine had no bite. In Wisconsin, an officer of the court, the "divorce counsel," the "guardian of the public interest in marriage," was supposed to investigate the facts in divorce cases, and report to the court if either spouse had committed "any pertinent marital misconduct."[25] The court was then supposed to take this information into account—including information about recrimination. But the divorce counsel told the researchers that he had reported "mutual misconduct and recommended denial of divorce ... in more than 100 cases." The court ignored him in all but one of these cases. Moreover, in only 44 out of 567 divorce cases studied in the county did defendant raise the issue of "plaintiff's marital misconduct." In thirty-five of these, the divorce was granted—though mostly to the defendant. In a few cases, the parties reconciled, or the records were simply incomplete. In none was the case dismissed, on the grounds of "recrimination, connivance or provocation." And yet these doctrines, "if strictly applied," would "have barred relief in practically every case."[26]

The model for the Wisconsin "divorce counsel" was probably the "King's Proctor," an officer in England, whose job it was to sniff out (and prevent) collusion and other flaws in divorce proceedings. In 1915, Tennessee created the office of "divorce proctor," with power to "investigate the charges" in divorce cases, for a fee of $5 per case.[27] In Oregon, the District Attorney was supposed to see that there was no fraud or collusion in divorce cases, whether or not the defendant contested.[28] In West Virginia, the duty of the "divorce commissioner"—a person of standing in his profession and of "good moral character"—was to investigate divorce suits, and take steps necessary to prevent "fraud and collusion in divorce cases."[29] One proctor, W. W. Wright, in Kansas City, supposedly reduced the divorce rate in that city by 40 percent.[30] But this, if true, must have been very exceptional. For the most part, these officials accomplished nothing. Collusive, consensual cases continued to be the norm.[31] The courts endlessly repeated the mantra that collusion was an evil, and that courts should not grant divorces if the case even smelled like collusion. But this was, basically, nothing but talk. In Illinois, for example, in a study published in the 1950s, Maxine Virtue (wonderful name) concluded that almost all divorce cases were collusive. In the typical case, the plaintiff, a woman, accused her husband of cruelty; he beat her, slapped her, abused her. Virtue noted the "remarkable" fact that "cruel spouses" in Chicago usually struck their wives "in the face exactly twice." The wife's mother, sister, or brother typically backed up this story.[32] In Indiana, until the 1950s, judges were supposed to refer to prosecutors all cases where the defendant did not show up or defend himself

against a divorce. The prosecutor's duty, at that point, was to enter and defend the case, if there was any suspicion, God forbid,
of collusion. But these were empty words. In practice, Indiana
was no different from any other state. Almost all divorces were
uncontested, undefended, and the prosecutor never showed up.
Divorce was available almost "for the asking."[33]

In short, most divorces were in fact consensual—at least in
some sense. Both parties wanted the divorce, or at least were
willing to let it happen. But this does not mean there was nothing else in the background—a wife disgusted with a drunken
or abusive or unfaithful husband, for example; a woman whose
marriage was so wretched that she felt obliged to ask for divorce.
William Goode, in his classic study of divorced women in De-
troit in the 1950s, concluded that the husband was usually "the
first to desire a divorce"; but that he had also adopted, "whether
consciously or not," a "line of behavior" that forced the other to
want a divorce.[34] That a case was uncontested meant only that
the parties had agreed "to spare themselves the extra expense
and humiliation" of trial. All issues had been "hammered out in
brutal negotiation in the offices of their respective lawyers."

It is surprisingly difficult to tell how many cases were actually
contested.[35] Clearly there were not very many. In Maryland, for
example, of 3,306 cases filed in 1929, answers were filed in 44.1
percent of them; but there seemed to be a real contest in only 5
or 6 percent of the cases. And in many of those, the dispute was
over alimony or custody or the like, not over the divorce itself.
The researchers suggested that actual contest over the divorce
itself accounted for "no more than one suit out of every forty
or fifty filed."[36] Plaintiffs overwhelmingly won their cases. Between 1948 and 1950, 14.8 percent of divorce cases nationwide
were contested; but many were contested for strategic reasons; in
fact the plaintiff was successful "in all but a handful of suits."[37] In
San Mateo County, in the 1950s, the results were pretty much the
same. Wives who were plaintiffs won 96 percent of their cases.
Men who were plaintiffs won 78.2 percent.[38]

Most of the twentieth century, then, was the age of collusion.
Divorce was a dual system. The real law of divorce was a pious
(or impious) sham. Yet a more liberal divorce law was out of the
question in most states. The forces of morality shouted down any

such suggestions. Legislatures did not dare to offend the moralists. Hence, the formal law seemed unchangeable—petrified, frozen into weird, archaic shapes. Divorce had become a ritual—stylized, stereotyped, a kind of theater of the absurd.

One might imagine that men and women would find marriage inadequate in equal numbers. Or that more men would want a divorce—women, tied down with children, less chance at remarriage, and fewer economic opportunities, might cling to shabby marriages much longer than men. Goode's research suggests that this was in fact the case. But on the surface, the picture seemed the opposite. Figures differed from time to time and place to place, but everywhere women far outnumbered men as plaintiffs.[39] In 1930, 72 percent of the divorces were granted to women.[40] In San Mateo County, between 1950 and 1957, 84.1 percent of the plaintiffs were women.[41] Figures for 1950 show that, nationwide, wives received 72.5 percent of the divorces.[42]

After all, in collusive divorces, it was useful for a woman to bring the case. She would, of course, allege adultery, cruelty, or desertion. Women were expected to be victims; they were, to use a popular phrase, the weaker sex. It was humiliating for a man to claim that his wife had cuckolded him, or battered him with a frying pan, or had run off and left him behind. Moreover, since a woman was likely to end up with the children, and since she wanted or needed child support or alimony, she had to be cast in the role of the victim.[43] Dorothy Thompson claimed in 1949 that "chivalry" was also a factor. A man would not want his wife's name "besmirched," especially if he had children. So he assumed the blame.[44] Perhaps this was true at least once in a while.

Collusion followed the contours of the formal law. If the formal law—as in New York—insisted on adultery, then it had to be collusion about adultery. New York developed what has been called soft-core adultery. The husband would check in to a hotel. A woman (for some reason, she was usually a blonde) would come to his room. They would take off some of their clothes (usually not all). In a study of five hundred cases published in the 1930s, the man was naked in only twenty-three instances; in two he was wrapped in a towel, in 119, he was in his "B.V.D. or underwear"; in 101 in a bathrobe or dressing gown; the rest of the time, 227 cases, he was in pajamas. The woman was naked about twice as often: she was in a "negligee" 67 times; a nightgown 126 times; pajamas accounted for 73; bathrobe, 32; and "kimono," 68. In any case, there would be a knock on the door—a maid with towels, or a bellboy with a telegram. Then a photographer would burst in and take pictures.[45] The woman would then collect her fee ($50 was normal), and disappear. The photos would show up in court, as evidence of adultery. An article published in 1934 in a newspaper had the intriguing title: "I was the Unknown Blonde in 100 New York Divorces."[46]

Other states followed different patterns. In Ohio, "gross neglect of duty" was the favorite grounds in the early 1930s. Almost nobody alleged adultery.[47] If you believed the court records, husbands in Ohio were faithful but bad providers. In Philadelphia, too, husbands were either cruel, or deserted their families in droves, but they never strayed. A study of Philadelphia, Pennsylvania, between 1937 and 1950, found desertion in 46.9 percent of the cases, 29.7 percent alleged "indignities," and 16.8 percent, indignities and cruelty.[48] "Cruelty" was alleged in 85 percent of the petitions in Linn County, Iowa, between 1928 and 1944. Here too, adultery barely appeared in the records.[49] In states with longer lists of grounds than New York, plaintiffs made the less stigmatic choices. In some of these states, adultery was a crime. But adulterous husbands almost never went to jail. In Massachusetts, if the plaintiff alleged adultery, the judge was supposed to pass this information on to the district attorney, along with a "list of witnesses." Apparently the district attorney never took the slightest notice. In 1947, the probate judges of Massachusetts recommended getting rid of this provision. It was an "unnecessary expense and ineffective." The legislature repealed it in 1948.[50]

Divorce on the Move

There were other ways around the formal law. New York, as we said, allowed divorce only for adultery. A resident of New York, with time and money, could go to a state where the laws were much less fussy. To do this, of course, you had to establish residence in the other state. But some states were eager to oblige. Today we have eco-tourism, and sex tourism; in the past there was a flourishing business of divorce tourism. States that wanted the money from divorce tourism lowered their residence requirements, and inflated the grounds for divorce.

A number of states had tried this. But the winner, in the long run, was Nevada. "Going to Reno" became almost synonymous with divorce. Divorce, like gambling, was a way to make money in this barren, desert state, with no real economic base. But even in Nevada, a state where moral considerations, to put it mildly, rarely interfered with pursuit of the dollar, the issue evoked controversy. Women's groups, clergymen, and others railed against easy divorce. In 1913, they demanded a strict one-year residency law. Their victory was short-lived. The residence requirement dropped to six months, then three months, then (in 1931), to six weeks.[51] The census figures for 1929, 1930, and 1931 showed the results quite clearly. In Nevada, there were thirty-eight or so divorces, for every 1,000 residents—more than ten times higher than Oklahoma, the next highest state.[52] In 1946, in a burst of postwar divorces, Nevada crested at 143.9 divorces per 1,000 inhabitants; in 1950, there were fifty-five per 1,000. This was still more than fifteen times the California rate—and more than fifty times the rate in New York, the state with the lowest divorce rate and, not by coincidence, the strictest divorce laws.[53] In the late 1940s, the Nevada legislature allegedly considered a bill to allow divorce by slot machine.[54]

In 1959, Eddie Fisher, the singer, wanted to divorce his wife (Debbie Reynolds) in order to marry Elizabeth Taylor.[55] Fisher and his wife lived in California; but California required a one-year waiting period before remarriage. Nevada required only a six-week residency period. A forty-four night gig at Las Vegas's Tropicana Hotel as a nightclub singer did the trick for Eddie Fisher. (At the close of the third season of the acclaimed television show *Mad Men*, set in the 1960s, Betty Draper was on a plane to Reno—to begin her six-week stay that would allow a quickie Nevada divorce from philandering husband Don and an immediate remarriage to Henry Francis.)

In a federal system, divorce tourism ran a certain risk. Were these six-week wonders in Nevada really valid? Nevada wanted the divorce business; but strict states wanted to protect their citizens—and their laws—from the laxer moral views of divorce.

States, under the "full faith and credit" clause, were supposed to honor judgments of sister states. Did they have to recognize quickie divorces and remarriages in Nevada? Or anywhere?

Two cases in the 1940s involved the tangled affairs of squabbling couples in North Carolina. North Carolina, like New York, was a very hard-nosed state. Divorce was basically only for adultery. Mr. Williams, who had a wife and four children in North Carolina, went to Nevada and checked in to the Alamo Auto Court, on the Las Vegas–Los Angeles Road. So did a Mrs. Hendrix, also of North Carolina. They stayed for six weeks, and each filed for divorce. Notice was published in a Las Vegas newspaper; and copies of the summons and complaint were mailed to the outraged spouses in North Carolina. Williams and Hendrix got their divorces, and immediately married each other in Nevada. But when they returned to North Carolina, they were accused of bigamy, arrested, and convicted.

The U.S. Supreme Court reversed their convictions.[56] The Nevada divorce was valid under Nevada law; and therefore, under the full faith and credit clause, North Carolina had to give effect to the judgment of divorce, even if it would not have permitted a divorce under the same circumstances. But Williams and his new wife were by no means out of the woods. The case went back for retrial. Again, Williams and Mrs. Hendrix were convicted. But this time, the conviction was based on a slightly different theory. The Nevada divorce was said to be invalid because Williams and Hendrix never intended to make a home in that state. Their "residence" in Nevada was fake; and this meant that Nevada had no jurisdiction over them in the first place. And this time, the Supreme Court affirmed the decision.[57] What was the difference between *Williams I* (1942) and *Williams II* (1945)? Only that in *Williams I* (according to the Supreme Court), North Carolina assumed the right to disregard Nevada's decree, without challenging its validity. In *Williams II*, North Carolina did precisely this—that is, challenged the validity of the divorce under Nevada law—and prevailed. Presumably, Williams and his new wife, Hendrix, went to jail.

Some divorce locales were even more exotic than Nevada; Mexico was one of them. According to one estimate, between the First World War and 1929, about two thousand American couples were divorced in Mexico.[58] In 1929, it was reported that the

Mexican state of Campeche was a huge divorce mill: For a fee ranging from $600 to $1,500, a quick divorce could be had.[59] There was apparently another surge of Mexican divorces in the 1960s. In 1963, Sybil Burton divorced her husband, the actor Richard Burton, by proxy in Mexico. A local lawyer, in Jalisco, appeared for her in court; the ground of the divorce was "cruelty." Burton was then free to marry Elizabeth Taylor. This was the second time migratory divorce freed up a husband for her. The Burtons thus became "one of the 10,000 or so non-Mexican couples" who, each year, "consummate a Mexican divorce" in a "ritual that has been called 'serial monogamy.'" Mexican divorces were quick, cheap, and easy. Mexico granted instant residency; and a divorce could be granted in minutes.[60] But most attorneys (and courts) felt these divorces were not valid in the United States. This apparently did not stop people from crossing the border for a quick divorce. A song sung by the country music singer Ry Cooder put it this way:

> Down below El Paso lies Juarez
> ....
> An old adobe house
> Where you leave your past behind
> ....
> One day married, next day free
> Broken hearts for you and me
> It's a sin for you to get a Mexican divorce.[61]

Other jurisdictions, too, tried to get a share of this rich source of business. In 1944, the legislative assembly of the Virgin Islands reduced its residency requirement to six weeks. For a brief period, business was booming; but this ended in 1955.[62] The legislature of the islands, the Supreme Court said in *Granville-Smith v. Granville-Smith* (1955), had no authority to pass laws except about local affairs; enticing divorce tourists was no local affair.[63] Justice Clark dissented; the "only practical effect" of the holding, he said, "would be to make New Yorkers fly 2,400 miles over land to Reno instead of 1,450 miles over water to the Virgin Islands."[64] Haiti and the Dominican Republic also entered the business. A "weekend in Haiti can include a divorce," according to an article in the *New York Times* in 1986.[65] An attorney advertised in the *Washington Post*, in 1979, that he could give "legal advice" for "mutual consent divorces" in the Dominican Republic: "Divorce granted within 24 hrs of arrival in the Dominican Republic."[66] A lawyer in Guam, on his website in 2008, gave "six reasons why a divorce from Guam U.S.A. is better than a Caribbean divorce." Divorce in Guam was quick (two weeks); meanwhile, you enjoyed an "American vacation paradise" in a clean, modern, and *American* locale, with "extraordinary hotels, nightlife, diving, golf and beaches," a "corruption-free U.S. legal system," and a valid decree in the English language. The Caribbean mills, on the other hand, are "wretched, impoverished and dangerous.... Sanitation is generally poor, and disease is rampant."[67]

Divorces from all of these exotic locales were legally dubious. But if nobody complained, then these divorces were, in effect, perfectly valid. Only an occasional disgruntled ex-spouse made trouble. The Supreme Court, in *Estin v. Estin* (1948), gave some protection to spouses—it refused full faith and credit to aspects of a divorce decree that dealt with property division and support.[68] The rulings in *Williams* were confined to the judgment of divorce, and were a warning signal about migratory divorce. But, for the most part, nobody bothered the thousands who went to Reno or Las Vegas for a divorce, just as nobody bothered the tens of thousands whose divorces were based on pious perjury in court.

Creeping Decay

For most of the twentieth century, this jerry-built structure persisted. The law seemed stuck in place. Yet, when one looks a bit more closely, by the middle of the century, the old system was showing signs of wear. In 1966, for example, New York finally revised the law of divorce, and added "cruel and inhuman treatment" to the list of grounds for divorce.[69] Slowly, a kind of creeping no-fault system began to emerge. By 1950, perhaps twenty states allowed divorce, without grounds, after a certain number of years of separation: in Arizona, Idaho, Kentucky, and Wisconsin, five years; in Rhode Island, ten; in Arkansas and Nevada, three; in Louisiana and North Carolina, two.[70]

In most states, this provision was little used. Why postpone a divorce for several years, when a few white lies could you get one more quickly?[71] But creeping no-fault had a significant symbolic meaning. These statutes admitted, in effect, that some marriages were dead, and should get a decent burial, with or without "grounds." In 1933, New Mexico took a further step. It amended its statute to include, as grounds for divorce, "incompatibility."[72] To say that a couple is "incompatible" means, in plain English, that they cannot get along. An amendment of 1953 made this explicit: there is incompatibility when, "because of discord or conflict of personalities, the legitimate ends of the marriage are destroyed preventing any reasonable expectation of reconciliation."[73] A sensible rule, but it blasted a hole in the traditional theory of divorce.

Nevertheless, the collusive system was still alive in 1970 and, despite grave faults, it did function in a rough and ready way. As Max Rheinstein wrote, in 1972, "consent divorce" was "freely available," no matter what the official law said or did. If people were willing to undertake "expensive travel," or tell a lie or two, consenting adults could have their divorce.[74] The system had a way to deal with the few *contested* divorces, too—though this was messy and unsatisfying.

But the system became increasingly unsatisfactory. To begin with, it was expensive. And hypocritical. Most family lawyers hated the dirty secrets and the lying. The laws "stink," as one New York lawyer put it. Others called the laws "inhuman" or "stupid."[75] In 1948, a New York grand jury denounced the "stench" from the "fraud, perjury, collusion and connivance" in divorce. District Attorney Frank Hogan cracked down on the fake adultery racket. He arrested one Max Zuckerman, a "private detective and a former process server," and Sarah Ellis, a young mother, who had been the "unknown woman" in about thirty-five cases.[76] These raids brought headlines, and shabby glory to the prosecutors. But they hardly made a dent in the divorce racket. Still, people were questioning the very existence of the dual system. Queen Victoria was dead. Society in 1970 was a society of cohabitation, of the so-called sexual revolution—and the age of expressive individualism.

It was a period of expressive marriage as well, which went beyond companionate marriage, a period in which millions no longer saw marriage as a yoke of reciprocal duties, or as a sacrament, but as a means of personal fulfillment. In a time dominated by "the pursuit" of "individual happiness," marriages came to be "regarded as exclusively personal affairs,"[77] in short, paths to self-realization. Conservatives never stopped resisting easy divorce; but their backs were more and more against the wall. As Dorothy Thompson, writing in the *Ladies' Home Journal* in 1949, put it, the divorce laws were simply barbaric. If life together was "intolerable," why not allow divorce by "mutual consent"? Marriages do fail: a "boy" whose mother was an "excellent housekeeper," marries a "career girl" with "lovely legs," but who never washes the dishes. Or a "boy" who grew up in a "lusty, warm, amusing" home marries a girl who is "dull and boring," and makes him wipe his shoes at the door. Why force these couples to stay together?[78]

Many experts wanted to get rid of collusion and replace it with something more "therapeutic," something more in tune with human and family values.[79] Los Angeles County established a Court of Conciliation, led in the 1950s by Judge Louis Burke. The Court had "jurisdiction over all persons having any relation to the domestic controversy." This meant it could even call in "third party 'paramours'" and tell them to quit their paramouring. The aim was to save marriages. The parties would (hopefully) sign a "Reconciliation Agreement." This was in theory enforceable. Violators could go to jail for contempt, which occasionally happened.[80] In a supposedly "typical" agreement, the husband would promise to support his wife, and take care of the "outside of the home." The wife was responsible for the "inside"; she cooked and handled laundry (though the husband was supposed to "share" in the work, if his wife had a job). Wives were expected to do more "giving" in the course of the marriage; but, at least in Judge Burke's view, women were "happy" to "sacrifice" for husband and family. Husbands and wives should also refrain from giving each other the "silent treatment." He was not to "maintain late and unusual hours," and should "take out the wife for dinner" or the like, "at least once a week." He was entitled to reasonable "pocket money" for golf expenses and snacks. She was entitled to "pin money" for the beauty parlor and cosmetics. Mealtimes should be times of "great peace and calmness." Both should try to control their tempers. Sexual intercourse, we learn, "provides a safe and healthy outlet for passion." But it should be done in "moderation." Twice a week seemed a good average, and "should not be considered excessive." In the "first stages of intercourse," tenderness was essential, because a woman is not "aroused" as quickly as a man. But she had duties, too: she should "respond to her husband's efforts in lovemaking" and not "act like a patient undergoing a physical examination." Both husband and wife should avoid "uncleanliness, overweight, vulgarity, or carelessness in dress." And both should be patient with the normal wear and tear on their bodies with the passage of time: "baldness, wrinkles, denture difficulties, arthritis."[81]

The Conciliation Court rested on familiar assumptions. Divorce was bad for children, for couples, for society—though sometimes unavoidable. The idea was to slow down the rush to divorce. In Chicago, Judge Julius Miner proposed a sixty-day cooling-off period; and in 1955, it was enacted into law. But lawyers quickly found a way around the law. "They ask the court to waive the sixty-day period because of an emergency"—perhaps the wife needs money for the kids right away. The judges grant this waiver "in nearly every case." Judge Miner also proposed a "clinic of counselors, social workers, psychiatrists and clergymen," who would try to save marriages during the cooling-off period. No such clinic emerged.[82]

It was (official) policy to prevent hasty divorces, and encourage conciliation. This policy undoubtedly lay behind the notion of the interlocutory decree (or decree *nisi*). In states with interlocutory decrees, divorce was a two-stage process. The first judgment was "interlocutory," or provisional; it became final only later— usually six months; but a full year in California and a few other states. Usually this second stage happened automatically, when the time was up; in a few states, the parties had to ask the court to finalize the divorce.[83] Fans of classic movies will recognize the interlocutory decree as a plot device in *The Awful Truth*, with Cary Grant and Irene Dunne (1937). Early in the movie, the two divorce; but they reconcile at the end (as we knew they would), just before the decree becomes final. But this rarely occurred outside the movies. The legislature refused to end the practice in 1933, even though a member of the assembly reported he had "handled about 200 divorce cases as an attorney and that in only five or six cases had reconciliations been effective."[84] There were claims that some programs worked—Judge Alexander's family court in Toledo, for example, also in the 1950s.[85] But failure was the normal outcome. The Conciliation Court was voluntary, and perhaps did save marriages—*if* a couple actually did go for counseling.

But by the time most couples appeared in court, they did not want therapy or conciliation. They wanted a divorce. All conciliation plans, all plans for saving marriages, came up against the hard rock of reality. The couples wanted *out*. Or, at least *one* of them wanted out; and the other one would not or could not resist. Consensual divorce, by hook or crook, was a fact. In a period that emphasized personal growth and satisfaction, the old system could not survive.[86]

No-Fault

Nor did it survive. The *legal* story of divorce in the twentieth century was basically of how this dual system decayed—at first rather slowly, then, after 1970, in almost a helter-skelter rush.[87] Change started with a bang, in 1970, when California enacted the first so-called no-fault statute. The statute got rid of the very word "divorce," and changed its name to "dissolution of marriage." It provided that a court "may decree" a dissolution if "irreconcilable differences" have caused the "irremediable breakdown of the marriage."[88] The reformers who drafted and lobbied for this law clearly intended that the court would not be a mere rubber stamp. The law defined "irreconcilable differences" as "those grounds which are determined by the court to be substantial reasons for not continuing the marriage."[89] This seemed to be asking the court to conduct some sort of hearing, and make some findings of fact. Indeed, the statute went on to say that "If from the evidence at the hearing, the court finds that there are irreconcilable differences," it can order the dissolution of the marriage. The court could also continue the case for thirty days, if there was a "reasonable possibility of reconciliation."[90]

This is not really divorce on demand—at least not if you read the text literally. But as is so often the case, the text is no guide to what actually happened. Almost immediately, the hearings disappeared, the thirty-day continuances disappeared, the taking of evidence disappeared, conciliation disappeared. The statute came to mean simply this: if either party wanted out, and for any reason, the marriage was over. The judge *was* reduced to a rubber stamp. Conflict could (and did) remain over property, support payments, and child custody. But the divorce itself was no longer an issue. No-fault was not just consensual divorce. It was unilateral divorce. It does not matter if the other spouse says no. There is no defense to a petition for a no-fault divorce. Divorce is available for the asking.

It was as if a dam had broken. In 1971, Iowa and Minnesota followed California's lead.[91] Soon other states rushed to climb on the no-fault bandwagon. Many states, like Minnesota, simply wiped out the old grounds for divorce. Another group added "irretrievable breakdown" to their list of grounds for divorce.[92] A few states—Nevada was one—used the concept of "incompatibility" to reach the same result.[93] In Pennsylvania, if both parties agree that the marriage is "irretrievably broken," they can divorce by consent almost immediately. But even without mutual consent, a no-fault divorce can be granted after a two-year separation.[94] In most states, not only did a law of the California type carry the day, but the results were also the same as in California: not consensual, but unilateral divorce.[95] In Nebraska, a survey in the 1970s of nearly 10,000 divorce cases failed to find a single one in which a divorce, which one spouse wanted, was refused.[96] In Iowa, too, the result was exactly the same.[97] Divorce (or "dissolution of marriage") is on the whole easier and cheaper in the United States than in most other countries; but many European countries have been moving in the same direction. In Germany, for example, couples can divorce if their marriage has broken down; and a year's separation is conclusive proof that it has. They can, in fact, divorce even earlier, if both parties consent. Divorce law in the Scandinavian countries is similar: after a period of separation (usually a year), it is essentially no-fault divorce.

Why did all this happen? What was it that changed in society, in family life, or in social structure? What was the impact, for example, of the so-called sexual revolution? Some social influences seem pretty obvious. Others, less so. The United States, for example, is an exceptionally religious country. If anything, it seemed even more religious, more fervent, more devout, at the end of the twentieth century. Millions still defend what they call traditional family values; and seem to shrink with horror from the very idea of gay marriage. Divorce is forbidden to Catholics; and distasteful to many others. But statistically speaking, states full of Catholics, states full of conservative Baptists, and the wild and funky regions of California and Nevada, all seem to indulge in divorce. (Today, in fact, divorce rates are highest in the so-called Bible Belt.) Were Americans simply hypocrites?

Divorce law has always been legally more complex than marriage law. Thousands of lawyers make money out of divorces and divorce settlements. Nobody makes much money out of marriage laws. Yet divorce *depends* on marriage. Divorce is marital breakup. The ethos of divorce flows from the social ethos of marriage. To understand divorce, we must look to changes in the *social* meaning of marriage, which we explored in chapter 2. At the beginning of the twentieth century, most people at least gave lip service to traditional values and traditional ideas about marriage. And what many couples expected out of marriage was not totally beyond reach. Moreover, divorce carried a certain stigma; and was, at best, a last resort. "Living in sin" was, well, a sin— and a scandal besides. Children born out of wedlock carried the stigma of bastardy. Of course, many people violated the rules. Not many flaunted them, however.

Yet traditional marriage *was* already shifting, in subtle ways in the direction of what can be called companionate marriage. Traditional sex roles were eroding. Couples were supposed to be close to each other, best friends as well as lovers. The man was still the head of the household. But the *ideal* marriage was supposed to be a partnership—a union of (more or less) equals. Of course, true partnership within the family was still rare. But the theory in itself put a strain on traditional marriage. Men and women expected more from each other. When expectations are not met, intimacy could become "suffocating," and demands "unbearable." Divorce became a kind of "safety valve" that made the system "workable."[98] And divorce was the gateway to remarriage. If remarriage, as the cynical phrase puts it, is the triumph of hope over experience, then divorce is one of the ship's essential pilots. Still later, as we have seen, came what Andrew Cherlin has called expressive marriage—along with even more pressure for easy divorce. Indeed, no-fault divorce represents the absolute triumph of expressive marriage—or, to put it another way, a sign of how fragile expressive marriages can be.

New York was the lone holdout on true no-fault divorce until the twenty-first century. It finally joined its sister states in 2010. Until then, the legislature had rejected numerous no-fault proposals over the years, clinging to the old system, with all its faults and frustrations. It not only maintained, as many states did, a fault-based option; its only no-fault option was a one-year separation pursuant to a formal written agreement resolving all issues related to money and children. And to add insult to injury, the fault-based grounds were construed strictly, meaning that couples sometimes litigated their divorces all the way to the state's highest court and were still denied.[99] In 2009, Novel Davis filed for divorce against her husband of forty-one years, Shepherd Davis, on grounds of abandonment. They were still living in the same house, but, she claimed, he had abandoned her socially. He refused to celebrate holidays or birthdays with her, or eat meals together, or go to family functions or movies, restaurants, or church together; he removed her "belongings from the marital bedroom." But this sort of "social abandonment" was not "abandonment" within the meaning of the divorce statute; to prevail she would have had to prove that, for a period of one year, he moved out, locked her out, or refused to have sex without justification (and despite repeated requests).[100] The court rejected the idea of "social abandonment" to avoid a back door to no-fault divorce. This approach left Novel Davis married, the same fate that had befallen other unsuccessful divorce plaintiffs in the supposedly modern era in New York.[101]

The new law will put an end to these marital life sentences. It maintains the divorce code's traditional structure, but adds an additional ground for divorce when "[t]he relationship between husband and wife has broken down irretrievably for a period of at least six months, provided that one party has so stated under oath."[102] This establishes unilateral divorce, as well as no-fault divorce for couples who can agree to part ways, though issues of property and custody can remain.

What did no-fault accomplish? One result is clear. It swept away the lying and the perjury and the squabbling over "grounds" for divorce. It eliminated collusion once and for all. It wiped out all the defenses—recrimination, condonation, and the rest. Many reformers wanted to legitimate consensual divorce— divorce by agreement of man and wife. But it was *unilateral* divorce, a much more radical change, that actually occurred. Any partner could end a marriage, at any time, and for any reason, or no reason at all.

Divorce—or, dissolution of marriage—thus became quicker and easier to get. And cheap—even, at times, extremely cheap, especially if you bought a do-it-yourself handbook on divorce; or patronized a company, like the one that promises a "premium online divorce" (an "easy, accurate, and up-to-date" service, available for an "uncontested divorce"). Completed documents could be "ready for filing in less than 1 hour." The price (as of 2010) was a mere $299; or two monthly installments of $157.[103]

Did cheap and easy divorce increase the actual divorce rate? The evidence is skimpy and conflicting.[104] But does this matter? Divorce is a way to dissolve a marriage, legally. Many people, now and in the past, have pointed to easy divorce as one of the reasons for the erosion of the family. But this confuses cause and effect. A happy marriage does not end because divorce is available at bargain-basement prices. Marital failure and family breakup breed divorce, not vice versa. A more difficult and controversial question is whether no-fault has made women worse off. Here too, the evidence is conflicting. We deal with this issue—the economic consequences of divorce—in chapter 9.

ANNULMENT

Annulment is another way of ending a marriage. Annulment wipes a marriage off the books, as if it never existed. This is, as we said, appealing to devout Roman Catholics. The Church forbids divorce and remarriage, but if a marriage is annulled, then the parties can remarry, since (in the eyes of the Church) they were never married to begin with.

A Catholic annulment is not the same as a legal annulment. A Catholic annulment requires a proceeding in church tribunals. These tribunals grant about 40,000 annulments per year, up from a mere 368 per year in 1968.[105] A couple can have a Catholic annulment without a secular annulment; and vice versa.

In American courts, annulment proceedings are much less common than divorce proceedings. The formal rules have always been—on the surface, at least—quite strict. Annulment is possible only when something was radically and fatally wrong with the marriage from the very beginning. A decree of annulment tears up a marriage "by the roots."[106] State statutes list various "grounds" for annulment—typically bigamy, impotence, infancy, imbecility, incest, fraud, and duress—the flip side of the "impediments" to marriage we discussed in chapter 1.

The law of annulment distinguishes between "void" and "voidable" marriages, based, at least loosely, on the severity of the marital defect. Under the Oregon Code of 1930, for example, an incestuous marriage was absolutely void. The same was true if a person married someone with "one-fourth or more of negro blood."[107] Or if the marriage was bigamous. These marriages were invalid even if no court ever formally nullified them. Still, victims of bigamy often asked for annulments, probably to make the matter official, even though their marriage was already "void." Josephine Mendes, a "petite film actress," who had "one of the smallest pair of feet in the film colony," married Joseph Y. Fernandez, in Tijuana; she found out he already had a wife, and child; she then left him and got an annulment, in September 1935.[108] And in 1943, John A. Blackadder, owner of a detective agency, got an annulment from his wife, Idelia, even though they had been together for nineteen years. Idelia told him her original husband had been killed in the First World War, but he turned out to be "very much alive."[109]

Certain other kinds of marriage, however, were merely "voidable." These marriages could be annulled; but unless and until this was done in court, the marriage was treated as valid. A marriage in Oregon was "voidable" if either party was "incapable" of entering into a marriage contract, "or assenting thereto, for want of legal age or sufficient understanding"; or where consent was "obtained by force or fraud."[110]

Very hasty marriages, marriages of people who were so drunk they had no idea what they were doing, marriages that were thought of as jokes, are all examples of marriages that could lead to annulments. In Atlanta, in 1924, an eighteen-year-old woman claimed she was "drugged while on an automobile ride" and was only "semi-conscious" during her wedding.[111] In San Mateo County, California, in 1952, Linda Moyers left her husband, Eugene, one day after they got married in Reno, claiming she was dead drunk during the ceremony.[112] In 1908, Alexander Vazakos, a Greek student at Columbia University, wanted to annul his marriage to Luise Xenia, who was nearly sixty years old. In Greece, Luise was giving him German lessons; she hypnotized him, so that his "sense left him," and he "felt compelled to obey her wishes." He ran away from Athens to the United States; but Luise followed him.[113] All of these annulments were granted.

Young hasty marriages have always been in danger of annulment. More recently, there seems to be a rash of hasty celebrity marriages, followed by second thoughts and annulments. The singer Britney Spears married a childhood friend in 2004 and the next day filed for annulment. Her claim: she "lacked understanding of her actions," and was "incapable of agreeing to the marriage"; the two did not "know each other's likes and dislikes" or their wishes about children, and were in general completely "incompatible."[114] She got her annulment. Darva Conger married Rick Rockwell, on air, at the end of a TV show, *Who Wants to Marry a Millionaire?* Rockwell really *was* a millionaire, but he was also a man who had been restrained by a prior girlfriend who alleged domestic violence. Annulment granted. Actress Carmen Electra and Dennis Rodman, a professional basketball player, annulled a drunken marriage; Renée Zellweger annulled her short-lived marriage to country crooner Kenny Chesney, citing unspecified "fraud."

Annulled marriages were typically short.[115] There were occasional exceptions—the Blackadder marriage, for example, mentioned above. Some sort of record was probably set by Herman Rosenblat, who told his sad tale in Los Angeles in 1931. He had been married thirty-seven years, to a wife who was "mentally unbalanced." All those years, out of "deep and enduring love," he had persisted, hoping for a cure. Finally he gave up. The wife was now in an institution. The judge granted the annulment.[116]

Under some statutes, parents of underage spouses can petition for annulment, perhaps even when both bride and groom object.[117] A California father, in 1900, tried to annul the marriage of his underage daughter. He failed, after he confessed in court that he "had so many children" that he was unsure of his daughter's actual age.[118] Judges sometimes annulled unconsummated marriages, especially when the bride (or groom) was very young.[119] Physical impotence was grounds for annulment in most states. Florence Walter complained that she and her husband had tried, and failed, to have intercourse, even though she did "all that a woman could do to assist him." She said his private parts were correctly formed, "if rather small."[120] Ethel Lipscomb sought an annulment because, she claimed, her husband's long history of obsessive masturbation had left him impotent. In both cases, the judge granted annulments.

Fraud—basic lies about some critical fact—was also grounds for annulment. Dora Monte of Los Angeles married Stanley Carr in October 1918. Carr, it turned out, was underage; and a "lounge lizard." He was an "expert fox trotter," but he also told lies about money and about a supposed large income from his father's estate. When Dora found out the truth, she left him "at once," and got an annulment.[121] Lack of mental capacity was grounds for annulment as well. As we saw, early in the twentieth century, states tried to prevent the marriages of people with mental disabilities. Even today, every state requires some minimal level of mental competence for marriage. But the legal standard is extremely low—lower than for virtually any other legal act. Even a person in an asylum, or under a conservatorship, or legally incompetent to write a will, may be competent enough to marry.[122] All that is needed is some sort of understanding of what a "marriage" is.[123]

In most states, annulments have been uncommon—certainly as compared to divorces. At the beginning of the century, in Alameda County, California, only 1 or 2 percent of the petitions to end a marriage asked for annulment rather than divorce.[124] In Maryland, in 1929, there were 1,973 petitions for absolute divorce, and only 30 for annulment; in Ohio, in 1930, there were nearly 6,500 petitions for divorce, and only 38 petitions for annulment.[125] In Iowa, in 1967, there were 6,018 divorces; and 46 annulments.[126] But in San Mateo County, between 1950 and 1957, 12.3 percent of the petitions for dissolution asked for annulment.[127] Some 36 percent of the plaintiffs in these cases were men, compared to 15.9 percent in suits for divorce.[128] It is unclear why so many men in this county wanted their marriages annulled.

Like divorce cases, annulments were much easier to get when the other party failed to contest. In contested cases, courts could be tough. In a Massachusetts case from 1934, Pauline Maier Hanson told a pathetic tale: she was underage, and had been bamboozled into marrying young Hanson. He told her he would lose his job if she did not marry him; his salary had been raised because he was going to be married; and if she would go through with the formalities of marriage, they could get it annulled the next day. They got married, she went home, and her family (not surprisingly) flew into a rage. Hanson, to add injury to insult, suffered from a venereal disease. Pauline claimed duress and fraud; and said they had had no "sexual relations." The trial court granted an annulment; but the appeal court reversed. This court saw no real duress; the so-called fraud did not go "to the essence of the contract." Marriage, said the court, "is not something to be swept aside lightly."[129]

In New York, on the other hand, marriage apparently *was* something that could, at times, be swept away lightly. New York was the exception to the general rule that annulments were tough and uncommon. In New York, prior to the 1960s, as we saw, adultery was the only grounds for divorce. This led to what we called soft-core adultery, and to migratory divorce; but also to a high demand for annulment. New York was to annulments what Saudi Arabia is to oil. Apparently, there were almost as many annulments in New York as there were divorces, at least in some parts of the state. In New York City, in 1946, out of 11,802 "dissolutions," no less than 4,169, or 35 percent, were annulments.[130] And the courts, it seems, were quite willing to bend the law (or, more accurately, to bend normal doctrine about annulments). In New York courts, for example, "fraud" was a more elastic concept than it was in other states. In 1919, Mrs. Barbara Grube, of the Bronx, wanted her marriage to Edward annulled. He had told her he was a "true blue" American; but she found out he was an "alien enemy." This "fraud" made Barbara herself an "alien enemy in the eyes of the law." A judge granted the annulment.[131] Women also demanded annulments if they discovered their husbands were anarchists, or Bolsheviks, or Communists; or if husbands lied about health, or "chastity, professional status, and financial standing"; or if they concealed facts about "mental illness, atrophy of private organs, criminal record, and illegal presence in the country"; or made false promises to "establish a home," or to "have children," or to follow the spouse's religion, and so on.[132] Appellate courts were sometimes reluctant to grant these annulments; but most cases never got that far. In general, New York courts were quite accommodating.

Other states were and are less willing to stretch the meaning of fraud. A marriage contract, as one writer put it, "is more difficult to avoid because of fraud than ordinary contracts."[133] Courts by and large have taken a kind of "buyer beware" approach to fraud; they refuse to nullify marriages for "blind credulity" to statements made during a courtship.[134] In a California case, *Marshall v. Marshall* (1931), the husband had lied about his money and about his ability to support her in the style to which she was accustomed. But this, according to the Supreme Court of California, was not the kind of "fraud" which entitled her to an annulment. Annulments were for "extreme" situations only, those that struck at the heart of marriage.[135]

Fraud, in official doctrine, referred only to misrepresentations about the "essentials of the marriage"—definitive aspects like sex and procreation. In a Massachusetts case, Michael Reynolds wanted to annul his marriage to Bridget, who, in the six weeks they had known each other before marrying, had passed herself off as "chaste and virtuous." But, in fact, she was pregnant with another man's child at the time of the marriage. Here the wife's pregnancy undermined her husband's implicit "right to require that his wife shall not bear to his bed aliens to his blood and lineage." And, as a pregnant woman, she was "incapable of bearing a child to her husband at the time of her marriage," and thus "unable to perform an important part of the contract."[136]

Courts also seemed willing to grant annulments in cases of sterility and undisclosed venereal diseases, which also related to the "sexual relations that are at the heart of the marriage."[137] But they were reluctant to go further, until recently. Some modern cases have moved toward a more subjective test for fraud—one that asks whether a misrepresentation was essential to *this* marriage. Would the truth have been a deal-breaker for this particular deceived spouse? If so, it might justify an annulment on grounds of fraud, even if other marriages could continue happily under the same circumstances.

In *Wolfe v. Wolfe*, an Illinois case from 1979, the wife claimed to be a widow, and even showed a fake death certificate. In fact, she was divorced.[138] The husband, a strict Catholic, insisted he would not have married her, had he known the truth. "What is essential to one marriage may not be equally significant to another," according to the court. Fraud had to be judged on a case-by-case basis. The court granted the annulment—even though the parties had lived as husband and wife for several years, and had a child—because the marriage "would not have occurred but for the fraud." In a recent Colorado case, *In re Marriage of Farr* (2010), a court took this even a step further—granting an annulment to a woman who says she only remarried her ex-husband because he told her he had a terminal illness. She did not want him to die alone and thus agreed to the remarriage, but cried foul when he just kept living. The fact that the wife relied on her husband's false representation of imminent death meant that it went to "the essence of the marriage."[139]

Some courts have towed the traditional line,[140] but there is a palpable shift toward this more subjective understanding of fraud. The shift evidenced in cases like *Wolfe* and *Farr* goes hand-in-hand with the move toward individualized or expressive marriage. Like no-fault divorce, modern annulment law has started to reflect the notion of marriage as a vehicle for personal happiness. A person lured into a marriage under false pretenses, even those that bear only on individualized expectations for happiness, has been deprived of that shot at happiness.

Annulment cases, as we said, were never common, except in New York.[141] No-fault made annulments even less common. Even in New York, which did not have unilateral no-fault until 2010, less restrictive divorce laws have reduced the need to stretch the concept of annulment. In general, in the age of no-fault, divorce is so quick, easy, and cheap ("as easy as buying a package of gum," as an attorney in Iowa put it)[142] that many couples apparently decide that annulment is not worth the bother. The states, by and large, have cut down the differences between divorce and annulment. Children of annulled marriages are still legitimate. Most states authorize courts to divide property and award alimony on the same terms in annulment cases as in divorce. In a few states, however, spouses have fewer economic rights after annulment. And prenuptial agreements may not take effect if a marriage is annulled.

Annulment can still be tempting, to be sure, for people with religious scruples against divorce. There are companies in Nevada which, at least according to their ads, do a brisk business in annulments. One company (it promises "Quick Legal Solutions with a Human Touch") charges $767 for an ordinary annulment—"With Children add $25.00 per child. With Property add $25.00"; a "Missing Spouse" would cost $250 extra. The company claims a 99.9 percent "Success Rate."[143]

COVENANT MARRIAGE

The law of marriage and the law of divorce are twin bodies of law. Divorce depends on the social construction of marriage; it is intimately connected to the law of marriage as well. We live in a period of easy divorce. It is easy to get married, and easy to get out of marriage.

This situation is anathema to many people, especially deeply religious people with strong feelings about "traditional" values. Easy divorce seems to destroy the sacred foundations of marriage. It leads, they feel, to dry rot in family life; and it erodes the pillars on which society rests. Divorce rates are high; and so are rates of family pathology. Easy divorce is a convenient scapegoat. Toughening the law of divorce might seem one way to fix the situation. Somewhat surprisingly, this takes the form of a backlash against the normal way of getting married.

Louisiana pioneered by creating a new form of marriage, the so-called covenant marriage, in 1997. Couples could choose between ordinary marriage and the new covenant marriage.[144] Couples in covenant marriages give up the right to no-fault divorce. Their marriage is to be a "lifelong arrangement."

In fact, couples in a covenant marriage are not really married for life. They can get a divorce, but not so easily. They must have grounds, just as it was before no-fault—adultery, desertion, physical or sexual abuse, or a felony conviction—or a lengthy period of separation. Couples in a covenant marriage also have to agree to marriage counseling, before they can go to divorce court. Covenant marriage appeals to some couples; but it has not caught on—either in Louisiana or elsewhere. Two states, Arizona and Arkansas, enacted their own version of covenant marriage.[145] Everywhere else, it failed to be adopted.[146] And even in Louisiana, according to a study published in 2001, less than half of the population even knew there was such a thing; and hardly anybody knew anybody who was actually in a covenant marriage. Clerks were also fairly ignorant; and about two-thirds of them never even mentioned this option to people applying for a marriage license. In any event, according to the clerks, few couples seemed to show much interest.[147] This lack of interest may reflect a general tendency of couples to underestimate their own risk of divorce—most put their own chances at or near zero, even though most also know that the overall rate of divorce hovers near 50 percent.[148]

The situation was similar in Arkansas. As of May 20, 2000, only four out of 11,037 marriage licenses issued were for covenant marriages; five couples converted their marriages to covenant marriages. From 2002 to 2004, there were 111,736 traditional marriages in Arkansas; only 562 couples opted for covenant marriage; 206 couples converted their marriages to covenant status.[149] In November 2004, the governor of Arkansas, Mike Huckabee, a former minister, announced that he and his wife planned to convert their marriage into a covenant marriage during a mass ceremony on Valentine's Day.[150] He clearly hoped to start a parade of conversions and new covenants. But not much happened.

There is a "Covenant Marriage Movement," not aimed at changing the law, but at achieving the goals of covenant marriage, through working with individual couples. Phil and Cindy Waugh are its executive directors; according to their website, in 2001, "God spoke to Phil ... and called the two of them to serve" the movement; God asked them "to join hands and hearts in transforming the present divorce culture."[151] In some cities, members of the clergy have agreed, on a voluntary basis, to do premarital counseling. The goal is to give people ideas and information that might help build successful marriages. Another goal, for many of the ministers, was to lower the divorce rate, and to promote chastity outside marriage and faithfulness inside marriage. A number of communities have established "community marriage policies," and some claim a measure of success in reducing the rate of divorce.[152] Nobody could object, one supposes, to premarital counseling, although most people do not want to be forced into it. South Carolina uses a carrot rather than a stick. Couples who "successfully complete a qualifying premarital preparation course" can receive a $50 "non-refundable state income tax credit."[153]

Covenant marriage might become more popular. It is, after all, a relatively new idea and few people know about it. If it spread, would the divorce rate go down? Probably not. Covenant marriage simply puts divorce law back where it was before the no-fault revolution. Would couples really feel themselves bound, in a covenant marriage, if they fell out of love, or if the marriage became hollow and unfulfilling? In the twenty-first century, that seems unlikely. People who choose covenant marriages are likely to be couples who would stay together through thick and thin, with or without no-fault. A study in Louisiana, in 1999–2000, found that couples who chose covenant marriage were (no surprise) "far more religious and traditional in attitudes" than other couples. They reject cohabitation. They believe in conventional, old-fashioned gender roles. Jennifer and Jason Barton, who now live in Tennessee, were married in Louisiana, and have a covenant marriage. Jennifer, a "stay-at-home mom," thinks marriage is not "something you can take back to Wal-Mart for a refund if it breaks"; instead, "God designed marriage as a covenant."[154] Covenant marriage, then, "appeals to a small, distinct group" which differs in "important ways" from other couples who get married. The study concluded, then, that covenant marriage had little chance to spread to "a larger, more diverse population."[155]

MARRIAGE PROMOTION MOVEMENT

The marriage promotion movement is another modern development that grew out of dissatisfaction with our modern culture of divorce. It is a grassroots movement to strengthen marriage. A coalition of conservative family policy groups, led by the Institute for American Values, has led the way. In "The Marriage Movement: A Statement of Principle," the group declares that "the divorce revolution" and the "unwed-childbearing movement" had failed. The goal was to "turn the tide on marriage and reduce divorce and unmarried childbearing," so that "more children will grow up protected by their own two happily married parents," and more "marriage dreams" of adults "will come true."[156]

Government is also involved in promoting "healthy marriage." A public service poster, on Long Island Rail Road and D.C. Metro trains, shows a young African American couple lying in bed together. He is asleep, clutching his wife, and appears to be snoring. She is awake, her eyes rolling, and she glares at him. The tagline for the ad is: "He may not always be charming, but he's always your prince." Smaller type warns: "Engagement ring, wedding ring, snoring? It takes more than love to make marriage work. But whether shouldering a cuddle or a good cry, he'll be by your side." Tiny print at the bottom gives the source of the ad: the federal Department of Health and Human Services (DHHS) and TwoOfUs.org.[157]

These campaigns are meant to shore up marriage. President George W. Bush made marriage promotion a focus of his administration. A week in November 2001 was designated as "National Family Week." A "Healthy Marriage Initiative" was designed to "promote policies" that would "strengthen the institution of marriage and help parents rear their children in positive and healthy environments."[158] The president turned over the reins to Wade Horn, a conservative family policy advocate and spokesperson for the "responsible fatherhood" movement; Horn became assistant director of the Administration for Children and Families (ACF). Horn believed strongly that the government should take a "pro-marriage" position: "I don't want to play Cupid. This isn't about telling anybody who should marry who. But when you have a couple who say, we're interested in getting married, or who are already married, it's about helping them develop the skills and knowledge necessary to form and sustain healthy marriages."[159] Healthy marriage, advocates of this movement feel, might cure the ailments of the American family, and solve "America's most urgent problem," the "decline of the two-parent, intact marital family.[160]

Marriage promotion was already a federal budget item. It figured in the overhaul of the welfare system in 1996, under President Clinton. Congress declared that "[m]arriage is the foundation of a successful society," and an "essential institution" for promoting the interests of children.[161] Every federal budget since then has included a line for strengthening marriage; and every state has taken policy initiatives "aimed at promoting marriage, strengthening two-parent families, or reducing divorce."[162] The Personal Responsibility and Individual Development for Everyone Act of 2005 (PRIDE) reaffirmed the federal commitment to promote marriage, but also included provisions to address concerns about domestic violence—reflecting the idea that women should not be forced or cajoled to stay in abusive marriages.[163] The Deficit Reduction Act, passed the same year, allocated $150 million per year for the promotion of marriage.[164] The money is used for marriage education programs, public advertising campaigns, "responsible fatherhood" programs, marriage mentoring programs, and research relating to marriage and the well-being of families, among other things. Anticipating possible objections, the government's marriage promotion website makes clear that the Healthy Marriage Initiative is *not* about "coercing anyone to marry or remain in unhealthy relationships," or "limiting access to divorce"; it is not billed as a "panacea for achieving positive outcomes for child and family well-being"; and is certainly not a "federal dating service."[165]

Marriage promotion seems to assume that marriage is the cure for deep social problems—like childhood poverty. But is it? The real reasons why the family is troubled—and why some women and men reject marriage—lie much deeper in society. One reason, surely, is that new concepts of marriage, among both men and women, put so much strain on marriage that it often becomes brittle and tends to crumble into dust. No-fault divorce is not a solution to the problem of sick families, of course. But it is a reflex of families in trouble—a social admission that forcing people to stick to an unfulfilling marriage is simply pointless in this day and age. The covenant marriage and the marriage promotion movement themselves may be implicit admissions that easy divorce has become part of the general culture; for now, major changes in divorce law, aimed at tightening the binding ties, seem politically quite out of the question.

Dollars and Sense:
The Economic Consequences of Divorce

DIVORCE CAN SWIFTLY end a marriage, but the economic consequences can last a lifetime. As with many aspects of family law, the law governing the economic consequences of divorce underwent a dramatic shift during the twentieth century. In broad brush, husbands lost exclusive control and ownership of property during and after marriage; more and more they had to share ownership during marriage with wives, who had strong claims to property upon dissolution; the common-law tradition that relied on strict (and unequal) gender roles shifted to a more egalitarian approach. Yet even under the modern rules, women suffer more financially than men after divorce.

These changes, despite their importance, took place quietly, with little fanfare. Also, in a way, modern law was shaped not only by the way in which gender roles have changed, but by the way they have remained the same for many couples. The common-law system assumed that women would stay home as housewives and this was mostly true. Modern law has to take into account the persistence of traditional patterns, in which still more women than men never work, quit working, or work less in order to keep house and raise children, and therefore have less wealth and earning power than their husbands.

In this chapter, we consider developments in the law of property division and spousal support, with some attention to such private arrangements as antenuptial agreements. The story, then, is mostly about couples with money—though usually one or both spouses will have to do with less after the divorce. And if there is no money, there is nothing to fight over, nothing to divide.

There are two basic questions: who gets what right now (property division), and should either spouse share in the other's future earnings (spousal support). The answers are far from simple. These issues are "the main concern in divorce negotiation in lawyers' offices and the major time in litigation," particularly since no-fault divorce eliminated most fights about *whether* a marriage would dissolve.[1]

THE COMMON-LAW SYSTEM OF PROPERTY RIGHTS
OF HUSBAND AND WIFE

The common-law system of marital property had two defining features: coverture during marriage, and a title-based system of distribution at divorce. As we discussed in chapter 2, the principle of coverture suspended the wife's legal identity during marriage.[2] For all practical purposes, husbands controlled family property. Husbands were supposed to support their wives, but the doctrine of marital privacy usually made this duty all but unenforceable.[3] However, once coverture was abolished by the Married Women's Property Acts, married women could own property, and earn money, in their own right.

But what happened after a divorce? The common-law system revolved around a basic, if crude, principle: eat what you kill. In so-called separate property states, everything in the husband's name went with him; everything in the wife's name with her. Spouses, in other words, did not acquire ownership rights in one another's property simply because they were married.

When combined with coverture, the title-based system was potentially devastating for wives. Although the system spoke of "separate property," coverture prevented wives from holding or acquiring separate property during marriage. They had usually turned premarital property over to their husbands upon marriage, and any property acquired during marriage was at least initially in his name as well. Thus, when the time came to divide property, a court could award most or all of the property to the husband. Some courts, it seems, often split property between spouses—disguised as "alimony," or simply by ignoring formal law. But without a system that clearly authorized redistributing property, wives could be left destitute.[4]

Coverture disappeared, but the title-based system remained. The shift from an agricultural to a wage economy further stratified gender roles. In an industrial society, men, by and large, brought home the bacon; women worked at home. A woman

193

who brought property into the marriage kept hold of it, but most women had no such property. South Carolina (once it allowed divorce at all) was unique in applying a "special equity" doctrine, which allowed courts to grant a wife a share of her husband's property upon divorce if she could prove she had made financial or other contributions that helped her husband acquire it.[5] This was an exception to the rule that ownership flowed from title, but did nothing to alter the basic problem—wives had little chance as an initial matter to hold or acquire title to property.

COMMUNITY PROPERTY: AN ALTERNATE SYSTEM

Eight states, scattered across the South and West, rejected the separate property system that drew a solid line between "his" and "hers."[6] They followed, instead, a system of "community property." The basic principles of community property—inherited from Spanish or Mexican law—change the way property is held during marriage *and* the way it is divided upon divorce or the death of either spouse.[7] The property of a married couple is, on paper anyway, divided into three categories: his separate property, her separate property, and community property. Separate property includes premarital property and property acquired during marriage by gift, inheritance, lottery, personal injury lawsuit, or from any other "unearned" source. Community property is every dollar earned by either spouse during the marriage and property acquired with those earnings. During marriage, separate property is controlled by its owner unless it has been "transmuted" into community property or given as a gift to the other spouse. Community property, however, is owned 50/50 from the moment of acquisition. Each dollar of his paycheck is theoretically split in equal shares, whether or not she also works or contributes in any tangible way to his earning power.

The community property rules at divorce flow from the rules during marriage. When they part, each spouse keeps his or her separate property, and, under the traditional approach, they split the community property 50/50. As we will see, three states still adhere to this strict approach;[8] five allow deviations based on equitable factors.[9] Community property treats husband and wife as a unit. Because it pays no attention to who earns property, it is better at accommodating "traditional" marriage, in which men earn more than women do, as a rule.

ALIMONY IN THE COMMON-LAW SYSTEM

Historically, courts in all states could award alimony to wives, in a divorce or legal separation. In 1931, every state but four had a statute expressly authorizing alimony for wives in divorce cases.[10] Three of those four states had some other mechanism to deal with wives' economic needs (the fourth, South Carolina, had no alimony because it had no provision for divorce).[11] A husband's duty to support his wife survived the end of the marriage.[12] The husband in the old days was a "substitute for a pension or social security"—his money prevented a wife who had never worked from becoming a "public charge."[13] Alimony was supposed to strike an "equitable balance between the needs of the dependent spouse and the ability of the supporting spouse to pay."[14] But there were restrictions until the 1970s.[15] In some states, a husband's fault was the precondition for an alimony award. Oklahoma, for example, permitted alimony only if the divorce was based on the "husband's aggression."[16] Most states simply authorized alimony for any "plaintiff." But in all but seven states, a "guilty" wife—especially an adulteress—was barred from collecting alimony.[17] A review of one hundred alimony awards appealed in the 1930s showed that a "guilty" wife almost never received alimony, particularly if she was "divorced for her cruelty, adultery, or desertion."[18] This preoccupation with fault would abate later in the century, but never fully disappear. And in California, if the wife had a sufficient "separate estate" or there was sufficient community property to provide for her, the court could deny her any support.[19] In most jurisdictions, alimony terminated if the wife died or remarried.[20] A dead woman needs no support; and a new husband took over the duty of providing for support.

Alimony, in any event, was never automatic. Whatever the statute said, the size and duration of awards were (and still are) almost entirely a matter of judicial discretion. A few states limited awards to a certain percentage of a husband's income;

most simply authorized "reasonable" or "just" or "equitable" or "proper" amounts.[21] In practice, few wives were granted alimony awards; most ex-husbands failed to pay; and ex-wives rarely went back to court to try to collect their money.[22] Federal government data from the late nineteenth century showed that alimony was awarded in 9 percent of divorces.[23] Later studies and surveys agreed on low frequencies; alimony was awarded in no more than 15 percent of divorces.[24] In Ohio, in the 1930s, alimony was awarded in 10.5 percent of cases; but in 74.5 percent of the cases in which women won custody of minor children.[25] In Alameda County, California, in the early twentieth century, alimony was awarded in only 7.6 percent of the cases where the couple had no children.[26] In general, alimony never served as an effective financial backstop for women.

EQUITABLE DISTRIBUTION: A MODERN SOLUTION?

Equitable distribution is the "modern" answer to the unfairness of the traditional system of allocating property at divorce. A judge, basically, can ignore legal title, and redistribute property in the name of fairness.[27] Many states had "some form of equitable distribution as early as the 1930s."[28] But these early statutes were vague and left everything to judicial discretion. Fault was the dominant guiding principle in property division, as it was in alimony law.

With the spread of no-fault divorce in the 1970s, a broader approach to equitable distribution took hold in all separate property states. Equitable distribution statutes have survived any number of legal challenges; courts have uniformly ruled that states have the power to reallocate property between husband and wife upon dissolution of marriage.[29] By the mid-1980s, the common-law system of allocating property at divorce based solely on title was finished.

Mississippi was the lone holdout; it never authorized equitable distribution by statute. But courts in that state had been quietly dividing marital property for some years, and the state's highest court finally adopted a formal set of guidelines for equitable distribution in *Ferguson v. Ferguson* (1994).[30] Linda and Billy Ferguson married when she was seventeen and he was twenty-one.

They lived in Chunky, Mississippi, throughout their twenty-four-year marriage, raising two children, Tamatha and Bubba. Linda worked as a homemaker and beautician; Billy was a cable repair technician. Linda sued for divorce, on grounds of adultery; Billy's paramour admitted the relationship and presented tape recordings of their conversations.[31] The couple had little in the way of cold, hard cash. But Linda asked for equitable distribution of Billy's assets: his vested pension plan with Bell South. Billy insisted that Linda "in no way contributed to their acquisition" and "nothing was ever issued in her name." But the divorce court, and the Mississippi Supreme Court, held that Linda was entitled to an equal share of assets "accumulated through the joint contributions and efforts of the parties"; "domestic services" counted. The "non-financial contributions" of "traditional housewives" had to be taken into account.[32]

In general, concern for non-economic contributions to marriage was a driving force in developing modern laws on equitable distribution. A 1979 survey of state divorce laws found that twenty-two states formally recognized contributions such as childcare, housework, cooking, and so on, when dividing a couple's assets at divorce; other states listed factors that were broad enough to encompass such contributions.[33] Property division, as one court put it, augments the "inherently precarious" support that alimony furnishes; and remedies the "grave wrong" of ignoring the wife's "supportive role" in the home, which contributes to the accumulation of marital assets.[34]

Women and Wage-Earning

Married women today have full *legal* rights to earn wages and acquire property. Thus, if men and women engaged in roughly equal amounts of wage-earning work, and were paid equally for that work, a title-based system would create no particular unfairness at divorce. But the social reality is quite different. More and more women are in the workforce, especially since the 1950s; yet women are still much more likely than men to forego higher education or professional schooling or to drop out of the workforce episodically or permanently to devote themselves to household work and childcare. According to 2008 data, just over 60 percent of wives are in the paid labor force.[35] A few decades earlier, the percentages were the reverse. But still, there are a significant numbers of wives without wages. Wives today contribute 35 percent of income earned by married-couple households.[36]

Change in work patterns by gender is not moving only in one direction. On the one hand, the composition of the labor force is shifting in favor of women; a majority of new entrants to the labor force are women, and men were disproportionately on the receiving end of layoffs during the recession that began in 2008.[37] As of 2009, women were "poised to surpass men on the nation's payrolls, taking the majority for the first time in American history."[38] On the other hand, a Pew Research Poll found that the number of working mothers with minor children who think "full-time work is the ideal situation for them" actually declined between 1997 and 2007, from 32 percent to 21 percent.[39] Almost as many working mothers said they would prefer "not working" to "full-time work." The number of stay-at-home fathers has increased recently; but the number is still tiny. In 2007, of more than 23 million married-couple households with children under fifteen, 5.6 million included a stay-at-home mother, while only 165,000 included a stay-at-home father.[40]

Even for women who work, there is a persistent gender gap in wages. A woman, on average, earns seventy to eighty cents for every dollar earned by a man.[41] The pay gap is especially pronounced for African American women and Hispanic or Latino women.[42] The gender wage gap exists at every level of earnings, but is largest at the top of the earnings spectrum.[43] Although the wage gap today is narrower than in the 1970s, when it was fifty-nine cents on the dollar, most of the change took place during the 1980s, and studies show little additional progress since 1990.[44] Moreover, the disparity in men's and women's wages grows throughout the employment lifecycle. Women at the beginning of their careers earn less than men; and the disparity is even greater for women in their forties and fifties.[45] In their prime earning years, women earn only 38 percent of what men earn over a fifteen-year period.[46]

At least some of the wage gap can be attributed to sex discrimination and stereotyping.[47] Perhaps ironically, even when women do not take time out from the workforce to tend to domestic responsibilities, employers pay them as if they do. Employers penalize women for expected leaves in excess of what those women actually take.[48] There is also a well-documented "wage premium" for married men, but not for married women, and a wage penalty of 10–15 percent for women who have children.[49]

When women get divorced, they often find they have very little property in their own names, and have suffered irreparable harm to their earning capacity. Hence, popular books urge women to "Get to Work."[50] Leslie Bennetts has argued that "choosing economic dependency as a lifestyle is the classic feminine mistake."[51] But the problem remains. Equitable distribution, which recognizes both economic and non-economic contributions to the household and its accumulated property, is a partial solution. Equitable distribution, thus, in a way, responds to the persistence as well as the decline of traditional gender roles.

Defining "Fair"

At the core of modern equitable distribution statutes is at least a thin commitment to the "partnership principle"—the idea that spouses are partners who should share the gains or losses equally if the partnership dissolves. Spouses should be rewarded for their contributions, no matter what form the contributions take. Economists have tried to put a price tag on the value of homemaking services. Judges, under state statutes, have broad discretion to value these services, and to weigh them against competing factors. Judges may also try to gauge future financial need—what it takes to maintain status and standard of living, and the cost of job training for those who have stayed out of the job market. Modern statutes tend to list factors judges might take into account, but judges still have enormous discretion.[52] Fault, too, can sometimes play a role in these awards, as we will see.

During a divorce proceeding, property is retroactively labeled as "separate property" or "marital property," depending on when and how it was acquired. "Marital property" is defined much like "community property": property earned by either spouse during marriage. Separate property, more or less, is everything else. Once a couple's property has been inventoried and classified, each piece is assigned a value and allocated according to the statutory guidelines. Some states allow both separate and marital property to be equitably distributed; others provide that separate property automatically stays with its owner. The

Uniform Marriage and Divorce Act (UMDA), promulgated in 1970, takes the former approach.[53] Only six states formally adopted the UMDA, but it nonetheless reflected and reinforced the modern trend toward more equal property-sharing at divorce.[54] Over time, the outcomes produced by equitable distribution rules and community property rules have started to converge. In most states, regardless of the governing system, judges presume that marital property will be split more or less evenly, but have some power to deviate based on equitable factors. But despite this convergence, only in community property states do spouses gain ownership rights *during* marriage, and not just at divorce or death. The joint "ownership" in separate property states is at best a system of deferred community property, where rights do not kick in until the marriage ends.

It is hard to know exactly what effect the modern laws have. Courts tend "to divide property equally in the case of long-term marriages (fifteen years and longer)"; they are much "less likely to presume equal division" for those lasting only a few years.[55] The family home usually goes to the custodian of the children, but this has become less certain over time.[56] There is no question that distribution of property now is fairer than in the past. But fairness comes at a price: the modern approach increases the complexity and cost of divorce litigation. It has fundamentally changed the nature of divorce lawyering.[57] The system often turns divorce litigation into a "full-fledged trial often lasting several days, replete with expert witnesses, economic and financial analysis, and multiple tax questions."[58] Time and money are spent on hide-and-seek for assets. Billy Ferguson, whose case we discussed above, managed to spend down all but $600 of the more than $33,000 he held in an employee savings account after his wife, Linda, filed for divorce. He admitted withdrawing the money, but claimed he had spent it all. His girlfriend testified, however, that he told her he had hidden it away.[59]

LIMITS ON THE SHARING PRINCIPLE: THE PROBLEM OF HIGH-INCOME FAMILIES

Lorna and Gary Wendt had been high school sweethearts back in Wisconsin. After thirty-one years of marriage, Gary Wendt was an executive worth approximately $100 million. He then left his wife (ironically, for an *older* woman). Lorna was the consummate corporate wife—she kept the house, raised their children, played hostess at dinner parties, orchestrated charity events, relocated on command, and went along on trips. *Her* career consisted of managing *his* career.[60] He offered her $10 million, which she turned down. Her claim in a nutshell was this: "Marriage is a partnership, and I should be entitled to 50%. I gave thirty-one years of my life. I loved the defendant. I worked hard and I was very loyal."[61] Some critics wondered why a woman in her late fifties, with no children still at home, needed more than $10 million. She admitted she could get along on that amount, but asked, "Why should he get $90 million? I entered this marriage as a partner. I don't know when he decided that it was not a partnership." [62] Gary, she said, "wanted to buy out my partnership, and I didn't want to be bought out. It's like a hostile takeover—he offered me a very small percentage, and I said that's not the price of a buyout."[63]

This case tested the limits of the partnership principle. Does a spouse get half even when much less would be more than sufficient to maintain her lifestyle? In fact, courts almost never divide property equally when there is so much of it. They do not buy the partnership idea; and settle for an amount sufficient to maintain the wife at the level she lived during marriage. The trial—covered extensively in the media—lasted eighteen days and produced a judicial opinion that was more than five hundred pages long.[64] In the end, Lorna got $20 million. This was hardly an equal partnership, but it was more than she had been offered. Lorna Wendt became a mini-celebrity, and a spokeswoman for corporate wives who found themselves unexpectedly dumped.[65]

ALIMONY IN THE MODERN ERA: A REMEDY
WITHOUT A THEORY?

Two major developments have altered the legal treatment of alimony: new norms of sex equality and no-fault divorce. In *Orr v. Orr* (1979), the Supreme Court struck down an Alabama law that said husbands—but not wives—may be forced to pay alimony.[66] Alabama had argued that alimony was designed to provide for needy spouses, and that gender was a good proxy for need. Their rule also compensated for past discrimination in marriage, which left women unprepared to compete in the workplace. In fact, women *were* more likely in 1979 to be economically dependent on their husbands than vice versa, and ex-wives very likely did suffer reduced earning capacity because of marriage (as many still do today). But individualized hearings could smoke out need regardless of gender, and the Court refused to stereotype women as dependent, even if, by and large, they were. This decision was part of a larger move to purge family law of rules that formally enforced or presumed gender-based roles for husbands and wives.

Orr marked the end of gender-based alimony statutes and awards. It also meant that alimony could no longer be justified as an extension of the husband's duty of support. During the same decade, no-fault divorce was becoming the norm, introducing new ideas about the role of marriage—and remarriage—in individuals' lives. Individualism, and expectations for happiness even at the expense of the family unit, began to triumph. No-fault divorces, which tend to be quicker, cheaper, and less messy than fault divorces, may have reduced acrimony in divorce. But they also fueled a clean-break theory—the idea that couples should be able to end a failed marriage, go their separate ways, and, perhaps, find happiness in a better marriage. Lifelong alimony was inconsistent with this ideal.

Formal gender neutrality and no-fault made it easy for courts to limit or reduce alimony awards drastically. These awards were already sparse and meager. Courts more and more showed their dislike for the very idea of alimony—the idea that a spouse, especially the husband, had "a continuing economic responsibility for the other after divorce."[67] Some courts felt this notion was based on an outdated concept of marriage. One court said it impeded a man's future freedom, and, as for the woman, it might encourage her to "live a life of physical and mental indolence."[68] Awards, according to this court, should be based not only on the "needs of the rejected wife," but on "what the man can afford to pay," giving both "the opportunity to make a new life on this earth." The court noted the "profound and deep social change" wrought by "women's liberation," and the resulting increase in work opportunities for women. A divorced woman, in short, should get a job. Some feminists agreed; ex-wives needed to become independent. Property division was better than alimony. Assets acquired during marriage were the product of the efforts of both spouses; they should be divided, and then each should go his or her merry way.

Alimony thus shifted from lifetime support to short-term, "rehabilitative" awards.[69] Some states went as far as to prohibit permanent awards altogether. But in most, permanent alimony was technically available, but in practice reserved for women married a long time and "of no skills," with a "debilitating infirmity," or "of advanced age."[70] Other dependent spouses could receive alimony for a limited time, often keyed to the time necessary to obtain a particular educational degree or find a decent job.[71] This narrower type of alimony tries to balance a woman's genuine need to be "rehabilitated" from dependency, and the desire to give divorcing couples an unencumbered future.

But the renunciation and critique of alimony in the 1970s may have been too hasty. New studies suggested that divorce left women worse off than men. Lenore Weitzman claimed that, one year after divorce, the average standard of living of men had gone up by 42 percent; the standard of living of women had gone down by 73 percent.[72] Her methods and analysis of data have been severely criticized, as has the fact that she blamed these effects on no-fault divorce. But poverty in female-headed households was real enough.[73] Most studies and surveys concluded that divorce imposed harsher consequences on women and children than on men.[74] In fact, the economic situation of women and children, it seems, "was bad before no-fault, and it continues to be bad now."[75]

Property redistribution was supposed to level the financial playing field after divorce. But most divorces occur early in marriage, and the net value of most marital estates is relatively small. Real estate, cars, or furniture were the most common types of property transferred.[76] Not stocks, bonds, or huge piles of cash. According to 1990 census data, only 32.3 percent of divorcing women received any property settlement at all, down from 44.5 percent in 1979.[77] And the median net value of most marital estates, according to a 1994 article, is under $25,000.[78] Spousal support was, in short, still badly needed in some cases.

Courts again began to acknowledge the hard fact that most divorcing couples do not have enough assets to support two households and that primary caregivers suffer the most. In one case, Rosalie LaRoque, married twenty-five years, had raised five children and earned only $5,600 in outside income during her marriage. The trial court gave her small monthly payments for eighteen months. The Wisconsin Supreme Court considered this stingy and unacceptable. A "career as homemaker—although of economic value to the family and society—all too frequently does not translate into money-making ability in the marketplace."[79] The court awarded her permanent alimony.

Today, alimony statutes resemble equitable distribution statutes. They authorize judges, in general, to make "just" or "equitable" awards, sometimes guided by a list of relevant factors.[80] In some states, judges must first make a threshold finding that one spouse was a "provider" and the other was a "dependent" in order to award alimony at all. The American Law Institute's Principles of the Law of Family Dissolution, which we introduced in chapter 6, shift the focus away from need; they suggest instead that awards be designed to compensate for specific losses incurred in marriage—for example, losses in standard of living, when a spouse after a long marriage has few skills and little money; or reduced earning capacity, because of child care duties.[81] In general, today, permanent alimony remains taboo except in cases of very long marriages. Judges are reluctant to impose alimony at all, particularly if property division can be used to balance out the parties' financial positions.

It may well be that alimony payments declined after no-fault was introduced. In Georgia, before no-fault, 15.4 percent of wives received an award of alimony, with a median value of $150 per month. After no-fault, the frequency fell to 10.9 percent, and the median to $94 per month. Similar results were reported in Washington State, and in New Haven County, Connecticut.[82] However, as we saw, spousal support awards have always been the exception rather than the rule. In Vermont, in 1982 and 1983, only 7 percent of spouses received alimony awards, while less than 2 percent received "permanent" alimony.[83] National data during that same period show that alimony was awarded in 12–16 percent of cases, varying significantly by length of marriage.[84] (More current data on alimony awards are sparse; the federal government abruptly stopped collecting state data about divorce in 1995, after a century of compiling a very useful data set.) Women who have been married for at least fifteen years are the most likely to receive spousal support.[85] Divorced or separated women in 1990, according to census data, received alimony in 15.5 percent of the cases.[86] Women over age forty were twice as likely to receive an alimony award as women under forty, consistent with the view that alimony should be reserved for older women who cannot be "rehabilitated."[87] But the brute fact remains: despite all the theorizing about alimony, its importance is limited—few women get it; and few of those who do get very much.

THE PROBLEM OF NEW PROPERTY

No-fault divorce, as we mentioned, rested on a "clean-break" principle that influenced alimony and property distribution. Divorcing spouses were supposed to get on with their lives, as best they could. Yet, even during a short marriage, one spouse sometimes greatly enhances his earning power, while the other drastically reduces hers by staying home with the children. Earning power is often the most valuable asset of the marriage. If so, then it is unfair to confine the distribution to traditional property, and without taking future earnings into account. Hence, modern divorce law has begun to focus on "new property"—things that can't be touched or held, but nonetheless have economic value: pensions, business goodwill, professional licenses, and professional degrees.

Until the late 1970s, courts routinely viewed pensions as indivisible. But a person earns a pension, like a salary, through work. Logically, under partnership or community property principles, pensions should accrue to both spouses. By 1979, a survey of state laws noticed a trend toward recognizing "spousal claims to an interest in retirement and pension benefits upon divorce."[88] Many states had yet to consider the question, but they eventually came around, and pensions are now routinely divided at divorce. Valuation can pose a challenge—pensions may or may not be vested at the time of divorce, and may be of uncertain future value. For the vast majority of pensions covered by a federal law, the Employee Retirement and Income Security Act (ERISA), courts can impose "a qualified domestic relations order" directly on the plan administrator, which allows payments to be made directly, when the pension matures, to the non-employee ex-spouse.[89] This resolves many of the problems that arise from sharing future pensions with an ex-spouse.

If one spouse helps put the other through law school or medical school, should the degree itself be considered marital property? Only one state, New York, has ruled yes on this question. Michael and Loretta O'Brien were teachers when they got married. Michael then finished college and medical school; Loretta worked to help put him through school. When they divorced, his medical degree was essentially their only asset. In *O'Brien v. O'Brien* (1985), the highest court in New York decided that the value of the degree could be divided, if both husband and wife had contributed to the process of getting it.[90] Of course, a professional degree cannot literally be divided; Loretta could not set up shop as a doctor. But a judge can order a doctor husband to pay money to an ex-spouse. Loretta O'Brien was a kind of "equity investor" in Michael's education; she was entitled to her share—part of the difference between what he would earn as a surgeon, and what he would have earned as a school teacher. Many states have rejected this approach. But some take the facts into account when figuring the amount of spousal support. Some states allow a kind of "reimbursement alimony"—paying spouses like Loretta back for what they actually spent on their husbands' education, or for their own lost opportunities. This of course results in a much smaller payback than under the *O'Brien* formula.[91]

MARITAL FAULT AND MONEY

"Fault" has disappeared from divorce in the no-fault age. But does—and should—fault play a role in decisions about property and spousal support? Theresa Havell divorced her violent and abusive husband, Aftab Islam, after twenty-one years of marriage. One morning, he attacked her with a barbell; the children and a housekeeper tried to stop him, but by the time the police arrived he had smashed her teeth and jaw, and she suffered permanent, debilitating injuries.[92] Islam eventually went to jail. Havell and Islam were very well-off financially; both had been successful investment bankers (before the fall of Wall Street), she even more so than he. The net marital estate was worth approximately $13 million.

No-fault had not yet come to New York; and Havell asked for divorce, on the grounds of cruel and inhuman treatment. Should his cruelty also have economic consequences? Most states consider fault as a factor, if the misconduct had some sort of economic effect. For example, if the husband gambled away part of the marital estate in Las Vegas, he might get a smaller share of what's left.[93] Same, too, for a wife who intentionally dissipates marital property in anticipation of filing for divorce. But the states do not agree about whether other forms of marital misconduct should be relevant to property division or not. In almost half of the states, "fault" matters, in at least some cases, even if it has no economic consequences.[94] In states that treat marriage as something like a business partnership, the goal is an even split between partners; and fault is irrelevant. The Uniform Marriage and Divorce Act, in 1970, urged property division "without regard to marital misconduct," as if a partnership were being dissolved.[95] Other states still consider fault relevant, however. For them, the business analogy only goes so far; husband and wife have a personal relationship; and ignoring fault can sometimes lead to very unfair results.

New York's divorce statute generally directs courts to consider thirteen factors before deciding how to apportion marital property—factors like income and property; age and health of the spouses, and so on.[96] But courts are also permitted to consider "any other factor which the court shall expressly find to be just and proper." The Havell court admitted that "any other factor" does not generally include marital fault—unless the misconduct "shocks the conscience." In one prior case a husband had tried to murder his wife; in another, a man had raped his stepdaughter.[97] The *Havell* court gave the wife 95.5 percent of the marital estate, leaving Islam with almost nothing. Later cases in New York have taken fault into account, even in cases of less severe domestic violence.[98]

The line between ordinary and egregious fault is hard to draw. Howard and Lillian DeSilva married in 1997. She was a receptionist in the World Trade Center; he was a lawyer in the building. They had two children; he adopted her daughter from a prior relationship. In 2004, Lillian gave birth to a fourth child, Charles.

The couple began divorce proceedings, and Howard became suspicious, after family and friends joked that he and Charles looked nothing alike. He secretly arranged for DNA testing; it proved conclusively that Howard was not Charles's father. Howard demanded the lion's share of the marital property because of his wife's "fault." Howard lost; the court was not sufficiently shocked by Lillian's behavior.[99] Simple adultery, along with such transgressions as alcoholism, abandonment, and verbal harassment, were not "egregious fault." It can hardly be said, after all, that adultery "shocks the conscience," given survey data suggesting that at least 25 percent of married persons engage in it, at least once, and as many as 5 percent of children born to married women are not fathered by the woman's husband.[100]

Oddly enough, fault's role in alimony law is not always the same as its role in property distribution. Twenty states follow an ALI suggestion and refuse to consider marital misconduct in alimony issues; another eight only in rare cases.[101] Brenda and James Mani met in 1970, when she went to work for his business on a boardwalk on the Jersey Shore. After they married in 1973, they worked long hours together at the business. The business made a profit, but not enough to finance their "extravagant" lifestyle. Gifts of stocks and bonds from Brenda's father made up the difference. But the gifts were only for her; James had to sign a written waiver of all rights to the property. While still in their forties, the couple retired. Seven years later, Brenda learned that James was having an affair with a mutual friend. She filed for divorce, alleging adultery. By the time of divorce, Brenda's assets were worth $2.4 million; James's—including his share of marital assets—were worth, at most, a few hundred thousand dollars. The trial court awarded alimony to James, fixed at $610 a week. James appealed; he wanted more. Brenda argued that he should receive nothing. He was lazy; and, moreover, he did not deserve compensatory alimony. The appeals court refused to raise the award, citing James's "marital indiscretions." The New Jersey Supreme Court held that fault is irrelevant to alimony—unless it directly affected finances, or was so "outrageous" that "society" would not tolerate "continuing ... economic bonds between the parties"—a spouse who tried to murder the other spouse, or deliberately infected the spouse with venereal disease. James's conduct did not rise to this level.[102]

Despite the reluctance of New Jersey and other states to bring marital fault into alimony determinations, twenty-two states still permit full consideration of fault in this context. North Carolina goes even further—barring alimony to a dependent spouse who has committed adultery or engaged in any other "illicit sexual behavior," and requiring that alimony be paid if the supporting spouse was the philanderer.[103] (If both have strayed, the court has the usual discretion about alimony.) This kind of absolute rule is now fairly rare.[104] Marital misconduct, however, can affect the amount of the award in many states.[105]

Prenuptial, Postnuptial, and Separation Agreements

An increasing number of couples leave nothing in the hands of a neutral fact-finder. These couples are bound by a contract that spells out the terms of their divorce. Most of these are contracts made before marriage—prenuptial or premarital agreements; during marriage with the intent that it continue—postnuptial agreements; or on the eve of divorce—separation or dissolution agreements. All three types of agreements have become increasingly enforceable, part and parcel of the general shift toward individualized marriage—and customized divorce.

The usual purpose of premarital agreements is to fix what happens to assets if the marriage is dissolved by divorce, annulment, or the death of one spouse. Couples have entered into premarital agreements for centuries. But historically, courts were hostile to the very idea. Marriage was a legal "status," whose terms were dictated by the state, and regulated by the state; and which applied to all couples. But the courts today are much friendlier to such agreements. This shift is related to the more general trend we have mentioned: individuals and couples have gained greater power to fix the terms of their relationships, and greater control over their marriages—before, during, and after.[106] This long-term shift, from status to contract (as it were), is seen in all parts of family law—no-fault divorce, for example, epitomizes this same idea—and, in this case, the custom-made divorce.

In the past, well-to-do people entering into second or later marriages tended to execute premarital agreements, often to protect the inheritance rights of children from an earlier marriage.

Beginning in the 1960s and 1970s, however, more couples began to use these arguments to regulate the economic consequences of divorce, as well as those of widowhood. Richer spouses would have less to lose in a divorce situation, if they had such an agreement. But agreements that customized rights like alimony and property division challenged the state's authority to regulate marriage as a legal status; and courts were skittish about enforcing contracts that gave people an economic incentive to get divorced.

The traditional hostility to premarital agreements began to crack in the 1970s, in the age of no-fault, greater equality of women, and a sharp rise in rates of divorce and remarriage. Now every state agrees that couples *can* enter into enforceable prenuptial agreements that spell out the economic consequences of divorce. But should these contracts be treated just like all other contracts, or should there be special rules to govern them? Contracts generally are presumed to be enforceable; they are presumed to reflect voluntary exchanges, which both sides want, and which benefit them both. And parties are generally bound by their agreements. The worry is that these conventional rules, if applied to prenuptial agreements, might produce unfair results. For example, in a 1990 case from Pennsylvania, *Simeone v. Simeone* (1990), a neurosurgeon married a nurse.[107] His attorney drafted the agreement and presented it to the would-be wife without explaining her legal rights. The agreement limited alimony to $25,000 total, a paltry sum in the light of his very high income. The agreement, said the court, was binding, whether or not she understood the terms, and whether or not the agreement was fair. Freedom of contract is an important value; and parties should generally be able to rely on such agreements.[108]

The Uniform Premarital Agreement Act (UPAA), which was promulgated in 1983,[109] tried to encourage states to take a more uniform approach to enforcement. More than half the states have since adopted this act. The UPAA encourages enforcement of prenuptial agreements, but stops short of treating them like ordinary contracts. It provides that a spouse can block enforcement of a premarital agreement only if the spouse can prove that: (1) the agreement was executed involuntarily; or (2) the agreement was unconscionable, and it was signed without fair and reasonable disclosure of the financial circumstances of the richer party.

Although this calls for more scrutiny than under general contract law, these standards make it relatively hard to invalidate a pre-nuptial agreement.[110] It can thus leave some spouses vulnerable to an unfair or lopsided divorce.

In an Iowa case, Randall Shanks, a personal injury lawyer, presented his fiancée, Teresa (who worked for him), with an agreement, ten days before the wedding. It required her to waive all rights to share property and to receive alimony. He promised only to maintain an insurance policy, naming her as beneficiary. Teresa said she was not marrying him for his money; she asked only a few questions, and then they flew off to Jamaica to get married. When they got divorced, she challenged the agreement. The court rejected her arguments. Nobody forced her to sign; she had a "reasonable alternative," that is, she could have backed out of the marriage. Her claim that the contract was unfair fell on deaf ears. Since she received some benefit from the agreement, and since he also waived marital property and support rights, the agreement was not "unconscionable." Finally, although the court admitted she lacked full information about his wealth and his pension, the court felt she had enough "general knowledge" to make a decision to sign.[111]

These cases represent the modern trend. Courts lightly scrutinize the agreement, but parties entering into prenuptial agreements can generally have confidence the agreements will be enforced. But should we assume that an engaged couple is really like the ordinary buyer and seller? The parties may be emotionally vulnerable. Most of us are unable to make rational assessments about the chance of a divorce, before we even marry. In the light of these concerns, some states treat prenuptial contracts as at least somewhat special. They emphasize fairness as a condition of enforceability. There is procedural fairness—each party should make a full, fair disclosure of their wealth; independent counsel for both parties is also an element.[112] And there is also substantive fairness: the courts should assess whether the agreement is fair, not just when it was executed, but also at the time of the divorce.

The ALI Principles, which we mentioned in chapter 6, fall into this category.[113] Enforceability depends on meeting certain conditions. The agreement should be executed at least thirty days prior to marriage. Both parties should have a reasonable opportunity to obtain independent legal advice; if one party does not have a lawyer, the agreement should be written in ordinary language. Even when these conditions are met, enforcement can be denied in the interest of "substantial" justice. This approach draws a more nuanced line between sensible financial planning and exploitation of a weaker party.

Postnuptial agreements, executed some time during marriage and often after a period of marital discord, have crept into the realm of enforceability as well. They are far less common than prenuptial agreements, but when executed with some procedural safeguards to protect the weaker party, are likely to be enforced. The highest court in Massachusetts upheld a postnuptial agreement for the first time, in *Ansin v. Craver-Ansin* (2010).[114] Although the court worried about the possibility of a holdup game—one spouse threatens to leave the marriage unless the other agrees to reduced property or support upon any future divorce—it held that such agreements could be enforced as long as there was no fraud or coercion, both parties had the opportunity to seek the advice of counsel, and the agreement itself was "fair and reasonable." Recent cases and statutes from other states also allow enforcement of postnuptial agreements.[115] But these agreements are, as we discussed in chapter 2, generally restricted to the consequences of divorce. The Iowa Supreme Court in 2009 refused to enforce a "reconciliation agreement" that a couple signed after she discovered he was having an affair.[116] He promised to behave better—and to suffer a financial penalty upon divorce if he fell short. The court said the agreement went too far; the couple could not regulate their marriage through a contract to be used and "proved in the courts as if the matter involved the timely delivery of a crate of oranges."[117]

Separation agreements—entered into on the eve of divorce rather than marriage—are also increasingly popular among couples and courts. At one time, courts disapproved of such agreements on policy grounds.[118] But these agreements had an obvious appeal. Parties can cheaply, easily, and flexibly arrange their own divorce settlements. Studies also show that parties tend to comply better with these settlements, compared to litigated arrangements. There was a shift in the 1950s and 1960s in favor of enforcing these agreements, but only if they were substantively fair. Spouses were not treated as arms-length negotiators; they were in an intimate relationship, where one party might be able to take advantage of the other one. Careful judicial review was appropriate. Today, separation agreements are presumptively enforceable. Courts feel they should defer to the parties to promote "amicable settlement of disputes"; they should set aside only agreements that are "unconscionable."[119] Provisions on child custody are more closely scrutinized, to make sure they serve the "best interests of the child," and provisions for child support must be consistent with state guidelines; but in most cases, these deals regarding children are also approved.[120] One well-known study found that judges never review separation agreements, even those involving children, unless somebody objects.[121]

Separation agreements are now the rule rather than the exception. At least half of all divorce cases settle based on a written agreement between the parties. As few as 10 percent go to trial.[122] Divorced spouses thus, in most cases, make their own new, separate beds to lie in.

CONCLUSION

Today, states are inching toward true community property principles, by tinkering with laws about equitable distribution. Alimony continues to fade in relevance. Whatever the law provides, couples have to face the fact that divorce may reduce the standard of living of one of them, or both. Property and alimony fights can be bitter, emotional, long and drawn out; and with consequences neither party likes. H. Beatty Chadwick served fourteen years in a Pennsylvania prison, after refusing to turn over $2.5 million to his ex-wife, as a divorce court judge had ordered. He was released in 2009, seventy-three years old, and a cancer survivor. He still refused to reveal where he had hidden the money. The law permits imprisonment for civil contempt only so long as it seems likely to force the desired outcome. After fourteen years, the judge thought (probably correctly) there was "little chance" of that.[123]

Chadwick is an extreme case. But divorce is painful and family law has no real remedy for the pain. Or for the poverty. Two households are much more expensive than one. The luxuries of an intact household often cannot continue after divorce. Women who stayed home with children often have to go to work. In 1980, divorced mothers accounted for two-fifths of households living in poverty.[124] A 1997 census report found that 45 percent of children living with divorced mothers lived near or below the poverty level. The number of children in poverty goes up dramatically if children living with never-married mothers are also included.[125] Couples living below the poverty line are much more likely to divorce than those living above, and those couples obviously are less likely to have enough assets to support a decent lifestyle after divorce. Laws of equitable distribution and spousal support, thus, for most families, merely aim for a "fair apportionment of that disadvantage."[126]

The gender effects are stark. To a surprising degree, men and women cling to a traditional division of labor during marriage. Men invest in their careers during marriage; and they reap the benefits later on. Women invest in housework and childrearing. They suffer the economic effect of those decisions, too. The law today tries to strike a balance. But women will never come out of a failed marriage with the same economic status as their husbands, unless they pursue wage-earning during marriage on more or less the same terms. Nor, as we discuss in the next chapter, will most men emerge from marriage with the same ties to their children as their ex-wives will have developed.

Collateral Damage:
The Children of Divorce

THERE ARE MINOR CHILDREN in roughly half of all divorces. Who gets custody? Typically, both parents are fit; both have a constitutionally protected interest in rearing their children; but both have also chosen to live separate lives. Neither has a superior constitutional claim; and courts simply have to apply the state standard for handling custody disputes.[1] Along with fights about money, custody disputes are at the heart of many contested divorces.[2] This chapter will explore the rules and standards courts are supposed to use, in awarding custody; and how these rules and standards have shifted over the years. It will also explore the troubling issue of child support. Who is supposed to pay for the children left adrift after divorce? How are support awards enforced?

CHILD CUSTODY

From the colonial period through the middle of the nineteenth century, fathers had "an almost unlimited right to the custody of their minor legitimate children."[3] This reflected the general thrust of family law, which was essentially patriarchal. In case of divorce—a rare event—a father had the right to custody of the children; he could also, at least in theory, designate a guardian for the children, other than their mother, when he died.[4] The first women's movement, in the mid-nineteenth century, demanded equal rights to custody and guardianship of children.[5] Society, and gender relations, changed dramatically in the nineteenth century; and the law of parental rights began to reflect those changes. Judges began to adopt and apply a "tender years" doctrine to custody disputes, which presumptively placed children under age seven with their mothers. Older children were often placed with the parent of the same sex. The "separate spheres" ideology held that men and women had very different roles in society. Women were in charge of home and hearth; men were breadwinners and involved in public life. Children thus needed to be nurtured by the parent whose role they were destined to replicate.

This shift to a "best interests of the child" standard gave great power to judges, who had virtually no limits on their discretion.[6] By the opening of the twentieth century, every state followed some version of this test, but still with a strong maternal preference, at least for younger children. In the twentieth century, particularly in the second half, custody law and practice would undergo certain changes. Judges would have a bit less discretion, formal standards would be unisex; and shared parenting after divorce would become more popular.

The "best interests" standard has often seemed hopelessly vague. A 1966 Iowa case, *Painter v. Bannister*, often strikes people as a case where the standard went seriously awry. Harold Painter's wife and daughter were killed in a car accident. He left his son Mark temporarily with the wife's parents, the Bannisters, until he could get back on his feet. Harold remarried and tried to reclaim Mark; but the Bannisters refused to let go of Mark. An all-out custody war began; both sides tried to prove they could best serve Mark's interests. The Bannisters were good folks from Iowa, capable, in the court's view, of offering Mark a "stable, dependable, conventional, middle-class, middle-west" life.[7] Harold, who was something of a free spirit, could offer him a "more exciting and challenging home," and an "opportunity to develop his individual talents." But the home would be "romantic, impractical and unstable." Harold lived in an unpainted house (unpainted by choice), with a yard full of "uncut weeds and wild oats." Harold took a "Bohemian approach" to life, the court noted, and has "read a lot of Zen Buddhism."

A child psychologist, who spent twenty-five hours "acquiring information" about the case, claimed that Mr. Bannister had become a "father figure" to Mark, and that Mark was happy and well-adjusted.[8] The court in *Painter* was careful to make clear that it believed both Harold and the Bannisters were "fit" to raise Mark. But they chose the Bannisters, even though normally a fit parent has a virtually absolute right to keep his child. Harold wrote a book entitled *Mark, I Love You,* and Mark eventually chose to return to his father.[9]

Painter would come out differently today; as we discuss in chapter 12, the Supreme Court has strengthened the constitutional rights of parents, particularly when fit parents are pitted against non-parents. But the case illustrates some disturbing features of open-ended custody decisions—heavy reliance on psychological experts, loose propositions about what is most beneficial for children—and too much discretion in judges; the values of the Iowa judges obviously influenced how they defined the "best interests" of the child. *Painter* and other cases like it frightened legislators and policymakers into reining in the "best interests" standard by adopting rules rather than standards—simpler, more mechanical devices that ideally would be applied consistently from case to case, instead of the empty formula of "best interests."

Beginning in the 1970s, custody statutes began to enumerate factors to guide a "best interests" determination, or to adopt presumptions that would all but dictate the outcome in certain types of cases. Typical factors range from parental age and health to earning capacity, ability to nurture, and living arrangements. Children of a certain age might get to voice an opinion, too.[10] This does not eliminate judicial discretion, but it narrows the inquiry at least somewhat. At the same time, the maternal preference—formally recognized in some states, but informally lurking virtually everywhere—gave way to a gender-neutral standard in the 1970s. The ban on sex discrimination in the 1970s made it difficult, if not impossible, for states to defend sex-based classifications. The maternal preference was held to be unconstitutional, in favoring women and penalizing men who might be equally good parents.[11] As the Utah Supreme Court wrote in a 1986 opinion, the "tender years doctrine was perhaps useful in a society in which fathers traditionally worked outside the home and mothers did not," but it was now "unnecessary and perpetuates outdated stereotypes."[12] As one New York court observed, not all "mothering" need be done by a mother.[13]

In some jurisdictions, the maternal preference was gradually replaced by a "primary caretaker" preference, which emphasized the functional aspects of parenting.[14] Who made the children's meals? Who bought their clothes? Who changed their diapers?

Who planned birthday parties and play dates? Who took them to the doctor and got up with them in the middle of the night? Who remembered to give them the full course of antibiotics even after the infection was gone? That person—the primary caretaker—was best suited to have custody after divorce. Or at least it was a factor that weighed heavily in favor of the primary caretaker. This standard draws on the notion of competence—presumably the person who performed these often tedious and repetitive tasks would tend to do them better in the future—and continuity of care, a polestar of modern custody law.[15] This idea also applies to modification of custody: in most jurisdictions, a court cannot revisit the "best interests" of the child once a custody order is in place unless the circumstances have changed substantially, and sometimes only after a specified period of time has elapsed.[16]

Stereotypes about gender and parenting may be "outdated"; but the truth is, still, that most primary caretakers are mothers. That holds true even if they work outside the home. In a 2000 survey, eight out of ten working mothers reported that they do "far more of the household chores" than their husbands or partners; men who were surveyed in the same sample agreed.[17] Women tend to spend nearly double the number of hours on child care and housework that men do, even in dual-earner couples.[18] Hence, women still get custody in the vast majority of cases, even if fathers put up a fight; this is especially true for children under age five.[19] And, as Karen Czapanskiy has argued, courts could be said to promote actively "a gendered allocation of household labor" through various policies and doctrines, despite the appearance of gender neutrality.[20]

In a number of cases in the 1990s, fathers argued that mothers who worked full-time and relied on daycare or a nanny should be denied custody. A mother in a Michigan case lost custody because she put her baby in daycare in order to attend college classes, even though the child's father intended to rely primarily on his parents for childcare rather than to provide it himself.[21] But most cases, especially more recent ones, have refused to treat working mothers as inherently unqualified, just as they have ceased treating all fathers as less qualified to raise children.[22] A side story during the media firestorm surrounding the trial of O. J. Simpson for a brutal double murder was about the custody problems of Marcia Clark, the lead prosecutor.[23] Her ex-husband sued for a change in custody, arguing that her "grueling work-load was harming" their two young sons, leaving them "starved for affection."[24] In the end, Clark's husband dropped his petition; but some women have suffered because of career ambitions. Women who work long hours can lose custody if a court feels this means their children would be better served by a different custodial arrangement.[25] Sharon Prost, a lawyer for Senator Orrin Hatch, lost custody to her ex-husband because of her work schedule and professional commitments.[26]

Custody fights can be bitter, with both sides bringing up their heavy artillery.[27] (The Academy Award–winning film *Kramer vs. Kramer* [1979] depicted this on the big screen.) Despite all the rules and the standards, the discretion of the judge is still crucial. To be sure, the judge will give some weight to psychiatrists, psychologists, and social workers; there is sometimes a desperate effort to enlist "science" in these cases, in the vain hope of finding a clear answer to a question which essentially lies beyond the power of science to answer—which parent is most fit? We hear about the Millon Clinical MultiAxial Inventory, used to ferret out "personality disorders"; the Bricklin Perceptual Scales, designed "specifically for custody evaluations," and consisting of questions for the child, including "picture-drawing," and asking the child to complete a "story about how the family resolves disputes"; and the Ackerman-Schoendorf Scales for Parent Evaluation of Custody.[28] All of these have been criticized; all are probably at best weak guides to the solution of this often insoluble problem. Some courts have gone so far as to recognize "parental alienation syndrome," a controversial and dubiously scientific label for a common problem—one divorced parent's poisoning the children's minds against the other.[29]

Parental Behavior and Custody Disputes

An obvious question in assessing the relative fitness of parents is whether their lifestyle and conduct should be taken into account; sexual behavior, sexual orientation, and unpopular religious beliefs can be hot button issues in custody disputes, but the law over time has moved away from allowing them to control outcomes without proof of an effect on the children.[30] Recall the

Jarrett case, which we discuss in chapter 6: Jacqueline Jarrett's children were removed from her custody because she was living with a man to whom she was not married.[31] Cohabitation was still a crime in Illinois at the time, and the state's highest court saw no problem preferring the children's other parent, who was not demonstrating lax morality and showing open disrespect for the state's law. At no point in the case, however, did the court ask whether the children were being harmed, or even potentially harmed, by their mother's actions.

Jarrett was not alone in losing a custody battle because of sexual behavior. Although the sexual revolution was in full swing by the 1970s, custody law was relatively conservative; it clung to the view that certain types of parental behavior were *per se* disqualifying. But the tide did eventually shift toward the modern "nexus" standard. Parental behavior of any type is relevant to custody determinations only if there is a proven nexus between it and the children's well-being. A dissenting judge in *Jarrett* had argued for this standard, urging the court "to leave to the theologians the question of the morality of the living arrangement," and focus instead on the record showing that the children were "healthy, well adjusted, and well cared for."[32]

These same issues were raised in cases when one ex-spouse took up with a partner of the same sex, after an earlier heterosexual marriage. (Adoption by gays and lesbians is taken up in chapter 14.) Should a parent's homosexual relationship be grounds for denying custody or visitation rights? Courts at first viewed this kind of parental sexual behavior as *per se* disqualifying. Sodomy was still illegal in a number of states until the Supreme Court's 2003 decision in *Lawrence v. Texas*. Widespread social disapproval of homosexuality clearly played a role in custody cases. In a 1985 case, the Virginia Supreme Court held that the "father's continuous exposure of the child to his immoral and illicit relationship [with another man] renders him an unfit and improper custodian as a matter of law."[33] But in later cases, views of parenting by gays and lesbians generally became more tolerant.[34] A parent's sexual orientation was no longer a *per se* disqualifier. Instead, the focus was on the potential impact on a child's well-being. Courts thus looked for a nexus between a parent's behavior or lifestyle and the child's emotional, mental, and physical health. New trends in divorce law emphasized the freedom of men and women who divorce—freedom to start new lives, which might include relocating, pursuing new economic opportunities, and often a renewed search for romance. Courts in a few states are still dragging their feet, harboring at least a lingering suspicion that custody or visitation by a homosexual parent does not serve the best interests of the child. In 1998, the North Carolina Supreme Court affirmed a trial court decision removing children from the custody of their father because he was engaged in a homosexual relationship that "will likely create emotional difficulties for the two minor children."[35] But the strong trend is away from such views.

JOINT CUSTODY

Custody awards traditionally were of only one type: one parent was awarded sole custody, and the other was perhaps awarded "visitation." Sole custody basically meant decision-making power over all aspects of the child's life, and physical responsibility for all aspects of a child's care. But this arrangement often meant that relationships with the other parent were apt to deteriorate or disappear. One study of national data found that, after divorce, "[n]early half of all children have not seen their nonresident fathers in the past year," and many "have never set foot inside the houses of their nonresident fathers."[36] Children too are discontented; "[m]ore than half say that they do not get all the affection they need, and nearly as many say they are only fairly close or not close at all to their father." Many non-resident fathers tend to "behave more like pals than parents." The study concluded that in most families "[m]arital disruption effectively destroys the ongoing relationship" between children and the non-custodial parent.

The joint custody movement was one response to these negative effects of sole custody. California pioneered this new arrangement in the late 1970s. With joint custody, parents can share "physical" or "residential" custody so that children go back and forth from house to house (or, in some cases, the parents go back and forth between the custodial house and another residence).

Or they may just share "legal" custody, that is, both parents have a say in important decisions about education, religious training, and medical care.

In a few early cases, courts wondered if they had authority to order such a nonconventional arrangement, but most concluded that they did.[37] In 1978, only three state custody statutes expressly provided for joint custody as an option; by 1989, thirty-four states did. Joint custody became so popular in the 1980s that several states enacted presumptions in favor of it. Parents, in other words, if they wanted to avoid joint custody, had to prove that it was *not* the best arrangement for them or their children. But states have gotten over this infatuation with joint custody; they decided in the end that no single arrangement could be presumed best in all cases.[38]

Joint custody is in many ways harder to establish and maintain than the traditional arrangement. Parents must have the capacity to make decisions together—even though, after all, they have recently gotten a divorce. They must be able to afford two of everything—beds, clothes, toys, musical instruments, bikes—so that children do not feel they are living out of a suitcase. They must live close enough to each other so that the back-and-forth travel is manageable for children and parents. And the children themselves must be secure and stable enough to handle all the moving around. On the other hand, fathers with joint custodial rights are more likely to pay child support.[39] Children clearly benefit in most cases through stronger ties with both parents. But divorcing families are not all alike; and legislatures eventually decided to give back to the judges some of their discretion in deciding where the children's best interest lies. Courts may consider what the parents want, what they can do, what the children want (if they are old enough to have a say), the money situation, geographical issues, what will and what will not disrupt the children's education and social lives, and so on.

Joint *legal* custody is less difficult; but there is still plenty of potential for trouble. If one parent thinks the child needs a private school, and the other prefers a public school, who decides? Disagreements often led to the divorce in the first place, so it is hardly surprising that they continue afterwards. Some courts give the final say to the parent with physical custody; but the Michigan court, in *Lombardo v. Lombardo* (1993), gave judges the authority to resolve disagreements.[40] Neither solution is perfect; each can lead to litigation; each can also undermine shared decision-making authority.

Today, joint custody remains popular as an initial order, although studies suggest there is often some "drift" back over time to a more traditional arrangement. Robert Mnookin and Eleanor Maccoby found, in nearly half the cases in a study of cases from 1984 and 1985, that joint custody arrangements reverted to sole custody by the mother within three years.[41] Some feminists have criticized joint custody as favoring "the interests of non-caretaking fathers over caretaking mothers."[42] The American Law Institute has proposed a kind of compromise between sole custody and joint custody. The goal is to allocate custodial responsibility in proportion to the way it was carried out prior to the custody proceeding.[43] Thus, a father who spent time with his children mostly on the weekends should have parenting time on weekends, while a more involved father should have time with them perhaps every day.

PARENTAL OBLIGATIONS: THE DUTY OF SUPPORT

In chapter 12, we take up parental rights. But parents also have obligations with respect to their children. The increasingly formal nature of these obligations is among the more significant developments in modern family law. The growing number of children who do not live with both parents—nearly 30 percent in 2006, up from only 8 percent in 1960—makes child support law very important.[44] Current law binds fathers to children (legitimate or not). Also, the influence of the federal government has grown; and legislatures have been more active in rule-making than before.[45]

A formal obligation to support children, in modern law, is a reversal of common-law notions. Under common law, "the parent's duty to support was a mere moral obligation creating no civil liability."[46] But divorce codes expressly gave judges the authority to order support for children following dissolution.[47] And every state, by 1931, had both a civil law requiring support for children and a criminal law to penalize non-support.[48] On the criminal side, "family desertion" acts required men to support both spouses and children, including, in eighteen states, illegitimate children. In California, a father who, "without lawful excuse" did not provide food, clothing, shelter, and medical attention, for children (whether or not legitimate) was guilty of a misdemeanor.[49] In some states, mothers had equal obligations of support; in others, no mention was made of any obligation; or it was secondary to the father's. In California, the mother's duty arose only if the father was dead or incapacitated. Iowa law imposed criminal liability on mothers and fathers for non-support of a "legitimate or legally adopted child"; it applied the same rules to any parent having "custody of a bastard," but imposed a special set of rules on non-custodial unwed fathers.[50]

Today, the general obligation of parents to support their children is at least loosely enforced through the abuse and neglect system. On the civil side, parents must support their children, with some variation on whether mothers are equally liable, and whether illegitimate children are equally entitled to benefit.[51] Intact families, where children are raised by married parents, have always been by and large insulated from state intervention. These parents have the same obligations as unmarried or divorced parents; but the state does not look very closely into their level of support; and it does not intervene unless the parents are so neglectful that removal of the children from the home might be justified.

Child support can be awarded in paternity suits, which we discuss elsewhere, and in abuse and neglect proceedings, but for the most part the law developed out of divorce actions. For divorced couples, the duty of support changes. The duties of the custodial parent consist of day-to-day provisions for the child; this duty is enforced through abuse and neglect laws. For the non-custodial parent, the duty is enforced through a formal child support order.

Formal child support awards are not new; but they were not routinely imposed until the 1970s.[52] And even then, awards were made too infrequently and in amounts too low to provide much protection for the children who were supposed to benefit from them. According to one estimate, based on current guidelines, fathers in 1983 "should have been paying between $25 and $32 billion in child support; in fact they owed only $10 billion and paid only $7 billion."[53] And there were "great inequities" in awards;

the same courts and judges issued wildly varying awards.[54] It was a system of unbridled judicial discretion. By statute, states authorized courts to impose child support obligations on non-custodial parents, but gave only general guidelines on amounts (for example, "just and reasonable"); and did not make awards mandatory.[55] Judges tended to sympathize with non-custodial fathers, who often had no meaningful role in raising their children after divorce and yet were obligated to support them. A separate but important problem was the lack of sufficient enforcement mechanisms. Many fathers simply did not pay; this left many children of divorce in poverty.[56]

Child support, like most family law issues, had traditionally been left to the states; but Congress took an interest in the subject because it was tied to welfare programs, which the federal government subsidized. Many divorced moms and children depended on welfare, sometimes because fathers were not paying. The Aid to Families with Dependent Children program (AFDC 1935), which was eventually replaced by the Temporary Assistance to Needy Families (TANF 1996), was supposed to provide assistance to needy children living with a single parent. Dramatic changes in household arrangements—a huge increase in divorce and in non-marital parenting—brought about a tremendous expansion in the size and cost of the program.[57] These costs, rather than "social alarm over the plight of mothers raising children with insufficient support," put child support enforcement into the spotlight.[58]

In 1975, Congress created the Office of Child Support Enforcement as Part D of the Social Security Act ("the IV-D program"). This was the first time the federal government, and federal money, came to play a role in child support. In 1984, Congress took a bold step to reduce the dependency of children: it made state AFDC funding contingent on the adoption of methods to enforce child support.[59] In 1988, Congress, by law, made support guidelines mandatory; deviations were permitted only in narrow circumstances.[60] The federal law did not mandate any *particular* formula or guidelines; but the states, to keep their welfare subsidies, were required to ensure more adequate awards and greater consistency among them. The discretion of judges was limited. More money for children was supposed to end up in the hands of custodial parents. Consistency at least has by and large been achieved. A 1996 study of child support orders in eleven states found that 83 percent awarded the guideline amount.[61]

Children—this was the aim of the guidelines—were supposed to live as well as their parents lived. Property division and alimony (see chapter 9) are mainly left to couples to work out for themselves. But not child support. Judges have to stick to the guidelines, even if the couple agrees to a different amount. In a recent New York case, a separation agreement provided that the father could stop paying if his teenage son worked full time. The court refused to accept this arrangement. Parties "cannot contract away the duty of child support"; the contract had to yield to the "welfare of the children."[62] A child is emancipated, and no longer in need of child support, only when he is truly economically independent.

Under the stricter new approach, questions can be raised about "shirking"—are divorced parents under a duty to maximize their income, and thus maximize the amount of money they can use to support the children? Jane Chen was an anesthesiologist earning more than $400,000 a year. At the age of forty-three, she decided to "retire" and stay home with her three school-age children. She and her ex-husband, John Warner, also a well-paid physician, shared custody, alternating week by week. A court ordered Warner to pay $4,000 more per month in child support, to make up for Chen's reduced income. He objected, however, arguing that she was "shirking" her duty to support her children. The Wisconsin Supreme Court disagreed; Chen's decision was reasonable under the circumstances—and did not violate her obligation to support her children.[63]

However, most states do permit judges to calculate child support based on "earning capacity" rather than actual "income." For example, a father who quits his job immediately before appearing at a child support hearing, in order to evade an award, might still owe child support based on what a court believes he *could* earn. In 2005, a New York court held a father in contempt of court for non-payment of child support; he had finished law school and passed the bar exam, but never filed the necessary paperwork to be admitted to the bar. He decided, instead, to enroll in divinity school.[64] That he "does not want to be a lawyer" was no defense to his failure to keep up with his child support obligations. The amount owed would be based on his "potential," not "his voluntary seeking of another degree." But was this different from Chen's decision to give up a big salary in order to spend more time with her children?

Many families still elect to have one parent stay home with young kids. Usually, this is the mother, even though women today have many job opportunities.[65] She makes this choice because she trusts her husband to provide for the family as a whole. But trust is often lacking after a divorce; and conflicts can arise when one parent's work or lack of work affects the other parent's duty to pay child support. Because both mother and father have a legal duty to support their children, the court is thus invited to scrutinize, and perhaps override, a decision that most parents assume should be private. Courts retain jurisdiction over child support and custody awards until the children reach at least age eighteen. Parents can be judicially overruled throughout that time, on many important life decisions—whether, where, and how much to work; whether to relocate; and even whether to become involved with another adult.[66]

No law and no judge would say anything about a married woman who chose to stay home with the kids. Nor even about an extremely rich husband who made his kids live like paupers; or a middle-class family that decided not to pay college tuition for the kids. An intact family has the luxury of making almost any decision about work, income, and expenditures that it sees fit—so long as this does not constitute "neglect." But divorcing families do not have this autonomy. In some states, courts have the discretion, for example, to compel a non-custodial parent to contribute to college tuition, even though no such order would be issued against a married parent. The Supreme Court of Iowa ruled, in one case, that the legislature could authorize judges to issue orders for tuition payments. Most married parents support their children through the college years; but even "well-intentioned parents," who do not have custody, "sometimes react by refusing to support them as they would if the family unit had been preserved."[67]

In the end, the court honored Jane Chen's decision to stay home. Even in the strict world of child support laws, there is some sympathy for stay-at-home mothers. In some states, child support laws expressly exempt a "nurturing parent" with young children. In Louisiana, for example, earning power is not to be imputed to the primary caretaker of children under age five.[68]

High-income families pose a challenge for child support guidelines. Does any child really need 25 percent of a professional basketball player's income? States often cap the amount of income subject to guidelines, but give judges discretion to give more, if the children would benefit. High-earners likely to have huge income swings in their career—professional athletes, for example—are sometimes ordered to set up a trust for future support of their children. Child support guidelines in the states vary greatly as to the treatment of high-income families.[69]

Second marriages and blended families also pose problems. There is a limit to how many 25 percent slices can be carved out of a person's income, and still leave him (and perhaps a new wife) enough to live on. Former NFL running back Travis Henry has fathered nine children with nine different women (he claims some of them "trapped" him by lying about birth control). He has a child support order for each one; payments come to some $170,000 per year. He is no longer on the team, no longer earning millions; he has fallen behind on many of his obligations; at least once he had to go to jail for failing to pay.[70] An appellate court upheld an order requiring him to put $250,000 in a trust fund to secure future child support payments.[71] States generally give priority to children of a first marriage; they refuse to reduce early support awards in order to bolster later ones.[72] This is designed, at least in part, to deter men from having more children when they are already unable to support the ones they have.

CHILD SUPPORT ENFORCEMENT

Congress not only aimed to mandate guidelines for child support, but also to facilitate enforcement of awards. Child support has thus become a hybrid federal-state area of law—an unusual feature for family law. Congress has used both the carrot and the stick. States get performance incentives to improve collection rates. Mothers get incentives if they cooperate in establishing paternity—the first step toward getting a child support award.[73] States, in turn, pass tougher laws for parents. Modern technology and various registries help courts, welfare agencies, and custodial parents track down so-called deadbeat dads when they move or change jobs. Government agencies give custodial parents help in this search, in establishing paternity, and in getting and enforcing child support orders. Deadbeat parents can lose their driver's licenses. Their wages can be garnished. In extreme cases, they can go to jail. A parent who has more than $10,000 in unpaid child support for a child in another state can be charged with a federal felony.

Lawmakers and candidates have responded to the cry for tough measures against deadbeat dads. Finding and getting money from "AWOL fathers" has been one of the most "successful—and bipartisan—social policy crusades of recent years."[74] The sheriff's office in one New Jersey county conducted a raid after Mother's Day in 1998, arresting 629 "deadbeats" (forty-one were women) and collecting more than $88,000 in back-owed support. Those who couldn't pay up were "sent to jail until they came up with the money or agreed to a payment plan."[75] And in 2002, federal agents conducted a "nationwide sweep" of deadbeat dads; the Bush administration had resolved to make aggressive use of federal criminal law to get men who "repeatedly flouted state court orders."[76] The targeted dads were not "dead broke" at all—among them were professional football players, psychiatrists, and restaurant owners. As a group, these dads owed more than $5 million in unpaid child support; some individual debts were as high as $297,000.

Rich dads are one thing; poor dads are another. The federal effort has focused on reducing welfare spending. Most of the money collected from poorer dads goes to reimburse the government for public assistance given to the children.[77] The family thus gets little or no benefit from these payments. Some efforts have been made in recent years to structure the laws in such a way as to promote ties between fathers and their children, and not just focus on repaying the government, and punishing wrong-doers.[78]

Despite federal intervention, a surprising number of eligible parents have no child support awards; or receive no money from the other parent. The U.S. Census Bureau has compiled information on child support since 1978. A 1981 Census report found 8.4 million women raising children of an absent father. Only 59 percent had a child support order in place. Twenty-eight percent of those who were supposed to receive payments that year did not receive a penny.[79] Poor women fared worse; only 39.7 percent of women below the poverty level had an award; and nearly 40 percent of those received nothing at all in 1981.

By 1989, almost 10 million women were raising children alone. The child support numbers had improved slightly. Fifty-eight percent of the single mothers had a child support award (a slight decline from 1981), but of these, only 24 percent were getting nothing. Among poor women, the rate of awards had increased (43.3 percent) and the rate of non-collection had decreased (31.7 percent).[80] In 2001, single mothers numbered 11.5 million; but 63 percent had a child support award; and only 25 percent of those received no payments.[81] The Census Bureau also had data on single fathers. Only 38.6 percent of those had a child support award, and 34 percent of those with awards received no payments.[82]

Legally, there is no connection between visitation rights and child support.[83] But fathers with formal custody or visitation rights are, in fact, more likely to fulfill their financial obligations.[84] Race and socioeconomic status seem to influence the likelihood of getting a child support award, but not the rate of collection, to any significant degree. According to the most recent data, white custodial mothers were twice as likely to receive a child support order as black or Hispanic custodial mothers.[85] The percentage of custodial parents who work full time has increased steadily, to 55 percent in 2001; another 28 percent work part-time or part of the year. At the same time, the welfare rolls have steadily declined. The percentage of custodial parents receiving public assistance dropped from 41 percent to 28 percent between 1993 and 2001. Mothers were much more likely to need welfare than fathers.[86] The number of single parents living in poverty declined as well, from 33 percent in 2003 to 23 percent in 2001; still, poverty plagues single-parent families at four times the rate of married-couple families.[87]

The (in)effectiveness of the child support system also affects the way women and children fare after divorce (we deal with this in another chapter).[88] And the awards under current guidelines are too low; raising children is expensive.[89] The system does play a "non-trivial" role in reducing poverty rates, and helping divorced women with children,[90] but it still "falls far short of its potential to transfer income from noncustodial to custodial families."[91] The number of children being raised in unmarried or single-parent households keeps going up; and with it, the importance of laws and practices relating to child support; and the modes of enforcing these awards.

All social trends have winners and losers. The big social trends we discuss in this book—the loosening of traditional ties, the increasing empowerment of women, the growth of expressive individualism—have naturally produced a crop of winners and losers. In this chapter, we looked at a significant class of losers: the children of divorce. They face the job of adjusting to the new reality, of living with only one parent. And they also face a significant loss of economic stability. Probably there is no perfect solution to the problem—and perhaps not even an imperfect one, as we saw in this chapter.

PART FOUR

THE OLD AND THE NEW GENERATION

✳

The Extended Family: Elder Law and the Law of Inheritance

DESPITE ALL THE CHANGES throughout the twentieth century, families are still the bedrock of society. Family life is where children are raised, where men and women commit to each other. Family life involves nurturing, caring, loving, and sex; all in functional and dysfunctional ways. But, as we have seen, family life is also about money. Families are economic units as well as social units and units of intimacy. In the typical family, one or more of the members works, and earns money. And, also in the typical family, the money is shared with other members, though the patterns of sharing and not-sharing can be extremely complex.

Family members not only earn money from work; some family members also inherit money from dead relatives, or get gifts from living ones. Other members give money away, during their lifetimes, or after death. Parents obviously have to pay for everything small children need; and when the children get older, parents who have money might pay for a college education, might support the children as they are getting established, and might help them out with the down payment on a house. Grown children sometimes support old, sick, and destitute parents. When a family member dies, typically he or she leaves whatever money or assets remain to members of the family. Studies of inheritance patterns—no surprise—show this clearly. In terms of inheritance, blood is definitely thicker than water. For the most part, money goes to widows, widowers, and children.

In books, and in law school curricula, family law and the law of succession (the law about wills, trusts, and other ways of passing money from the dead to the living, or from the living in contemplation of death) are treated as entirely different subjects. They are also quite separate in the world of legal practice. General practitioners may handle a woman's divorce, and then later on her estate. But there are "family law" firms that do not deal with inheritance; and "estate planning" firms that would not touch a divorce. Separating the two fields may make sense in various practical terms, but it ignores one of the important social roles of the family. Hence, in this section, we will ignore these artificial boundaries, and deal briefly with succession, as it impacts family life and family law.[1]

INTESTATE SUCCESSION

Within limits, American law allows people to leave their money however they wish, and to whomever they wish. (The big exceptions, as we will see, are the claims of husbands or wives; in almost all states, it is hard to cut a spouse off entirely.) But disposing of your property at death, generally speaking, has to be done in formal ways. As everybody knows, the main way to do this is through a will.

But what if the dead man or woman never bothered to execute a will—many people don't. In 1900, most people probably died "intestate," that is, without a will. In San Bernardino County, in 1964, two-thirds of the probated estates had wills.[2] But even today, despite the popularity of the will, a significant portion of the population will die fully or partially intestate. In such a case, the law steps in and dictates what happens. This is the law of intestate succession. The rules vary somewhat from state to state, but the general principle is the same, and has been the same for a very long time: the closest relatives inherit. Nowhere would an uncle be preferred to a daughter, or a cousin preferred to a brother. Nowhere would the law look for the dead man's best friend, or next-door neighbor, in preference even to a cousin in Australia. There are distinctions, too, between big estates and small estates. If you leave less than a certain amount of money, and you have a spouse and children, they will probably take it all. Freedom of testation, like some other freedoms in modern societies, is mostly freedom for people with money.

The rules of intestate succession have been fairly stable, but two changes over the twentieth century are worth noting here. First, the law more and more favors a person's spouse. If you go back in time far enough, a widow (say) had very limited inheritance rights. She was not an "heir" and thus not entitled to an outright share of her deceased husband's estate. In old England, a widow's right was called *dower*; and it consisted of an interest in one-third of his land—though only as long as she lived. (Husbands had a parallel, though not identical, right called *curtesy*.) The right of dower was superior to creditors, but the widow had no power to dispose of the land after she died. The rules of inheritance strongly favored the bloodline. Property was supposed to stay within the family. And a widow, after all, was not really part of that family. Moreover, as we have seen, a woman lost control over her *own* property when she married. Her husband took over, and her rights were no greater than the rights of an incompetent adult or a very small child. She could not sell it, or leave it behind by will.

Dower was largely abolished in the nineteenth century. For an estate with no will, it was replaced with an intestate share—a fixed percentage of real and personal property, outright. This meant, of course, that she could dispose of it by will. And, by the end of the nineteenth century, the legal disabilities imposed on married women with respect to property were essentially gone. The twentieth century continued the process of empowering a man's widow (and a woman's widower). Today, in some states, if a man dies without children (and no will), his widow takes everything; this is the situation, for example, in Florida.[3] In some states, the surviving spouse gets it all even if the decedent leaves behind children, as long as the widow or widower is also a parent to those children.[4] In virtually all states, the surviving spouse can claim a significant share of whatever the deceased left behind, regardless of who else survives.

The second change is to disfavor distant relatives. The old rule gave the estate to the closest living relatives—even if they were not particularly close. If a person died, without immediate family, and only a distant cousin or two, the distant cousins inherited. These were the so-called laughing heirs—relatives who had no emotional ties to the deceased, no grief at the death, and for whom inheritance was a lucky windfall. Everybody has *some* relatives, but it can be hard to find them. When Howard Hughes, who was ultra-rich, died without a will, and no close relatives, all sorts of people—five hundred in all—came out of the woodwork to claim a share of his estate.[5] But today, in many states, the laughing heir has nothing to laugh about. Nobody more distant

237

than descendants of a grandparent can inherit. This is the approach counseled by the Uniform Probate Code and now followed in many states.[6] If no such persons exist, the state government inherits; the property, as the legal term has it, "escheats" to the state.

As usual, legal change parallels social change. These two developments have shifted emphasis away from the bloodline, to what is the norm in American family life—the nuclear family, or what one might call the family of affection and dependence. For most people, nobody is emotionally closer than a wife or husband. The children, who during their early years are totally dependent on their parents, come next. Then come parents and siblings. Close ties with more distant relatives are not common in this country. We are a nation of small families and rolling stones.

Blood is still important, of course, but in some regards, less so than in the past. The common law, for example, recognized no such thing as adoption of children. You were a blood child or nothing. Even if your parents were dead, and you lived with some other family, and they treated you as if you were their child, you had no inheritance rights if your new "parents" died without a will. Formal adoption came into the law in the middle of the nineteenth century (in England, not until 1926).[7] In the twentieth century, inheritance rights of adopted children became stronger—they came to parallel, more or less, the rights of "natural born" children. The other side of the coin is that formal adoption cuts off the inheritance ties between an adopted child and her birth family, with only minor exceptions. (We discuss the legal effects of adoption in chapter 14.)

In a way, the law about illegitimate children makes the opposite point. Here blood has come to matter *more* than in the past. Originally, illegitimate children inherited nothing. They were, as the phrase went, *filius nullius*—the child of nobody. By the end of the nineteenth century, they became the children of somebody—their mother—with the same right to inherit from the mother as a legitimate child.[8]

And not only children of their mother, but very often of their father as well. Rights to inherit from a father have grown stronger during the twentieth century, but there is a great deal of variation from state to state, and from period to period. In Illinois, for example, in 1953, an illegitimate child was "heir of the mother," but from a father only if he married the mother and "acknowledged" the child.[9] States now grant broader inheritance rights to illegitimate children, in large part because the Supreme Court has, on constitutional grounds, disapproved of laws drawing sharp distinctions between children based on legitimacy or between mothers and fathers based on marital status. In 1968, in *Levy v. Louisiana*,[10] as we noted, the Supreme Court struck down a law that prevented illegitimate children from claiming tort damages when their mother was killed. In later cases on the inheritance rights (or non-rights) of illegitimate children, the Supreme Court waffled and wobbled. But *Levy* made it clear that, beyond some point, states were not allowed to discriminate against illegitimate children.[11]

Today, in many states, illegitimate children share in a father's intestate estate, if the father has admitted he is the father; or if a court order says he is, and orders him to pay child support. In Alabama, an illegitimate child inherits from his father if the "paternity is established by an adjudication before the death of the father or is established thereafter by clear and convincing proof."[12] And Washington State has gone all the way: "For the purposes of inheritance to, through, and from any child, the ... parent-child relationship shall not depend on whether or not the parents have been married."[13]

The intestate succession laws are rigid and unyielding in one essential regard. If a woman dies, survived by four children (and no husband), the children will share equally in her estate. The loving son will get the same share as the estranged daughter who has moved to Hong Kong. The rich daughter will get the same share as a poverty-stricken son who suffers from a chronic disease. Other common-law countries have amended their rules so that judges have some discretion. In England, courts can order a "reasonable" provision for members of the immediate family, on the basis of various criteria, despite the intestacy statute—and even despite the provisions of a will.[14] There is little sign of this kind of flexibility as yet in the United States. In Illinois, however, a close family member can make a claim (for a limited amount) against the estate, if the petitioner was "dedicated" to the care of a disabled person who then died, and if the petitioner lived with the person and helped out for at least three years.[15] Up to now, this is as far as the law has gone toward making merit a criterion for dividing an estate. The rules today may be strict and inflexible; but they work, and courts feel it would be a nightmare to unsettle the situation.

As we saw elsewhere, modern inheritance law has also come to recognize new kinds of family life. At least this is so in an important group of states. In states that recognize gay marriage or a marriage-equivalent status, a surviving same-sex spouse of course can inherit. Other states offer a status that is not equivalent to marriage, but still bestows inheritance rights on registrants. In California, the domestic partnership law did not at first include inheritance rights. Jeff Collman, a flight attendant, lived with Keith Bradkowski, his registered domestic partner. Collman died when his plane crashed into the World Trade Center on September 11, 2001. Bradkowski had no claim on his estate.[16] Shortly thereafter, California changed its law, to strengthen the rights of domestic partners; and these rights now include virtually all the rights of marriage, including the right to inherit.[17]

But without such laws, a surviving partner is probably out of luck. In a New York case from 1993, the deceased, William Cooper, was gay. He left the bulk of his estate to a former lover; his current lover, Ernest Chin, was dissatisfied with what he received under the will. He tried to renounce the will and claim a share in the estate, on the grounds that he was a "surviving spouse." He had lived, he said, with Cooper "in a spousal-type situation. Except for the fact that we were of the same sex, our lives were identical to that of a husband and wife. We kept a common home; we shared expenses; our friends recognized us as spouses; we had a physical relationship." The court denied the claim.[18] New York courts, more recently, have come to recognize inheritance rights of same-sex partners, if they were legally married in another jurisdiction.[19] But on the whole, inheritance rights still follow marital status, however. Unmarried partners, regardless of sex, almost never collect through intestacy.

THE WILL

The will is an ancient document, and a very well known one. Most people with money, esp cially older people, know that it behooves them to make out a will; the wealthier they are, the more likely they are to have one. The law gives them a pretty free hand to dispose of their wealth as they see fit.[20] Children, as we shall see, can be freely disinherited. The only big exception to freedom of testation is whatever rights the surviving spouse may have. (Women tend to live longer than men, marry older men, and have less money than men, so disinheritance is primarily a problem for widows.)

Can a man cut his wife out of his will? The answer is clearly yes in Georgia. Widows have no claim to a share of the estate in Georgia. The blunt statute plainly gives a person the right to "make any disposition of property" by will, to the "exclusion of the testator's spouse and descendants."[21] So much for southern chivalry. No other state is so crass, however. Everywhere else, the surviving spouse has some protection against complete disinheritance. In community property states, a surviving spouse automatically owns half of whatever the "community" owns.[22] The "community" is husband and wife, and "community property" is what they have each earned during marriage; obviously, the longer the marriage, the more likely that all of the property is "community" rather than separate property. To the extent the community has assets, neither spouse has the power to leave the other one penniless through disinheritance.

In "separate property" states, surviving spouses have a different form of protection against disinheritance. Dower was the old form of protection. For estates with a will, it was replaced with the elective share. The widow lost the protection from creditors, but gained an outright interest in the estate. If a husband tries to disinherit his wife (or vice versa) by leaving her nothing in the will, or less than her legal share, the widow can "renounce" the will, "elect" her statutory share, and take that slice of the estate. In other words, she is entitled to something, will or no will. In most states, the "elective share" amounts to a third of the decedent spouse's probate estate. (And, as with the spousal share under intestacy laws, the elective share is restricted to legal spouses in every state.)

A long series of twentieth-century spouses—mostly husbands—tried to find some way to disinherit wives they had come to hate. One trick was to execute a trust, put all the money into the trust, and give the widow no rights to the trust. The man then makes out a will, disposing of a non-existent estate (all the assets are in the trust) and leaves her a half or a third of an empty vessel. Does this trick work? In 1930, New York State abolished dower, and gave widows a sizeable share of a husband's estate. This was not to the liking of Ferdinand Straus, a wealthy insurance broker, whose marriage to Clara Dorner Straus was, to say the least, unhappy. Clara sued him for divorce; he countered with a claim for annulment. But when he died, in 1934, they were still legally husband and wife.

No doubt on the advice of a clever lawyer, Ferdinand transferred everything he owned into a trust, three days before his death. He kept the right to revoke the trust, and the right to receive the income, as long as he lived. He left Clara by will enough of a share of his "estate" to satisfy the statute (he thought). But his "estate" consisted of almost nothing: all of his assets were in the trust, and did not pass under the will. At his death, he and Clara were separated; she was living in a hotel, and had trouble paying the rent, even though she was (in her eyes) the widow of a very wealthy man.[23] She brought suit, and in 1937, in a case called *Newman v. Dore*, the New York Court of Appeals ruled in her favor. Ferdinand's transfer of assets into the trust was "illusory"; it was "a mask for the effective retention by the settlor of the property which in form he had conveyed."[24] It could not work, as against Clara; she was entitled to her share of the assets in the trust, as if they had remained in his probate estate.

Lawsuits in a number of states presented similar issues. Angry or spiteful husbands tried other kinds of trusts, joint bank accounts, insurance schemes, and other devices, trying to succeed where Ferdinand Straus had failed. Generally speaking, the courts were unsympathetic. They used various rationales to thwart these plans. Many courts found unappealing the notion that such transfers were "illusory," but they were able to find other doctrines they could use to frustrate the dead man's wishes, and give the widow her share.

The basic problem lay in the distinction between a *probate* estate—the property that passes under a will or through intestate succession—and other kinds of property, such as inter vivos trusts, joint accounts, and life insurance policies, which do not. Some modern statutes have created a new concept—the "augmented" estate—and they give the wife her share of this "augmented" estate.[25] Essentially, the idea is to add to the nominal estate the value of assets transferred out of the probate estate, insofar as the scheming husband (like Ferdinand Straus) kept power and control over them, or made transfers right before death. Transfer into living trusts, and joint bank accounts, or gifts within one year of death, can be treated as part of the "augmented" estate. A bitter and crafty husband can probably still accomplish his purpose; but it is harder to do than before. The best way is the most radical: actually give your money away while you are still alive.

In any event, these tricks are mostly for the well-off. In very small estates, as we mentioned, there is no point trying to disinherit a spouse. Widows (and minor children) will automatically inherit. Statutes also give surviving spouses certain absolute rights, will or no will, and whether the estate is solvent or insolvent estates. Support during the probate process is one such right. Homestead protection and personal property set-asides are two others. In Wisconsin, for example, as of 1915, the widow (and the statute specifically said "widow") had a right to "all her articles of apparel and ornaments ... family pictures ... household furniture," and "all provisions and fuel on hand provided for family use," up to $200 in value. She and the minor children were also entitled to a "reasonable allowance" during the probate period (if the estate was insolvent, this period could not last more than a year). And if the estate was worth no more than $1,000, the whole of it could be distributed to her.[26] Most states have a provision for small estates which is roughly similar, though the definition of a small estate has changed with the value of the dollar. In California, the threshold amount was $2,500 in the 1930s, $3,500 in 1959, $5,000 in 1961, and is now $20,000.[27] In Connecticut, during the probate period, the surviving spouse "or family" is entitled to the use "of any motor vehicle maintained by the decedent during his lifetime as a family car."[28] In Oklahoma, exempt property includes a church pew, a cemetery plot, and the family Bible.[29] In New York, it is possible for a surviving spouse to get as much as $92,500 in exempt property, if the decedent spouse owned sufficient assets in every category.[30] A surviving spouse there is entitled to both a tractor and a lawn tractor, if both were owned by the decedent, and are worth less than $20,000.

The right to the "homestead" has tended to shrink over the years. In some states, it is no longer literally the right to stay on in the family home. In Wyoming, the widow and children enjoy a homestead exemption, but only up to the value of $30,000.[31] The dollar goes further in Wyoming than in, say, Manhattan; but even so, the crudest shack in Wyoming should be worth more than this. At the other extreme is Florida, where, until 2010, a huge mansion and its grounds was exempt from creditors, with no limit on value at all, as long as the surviving spouse stayed alive.[32] In California, the homestead right is "only for a limited period"; in no case can it last past the "lifetime of the surviving spouse, or, as to a child, beyond its minority."[33]

It may be hard to disinherit a spouse; it is absurdly easy to disinherit children. In 1900, and for much of the century, all you had to do was say so in your will. If you made no mention of the child, the child took an intestate share. The California statute, for example, puts the matter this way: if a testator "omits" to provide for a child, the child takes a share "unless it appears that such omission was intentional."[34] But if you say, "I leave nothing to Ezra," or "nothing to my children," it's obvious that the omission *was* intentional; and the child is entitled to nothing. By 2000, in many states, you did not even have to make any mention of the child. If you said nothing, the child inherited nothing. Only children born or adopted after the date of a parent's will had some protection.[35] European countries that follow the civil law give children a share of the estate, regardless of what the parent might want. Louisiana, our only civil law state, had a similar rule; a child could be disinherited only if the parent had good reason to do so. But even Louisiana abandoned this rule in the late twentieth century. Only children under age twenty-three, or disabled, have a claim.[36] In all other states, minor children may have support rights while the estate is in probate, or access to a small amount of cash or property through "set-asides," discussed earlier, if there is no surviving spouse; adult children, however, can claim nothing.

This situation seems, at first blush, a bit anomalous. The law more and more emphasizes the nuclear family. Child support laws have been dramatically strengthened and more robustly enforced. Illegitimate children and adopted children have gained more and more rights under intestacy laws. Yet the right to disinherit children shows no signs of abating; quite the opposite. A parent can disinherit a minor child he would be forced to support if alive. Only a tiny number of states permit child support orders to be enforced against a dead parent's estate.[37] Why should it be so easy to disinherit children? The rule does, in fact, make sense for many families. If a man dies, leaving a wife and small children, he would normally prefer to give all the money to his wife. She needs the money to care for the children. Money left to minors is a bad idea. A guardian has to be appointed; this is expensive and irksome. And most estates are modest—the more shares allotted, the less likely a surviving spouse will have enough to live on. Second marriages pose a more troublesome question, especially when there are children from both marriages. But the law remains wedded to the idea that we need a single, inflexible rule. If so, a case can be made for the particular inflexible rule the common law has chosen.[38] The ability to disinherit children is consistent with the American system, which privileges "freedom of testation" over almost everything else. And, unlike a surviving spouse, children generally do not contribute to the earnings and wealth of the family; this makes a forced share that overrides the testator's estate plan harder to justify.

Parents can easily disinherit their children. But do they? Studies of wills show plainly that most parents don't—unless they have a surviving spouse. For example, one testator, Mike Schiro, in San Bernardino County, California, in 1964 left everything to his wife Jennie, and "nothing to our four children, as I know their mother will take care of them."[39] Typically, money gets left to immediate family; usually, if a person has children, the children are left equal shares—either initially, or upon the death of a surviving spouse. A 1979 study of wills in Bucks County, Pennsylvania found that 63 percent of testators with estates less than $120,000 left the estate entirely to the surviving spouse. The bigger the estate, the more likely it was to be divided into more shares.[40] Some people, of course, leave money outside the family—to friends, or employees, or to charity. But relatively few wills actually leave money to charity. All of the studies show this; and the finding is consistent over time. In Essex County, New Jersey, in 1900, there were only two charitable gifts in a study of 150 wills; in King County, Washington, in 1975, only 6.8 percent of the estates made charitable gifts; and in San Bernardino County, California, in the 1960s, only 7.9 percent.[41] These figures in fact overstate the number of charitable gifts. Some of the gifts were contingent (that is, they went into effect only if some relative died childless). Others were in the estates of people who died without close relatives. Very wealthy people, to be sure, often set up foundations. But for the rest of us, charity, apparently, begins and ends at home.

Wills can be contested, of course. A few will contests, in every period, have been flashy and flamboyant, even spectacular. But studies of the probate process confirm that will contests are actually quite rare. For most estates, there is no point to contest a will. A woman dies, survived by three children; and she leaves them her money in equal shares. No one has any interest in contesting. But contests are rare even with "unnatural" wills (those that ignore the "natural objects of one's bounty"), partly because there are many legal hurdles in the way. Still, if a will leaves more to brother John than to sister Kate, a testator is asking for family trouble. Not for himself—he is dead, after all—but there is real danger that John and Kate will no longer be on speaking terms. The death of a parent or parents often means the end of a close-knit family; all the more so, when a foolish or vindictive will—or even a just but harsh will—sets the stage for a bitter family quarrel.

Will contests often reflect the complexities of modern households: divorces, second wives, blended families. Seward Johnson, heir to a huge fortune, and father of quite a few children by a former wife, took a fancy to Basia, a much younger woman from Poland, who acted as his cook and chambermaid; he married her in 1971, and when he died in 1983, his will left her the bulk of his enormous estate. The children screamed "undue influence," and began a long, complex, and sensational lawsuit. Their case was flimsy; and the trial ended with a settlement. The children got some money—$3 million each; but Basia Johnson kept the bulk of the estate.[42] She apparently managed it well; as of 2009, she was listed as number 113 on the Forbes list of the world's richest people. Her fortune was estimated at $2.8 billion.[43]

A family dispute lurks behind almost every will contest.[44] Children left out of a will, or who get less than they feel they deserve, may complain about "undue influence" as in the Seward Johnson case. In 1903, two sons of Joseph Olcott, for example, complained of a sister's "undue influence" on their father. She conducted séances (they said) and acted as a medium—receiving, for example, a message from their dead mother, who told Olcott to leave his money to the daughter, "as the sons would be successful in business, and would be able to provide for themselves." Despite this claim, the will was admitted to probate.[45]

To contest a will, you need grounds; "undue influence" is one; or you can claim that the poor old testator had lost his senses and therefore the will was invalid. Many contests are based on "lack of capacity," a polite way to say mentally incompetent. The mental infirmities of some of the elderly are, alas, real; and these infirmities open the door to potential exploitation by caregivers, or others. There are hundreds of cases in which disappointed heirs challenged a will because of the alleged lack of capacity of the testator. In one New York case, in 1906, Charles H. Heyzer, who died in 1904, left everything to a woman he lived with for many years. His "actual wife" and his children (all of them adults) lived "a few blocks up the avenue." A jury, no doubt disapproving of his domestic arrangement, decided he was "not in his right mind when he made out his will," shortly before he died. But this decision was reversed on appeal: there was no evidence of "mental infirmity" whatsoever; Heyzer, separated from his wife for many years, had little or no contact with his children, and his live-in partner "had been true and loyal" and "had devoted her life to him."[46]

The vast majority of will contests fail. But they do open the door a crack for sympathetic juries, as in Heyzer's case. Juries can sometimes throw out a will that offends their sensibilities. Louisa Strittmater, a radical feminist in her day, left her money to the National Women's Party in the late 1940s. Louisa was unmarried. She was, admittedly, somewhat eccentric; but seemed to manage her property well. Still, her description of her father as a "corrupt, vicious ... savage," and of her mother as a "Moronic she-devil" along with her "morbid aversion to men" was enough to doom her testamentary plans.[47] And in a 1964 case, Robert D. Kaufmann bypassed his brother and other relatives, and left his money to Walter Weiss, his housemate and very likely his lover. The will failed on the grounds of undue influence—"insidious, subtle and impalpable."[48] Both of these cases would probably come out differently today. As public opinion shifts, so does the very definition of a family, and the notion too of what is or is not "unnatural." The law follows along, sometimes swiftly, sometimes not. There is certainly greater tolerance today for unmarried couples. And, if one can believe a 2005 poll in Indiana—one of the more conservative states—a majority of the population of that state (53 percent) would be in favor of "legislation giving inheritance rights to same-sex couples."[49]

"Undue influence" or an "unnatural will" were, to say the least, vague and malleable concepts. A few statutes were more blunt and open about offensive wills. In South Carolina, for example, anyone who "begets" a "bastard child," or who lives "in adultery with a woman," even though he has "a lawful wife of his own," was not allowed to leave the woman and her children more than a quarter of his estate.[50] This statute has vanished from history; but even today, under Indiana law, if you leave your wife and live in adultery, that costs you any right to inherit from your suffering spouse.[51] Abandonment or adultery will cause a surviving spouse in North Carolina to forfeit all inheritance rights.[52] And in New York, a spouse is disqualified from inheritance if he or she "abandoned" the deceased, or if, "having the duty to support the other spouse, failed or refused to provide for such spouse though he and she had the means or ability to do so."[53] Practically every state has a statute, too, which quite reasonably provides that you cannot inherit from a family member whom you murdered.

Many states at one time also had so-called mortmain statutes. These laws were designed to protect families against a dying man's fear of hellfire. A gift to charity was invalid, if the will was made too soon before death or if the will gave too big a share of the estate to charity. Only the immediate family, however, had the right to complain. These statutes were probably based on the fantasy of an evil priest or minister, preying on the sick and the dying. These fantasies have obviously faded. In the course of the twentieth century, these statutes were repealed or invalidated, one by one; and by 2000 none were left.[54]

TRUSTS

The trust is an ancient device, with medieval roots. But it flourishes in modern times, because it has proved to be useful and adaptive. Essentially, a trust is a device that splits ownership of assets into two separate aspects or functions. The *trustee* holds and manages the assets (and officially "owns" the assets); but everything the trustee does is supposed to be on behalf of one or more beneficiaries.

A person can set up a trust for anybody—a friend, a neighbor, employees, people whose name begins with Z. But, practically speaking, trusts are *family* arrangements. They are also very flexible devices. You can do with them more or less what you wish. Rich people commonly leave some of their assets in trust. They can specify as such in their wills, or they can set up a trust that goes into effect while they are still alive. Basically these trusts fall into two main types. One type is essentially nothing but a more complicated way to give money and other assets to somebody else. Once the trust is set up, the assets no longer belong to the settlor (the creator of the trust). Now they belong to the trustee and the beneficiaries.

Why give away money in this form? There are many reasons. If you want to transfer money for the benefit of a child, a trust is a good way to do it. The same is true for gifts on behalf of relatives who simply can't manage their own money—they might be developmentally disabled, for example. Or it can be set up for a relative if the settlor is afraid the relative might squander or mismanage the money. The trustee can be a friend, a competent relative, or a professional manager (often a bank or trust company); or some combination of these. Once she sets up the trust, the settlor can rest easier, knowing that the money is (relatively) safe from harm or mismanagement; or from the folly of the beneficiaries.

But many "living trusts" have quite a different aim. John and Mary, husband and wife, who are getting along in years, might set up a trust, and transfer some or all of what they own into the trust. They can name themselves as trustees; or perhaps ask a bank or a lawyer or a friend to do the managing. In this "living trust," they will reserve the right to change their mind, amend the trust in any way they wish; or, if they feel like it, undo it altogether. The income from the trust will go to them as long as they live. When they die, the trust property will go to other members of the family, whom they name in the trust as "remainder" interests.

Functionally, this is very similar to a will. But in some ways it is better than a will. For one thing, the assets won't have to go through the probate process when the settlor dies. If the trust is professionally managed, the settlor avoids the headache of dealing with the assets and making investment decisions. These "living trusts" became extremely popular in the last half of the twentieth century. This was partly a result of aggressive marketing, and partly because of literature that depicted the probate process as a sinkhole of expenses, which would deplete the estate for no good reason.[55] This is, to say the least, an exaggeration. But the customers for these trusts, frankly, did not always know what they were buying, or why. Nonetheless, for many families, the "living trust" *is* a handy and useful device for estate planning purposes.

The living trust is only one of a number of devices that act as will substitutes. Another is the so-called Totten trust, which dates from the very beginning of the twentieth century.[56] This is hardly a "trust" in the usual sense. It is simply an arrangement with a bank. The "donor" deposits money in a bank account. She keeps total control over the account, but also specifies that, if and when the depositor dies, any money left in the account will go to one or more "beneficiaries." This has been called the poorman's will. In the course of the twentieth century, almost all of the states came to accept the Totten trust. There were, to be sure, technical arguments against the device. After all, it (like living trusts) is suspiciously like a will, but without the formalities (witnesses, for example) that the law requires for a valid will. But the courts ignored these arguments.

In the twentieth century, in general, more and more people used will substitutes. There was an important shift in the social function of wills, and of inheritance in general. People were living longer and healthier lives. If a man lives to be eighty, and his wife to be ninety, their heirs—their children, usually—may well be themselves middle-aged or even older. As we mentioned, parents (if they can afford it) often help put their kids through college. Nowadays, this can be an expensive proposition. They may help children with down payments on houses. Thus, as John Langbein has pointed out, for many middle-class families, transfers of money, during the lifetime of parents, has become in some ways more important than actual inheritance.[57]

The Dead Hand

A will, or a will substitute, dictates what happens to a person's property at death (or before, in the case of some lifetime trusts). In this sense, the dead hand controls the fortunes of the living.

The dead hand can try to impose stern conditions on beneficiaries. One David Shapira left money to his sons, but only if they married Jewish girls, and within seven years after his death. One son claimed that this condition restrained his right to marry, and was against public policy. But a court in Ohio (1974) upheld the will.[58] The dead hand also can, if it wishes, tie up the property for some considerable length of time. A man can leave money to a trustee, to pay the income to his children for as long as they live, and then to the grandchildren. In this case, his children will have no way to get their hands on the principal as long as they live.

How long can a person tie up her estate in this way? An extremely technical rule, invented by the courts, and called the rule against perpetuities, essentially provided an answer. The details of the rule were maddeningly complex. The upshot was, however, that about eighty years or so was the practical maximum. After that, the dead hand had to relax its grip. The rule dates roughly from the beginning of the nineteenth century. In the twentieth century, it was reformed in many states to make it simpler to use. And, in a startling development at the very end of the century, some states got rid of it altogether. This means that in these states—Delaware is one—a man can set up a perpetual trust, a trust that never ends, and keep the estate "tied up" in his family, for centuries—perhaps forever, if there is a forever.[59]

Why did this happen? Basically, it began with a few states that decided to entice trust money into their state by relaxing some of the rules. Then other states copied, either to attract money on their own, or to defend themselves from the other states. It is too early to tell if perpetual trusts will become some kind of modern craze, like the hula hoop. It is, after all, only a toy for the rich. Whether rich people will relish the idea of controlling family money for generations to come is something we have yet to find out.

OLD FOLKS AT HOME ... AND ELSEWHERE

The family, in the twentieth century, had both gains and losses. Illegitimate children, adopted children, and couples in committed relationships were, in a sense, added on to the traditional or classical family, socially and legally. What was lost, on the whole, was the extended family—close relations with brothers and sisters, and with elderly parents, perhaps other relatives as well. There are societies where third cousins have a bond; but the United States is not one of those societies. The nuclear family has become everything; the family of origin, much less; the extended family, hardly anything at all.

We have dealt with (and will deal with again) the position of children in law and society. In this section, we look at the legal and social fate of those members of the family at the other end of life, members in their golden years which, for many of them, are not golden at all. Two themes will be stressed. First, responsibility for elderly relatives, specifically old parents, has shifted from the family to the state. A second theme is, in part, a consequence of one of the century's great achievements: medical miracles, which added years of life to the average person. These miracles have brought tremendous advantages; but they have also had their side effects. One of these costs was the increasing number of people who lived perhaps *too* long, and who found themselves, in the twilight of their lives, unable to take care of themselves and their property.[60]

Quite a few states began the twentieth century with statutes that made adult children responsible for their parents. Many of these lumped the duty of parents to children together with the duty of children to parents. Most people, surely, would consider it a moral obligation to help out old parents. But is it a legal obligation? In the age of Social Security, a number of states eliminated laws that made children responsible—Nevada did this in 1943, Washington State in 1949 (but restored it later), and Alabama in 1955. But other states passed or strengthened their laws. In 1956, all but ten states had some sort of law on the books making children responsible for impoverished parents. These laws remain. The current North Dakota statute, for example, makes it the "duty of the father, the mother, and every child of any person who is unable to support him or herself, to maintain that person to the extent of the ability of each."[61]

The later trend, however, was to do away with these statutes that made children financially responsible for parents. Today, more than twenty states have no formal rule imposing this liability. In seven states, there are criminal statutes, but no civil statutes. Theoretically, then, in these states, you can be put in jail for failure to support the old folks, but cannot be held liable in a civil suit. About half the states have civil statutes; but one law review writer called the duty to support parents "America's best kept secret."[62] There is little evidence that *any* of these statutes are actually enforced, except sporadically. Thus, the moral obligation is the only one that counts. And that obligation has probably weakened considerably, because the extended family is also weaker. Older people do not expect their children to support them. They do not expect to live with their children in their declining years. Many of them do not want to.

As the family ties got weaker, the state stepped in. A number of states began to experiment with old-age pensions: Arizona, Alaska (1915); three states in the 1920s (Pennsylvania, Montana, Nevada). Pennsylvania's statute and Arizona's were declared unconstitutional. After 1929, many more states joined the parade. Mostly, the statutes were only for poor people; and some states never joined in. The state laws were not, in general, successful. But they responded to a real felt need. The 1930s were also the period of the Townsend Plan. Dr. Francis E. Townsend proposed pensions for everybody over age sixty—$200 a month. How was this to be paid for? Townsend's suggestion was a national sales tax.[63] The plan was in fact totally beyond the financial means of government, state or local; but it was enormously popular, and millions of people joined Townsend Clubs. Members of Congress were "deluged with letters from members of the ... Clubs" in 1934 and 1935.[64]

The Social Security Act (SSA) was in part a reaction to the popularity of the Townsend Plan. It was, in any event, one of the jewels in the crown of the New Deal. It went into effect in 1935. This was a period of enormous unemployment. The SSA was designed to kill two birds with one stone. It would remove older workers from the job market, making room for younger workers. And it would benefit, not only the elderly, but also their children, who would otherwise be morally or legally bound to support them.

The Social Security Board's Bureau of Research and Statistics estimated that, as of the end of 1936, between 40 percent and 50 percent of the men and women over age sixty-five depended for support on friends or relatives. The United States was no longer an agricultural society, where life "is centered around a family unit," and where the old are treated with "obedience, veneration, even love and worship." In an industrial society, the old are "less agile, less productive than youth."[65] And family could no longer be depended on. For one thing, some 20 percent of the population either had not married, or had no children. And, as one author put it, "what happens when, in the absence of personal resources, even children fail, are unable and unwilling, or simply are not there?" The "gruesome" answer was "the poorhouse."[66] Stephen Young of Ohio, during the debates, made the same point: many old people were "destitute. Their sons and daughters, lacking jobs in many instances, cannot help."[67]

The basic elements of the Social Security Act are still in place; but there have been some significant changes. In 1939, the Act was amended to provide benefits for surviving spouses, and for dependents (children, mainly), so that SSA became in fact as well as in theory a family program. Originally, too, you lost your benefits if you did not retire, and you were only allowed to earn small amounts of money and still keep your benefits. This was the so-called retirement earnings test (RET). In 1950, this aspect of the law was removed for workers over seventy-five. In 1954, the age was reduced to seventy-two; and later amendments, in 1977 and 2000, essentially removed the RET. From 1956 on, SSA included a provision for disabled workers over fifty; in 1960, the statute was amended so that disabled workers of any age were covered. And Congress has, over the years, increased the benefits considerably (and raised the taxes needed to pay for them).

In 1965, Congress passed laws that established Medicare and Medicaid. Medicare is a program that pays for healthcare costs of men and women who are over age sixty-five. Medicaid is a program of public help for people too poor to afford health care. The same point can be made about Medicare that was made about Social Security. The primary beneficiaries are, of course, men and women who are over sixty-five. But the benefits also flow to their children and grandchildren. No longer do they have to worry about paying hospital bills for older members of their family. This too, then, is part of a long-term trend, which has shifted the burden of responsibility for elderly away from the family, and onto the state's broad shoulders.

This of course, erodes much of the support for laws that make children responsible. The relevant programs include not only Social Security, Medicare, and Medicaid (1965), but also the Food

Stamp program (1961); housing subsidies for the elderly; and supplemental benefit programs adopted in the 1970s. In 1991, the federal government spent $387 billion on programs for the benefit of the elderly, all of which "reduced financial burdens on children ... and ... lessened the perceived need for filial responsibility laws."[68]

Indeed, the enactment of Medicare and Medicaid stimulated some states to get rid of these laws. Medicaid rules do not allow states to shift the burdens to the family of the person helped. The rules make the finances of family members irrelevant. The only exceptions are spouses, and children under twenty-one (who would rarely be able to help). In a few states—notably South Dakota and Pennsylvania—the filial responsibility laws are not dead letters. But they are dormant in most.

ELDER ABUSE

Elder abuse is a form of domestic violence, usually against hapless old folks who live with their families. No doubt elder abuse has a long history; but for most of the twentieth century, if it was a problem, it was hardly mentioned. In the 1970s, some states passed laws which required the reporting of elder abuse by healthcare providers, social workers, and so on. Adult Protective Services Acts set up administrative structures, similar to those designed to protect children.

In 1981, a report by the House Select Committee on Aging brought the problem of elder abuse out in the open. According to the report, abuse of the elderly was a "widespread, serious and growing" problem.[69] But it was often hidden in the shadows; elderly people did not like to report abuse, either because they were afraid, or because they did not want to make trouble for the family. The report cited some horrible examples—elderly people beaten, neglected, and robbed, by their own children or grandchildren. A year later, a Chicago newspaper reported a "growing" but "unseen" problem of "battered elders."[70] A judge claimed that there were "probably four times as many abused elderly" as there were "abused children."

Domestic violence laws may help; but criminal law is a blunt weapon against neglect. In one horrendous case, decided by the

Texas Court of Criminal Appeals in 1989, Ray Edwin Billingslea was charged for criminal neglect of his mother.[71] Billingslea, his wife, and his son, lived in a small frame house in Dallas, together with his ninety-four-year-old mother, Hazel. They told Hazel's granddaughter, who was close to her, to mind her own business; and prevented her from visiting. The Adult Protective Services agency was alerted; when people came to the house, what they found was truly nauseating. There was a "strong, offensive odor of rotting flesh." Poor Hazel was lying in bed, nude from the waist down, moaning, her body covered with bedsores that at some points "appeared to have eaten through to the bone." Maggots "were festering in her open bedsores." She was removed from the house, but soon died.

Texas law made it a crime when someone "intentionally, knowingly, recklessly, or with criminal negligence, by act or omission," engaged in conduct that causes "serious bodily injury" to an "individual who is 65 years of age or older." Billingslea was convicted; the conviction was overturned, on somewhat technical grounds. The court was clearly troubled by the notion that an "omission" can be a crime, except in cases where there is a statutory duty to act, which was (they said) not the case here.

In many cultures—and indeed, perhaps, in our own culture, in the past—the duty to care for sick and elderly parents would seem obvious. And in many cultures not doing so would be almost unthinkable. Billingslea's behavior seems monstrous. Yet, despite Medicare, elderly people today can create a real family dilemma; old and sick parents sometimes impose a terrible burden on their children, who are often middle-aged themselves. Very few people have the money for full-time caregivers. Longevity can be a mixed blessing. Half or more of the people who reach the age of ninety suffer dementia. Caring for these people is no fun. Because dealing with old people can be thankless and unpleasant, cultural barriers against abuse have eroded. Indeed, the National Center on Elder Abuse, citing a study by the National Research Council, estimated that between one and two million Americans (as of 2005) had been injured, exploited, or mistreated by "someone on whom they depended for care or protection." There are estimates, too, that only a small proportion of instances of abuse come to the attention of authorities;

and, as far as "financial exploitation" is concerned, less than one out of twenty-five instances are reported.[72]

If a man kills his father or mother, or any other relative, he is not allowed to inherit from the victim under so-called slayer laws. But only California has gone one step further: you also cannot inherit if you abuse. The statute disinherits anybody shown "by clear and convincing evidence" to be guilty of "physical abuse, neglect, or fiduciary abuse of … an elder or dependent adult."[73] This statute is apparently unique. Illinois had no such law; but, in a case from 2002, a court stretched a bit its slayer statute, which barred inheritance by someone who "intentionally and unjustifiably causes the death of another." Ira D. Malbrough was a rich man; but in his old age he was blind and a stroke victim, completely dependent on his wife, Graciella. Allegedly, she neglected him totally; caregivers even found him at home with his "oxygen machine turned off, leaving him unresponsive with blue lips and fingertips." His brother began guardianship proceedings. Ira was removed to a hospital, but soon died of renal failure and congestive heart disease. The brother then contested Graciella's right to inherit. The trial court dismissed the case; but the appeal court reversed. The facts alleged, if true, would support a judgment that Graciella had in fact caused her husband's death.[74]

GUARDING THE RIGHTS AND THE WEALTH OF THE OLD

Protective services laws are designed to deal with the problem of elderly people who are victims of physical or mental abuse; or gross neglect. There are ways to deny inheritance rights to murderers and women like Graciella Malbrough. The criminal law can, perhaps, deal with outright physical abuse of the elderly.

But these are extreme cases. There is a much broader group of the elderly who need help in life. These are the people who become dimmer and frailer with the years; short-term memory begins to fail; checkbooks get lost; bills are not paid; the house, if they live alone, becomes dirty and neglected; it gets harder to shop, to buy clothing, or even to take a shower and get dressed. Clearly, these men and women are no longer able to cope. What is to be done?

As the population ages, this is a serious and growing problem. It is also a problem for families. The law has a role, though obviously a subordinate one. Somebody must be authorized to act on behalf of, and for the benefit of, people who are not legally competent. One legal issue is the nasty question of deciding *when* a person has slipped over the line and become "incompetent." For many elderly people, this is a very gradual process. The question can come up in many legal contexts. Was old Mrs. Jones competent when she signed this will? Was old Mr. Jones acting as a rational person when he gave away money to his next door neighbor? "Civil capacity" is a legal concept; evaluating it, and reaching a decision, concern matters that may be among the "most personal ... in one's life: what procedures will be done to your body, where you will live, with whom you are intimate with, how you spend your money."[75]

Capacity to enter into contracts or make a will is important. But also important is the more general question: has a person slipped so far that some kind of arrangement must be made for care and for handling financial matters. Legally, there are various solutions to the problem. One solution—which requires advance planning—is the durable power of attorney. An ordinary power of attorney ends if the person who executed it becomes incompetent (or dies). But a "durable" power springs into life precisely when the person who signed it becomes incompetent or otherwise unable to manage for herself. A "durable" power can also be made specifically for healthcare decisions, which gives someone else the right to make major decisions of this kind, or even to pull the plug.

The most drastic solution, perhaps, is to put a person under some form of guardianship. The rules vary from state to state. The law also distinguishes between guardians of the person—those who have physical custody—and guardians of the estate, who manage the property. ("Guardians" in some states are called "conservators.") Of course, one person can and often does act in both capacities. Or a relative can be guardian of the person, and a bank, or an attorney, or some friend, can act as guardian of the estate.

Guardianship arrangements of this sort go back a long time. They did, however, change greatly in the twentieth century. The changes tended, on the whole, to go in one direction: more procedural safeguards, and more rights for the ward. Under the older statutes, once a guardian was appointed, the ward had basically no rights at all. The guardian was, of course, supposed to act for the ward's benefit; and this right was in theory enforceable. But the ward was in other regards legally helpless. He could not make a will, enter into contracts, or do any of the things that normal people do.

Gradually, the legal posture changed. The general principle is to give the guardian only so much power as is absolutely necessary; and let the ward continue to live and do, as much as he can. So, for example, the New York law of 1972 added many new safeguards. If you apply for a conservatorship, the proposed ward has to be present, unless he cannot attend "by reason of physical or other inability." The court could appoint a guardian ad litem to represent the ward's interests. Later on, appointment of a guardian ad litem was *required*. In 1992, a new law was passed, which stated explicitly that the guardian would have only those powers that were absolutely necessary—" the least restrictive form of intervention."[76] This law also provided for a "court evaluator" to help investigate the need for a guardian.

The laws of other states underwent very similar evolutions. Sometimes evolution was helped along by court decisions. In Iowa, for example, an important case decided in 1995, *In re Hedin* (1995),[77] declared the existing guardianship statutes void, on the grounds that they were unconstitutionally vague. The court insisted that the guardian must exercise only those powers that were absolutely necessary (the least restrictive intervention criterion).

The statutes, if you take them literally, are now full of safeguards for the ward. In California, for example, from 1977 on,[78] a special official, the Court Investigator, will visit the ward before the hearing; and will also review the conservatorship every two years. California law, like the law of other states, has been moving more and more toward a looser, more flexible—and minimal—system. The system remains, however, highly discretionary. There are forms and procedures; but in the end, power resides in the conservator—and the judge. Conservatorship, moreover, is extremely local; and is a very low-visibility process.[79] It is perfectly possible that it works well and efficiently in County A; and is thoughtless and slipshod in County B. How the elaborate safeguards actually work out in practice is hard to know. There is very little research on the issue. That there are abuses, in some places, seems unquestionable.

The underlying problem is quite intractable. Even rich, famous people can be at risk if they are old, frail, confused—and vulnerable. When Groucho Marx was in his eighties, he fell into the clutches of a youngish woman, Erin Fleming, upon whom he became totally dependent. She was domineering and given to outbursts of rage. The household lived "in holy fear" of her. She tried to convince him to break with his daughter and grandchildren. Possibly she kept him drugged. Battles raged over the right to act as his conservator; and after his death, over his estate.[80]

Groucho Marx was not alone. The artist, Georgia O'Keefe, who was over eighty at the time, took in a young potter, Juan Hamilton, who was twenty-six, "with large, wary brown eyes and long, thick, dark hair in a ponytail."[81] She became very dependent on him; and gradually, he gained power over her property; Hamilton had power of attorney, and was the beneficiary of various provisions in O'Keefe's wills and codicils—made when she was in her nineties and had failing eyesight. After she died, lawsuits attacked the validity of two codicils; the case was settled out of court.[82] And Sir Rudolph Bing, former General Manager of the Metropolitan Opera of New York, at eighty-five, and suffering from Alzheimer's disease, married a woman named Carroll Douglass, forty-seven, who was herself a "sick, disturbed woman," and who at one time had had a "romantic and unreasonable fixation" on the Pope. A conservator for Bing's estate sought, successfully, to have the marriage annulled. By that time, most of Bing's fortune had been dissipated.[83]

These three instances were newsworthy, because the victims were newsworthy people. It is impossible to tell how many instances of oppression or neglect occur beneath the radar. Dementia and physical frailty can create a nerve-wracking, painful situation for the family of old people—and an expensive one, to boot. The money needed to do the right thing by grandma is the same money that the family would inherit at death. A dollar spent on caregivers, nursing homes, and medical care is a dollar that will not pass to the heirs. As the population ages, the problem of the old, frail, demented—and wealthy—can only grow worse. The law, as we have seen in this chapter, has worked out over the centuries elaborate plans for disposing of property at death (or before death). More recently, it has worked out elaborate plans for safeguarding the rights and the assets of old but vulnerable people. The best shield and safeguard for the elderly, of course, is a loving, caring, and unselfish family. This is, alas, not something the law can easily provide.

Parents and Children: Rights and Duties

B.F. SKINNER'S NOVEL, *Walden Two* (1948), describes a utopian community that solves the "problems of the family," in part by handing children over to group care. "Home is not the place to raise children," Skinner wrote.[1] In Plato's *Republic*, children would be removed at birth, to be raised by the state. Wives and children were to be "common," and no parent was "to know his own child, nor any child his parent."[2] In the Israeli *kibbutz*, children were raised communally; parents had visiting rights, but the children lived and were cared for separately. (The practice was later abandoned.) In some ancient cultures, however, the role of parents went to the other extreme. Under Roman and Babylonian law and custom, fathers, in varying degrees, had legal authority to buy, sell, trade, and even kill their children, more or less at will.

American law follows a different path. Parents share at least some control with the state and a tiny bit with children themselves. It is no surprise, in the light of our journey through family law, that the law has empowered children—at least to a degree—and has defined not only *their* rights, but also what society and their parents owe them. This is a tricky area, of course, because children are, after all, children; they mature slowly into adulthood; and for much of the time they are just plain unable to care for themselves or enforce any "rights" they may have. Deference to parents is vast. They make crucial decisions about childrearing, including education, religion, health care, and discipline; they are in total control of day-to-day activities. Children almost never win when they challenge parental authority in court, hence the intrusion of the state, at least in a limited role. The state has a *parens patriae* power, which authorizes it to protect and promote the welfare of children. The state can override parental decision-making, but only when the parents are seriously violating their duties toward their children, when the health or well-being of a child is at risk.[3] And in most cases of doubt, the judgment of the parents will prevail. The state can remove children from the home only on strong evidence of harm or potential harm. This, at least, is the theory. There is perhaps a cost to this hands-off approach: the state does very little to support families that do *not* fall below the minimum standards.[4]

In this chapter, we look at the rights and obligations of those who have earned (or been saddled with) the legal status of "parent"; we look at state intervention in troubled families, and challenges to parental authority by third parties (grandparents seeking visitation rights, for example). We also look at children's procedural and expressive rights against the state, and the rights against their parents related to financial independence, sex, marriage, and reproduction.

Constitutional Protection for Parental Rights

Only in the twentieth century did the Supreme Court establish a constitutional basis for parental rights. In *Meyer v. Nebraska* (1923), Nebraska law banned instruction in any foreign language before ninth grade. A school teacher was convicted for teaching German to a child.[5] The state, said the Court, had a right to try to "foster a homogeneous people with American ideals," but this was not strong enough to override the parents' rights. Learning a foreign language was in no way harmful to children.[6] The right to "liberty" mentioned in the Fourteenth Amendment included a sphere of personal and family life that the state was not to invade without a compelling reason. Two years later, the Court followed this up in *Pierce v. Society of Sisters* (1925); here, the Court struck down an Oregon law making attendance at public school compulsory for children between the ages of eight and sixteen.[7] States were free to regulate schools, and the curriculum.[8] But it could not force children to be educated only in government-run schools. The child was "not the mere creature of the State"; this law encroached on the parents' rights to make basic educational decisions.[9] In *Prince v. Massachusetts* (1944), a child's guardian (her aunt) was convicted for allowing her niece to sell religious pamphlets on the street—a violation of state labor law.[10] The Court upheld the conviction; it admitted that the children had rights, but in this case the rights were not strong enough to override the state's interest in regulating child labor.

PARENTS VERSUS THE STATE: POINTS OF CONFLICT

This trilogy of cases supports strong, but not unlimited, parental rights. Parents have a constitutional right to make basic decisions for their (minor) children. This is not only legal dogma; it rests on a strong social norm. Parents are strongly presumed to act in the best interests of their children—and very often they do. But the rights have limits—legally and socially. To be sure, most families, especially white, middle-class families, will "simply never experience any form of intervention from the state."[11] But there are flashpoints of conflict between parental rights and the state's interest in child welfare: in education, religion, medical care, and issues of abuse and neglect.

Education and Religion

Compulsory education laws—something we take for granted today—constitute, perhaps, the most dramatic instance of state control over parenting.[12] Massachusetts was the first state to mandate school attendance (in 1852), and by 1918 all states had followed suit.[13] Most parents, of course, are glad to have free public education. They do not think of it as state interference at all. Challenges to aspects of these education laws have been rare. In one landmark case, *Wisconsin v. Yoder* (1972), the Supreme Court granted the Amish an exemption from compulsory education laws beyond the eighth grade.[14] It was convinced that forcing secondary schooling would threaten the religious way of life the Amish parents had chosen for themselves and their children. The religious rights of the Amish thus outweighed the state's interest in insisting on compulsory education. *Yoder* represents the outer edge of parental freedom, but still the protected sphere is fairly broad. Parents also have a constitutional right to choose a private school (often a religious school), so long as the state's regulations and minimum requirements are met.[15] Home schooling is another permissible alternative, and increasingly popular. As many as 4 percent of children nationwide are home schooled, and the number is growing quite dramatically.[16] An appellate court in California stirred things up, in 2008, by holding that home schooling is valid only if a credentialed teacher conducts it, but the ruling was reversed upon rehearing.[17] Parents in that state have a strong but not absolute right to home school their children.

Medical care is another potential point of conflict between parents and the state. In *Jacobson v. Massachusetts* (1905), the Supreme Court held that states can insist on vaccinations, in the interest of public health and safety.[18] In 1922, the Court upheld a Texas law conditioning school enrollment for children on proof of immunizations. The interests of public health overrode the rights of children (or, more likely, their parents).[19] Although there have been periodic bursts of anti-vaccine activism (one current controversy concerns a vaccine to guard against a sexually transmitted virus that can lead to cervical cancer),[20] state power to mandate vaccinations has been pretty universally held to trump parents' rights. Today, every state mandates certain vaccinations for schoolchildren. But there are always exemptions for those who object on religious grounds; less commonly, for "philosophical" objections.[21]

Parents have a general obligation to get medical care for their children; but have broad discretion to make specific medical decisions for them. Except in an emergency, medical providers cannot act without informed consent, and minors, generally speaking, lack the ability to consent for themselves. As with other parental rights, however, state and federal law holds parents to certain minimum standards. Medical neglect is clearly a form of child abuse. If neglect is suspected or proven, states can intervene to protect children either by overriding a parent's refusal of consent or by imposing criminal liability if the neglect causes harm.

The question is how to define "neglect." In one high-profile case, Joey Hofbauer was suffering from Hodgkin's disease, a cancer of the lymph nodes, lethal if untreated. His parents passed up conventional treatment—radiation and chemotherapy—and chose, in 1977, to bring Joseph to Jamaica to be treated with Laetrile, a natural compound found in apricot pits, highly touted at the time. Did this constitute legal neglect? The courts said no. New York's highest court accorded "great deference" to the parents' choice of treatment, as long as they provided a treatment "recommended by their physician and which has not been totally rejected by all responsible medical authority."[22] Laetrile, alas, was proven useless as a treatment for cancer. It had "no therapeutic benefit" for cancer patients. Although thousands of people used laetrile, the vast majority of them died.[23] It did not work for Joey, either; he died at age ten.[24] After the boy's death, his father described his son as "a pioneer whose purpose was to establish the right of parents to make these decisions for their children" and to keep the governor and "his faceless bureaucrats out of the family."[25]

The toughest cases in this area involve parents who refuse medical treatment for religious reasons.[26] There is no federal rule that a parent or guardian has to provide medical treatment, if this would violate religious beliefs. States are free to decide where to draw the line between neglect and religious dogma.[27] State courts tend to give parents latitude to refuse only if the condition is not life-threatening or the treatment is cosmetic in nature. But the cases are not entirely consistent.[28] The worse the outcome for the child, the more likely the state is to challenge parental authority. In one recent case, for example, Dale and Leilani Neumann had a diabetic daughter, Madeleine. They treated this solely with prayer. Madeline died at age eleven from complications of the untreated disease. Her parents were both convicted of second-degree reckless homicide. They were sentenced to serve thirty days a year in jail for six consecutive years, and as a condition of their probation, they had to promise to take their other children to doctors and hospitals when necessary. Reportedly, there have been "at least 50 convictions in the United States since 1982 in cases where medical treatment was withheld from a child for religious reasons."[29] Many of these cases involve Christian Scientists—a religion that tends to reject the healing power of modern medicine.

Child Abuse

The most common reason for the state to intrude on family privacy and parental authority is in cases of child abuse and neglect. This is not uncommon. In 2008, child protective agencies received 3.3 million referrals, involving 6 million children. Two million of the referrals were sufficient to justify an investigation or assessment. After investigation, nearly 800,000 children were found to be victims of abuse or neglect; of these, 1,740 had died from the effects of maltreatment.[30] State agencies can remove children from a household in which they are abused or neglected. But it is not always easy to tell exactly what constitutes abuse and neglect. There are disturbing signs of a double standard: poor children are more likely to be wrenched from their homes than rich children. Has a judge the right to remove an eleven-year-old girl from her family—poor Mexican migrant workers—and give her to a middle-class family, a family with a house and a swimming pool, if, in the judge's opinion, she would be better off? A Tennessee judge so ordered. The hope is that this was an aberration; but one cannot be sure.[31] The record with regard to Native American children has been particularly poor, and at times even scandalous. Removal to boarding schools (or outright adoption into white families) was part of a process of forced assimilation. Needless to say, the situation today is completely different. The Indian Child Welfare Act of 1978[32] gave power over the process back to the tribes themselves. For removal cases in general, the Supreme Court has insisted on strict procedural standards, strong evidentiary rules, and adherence to due process.[33] Still, the process is almost necessarily larded with high levels of discretion, and how it operates on the ground is hard to know.

The state's role in preventing or responding to child abuse and neglect has dramatically increased over the course of the twentieth century. Not that society—or the neighbors—ever approved of child abuse; but there was little in the way of a formal legal structure to address it. "Little Mary Ellen," an orphan who suffered terrible abuse at the hands of her adoptive mother, helped inspire a national movement to address cruelty against children. In 1874, Henry Bergh, the founder of the American Society for Prevention of Cruelty to Animals, asked a New York court to remove her from her adoptive home, even though New York law at the time made no clear provision for such an action. (Contrary to popular myth, her case was not litigated under animal cruelty laws on the grounds that she was "a member of the animal kingdom.")[34] Mary Ellen gave heart-wrenching testimony: she had on her head "two black-and-blue marks which were made by Mamma with the whip"; her "Mamma" cut her on the forehead with a scissors as well. But Mary Ellen "never dared speak to anybody, because if I did I would get whipped."[35] The court removed her from "Mamma" and placed her with the state department of charities. "Mamma" was prosecuted for criminal assault, and sentenced to a year in prison at hard labor.[36] (Mary Ellen, it seems, went on to have a remarkably happy life, marrying, having two children, adopting an orphan, and living to age ninety-two.)

After the case was over, Bergh and Elbridge Gerry capitalized on the media coverage of Mary Ellen's case to found the New York Society for the Prevention of Cruelty to Children, the first such organization in the country.[37] Its approach was "remarkably successful" and "spread like wildfire across the United States." The child cruelty movement could be criticized as a tool to impose Christian, middle-class values on the poor. But it did represent the first sustained effort to rein in parental rights. By the turn of the twentieth century, the right to challenge parental authority in maltreatment cases had become well-established. Over the course of the century, the child welfare framework became increasingly standardized and bureaucratized.

The federal government entered the picture in the early twentieth century. A White House Conference on children was convened in 1909; the United States Children's Bureau was established in 1912.[38] The Social Security Act of 1935 provided small grants to states to set up child welfare agencies.[39] The 1960s were another turning point. Child abuse gained traction as a serious and mounting social problem, as did the plight of children lingering in foster care. In 1974, Congress stepped up its intervention with the Child Abuse Prevention and Treatment Act (CAPTA).[40] To qualify for federal money, states were required to set up procedures for reporting and investigating child abuse. Today, in every state, certain groups of people—doctors, teachers, police officers, child care providers, and the like—are designated "mandatory reporters." In other words, they have a legal duty to act on suspicions of child abuse or maltreatment.[41] CAPTA also established the National Center for Child Abuse and Neglect, which collects data, performs research, and supports state efforts to eradicate child abuse.

The modern system for dealing with child abuse and neglect has two branches. The civil system protects children through temporary or permanent removal from their homes; the criminal system imposes punishment for the most serious forms of child abuse and neglect. Progressively broader federal laws have turned the child welfare system into a kind of federal-state "hybrid."[42] The federal government now funds a substantial portion of the child welfare services provided by the states; it also dictates many aspects of the way those services are to be delivered and the outcomes they are supposed to produce.

Because of various federal mandates, state abuse and neglect laws are all quite similar.[43] All fifty state statutes define abuse to include physical or sexual abuse. Many also explicitly include emotional abuse; some include abandonment, or substance abuse by parents. They define the point at which the state's interest is sufficient to justify overriding parental authority and establish procedures for intervening. Most states, prodded by federal law, provide for a so-called guardian *ad litem* or the like—a representative to look after the interests of children in abuse and neglect cases. Whether these provisions are effective is another question. The practice, if not the law, is chaotic, and varies wildly from state to state and even from county to county.[44]

"Neglect" is a parent's failure to provide for the child's basic needs, including food, clothing, shelter, education, and medical care (as we noted), despite the parent's ability to meet these needs. A parent's conduct (or omission) constitutes abuse or neglect if it causes actual or imminent physical, mental, or emotional harm. Neglect, by its nature, is more difficult to pinpoint than abuse. Without telltale signs of physical or sexual injury, it is hard to tell whether a parent has fallen below some minimum standard. The vague definitions in the law leave room for agency interpretations which can be troubling at times. For example, until 2004, New York City's Administration for Children's Service (ACS) apparently had a policy that children would be taken away from a victim of domestic violence, if she had allowed their children to witness the violence. A lawsuit challenged the policy, which a federal district court called a "pitiless double abuse."[45] The New York Court of Appeals agreed, in *Nicholson v. Scoppetta* (2004), that simply witnessing abuse does not justify automatic removal.[46] "Neglect" was a complicated issue; and it had to be dealt with on a case-by-case basis.

Parents have a wide zone of discretion in deciding how to punish children. As the old maxim has it, spare the rod and spoil the child. This is no longer fashionable; still, parents can legally use reasonable amounts of physical force to discipline their children; it is not usually "abuse" unless it results in serious injury. A mother who forced her child to suck her toes as punishment was within her rights,[47] but parents who scald, break bones, and seriously bruise children can face removal or criminal charges.[48]

Child abuse is, alas, not rare. Whether it is more common than, say, a century ago, or simply more often reported, is impossible to say. The fact that every level of government has some sort of program, agency, or plan for dealing with child abuse makes the issue more salient than before (like domestic violence in general, and elder abuse). Salient—but delicate. Taking children away from their homes has to be, legally, the last resort. Within living memory, programs of child protection were stained by racism, insensitivity, and prejudice against the poor. Perhaps this is still the case.

What happens to children *after* removal? Each state has its programs. In 1980, Congress passed the Adoption Assistance and Child Welfare Act, responding to concerns that too many children were in foster care, and that they were staying there too long. The Act gave the federal government a significant role in developing and overseeing child welfare services. The goal was "family preservation and reunification." But reunification of children with their biological parents is not always possible— or desirable. Later acts, like the Adoption and Safe Families Act (ASFA) of 1997, promoted quicker decisions on questions of termination of parental rights. The goal was to make children adoptable before they languished too long in foster care.[49] These changes did reduce the number of children entering foster care, and increased the number who exited (to be reunified with families or adopted), but an enormous number of children are still part of the system. In 2008, almost half a million children lived in foster care.[50]

The state is not always quick enough to act or forceful enough in its response to allegations of abuse. Sometimes scandal erupts when a child is beaten, burned, or stomped to death, and the state could have intervened, but failed to. The death of little Lisa Steinberg, in 1987, at the hands of her foster parents, created a firestorm of outrage and a wave of public breast-beating. There had been complaints and investigations; the city had checked and checked; and still little Lisa died.[51]

Joshua DeShaney was born in 1979. His parents divorced a year later. His father gained custody, and moved to Winnebago County, Wisconsin. In 1982, the father's second wife complained that the father was abusing Joshua. There were investigations by the county, and counseling for the father; but the child stayed in the home. Finally, the father beat the child so severely that he went into a coma. Joshua stayed alive; but with permanent brain damage. Joshua's mother sued the county, for "failing to intervene to protect [Joshua]" against a known "risk of violence." This, she claimed violated his constitutional rights. The Supreme Court was sympathetic; but it denied the claim in 1989. The facts of the case, said Chief Justice Rehnquist, were "tragic." But the Due Process Clause (the basis of the lawsuit) was basically a "limitation on the State's power to act." It did not require the state to protect its citizens against "invasion by private actors."[52]

No doubt the county—and child protective agencies—breathed a sigh of relief. Yet no matter how the case had come out, the problem was bound to remain. Timidity, bureaucratic red tape—and a genuine preference for leaving children at home—combine to make this issue peculiarly intractable, at least with current tools. The scandals continue. The home of John Hardy Jackson, a man with a long history of violence and child molestation, was licensed as a foster home, in Mountain View, California. The local authorities had "outsourced" oversight of foster care to a private agency, paid by the county. Jackson had a history of drunkenness, drug use, and child abuse. And he proceeded, systematically, to molest the children placed in his care. He had sex with the children, and made them have sex with each other. Finally, he was arrested, convicted, and sent to prison in 2010; and he lost a massive civil suit as well. But no doubt the damage to the children had been done.[53] Children living in dysfunctional or abusive families are a tragedy for themselves, and for society. There is never an easy solution. There is no real substitute for careful love.

"Baby Moses" Laws

The birth of a child is not always taken as a blessing. Killing the newborn is an old and well-known pathology. But a cluster of cases at the end of the twentieth century fueled talk of an "epidemic," set off a full-fledged moral panic, and evoked a strong legislative response. The public was shocked when Melissa Drexler gave birth in a bathroom stall at her high school prom, and deposited a bag with the baby and a stack of bloody towels in the bathroom trash can. Melissa fixed her hair and makeup before returning to the dance floor and requesting that the DJ play, perhaps fittingly, "The Unforgiven" by Metallica.[54] A maid discovered the baby. Drexler pleaded guilty to aggravated manslaughter and was sentenced to fifteen years in prison; she was released after serving three.[55]

Melissa was not alone. High school sweethearts Amy Grossberg and Brian Peterson were convicted of manslaughter after leaving their son in a dumpster behind the dilapidated hotel where he was born in 1996.[56] Karlie DiTrapani gave birth in the bathroom of her parents' Brooklyn home, and then left him to asphyxiate in a plastic bag in her dresser drawer. Her secret was discovered, as Amy Grossberg's was, when she needed medical attention for bleeding and doctors discovered evidence of a recent birth.[57]

These cases all resulted in criminal penalties, but also a "swift, widespread, and confident response at the legislative level."[58] Texas passed the first infant safe haven law in 1999, after a year in which thirteen babies were abandoned in public places, four of whom were found dead.[59] Within just a few years, every other state followed Texas's lead.[60] These "Baby Moses" laws focused on giving "mothers in crisis" an alternative: they could leave an infant in a safe place to be cared for. Ultimately, the baby could be placed with an adoptive family.[61] If the newborn baby were left in a designated "safe haven," such as a hospital, church, or police station, the parents would gain immunity from prosecution for child abandonment or neglect. These laws conjure up the image of old foundling hospitals, where mothers could push unwanted babies through a revolving window, ensuring their care and safety (and the mother's anonymity).

The guarantees of anonymity and immunity, as Carol Sanger observes, "make the whole scheme work." The slogan for New Jersey's safe haven program: "No Shame. No Blame. No Names."[62] Most safe haven laws apply only to newborn infants.[63] Nebraska's safe haven law, passed in 2007, originally contained no age limit—a serious omission. One father, whose wife had recently died, left nine children, ranging in ages from one to seventeen, at a local hospital.[64] Lawmakers quickly amended the law to limit it to newborns.[65]

How many newborn babies are killed, or abandoned? Neither state nor federal governments formally collect such data. An informal survey of major newspapers conducted by the U.S. Department of Health and Human Services in 1998 found 105 reports of babies abandoned in public places; thirty-three of them were found dead. Whatever the number, it is "miniscule in comparison" to the more than four million births that take place.[66]

Safe haven laws run counter to other trends in family law. They do not require, for example, that the mother provide any medical information on the baby or other family members. They also deprive biological fathers of an opportunity to protect their rights, since the mother and baby are entitled to complete anonymity. And though adoption is the ultimate goal, the laws are usually silent about procedures for adoption of an abandoned infant; the usual requirements regarding consent, notification, and revocation cannot practically be met.[67] Safe haven laws also permit parents to avoid financial obligations for children through anonymous surrender, contrary to the law's generally unforgiving approach to such obligations.[68]

These laws grew out of a moral panic;[69] however, they seem rather ineffective.[70] Relatively few babies are abandoned at safe havens. In Houston, for example, nine babies were abandoned in public places in the first four months after the safe haven law took effect. Not one was abandoned in accordance with the statute.[71] Many states claim that they have never had a "safe haven" drop-off. In New York City in 2006, six dead, abandoned babies were found despite the passage in 2000 of a safe haven law.[72] Still, in the eight years after the law was passed, 118 babies *were* abandoned at safe havens across the state of New York.[73] Some critics of safe haven laws complain that they condone irresponsible behavior; others find the laws "ineffective," and rife with "unintended consequences."[74] Safe haven laws illustrate, once more, that legal incentives sometimes work badly in family affairs. Do we really need these laws? The United States is a wealthy country, contraceptives are pretty generally available, and abortion is legal. Also, single motherhood is not so stigmatic as before; and "the institutions of adoption and foster care are well established."[75] Safe haven laws are another example of the impact of the media, of publicity, of scandals and incidents, on the making of law. In the United States, it was probably always the case that few unwed mothers killed their newborns and disposed of the tiny bodies in local rivers, streams, and garbage cans. Today, for the reasons mentioned, it is probably even less of a problem.

Poor Mothers, Poor Children

The American welfare system is a vast, dark, dreary, and difficult expanse of statutes, rules, regulations, and practices. Here we mention only one or two aspects of this system. Jill Hasday, who has treated this matter in detail, refers to the "bifurcated law of parental relations"; that is, one law for the rich and the middle class, quite another for the poor.[76]

In the early twentieth century, many children of poor families worked and slaved in factories and stores. The northern states—with heavy support from labor unions—passed laws against child labor (and to make kids go to school). But many factories fled to the southern states, which lacked child labor laws. This led to a demand for federal legislation. Congress obliged with a law banning the products of child labor from interstate commerce. But the Supreme Court struck this down, in 1918, in *Hammer v. Dagenhart*.[77] Attempts were made to amend the Constitution to permit child labor laws. Employer groups fought back; the amendment, they claimed, would take away the rights of parents, and "pauperize minors"; it would result in the "destruction of the boys and girls of the country." They blamed the idea on "Socialists, Communists and Bolshevists."[78] The campaign against child labor had to wait until the New Deal of the 1930s for its ultimate success.

From around 1911, some states began to enact mothers' pension laws, to help poor women who had children. Congress enacted the Sheppard-Towner Act, for the "promotion of the welfare and hygiene of maternity and infancy," in 1921; but it died in 1929. Here too the New Deal was a watershed; it created permanent programs of Aid to Dependent Children, later renamed Aid to Families with Dependent Children; superseded, in the 1990s, by TANF (Temporary Assistance for Needy Families). The underlying policy vacillated. At first, the idea was, these women need money so that they can stay home and raise the kids. The latest policy, under TANF, is the reverse: by God, they ought to work for a living.

All these federal programs handed much of their authority to the states. These programs, too, were not shy about intruding into the lives of poor families. Men were supposed to support their women. Women who had no husband were deeply suspect—unless they were widows, who could not be blamed for lacking a man. Some state laws were quite specific on this point: only women whose husbands were dead or who had deserted them were eligible. Divorced women were disfavored; and mothers of "bastards" were often completely shut out. The statutes said nothing about race; but the southern states, for the most part, made sure that none of the money, or very little, would go to black families.

Many states cut off aid if they found out, or suspected, that there was a man in the house, whether or not he was the father of the children. Women who received federal money were supposed to live clean, moral lives; or forfeit their rights. The Florida ADC law of 1959, for example, explicitly demanded "a stable moral environment" for children; a woman was ineligible if she engaged in "promiscuous conduct either in or outside the home."[79] Welfare workers often made surprise visits to the homes of ADC women; and woe unto any such woman, if investigators sniffed out evidence that a man had been hanging around (or if they saw, as in one case, a barefoot man running out the back door). None of this snooping ever applied to pensions under the more middle-class Social Security Act. Some states, in the 1970s, became less intrusive; and the demands for high morality lessened in the age of the sexual revolution. But, in general, the "bifurcated system" has never completely vanished.

Parents versus Third Parties: Grandparent Visitation

Parents have rights over their children; and the state has a residual role. Are there others who have claims? Sometimes—particularly after bitter divorces or the death of one parent—grandparents

275

feel themselves cut off from their grandchildren. The extended family may be decaying; but grandparents still play a huge role in the lives of millions of children.

All fifty states today have statutes granting grandparents, and sometimes other third parties, the right to petition for visitation rights—even when parents object. These statutes pit parental rights against the grief of grandparents who lose contact with their grandchildren. These statutes vary in substance and procedure, but they all give a court power to override a parent's decision to cut off contacts with relatives. Many of the laws require divorce or the death of a parent to trigger visitation rights for third parties; children of fractured families, it was feared, were losing touch with extended families, particularly the parents of the non-custodial parent.[80]

Tommie and Brad Troxel never married, but they lived together and had two daughters together. (Tommie had eight children in all.)[81] After the couple broke up in 1991, Brad moved in with his parents and often brought the girls to their house for his visitation weekends. When Brad committed suicide in 1993, his parents wanted to maintain the same type of schedule; but their mother agreed to no more than one visit per month. The Washington State statute permitted "any person" to petition for visitation rights, and authorized courts to grant these requests if this was shown to be in the "best interests of the child."[82] The trial court granted substantial visitation rights to the grandparents— more or less what a divorced dad might expect.

Tommie appealed; and in *Troxel v. Granville* (2000),[83] a somewhat surprising decision, the United States Supreme Court held that Washington's visitation statute was unconstitutional, at least as applied to Tommie. Under the Fourteenth Amendment— the Due Process Clause—the parents' right to "liberty" included rights over the care, control, and education of their children. *Troxel* expanded this right. The Washington statute, according to a plurality of the Court, was "breathtakingly broad." A third-party visitation statute must, at a minimum, give "special weight" to a parent's decision not to allow visitation. The Washington statute relied on that old standard, the "best interests of the child." This appeared to give equal weight to the preferences of the parent and third parties. But a fit parent must be *presumed* to act in the best interests of the child; and that includes the decision to block visits by grandparents. Before a court can order visitation rights, there must be at least some evidence to overcome this presumption.

After *Troxel*, courts in many states struggled with challenges to their own statutes—did they give enough deference to parental rights? Statutes in California and Minnesota expressly built in a presumption in favor of parental decisions. New York's visitation statute permits grandparents to petition for visitation if either parent is deceased or if "equity would see fit to intervene."[84] Lower courts have read this requirement as sufficiently protective of a parent's right to refuse visitation.[85]

Little Brittany Collier lived with her mother and her maternal grandparents, Gary and Carol Harrold, from birth to age two. Her father (who had never been married to her mother) had supervised visitation rights twice a week. Then Brittany's mother died of cancer. Her father petitioned for and won custody of Brittany. He took her from the grandparents' home and refused any further contact. They filed a request for visitation. Ohio law put the burden of proof on the party seeking visitation, and listed factors to be considered, including the wishes of a child's parent.[86] This emphasis on the parent's rights was enough to allow the court to avoid *Troxel*. The Harrolds, who had a longstanding and close relationship with Brittany, won the right to visitation.[87]

Cases like these continue to wind their way through state court systems with mixed results. The statutes, and *Troxel* itself, are, of course, signs of the times. There is no organized "grandparents'" lobby; but it is easy to form interest groups out of dispersed individuals with a common problem or interest. And the civil rights movements—starting with African Americans, then women, Native Americans, the elderly, the handicapped, prisoners, and all other conceivable clusters—make the idea of grandparents' rights more tenable. As do the increasing use of courts, constitutions, and judicial review to sort out rights and conflicting interests; the growing tendency of law to treat *individuals* as rights-holders, rather than families; and the increase in the number of what used to be called "broken homes." All this set the stage for a battle, in which *Troxel* was a kind of climax, but not a definitive resolution.

DE FACTO PARENTAGE: A NEW FRONTIER

Miffed grandparents are not the only ones who challenge parents' rights. Former stepparents, and, increasingly, gay or lesbian co-parents have also mounted challenges, insisting on the right to visit children that they have *functionally* parented, despite lacking a legal parent-child relationship. In the last forty years, more and more children have had relationships with adults other than their legal parents.[88] Whether the *law* can make room for these other adults, as the families themselves have, is still an open question.

The concept of "de facto" parentage recognizes that sometimes adults who are not legal parents nonetheless perform parent-like functions. Several states allow courts to recognize—typically in limited circumstances—the parental rights of a "de facto" parent. In a Washington State case (2005), Sue Ellen Carvin and her lesbian partner had agreed to become parents together. Sue Ellen was neither the biological nor the adoptive parent. But when the couple broke up, the Washington Supreme Court recognized Sue Ellen as a de facto parent.[89] The highest courts in several states ruled likewise in similar cases.[90] A few courts rejected the doctrine.[91] New York, in *Debra H. v. Janice R* (2010),[92] was one of these courts. Earlier, the court had ruled that only biological or adoptive parents could seek visitation (against the wishes of a custodial parent).[93] They were asked in this new case to revisit the question. Here two women had co-parented a boy from birth on. They separated; and the biological mother cut off all contact between her son and her ex-partner, Debra. But the court refused to adopt the doctrine of de facto parentage, in order to promote "certainty in the wake of domestic breakups" and avoid "disruptive battles over parentage," and over custody and visitation.[94] Nonetheless, there does seem to be a trend to recognize, in principle, that a non-parent adult may develop functional ties with a child that should not be lightly extinguished.

Former stepparents have also tried at times to use this doctrine. Generally, when a relationship is created by marriage, it ends when the marriage ends. So, without special protection, a stepparent becomes a legal stranger to her stepchildren when she divorces their legal parent. Some states provide for former-stepparent visitation by statute. In California, for example, a court may grant "reasonable visitation" to a stepparent, as part of proceedings to end the marriage that created the stepparent-stepchild relationship.[95] But visitation may not be ordered if it would "conflict with a right of custody or visitation of a birth parent who is not a party to the proceeding." This provision also must be applied consistently with *Troxel*, the case that carved out a very protective sphere for parents as against nonparents. But in states with limited or no visitation, former stepparents have sometimes claimed de facto parent status as a way to keep a legal link to their stepchildren. These claims, like those brought by lesbian co-parents, have met with mixed results. In a 2010 case, *Corbin v. Reimen*, the Washington Supreme Court ruled against an ex-stepfather, John Corbin, who was trying to maintain strong ties with his former stepdaughter.[96] Although he had fully participated in her upbringing, even after divorcing her mother; a former stepparent, the court felt, can never qualify as a de facto parent.[97]

The cases on de facto parentage illustrate how complex the modern family can be—and modern family law as well. Courts and legislatures have to grapple with the legal definition of "parent," along with the question, whether there can be more than two parents. In real life, multiple mothers and fathers do play roles in conception, childbirth, and childrearing. The rights and duties of children that come out of these tangled affairs will be complicated, puzzling, and challenging for the courts. In chapter 13, we explore the vexed questions of parentage posed by new family types and new technology.

CHILDREN'S RIGHTS

At one time, a book about family law would have had little or nothing to say about "children's rights." Children, in a sense, had no rights. It would be too crude to say that they were the property of their parents; but minors, in general, could not enter into contracts, make wills, or get married without parental permission (much of this is still true); and the parents had the absolute right to decide what children ate, what they wore, what games they played, what religion they followed, and the like. Which is also still true—up to a point.

In short, *parental* rights were dominant. This was socially as well as legally the case; and extended even to adult children. In countless Victorian novels (and *Fiddler on the Roof*), the plot turns (at least in part) on the desire of an adult son or daughter to marry, against the wishes of a parent. Mostly, the child had to give up the idea, no matter how painful; the only options were to talk the parents into the marriage; or rebel and risk total estrangement (and disinheritance).

This seems so yesterday. The opinion of parents, of course, is still important; but it no longer has a kind of sacred quality. "Children's rights" is a sub-field of family law. Under the United Nations Convention on the Rights of the Child, almost universally adopted, countries are required (Article 12) to "assure to the child who is capable of forming his or her own views the right to express those views freely in all matters affecting the child"; and those views are to be given "due weight in accordance with the age and maturity of the child." The child should also have "the opportunity to be heard ... in any proceedings affecting the child," either personally or through a representative.[98]

The United States shares with Somalia a dubious distinction: these are the only countries that failed to ratify this Convention—even though children surely have more rights in the United States than in many countries which eagerly (if hypocritically) signed on. Why should this be so? Martha Fineman thinks that conservatives (who are often a bit xenophobic) see in the Convention a threat to parental authority. If children have "an age-appropriate and gradually increasing right to self-determination," and the "ability to meaningfully participate in decisions that affect them," this might endanger the "very existence of the traditional family."[99] Of course, the "very existence of the traditional family" has problems that go far beyond the reach of some UN text.

Even without the treaty, there has been a great deal of action—some of it judicial—that has made "children's rights" a legal reality in the United States.[100] After all, empowerment was a watchword of the late twentieth century—for minorities, for underdogs in general. And the general trend, dissolving families into collections of individuals, affected children as well as adults. Moreover, the nature of childhood socialization changed as well.

Take, for example, the influence of school. Children learned to read and write in school, to add and subtract. They did finger-painting and sang songs. But the schools also indoctrinated. School and schoolyard were thus, in a way, powerful rivals of the family in molding and influencing children: what they did, how they felt, what they thought, what they knew. Occasionally, there were outbursts of dissent—over the teaching or non-teaching of religion; over disciplinary matters; over evolution; over alleg-edly dirty books; but for the most part, parents accepted the role of the schools. School introduced the child to the world of the peer group, as well as the world of the ABC's. In the twentieth century, radio and television also invaded the home; these intro-duced messages, ideas, images, and influences from outside, all of this as early as the first months of life. Then came the Internet, Facebook, Twitter, and the like. Parental authority, by the end of the twentieth century, had lost huge chunks of its monopoly over family life; and the shape, power, and influence of the traditional family had suffered serious damage.

But if children have "rights," what are they? Not the right to vote, for example; or the same rights of contract and labor as adults; or even the right to execute a will. Does a minor have a right to an abortion, without the consent or input of her par-ents? When and how can children be emancipated? For what crimes are children to be tried as adults? All these questions have been the subject of dispute and litigation. And which children have rights? Children's rights, logically, refers to the rights of minors—boys and girls under eighteen. Of course, a boy or girl of seventeen can raise issues, can need, enjoy, and act on rights, in a way that a newborn baby cannot. If a baby or a toddler has "rights," somebody else will have to enforce them. That can be, and often is, the state itself.

Minors and Intimacy

As we discussed in chapter 1, minors cannot marry without parental consent (and below age sixteen, as a general matter, they cannot marry at all). These laws have been upheld in the courts.[101] Some states add special requirements like premarital counseling.[102] And only one state, Illinois, explicitly provides that a minor can seek judicial approval instead of parental consent for underage marriage.[103] But in some states, parents and judges had to consent to underage marriages, especially for minors who are fifteen or younger. In a 1953 Pennsylvania case, Barbara Haven's father had given consent for her to marry her twenty-two-year-old stepbrother; because she was only fourteen, she needed court approval as well. The court thought this "attractive well-developed girl" was "physically suited for marriage"; and the boy was "a typical, fine American youth" who was "industrious and ambitious."[104] Yet it refused to allow the marriage. The legislature had adopted an age restriction, so that "one in the sunlight of youth ... should not walk precipitously into the marriage chamber." The "young lady's protestation of affection" was not compelling enough to override the legislature judgment that marriages require more maturity than that of a girl of fourteen.

Minors have had greater success in matters of sex and reproduction. In *Planned Parenthood v. Danforth* (1976), the Supreme Court struck down a statute that gave parents the power to veto a minor's decision to seek an abortion, if the female minor was mature enough to give informed consent.[105] But the Court took another look at the abortion rights of minors three years later, in *Bellotti v. Baird* (1979). Here they upheld a statute that required parental consent, but provided for a "judicial bypass"; the minor could go directly to court, "without first consulting or notifying her parents," to show that she was mature enough to decide on her own, or that in any event the procedure is "in her best interests."[106] In fact, most (though not all) petitions are granted.[107] At present, thirty-four states require parental consent or notification before a minor can seek an abortion; but every one provides the option of a judicial bypass.[108] The Supreme Court also held that minors have the right to get and use contraception.[109] Even more broadly, most states permit minors to seek treatment for drug use or sexually transmitted diseases; their access to health care trumps parental rights.[110]

Emancipation

Is there a way to free a minor from the authority of the parents? The common law allowed such a move. A minor who lived independently, and who was self-supporting, could be declared "emancipated" in a court proceeding. Emancipation freed the minor from parental rules and discipline, and also freed the parents from the obligation of support. Functional emancipation could be a defense to an action for child support. A minor who marries or enlists in the military is very likely to be treated as emancipated. In addition, about half the states have created a statutory mechanism that allows an older minor to petition for emancipated status, which, if granted, not only relieves the parents of support obligations, but also grants the minor some adult-like rights—like the right to buy and sell property or file lawsuits.[111] Because emancipated minors have sole ownership of earnings, and control their finances, some child stars and athletes, including actress Drew Barrymore, actor Macauley Caulkin, and Olympic gold-medal gymnast Dominique Moceanu, were successfully emancipated as minors.[112]

In 1992, Gregory Kingsley, a boy of twelve, took the idea of emancipation one step further—he petitioned to "divorce" his parents. He had no money to protect; he simply wanted the judge to end the parental rights of his "natural mother," and allow his foster parents to adopt him. Gregory's birth mother, an unemployed waitress, had given him up to foster care three times—because she was poor, she said; each time this was supposed to be only temporary. Gregory had, however, lived with his mother only seven months out of the eight years preceding the court case. There was conflicting testimony about his mother; and plenty of tears and raw emotion. In the end, the judge granted Gregory's wish, terminated his mother's rights, and gave the Russ family, his foster parents, the right to adopt him (as their ninth child). George Russ, the foster father, a lawyer, represented both Gregory and himself.[113]

Perhaps it was George Russ who thought up this unusual action in the first place. It certainly attracted attention, was featured on Court TV, and even gave rise to a television movie, *Gregory K.*[114] It was, of course, a rare and isolated action; but it would have been unthinkable in earlier times. And it reflects the growing recognition that children have rights even against their parents; that there are choices which children can legitimately make, even when their parents are opposed; and perhaps even at a relatively young age. Gregory, one must remember, was not seventeen, but twelve.

Children versus the State

Very young children cannot be tried for crimes. And since the early twentieth century, children who commit offenses are handled by a special institution, the juvenile court.[115] The first such court was established in Cook County, Illinois in 1899; but the idea soon spread across the country. In theory, this was not a criminal court at all, but something quite different. And, in fact, the juvenile court had jurisdiction over neglected and abandoned children, as well as children who had committed offenses. Children, in short, were special and needed special handling.

In theory, juvenile court was entirely benign and humanitarian. But it did represent the heavy hand of the state. And proceedings in juvenile court were quite informal. Because these were supposed to be places for helping out children, the children did not need lawyers, or the complications of due process. But this became more and more unrealistic. In 1964, in Gila County, Arizona, the authorities took Gerald Gault into custody. A neighbor had accused him of making an obscene phone call. On very flimsy evidence, Gerald—who was fifteen years old—was declared delinquent, and six years in juvenile detention stared him in the face. The Gault family objected, and went all the way to the United States Supreme Court. In *In re Gault* (1967), the justices agreed with the family. To send Gerald to a correctional institution, without procedural safeguards, the right to a lawyer, and the right to a proper hearing, violated his constitutional rights.[116]

Two years later, in *Tinker v. Des Moines Independent Community School District* (1969),[117] the Court went one step further. Tinker was a high school student, who wore a black armband in school to protest against the war in Vietnam. The school had a rule against this behavior, and suspended Tinker. The Supreme Court held that students had free speech rights. Schools had to honor these rights unless the students were disruptive—which Tinker was not. A whole flock of cases in the next years turned on the right of schools to control hairstyles and dress. Could schools stop high school boys from growing beards, moustaches, or long hair? The cases in federal court—there were 118 of them, between 1969 and 1978—split over the issue. Some judges dismissed these actions, as a sheer waste of judicial time; others saw an important principle at stake, and upheld the students' rights. (The Supreme Court never resolved the conflict.) Courts also struck down school rules which discriminated against married students. A local school board rule in Ohio barred any married student from playing sports, attending the prom, and from any extracurricular activities (this was also true for any boy who "contributed to the pregnancy of any girl"). A court struck down the law.[118]

These legal battles over "children's rights" are complicated; the results are confusing. But on the whole they reflect one of the master trends described in this book: more and more, the family ceases to be a unit, and dissolves into a collection of independent *individuals*. This of course is most true for adults—husbands and wives; adult children. But the logic applies to younger children as well. It is reflected, too, in educational policy. At one time, the basic thrust of education was to instill adult values into young people. Children were considered half-formed and miniature adults. The job of the school was to socialize them properly. Of course this is still a major task of education. But, more and more, schools stress the duty to bring out each child's unique talents and propensities; to look to the wishes and desires of each child. The old, regimented schoolhouse is no longer. Fixed desks are history. Children are encouraged to "show and tell," and to aim for their personal best. Family life is still a powerful influence; but it competes with the media, with the peer group, and with the mighty strength of mass culture. It is against this backdrop that the notion of "children's rights" has evolved.

Whom Do We Belong To?
Parentage and the Law

W<small>HO IS A PARENT?</small> Who is a child? For most people, the answers are simple and obvious. And yet, consider these recent events in our brave new world: Stella Biblis is conceived with sperm donated twenty-two years earlier by her father, then a teenager suffering life-threatening leukemia.[1] Or this: a sixty-six-year-old woman dies, two years after giving birth to twins conceived with donated eggs and donated sperm.[2] A 2009 federal government study on non-marital births found that nearly four in ten births are to unmarried women, almost twenty times higher than in 1940, but also 26 percent higher than just five years earlier.[3] A married man who donated sperm to a lesbian friend so that she and her partner could have a baby was ordered to contribute toward the child's college education eighteen years later.[4]

The world's first "test-tube" baby, "conceived in laboratory glassware," was Louise Brown, born in 1978, in Oldham, England.[5] Louise, now a mother (and a postal worker who has to put up with many "puns about 'deliveries,'") is the picture of normality. Since then, *in vitro fertilization* has created over a million babies.[6] Artificial insemination has a longer history; it was used successfully in humans at least since the 1950s, and more often in later decades. Reproductive technology has, of course, made possible the use of sperm donors, egg donors, and gestational surrogates; biological parenthood is now open to infertile couples, single women, and same-sex couples.[7] But these changes challenge the traditional rules of parentage. Family law has been forced to adapt to a world in which babies can be made without sex and with ties to multiple adults, whether married or not.[8]

As we saw in previous chapters, a "legal parent" has rights and obligations. A legal parent must support the child, but also has the right to decide what she eats for breakfast, whether she is taught to believe in God, and whether to permit her to be adopted by strangers. An adult who does not qualify as a legal parent can be shut out entirely. Legal parentage also determines economic rights—rights such as Social Security, inheritance rights, and standing in wrongful death lawsuits. Parentage law can thus make or break a family; and deeply affect the life of a child.

THE PLIGHT OF THE "BASTARD" CHILD

Historically, one central dividing line in the law of parentage was legitimacy. As we saw, under English law a child born to unmarried parents was *filius nullius*—literally, a child of no one.[9] Legally, the child had no family ties; and, as we saw, no inheritance rights. American law was less harsh than English law; if the parents of an illegitimate child later married, their marriage legitimated the child. Illegitimate children could also, as we mentioned, inherit from their mothers. But they had a somewhat lowly status, legally speaking, until at least the 1970s.

The financial obligation of the father, however, has a long pedigree. As early as the seventeenth century, "bastardy" laws imposed a duty of support on the parents of illegitimate children. These laws—in every state by 1900—were part of both civil and criminal codes. The goal was to establish paternity and coerce support, or marriage, from fathers. The point was to prevent these children from becoming a public burden.[10] The child's mother, a third party, or the district attorney could institute bastardy proceedings. In Arkansas, for example, in the 1920s, if the mother of a "bastard child" swore that Mr. X was the father, the judge could issue a warrant for his arrest. The judge could also, on his own, bring the woman in and require her, under oath, to give the name of the father, "or give security to indemnify the county; and if she refuses to do either to commit her to jail."[11] Under this law, the father could be charged with expenses for the birth, up to fifteen dollars, and between one and three dollars per month for child support.[12] In their early twentieth-century form, these laws "gave no rights to the father, only responsibilities."[13]

Illegitimate children at that time were only a small minority. A 1915 study estimated that only 1.8 percent of children were born to unwed parents.[14] In 1940, the number was still low—3 percent.[15] Illegitimate children were socially stigmatized; social services available to other mothers and children were denied to them. Life was hard for these children and their mothers. A study of illegitimate children born in Boston in 1914 found that "more than three-fifths would become wards of welfare agencies in the first year of their lives"; only a small number of "identifiable fathers were taken to court" (13 percent); and "only 7 percent were actually ordered to pay anything at all."[16]

Parentage for Legitimate Children

A child born to married parents was given the benefit of every doubt about legitimacy. A woman's husband was, in many states, conclusively presumed to be the father of all children born during their marriage, even if a shock of red hair or other traits made the milkman a more likely candidate.[17] For most of our history, there was no definitive way to prove or disprove fatherhood. Blood group typing was not used until the early twentieth century, and, even then, it could only *disprove* paternity. A fight over paternity was an ugly court battle for parents and children alike. The law preferred to assume that wives were faithful; and cut off further inquiry.

Even in the face of scientific evidence, courts were reluctant to bastardize children of a married woman. Three years after Robert and Joyce Prochnow married in 1950, he began military service. When he returned home on furloughs, "he found his wife notably lacking in appreciation of his presence." At least one witness testified that Joyce was extremely friendly with Andy, a more "fun" man. On March 12, 1954, Joyce flew to San Antonio to meet her husband; they spent one night together in a hotel and had sexual relations. The next day, she told him she was planning to file for divorce. She served him with papers a few weeks later. Joyce gave birth to a child a little over eight months after the hotel rendezvous; she amended her divorce complaint to ask for child support. Robert's experts testified that blood-grouping tests proved he was not the father of the child. Joyce testified, however, that she had not had sex with other men, and that Robert was the father of this ostensibly premature child.

Under Wisconsin law, blood-typing evidence was admissible, but not conclusive. The trial judge found, despite the evidence, that Robert was the father. The Wisconsin Supreme Court was suspicious. "Cynics," they said, "among whom on this occasion we must reluctantly number ourselves," might imagine that Joyce, finding herself pregnant, "made a hasty excursion to her husband's bed and an equally abrupt withdrawal when her mission was accomplished." But despite these suspicions, a majority of the "cynics" upheld the trial court's ruling.[18]

The case would come out differently today. DNA testing, the gold standard, can establish paternity (or rule it out) with near 100 percent accuracy. And it can do so unobtrusively, with cells collected from an inside-the-cheek swab of father and child sent through the mail to a lab. Still, biology does not always triumph. In *Michael H. v. Gerald D.* (1989), the Supreme Court upheld California's conclusive presumption that a woman's husband is the father of her children if they are cohabiting and he is neither sterile nor impotent.[19] Carole gave birth to a child, Victoria, while married to Gerald. The true father was her neighbor, Michael. Gerald was listed as the father on the birth certificate and, at least initially, believed he was her father. Carole went back and forth between the two men (and a third man) during the first few years of Victoria's life. Carole and Michael together sought paternity tests, which proved, with 98.07 percent accuracy, that Michael was the father. When Carole stopped letting Michael see Victoria, he sued to establish paternity and to gain visitation rights. Carole (and Gerald) refused. Michael lost. The Supreme Court chose to protect the marital over the non-marital family, allowing states to rely on their old presumptions about marital paternity. Most states continue to indulge the marital presumption in some form, though DNA testing exerts pressure for change.[20]

Richard and Margaret Parker married in 1996, and she bore a child in 1998. When the couple divorced in 2001, Margaret got custody; Richard was to pay child support ($1,200 a month). Richard later discovered, through DNA testing, that he was not the child's father; he claimed that Margaret had deliberately concealed this information. He asked a Florida court for damages, to compensate for past and future child support. The trial court threw out his case, and an appellate court affirmed; Richard would have to go on paying child support for somebody else's genetic child.[21]

Richard is not alone—a survey in the 1990s found that as many as 5 percent of all marital children are not the husband's child.

Earlier studies had actually suggested an even higher percentage.[22] But the law does not necessarily allow a man to disprove paternity, even when science is on his side. Florida's approach is typical. It permits a husband to challenge paternity—but only within narrow limits. He can challenge paternity during a divorce proceeding and, if successful, can avoid further parental obligations. But Richard raised this issue for the first time two years after the divorce (five years after the child's birth). Margaret asserted in her divorce papers that the boy was "a child of the marriage" and Richard did not object. Once Richard's paternity became part of the judgment, it was almost impossible to reverse because of a general rule barring relitigation of issues previously decided by a court. Judgments based on fraud are an exception, but only if the misrepresentation is "extrinsic" to the proceedings—related to an issue separate from the case, or which affects the ability of a party to appear in court. But Margaret's fraud was deemed "intrinsic" and therefore subject to challenge only within a one-year statute of limitations.

Florida's statutory scheme may seem hypertechnical, but it represents a common compromise between two goals: first, that children should keep emotional and financial ties with the men they believe to be their fathers; and second, that men should not be responsible for other men's children. A revised version of the Uniform Parentage Act (2002) endorses a similar approach, respectful of modern science, but also zealously protecting the interests of the child.[23] A man may disestablish paternity, even for children born during a marriage; but it must be done within time limits.[24] Genetic testing is the *only* evidence admissible to disestablish paternity; results are admissible only if all parties consent or if a court ordered the testing. Secretly grabbing a used Band-Aid and sending it to a lab is out of bounds. The point is to avoid intruding into the marriage, raking up sordid details about infidelity.[25] When the time to contest ends—whether because of the child's age, or the lapse of time after divorce or other adjudication of paternity—the parties have to let sleeping DNA lie.[26]

Disavowals of paternity are also not favored in cases of biological, but unwanted, fatherhood. Matt Dubay, a twenty-five-year-old computer programmer, challenged a court order directing him to pay $500 per month in child support. He had never intended to become a father. His girlfriend assured him she was medically unable to get pregnant; and was using contraception just in case. Nonetheless, they conceived a child together early in their relationship.

In court, he used an argument supplied by the National Center for Men (NCM), a nonprofit group with the stated mission to "educat[e] the public about how men are hurt by sex discrimination."[27] Women can avoid unwanted children through abortion; thus men should have the right to reject fatherhood. NCM styled this case "*Roe v. Wade* for men."[28] The federal courts in Michigan refused to take the bait.[29] Both the trial and appellate courts rejected Dubay's argument that the situation violated the Equal Protection Clause of the federal Constitution.[30] The Constitution only guarantees equal protection to those who are "similarly situated." Before conception, men and women have equal opportunity to avoid parenthood. Once a child is conceived, their roles and rights diverge. Dubay's argument, the court concluded, relied on a "false analogy" between the woman' right to abort and the father's (alleged) right to avoid the payment of child support. A woman's right to abortion derives from her right to bodily integrity and privacy; there is no analogous right for men. The right to privacy for men, one case has held, "does not encompass a right to decide not to become a parent after conception or birth."[31] There is no constitutional right to avoid "financial obligations to his natural child that are validly imposed by state law."[32] The highest court in New York, in a similar case, agreed.[33] The unwilling father might sue a woman for fraud, if she lied about infertility or contraception.[34] Winning damages in such a case would not directly affect payments for child support, but might force reimbursement by the mother.[35]

Courts genuinely dislike intruding into sordid personal affairs, consensual sexual relations, and decisions about reproduction. But they do not always abstain. Courts have, for example, long permitted victims of sexually transmitted disease or other dangerous conditions to sue the person responsible, if he or she intentionally lied about the disease or condition.[36] Claims of involuntary fatherhood, however, rest on very subjective evidence. It would be hard to prove who lied, and who relied. Would Dubay have avoided sex, if he thought pregnancy was a possibility? Or might a man in his position lie after the fact to avoid nearly two decades of child support payments?

Courts are reluctant in such cases to allow these claims of unwanted fatherhood because of the effect on children. Children should not suffer because their parents were indiscreet, or told lies; or because of the way they were conceived and born. Child support payments are based on parental income and children's needs; parental misconduct is irrelevant, and so is the fact that the parents did not want to have a child. There is also some palpable fear that unwanted children might end up on the welfare rolls.

UNWED FATHERHOOD

Before the 1970s, unwed fathers who wanted rights to their children faced many obstacles. But rapidly changing household demographics, including a skyrocketing number of children born out of wedlock, put pressure on a legal system that gave little or no recognition to the rights and duties of unwed fathers.[37] Since 1972, unwed fathers have gained some protection for their parental rights under the Fourteenth Amendment; at the same time, as we have seen, illegitimate children have gained their own rights. The harsh distinctions based on legitimacy have eroded. But unwed fathers still do not have the same rights as unwed mothers.

In *Stanley v. Illinois* (1972), Joan and Peter Stanley cohabited on and off for eighteen years and raised three children. They never formally married. When she died, the children became wards of the state and were placed with court-appointed guardians.[38] Unwed fathers had no legal rights as parents under Illinois law. Peter challenged the law. The Court agreed with him. The Fourteenth Amendment did not permit him to be presumed unfit, while an unwed mother would be presumed fit. The right to "conceive and to raise one's own children" was "essential"; and the constitution protects the "integrity of the family."[39] The state had argued that "most unmarried fathers are unsuitable and neglectful parents." But the Supreme Court felt that Stanley's children could be taken away only on proof of unfitness or neglect. *Levy v. Louisiana* (1968), as we have seen, foreshadowed this case;[40] after *Levy*, states could no longer try to penalize the children of unmarried parents, in order to deter sex outside of marriage.[41]

Stanley was hailed as a sex equality case,[42] but its immediate and lasting impact was on the law of unwed fatherhood. The code books were full of rules that distinguished categorically between unwed mothers and unwed fathers for purposes of inheritance, custody, adoption, and other rights. In 1979, the Supreme Court invalidated a provision of the New York Domestic Relations Law, which gave unmarried mothers, but not unmarried fathers, the right to consent to (or veto) an adoption of their child.[43] Abdiel Caban had fathered two children during the years he lived with their mother. Later, their mother got married, and she wanted her new husband to adopt the children. Abdiel refused. The state argued that "a natural mother" usually has a "closer relationship with her child … than a father does."[44] But the Court, in *Caban v. Mohammed*, rejected this notion, and insisted that unwed mothers and unwed fathers be treated equally.

The children in that case were eight and ten years old; the Court left open the question whether unwed fathers would have the same equal claim to newborn children. In *Lehr v. Robertson* (1983), the Court said no.[45] Unwed fathers (unlike unwed mothers) were not entitled automatically to full parental rights. They had to assert paternity and develop an attachment to the child. *Lehr* involved Jessica M., who was born out of wedlock to Lorraine Robertson and Jonathan Lehr. Eight months after Jessica's birth, Lorraine married another man. Lorraine petitioned for her new husband to adopt Jessica when she was two. The social service agency reported favorably on the adoption, and a court approved it. Jonathan went to court; the adoption was invalid, he said, because he had no advance notice of the proceeding.

At the time of Jessica's birth, New York, like many other states, maintained a "putative father registry." This registry permits unwed fathers to preserve their potential rights by notifying the state of their intent to assert paternity over a child, either before or after its birth.[46] Listed putative fathers, along with some others (for example, those whose names were on the birth certificate, or who were living openly with the child and its mother), were entitled to notification of adoption proceedings. Jonathan knew about Jessica's birth, and her mother's marriage; but he satisfied none of the formal criteria for notification. He did eventually file a petition for visitation and paternity, but not until after the adoption proceeding had begun, at which point it was ignored. Jonathan argued that a putative father's "actual or potential relationship" with his child was a "liberty" protected by the constitution. The statute also, he said, gave unwed mothers greater rights than unwed fathers.

The Supreme Court upheld the New York law. Jonathan's biological tie to Jessica was not sufficient, in the Court's view, to justify full protection of his parental rights. The Court distinguished between a "developed parent-child relationship," and a potential one. The biological tie offers the natural father a unique opportunity to "develop a relationship" with the child. If he "grasps that opportunity," and accepts some "responsibility for the child's future," he may "enjoy the blessings of the parent-child relationship." But if not, the Constitution will not "automatically compel a state to listen to his opinion of where the child's best interests lie."[47]

Unwed fathers still face obstacles to asserting parental rights. About thirty states have putative father registries; some were adopted directly in response to the Supreme Court cases, others came after high-profile fights by unwed fathers who had been left out of the adoption process. The rules governing these registries vary state by state; most impose time limits on registration—for example, within five days of a child's birth or prior to the beginning of an adoption proceeding.[48] Unwed fathers have other ways to protect their rights under state law; the statutes, however, tend to be rather strict.

Despite the increasing protection for unwed fathers, some high-profile cases have turned on the adoption of children without the father's consent. In two highly publicized cases in the 1990s, the children were ultimately returned to the biological father. A court forced adoptive parents to turn three-year-old Baby Richard over to a man he had never met.[49] The birth mother had told him the baby had died, thus preventing him from asserting his rights earlier.

Baby Jessica was born in Iowa, but taken immediately to Michigan by her adoptive parents. Her birth mother, Cara, had named "Scott" on the birth certificate as the baby's father; both Cara and Scott signed a release of their parental rights. The controversy began when Cara admitted she had lied; Scott was not the father. The real father was Daniel, who intervened in the proceedings when he learned he was Jessica's father. The court agreed that the adoption could not proceed unless Daniel surrendered his parental rights, or had forfeited his rights by abandoning the baby.[50] Neither had happened. Jessica, two and a half years old, was taken from her adoptive parents and returned to her biological father. Television news filmed the hand-off; the drama— and trauma—reverberated in legislative chambers and living rooms around the country. *Whose Child Is This? The War for Baby Jessica* was the name of a movie shown on television.[51] Daniel and Cara eventually married. The adoptive parents never saw Jessica again.

The fight for Baby Jessica wreaked havoc all around. The adoptive parents adopted another baby, but divorced five years later; the loss of Jessica "was more than our marriage could handle." The same month, Daniel and Cara announced that they, too, were getting a divorce.[52] Cases like Baby Jessica and Baby Richard moved some states to go back to the drawing board. They wanted to make sure that no unknown biological father would come out of the woodwork—a possibility that might deter some couples from adopting children. Iowa, Baby Jessica's state, changed the law to limit the time a birth parent might object to an adoption.[53] Under the proposed act, unwed fathers, to thwart a pending adoption, had to speak up quickly, and also demonstrate potential for good parenting.[54] Some states clearly overreacted. The Florida Adoption Act, passed in 2001, required unwed mothers to help ferret out putative fathers. It did this by requiring women—including minors—to publish in a newspaper, in "each city in which the mother resided or traveled, in which conception may have occurred," a legal notice containing her name, age, and physical description, as well as the physical description of any man who the mother "reasonably believes" may be the father and a list of the locations "in which conception may have occurred."[55]

Several mothers, "a woman who was slipped a date-rape drug," a "teenage girl who had sex with numerous classmates," and a third who "traded her body for drugs," filed suit, challenging the law as an unconstitutional invasion of privacy.[56] Adoption advocates warned that the law would bring adoptions to a halt; some mothers would clearly abort or choose to keep the baby rather than expose their sexual history to the public. A Florida appellate court struck down the law, on the grounds that the state had no compelling reason for imposing such an onerous and humiliating requirement on mothers.[57] Other states continued to look for ways to balance the rules about adoption procedures and goals, with the rights of unwed fathers.[58] The putative father registries look better on paper than in reality. As one commentator put it: "It's all smoke and mirrors. How can registries work if no one's heard of them? And it's just not reasonable to expect that men will register every time they have sex."[59] The same article reported that "fewer than 100 men register each year" in many states; the Florida registry in the year 2004 had "just 47 registrants for the 89,436 out-of-wedlock births." Moreover, registration in one state provides no rights if the adoption takes place in another. The parental rights of unwed fathers thus continue to be somewhat precarious, despite constitutional protection.

THE LEGAL TREATMENT OF SPERM DONORS

One of the earliest forms of modern reproductive technology was "AID"—artificial insemination by donor—used by married couples when the husband was infertile. Anonymous sperm donation, in the 1950s and 1960s, horrified some traditionalists. Bills were introduced in a few states to prohibit or even criminalize artificial insemination by donor.[60] These laws did not pass. Outrage gave way to quiet concern, and, eventually, to regulation. The Uniform Parentage Act (UPA), first proposed in 1973, and subsequently adopted by eighteen states,[61] provided, in a key provision, that an anonymous sperm donor was not the "legal father" of any resulting child, if a licensed physician handled the insemination of a married woman.[62] Such a provision would encourage donors; they could not be chased down for child support; and the woman did not have to live in fear of a "father" showing up out of the blue and demanding parental rights. The husband of a married woman was the legal father of the child, a presumption that could be rebutted only in exceptional circumstances.[63]

The UPA was substantially revised in 2002. The current version drops the requirement of a licensed physician. A donor has no parental rights whether the woman was married or not. The husband is still treated as the legal father of his wife's children conceived with donor sperm. But, a woman's unmarried partner could also be the legal father of donor-conceived children.[64] Today, sperm donation has become a "booming business."[65] The

California Cryobank offers, for example, a celebrity look-a-like service; customers can look for donors who resemble "actors, athletes, musicians, or anyone else famous enough to be found on the web."[66] But the legal treatment of sperm donors is in flux.[67] For example, as we will discuss in the next chapter, the tradition of anonymous donation is under pressure to change. The 2002 UPA also defines "donor" to include egg donors and applies the same rules. Outside of the UPA, however, very few states address the rights or parental status of egg donors, even though it has become an important, and somewhat controversial, aspect of alternative reproductive technology.[68]

SURROGACY

Surrogacy has ancient and storied roots. In Genesis 16, the Old Testament tells the story of Abraham, whose wife Sarah was childless. Sarah gave her handmaid, Hagar, to Abraham so that he could have a child. Abraham and Hagar conceived Ishmael the old-fashioned way, which predictably gave rise to jealousy and conflict. This is not the stuff of modern surrogacy, which relies instead on reproductive technology and a special set of rules about parentage.

A surrogate is a woman who gives birth to a child, usually for money, with the intent that someone else will raise it. In its first modern iteration—what we now refer to as "traditional surrogacy"—a woman conceived a child using her own egg and sperm from the husband of an infertile woman; if he was also infertile, from a sperm donor. The surrogate could be inseminated by a doctor or by "using a simple turkey baster."[69] The intent behind this arrangement, typically laid out in a written contract, was to give the child, at birth, to its father and his wife, who would become the legal parents.

But what if the surrogate refused to turn over the child? Is a surrogacy contract enforceable? This was the issue in 1988, when the Baby M case made national headlines. Mary Beth Whitehead conceived a child through traditional surrogacy—she provided the egg and the womb—for William and Elizabeth Stern.[70] Mary Beth was a high school dropout; the Sterns were highly educated professionals. William and Mary Beth signed an agreement that she would give up the child, and do whatever was necessary to relinquish her parental rights, paving the way for Elizabeth to adopt the child. Elizabeth, for perhaps fancied medical reasons, had decided not to become pregnant. William, who lost most of his family in the holocaust, wanted to "continue his bloodline."[71] Mary Beth was willing to become a surrogate out of sympathy— she wanted to "give another couple the 'gift of life.'" She also wanted to earn money for her own family.

The Sterns agreed to pay Mary Beth $10,000, due after delivery of the child. They also paid a broker $7,500 for facilitating the arrangement. After several unsuccessful attempts, Mary Beth became pregnant and gave birth to a child in 1986. But Mary Beth changed her mind, and refused to hand over the baby.[72] "Baby M's" early months of life were a roller coaster. Mary Beth pleaded with the Sterns to let her have the baby for a week to say good-bye. The Sterns were afraid Mary Beth might kill herself, so they reluctantly agreed. Mary Beth kept the baby, and ran away to Florida with her husband. For three months, the three of them were on the move. Mary Beth spoke at times with Mr. Stern, who recorded the conversations. The talks were about "rights, morality, and power," along with "threats of Mrs. Whitehead to kill herself, to kill the child, and falsely to accuse Mr. Stern of sexually molesting Mrs. Whitehead's other daughter."[73] The Sterns eventually found the Whiteheads and the issue ended up in court.

Despite all its practical and emotional complexities, the legal question was relatively straightforward: was the surrogacy contract valid and enforceable under New Jersey law? Surrogacy in this form was relatively new. There were no prior cases; and the legislature had never acted on the question. The *Baby M* trial lasted more than two months. At the trial level, the Sterns won. The contract was valid; the Sterns would get the baby, and Mary Beth's parental rights would be terminated. The New Jersey Supreme Court took an entirely different approach. Surrogacy was baby-selling. It was illegal under state law to buy a child, and pre-birth adoption contracts were unenforceable.[74] The court worried about the "impact on the child who learns that her life was bought," and the impact also on the "natural mother."[75] The surrogacy contract was against the law, and unenforceable. This left open the question of custody.[76] As between Baby M's natural mother (Mary Beth) and natural father (William), who should be granted custody? Mary Beth's behavior after Baby M's birth was worrisome. The Sterns' household seemed to promise a better home for Baby M.[77] Baby M would be placed with the Sterns. But Mary Beth was still her mother. She would get permanent visitation rights. Elizabeth Stern was, and would always be, only a stepmother.

The Sterns lost the surrogacy battle, but won the war—custody of Baby M. But the case had national reverberations. It provoked national debate, as "ethicists, feminists, theologians, lawmakers, and local men and women weighed in on surrogacy's moral, legal, and practical significance."[78] Surrogacy was, and still is, controversial; it seemed to reduce "procreation" to something "purchased in the marketplace and governed by the rules of contract law."[79] But some feminists defended surrogacy as an aspect of reproductive freedom.[80] Public opinion was mixed, but a poll taken after the initial Baby M ruling found that 74 percent of those surveyed thought the baby should have gone to the father, and 69 percent said that surrogate mothers generally ought to adhere to the agreements they make.[81] Other studies, however, found that surrogacy was "the least acceptable of all assisted reproductive technologies.[82]

The legal landscape quickly became speckled with laws for or against surrogacy, of many different types.[83] In the year after the trial court's ruling in Baby M, seventy-three bills were introduced in twenty-seven states—to permit, regulate, or prohibit surrogacy.[84] Most of the bills did not become law, but several states did ban paid surrogacy.[85] Many European countries also ban surrogacy, including the United Kingdom.[86] New York enacted a complete ban on surrogacy, with little opposition, in 1992.[87] But in many states, legislatures took no position on surrogacy, leaving it up to the courts. The California Supreme Court enforced a surrogacy agreement in 1993; the court held that the intended parents were the child's legal parents.[88] Surrogacy is flourishing in California, and in a number of other states—about a dozen in all—where it appears to be legal.

The New York law, which banned surrogacy, was the "political high water mark" of opposition to surrogacy.[89] The trend now is to permit, but regulate, these arrangements. This shift acknowledges that surrogacy serves a need: it is a way for infertile or gay male couples to have children with genetic ties to at least one parent. Laws banning surrogacy in one state just push parties to enter into arrangements somewhere else. Noel Keane, the intermediary who brought together Mary Beth Whitehead and the Sterns, had the same number of surrogacy clients a year after paid surrogacy was banned in New Jersey; almost half of these clients were from New Jersey.[90] The demand for surrogacy is there; along with growing sympathy for those who see it as their only path to parenthood.

Meanwhile, further scientific advances changed the game with the development of a new type of surrogacy. In "gestational surrogacy," the surrogate, or "gestational carrier," provides only the womb. She is implanted with an embryo created using in vitro fertilization. The egg and sperm might come from any number of sources—one or both of the intended parents or third-party donors. This type of surrogacy, used 95 percent of the time today, has "proved to be not only more attractive to the parties but more palatable to law makers and the public."[91] Studies show that surrogates "generally report being quite satisfied with their experiences," and they tend to form a relationship "with the couple rather than the child."[92]

A few states now explicitly authorize surrogacy, but regulate it.[93] In 2004, Illinois enacted the Gestational Surrogacy Act, which imposes strict requirements on all the parties involved.[94] A gestational surrogate must be at least twenty-one years old, and have given birth to at least one child already; she must receive physical and mental health evaluations, and legal counseling about the arrangements and its consequences. The intended parents must prove infertility, or some medical reason to resort to surrogacy.[95] The law also deals with legal representation and formalities of execution. The surrogate must be permitted to choose her own physician. The intended parents can bargain for important rights; for example, they can insist that the surrogate give up drinking and smoking; and they can dictate the type and frequency of prenatal testing and care. Finally, the Illinois Act confirms that the children born to gestational surrogates, under a contract that satisfies the legal requirements, are the legitimate children of the intended parents. Neither the surrogate nor her husband has any parental status vis-à-vis the child.[96] The Illinois statute is thus a compromise: it tries to answer objections to surrogacy (exploitation of women; baby-selling); and also tries to ward off battles over custody and parental status. The *Baby M* case had made headlines; in contrast, the Illinois act "generated modest media attention and little controversy; it passed unanimously in both Houses of the legislature."[97] Other states have passed similar laws in recent years.[98]

New reproductive technology evokes, at first, "horrified negation"; then comes "negation without horror, then slow and gradual curiosity, study, evaluation, and finally a very slow but steady acceptance."[99] This was what happened, apparently, to surrogacy. Data are hard to get,[100] but surrogacy seems to be growing more common. According to one source, 1,600 babies were born to surrogates who used in vitro fertilization between 1991 and 1999.[101] The American Society for Reproductive Medicine estimates that there were as many as six hundred births a year to gestational surrogates between 2003 and 2007.[102] Surrogates tend to be paid in the neighborhood of $20,000; additional money often goes to brokers and medical providers.[103]

Surrogacy contracts set out what the parties intend to achieve, in the hope that everybody will live up to his or her end of the bargain. They often include specific provisions that are almost certainly not enforceable, anywhere—for example, specifying under what conditions the surrogate will abort. But the agreements are important, whether or not they are legally enforceable. The vast majority of all surrogacy contracts are honored by both parties; as few as 1 percent of surrogates reportedly change their minds.[104]

In modern surrogacy, it may take as many as five people to "procreate": a sperm donor, an egg donor, a gestational carrier—and two intended parents. This complicates the question: who is a parent?[105] The living law—the thoughts and behaviors of actual people—provides some answers; and the formal law slowly but surely follows. In a very recent case, a trial judge in New Jersey held that *Baby M.* applies with equal force to *gestational* surrogacy agreements; it refused to enforce an agreement between two gay men and the sister of one who carried twins for them.[106] Although the surrogate was not the biological mother—an anonymous egg donor played that role—the court ruled nonetheless that she and the intended father who donated sperm were the legal parents of the children that resulted from the arrangement.

Posthumously Conceived Children

Young Robert Netting and his wife, Rhonda, were trying to conceive a child. But then Robert was diagnosed with cancer—and the chemotherapy, the couple knew, might render him sterile. So before beginning treatment, Robert deposited his sperm, to be used in the future for in vitro fertilization. Sadly, Robert died of cancer. But before he died, he made clear his intention that Rhonda could use his sperm after his death. She did, and ten months after Robert's death, Rhonda conceived twins. Rhonda filed to collect Social Security survivors' benefits for the twins—a benefit normally available to dependent minor children of a deceased wage earner. But were they eligible, since they were not conceived until after he died?

Family law has always taken into account children who were born after their fathers had died. Men can die and leave behind pregnant wives, especially in the bad old days of shorter life expectancies, and no antibiotics; and also in times of war. The law simply treats a child as "in being" from conception rather than birth, if conceived before the father's death, but born alive afterward.[107] Courts presumed that children born within 280 days of a husband's death belonged to him.[108] Such a child would have full inheritance rights. But common-law courts never imagined the case of a child *conceived* after its father died.

But now this is definitely possible. A man can deposit sperm during his lifetime, to be used later to inseminate a woman, or for in vitro fertilization. (The technology for freezing a woman's eggs is not yet as far advanced; and there are no reported cases of conception after a woman's death.) In 1999, doctors reported the first birth of a child conceived with sperm retrieved from a dead man. When Bruce Vernoff, a man in his thirties, died suddenly, his wife asked doctors to extract sperm from his body, which was done with a urologist, a needle, and a trip to the coroner's office. Thirty hours after his death, sperm was successfully harvested, frozen for fifteen months, and eventually used to impregnate his widow.[109] The doctor who performed the procedure, Cappy Rothman of the Center for Reproductive Medicine in Los Angeles, began harvesting sperm from dead men in 1978, but the 1999 case was the first successful birth from a post-mortem extraction.[110]

Posthumous conceptions raise many medical and bioethical issues.[111] They also raise an important legal issue: is the deceased donor a parent?[112] Is the child eligible for Social Security benefits? Can the child inherit? A federal court held that the Netting twins could collect Social Security benefits; Robert was their legal father.[113] Arizona's parentage law was worded in a way that led the court to decide that biological children of married parents were legally their "children," no matter when conceived. [114]

The question of parentage in the Netting case turned on Arizona law. Social Security is a federal program; but the law, in questions about survivors' benefits, allows each state to define "parent" and "child." The same federal court, in fact, recently reached a contrary conclusion in a case from California. The court felt that California's parentage law did not define "child" broadly enough to include children conceived after their father's death.[115] In an inheritance case, *Woodward v. Commissioner* (2002), in Massachusetts, the court developed a special rule for this class of children. The court wanted proof of the genetic tie, and proof as well that the dead parent had agreed to the posthumous conception of the child.[116] The court also left open the possibility of imposing some sort of time limitation, in order to balance two policies: one favoring inheritance by children; the other disfavoring rules that might muck up the probate process.

Legislatures in five states have passed laws allowing posthumously conceived children to inherit, if the parent gave written consent.[117] Two states, on the other hand, enacted statutes prohibiting such children from inheriting from the dead parent. New York recently amended its code to make clear that posthumously conceived children were excluded from protection against accidental disinheritance by a parent.[118] But most laws governing parent-child relationships, and those governing important benefits like Social Security and inheritance, do not contemplate or address the rights of these children.

Courts, by their nature, cannot dodge this issue, just as they cannot dodge the issue of surrogacy, or any of the other issues which the new technology raises. A court cannot say, "I have no idea how to handle this." The buck stops with them. They have to make decisions; and they have to deal with issues the legislature never foresaw—the issue, for example, of women who, as it were, have sex with the ghosts of dead husbands.[119] Paradoxically, then, this age of empowerment of individuals also empowers the judges, who find themselves in the center of controversy, forced to try to disentangle some of society's most stubborn knots.

This chapter has asked the question: Who is a parent? The answer has gotten cloudier over the years. Science has added new ways to make babies. And society has changed the way it defines parents and children. Biological and social parenthood compete for legal recognition. What results is both controversy and confusion, as we have seen. So if we ask, "who is a parent?" the answer is, "it all depends."

Chosen People: Adoption and the Law

As should be obvious by now, American families are formed, both socially and legally, in many ways. One of the obvious ways is through adoption. This chapter will trace, briefly, the history of adoption law; and take a look at some of the more tricky issues that surround this institution—cross-racial adoption, for example, and the role adoption plays in the formation of gay and lesbian families.

THE ORIGINS OF ADOPTION

Adoption as we know it today is a product of the middle of the nineteenth century. The common law had no provision for adoption (it was present in Roman law, and was carried over into the civil law systems of Europe). England did not provide for formal adoption of children until 1926.[1] Of course, in an age rife with orphans, adults often raised other people's children. But there was no formal, legal way to adopt.[2] Mississippi passed the first American adoption statute in 1846, and Massachusetts a more comprehensive one in 1851.[3] Every state eventually did the same, half within the next twenty-five years.[4] Adoption statutes were a "far-reaching innovation"[5] that made "parent-child relationships possible where blood could not."[6]

Some early adoption statutes simply tried "to ratify and record private adoption agreements"; others gave judges a role in the process.[7] Over time, the less intrusive statutes were repealed and replaced with more modern adoption procedures. The most important change, as Vernier noted in 1936, was to introduce into state law provisions for a thorough investigation into "the suitability of the child for adoption, and the capability and suitability of those desiring to adopt, to care for, and to rear the child."[8] California's first adoption statute was typical. A competent adult could adopt any minor at least ten years younger.[9] Consent was required from any spouse of an adoptive parent; from the child, if over the age of twelve; and from the biological parents of the child.[10] Only the mother's consent was required for an out-of-wedlock child, and none from any parent who had been "deprived of civil rights," or divorced for adultery or cruelty, or a "habitual drunkard," or someone "judicially deprived of the custody of the child on account of cruelty or neglect."[11] Today, the right to veto an adoption is an incident of legal parentage, which, as we have explained, may turn on more than biology and may be forfeited by unwed fathers who do not assert their rights soon enough.

The Industry of Adoption

Over the course of the twentieth century, the law and practice of adoption became more professional. Early statutes reflected conventional ideas about eugenics—building in steps to the process to determine whether the parents were fit, but also whether the *child* was suitable for adoption. A 1917 Minnesota law required the state board of control to examine the "conditions and antecedents of the child," to see whether the child was a "proper subject for adoption" and whether the proposed new home was "suitable." The statute also gave some protection to parents by including a sort of lemon law provision. Parents could petition to "annul an adoption," if the child unexpectedly should develop "feeble-mindedness, epilepsy, insanity or venereal infection as a result of conditions existing prior to the adoption."[12] Without such a statute, courts claimed they had no inherent power to undo an adoption. One couple in 1958 tried to cancel their adoption of a child who developed such severe behavioral problems and mental deficiencies that she had to be institutionalized. The Oregon court held that it could not undo an adoption, without statutory authority, except to protect the *child's* best interests or welfare.[13] Adoption might disappoint both parent and child, but it creates a permanent legal relationship. Some modern statutes allow adoptions to be undone, but usually only if an adopton agency intentionally misled the parents about health or other essential matters. In California, for example, adoptive parents can surrender a child, within five years of the decree, if the child has an unforeseen developmental disability that renders him or her "unadoptable."[14]

The modern remedy for deception by adoption agencies or brokers in most cases is money damages or fines, rather than abrogation of the adoption.[15] In a rash of cases in the late 1980s and 1990s, adoptive parents sued agencies for "wrongful adoption" or something similar. In the leading case, *Burr v. Burr* (1986), an Ohio couple was told that a "nice, big, healthy, baby boy," seventeen months old, had become available, because his unwed teenage mother, who had been living at home, was moving to Texas; and the "mean" grandparents refused to care for him. Virtually all of this was a lie. The boy had lived in two foster homes prior to the adoption, and his parents were mental patients at a local state hospital; the "healthy" boy had severe physical and mental disabilities, was deemed "educable, but mentally retarded," and at age nineteen was diagnosed with Huntington's disease, a fatal hereditary disease that would inevitably kill him within a decade. The adoption agency was found liable on a "wrongful adoption" claim and the parents won $125,000 in damages.[16] Adoption agencies are not, as a general matter, "guarantors of their placements"; only a "higher authority" determines whether the children grow up to be healthy and happy. But adoptive parents are entitled to information about the child they are choosing to adopt. The agency here had failed to do so—deliberately misinforming the adoptive parents.

Other courts reached similar results, sometimes simply by relying on the traditional tort of fraud or negligent misrepresentation.[17] Some courts restricted recovery to cases of intentional misrepresentation, but others allowed recovery even if the agency was merely negligent in failing to disclose known or knowable health risks.[18] These rulings came at a time when the idea of adoption secrecy was losing its grip. More and more, adoptive children and parents craved medical information; this made lies and omissions less tolerable, even if the motive was to find homes for hard-to-place children. No doubt in response to these rulings imposing liability, as well as the more general shift in favor of openness in adoption, every state now has a statute specifying when medical information must or can be disclosed to adoptive parents.[19] All adoptive parents in Ohio, under a 2002 law, must receive a standardized disclosure form, containing "all background information available on the child."[20]

During the second half of the twentieth century, as demand for babies outstripped supply, adoption became a much costlier and lengthier process.[21] A number of factors suppressed the supply of babies available for adoption. The sexual revolution was a major factor. Greater access to more effective contraception meant fewer unwanted babies. The declining stigma attached to unwed motherhood meant more such babies were kept. In 2002, for example, less than 2 percent of unwed mothers relinquished their babies for adoption.[22] The shortage of babies stimulated the growth of international and transracial adoptions (to be discussed later), and the emergence of black and "gray" markets for adoption.

Public agencies, private charities or nonprofits, and independent lawyers and brokers controlled the supply of adoptable babies. Many states made it illegal to adopt a baby outside of a certified agency. But outside the occasional crackdown, there was little enforcement. In 1949, two lawyers and a housewife were accused of running a "big-time" baby business; they brought babies from Florida and sold them in New York for $2,000 each.[23] Prosecutors claimed Miami was a "mecca" for unwed mothers—Florida had no "illegal adoption" law—and was thus an obvious target for baby-sellers. The defendants were charged under a new law making it illegal to profit by placing a baby except through an authorized agency. But defendants insisted they were merely trying to help out "desperate unwed mothers and desperate childless couples." In 2010, a Long Island lawyer was convicted of thirty-seven charges, and sentenced to ten to twenty years in prison, for an adoption scam in which he promised numerous couples babies that did not exist. He used fake sonograms and non-existent birth mothers to steal more than $300,000 from families whose desperate hopes for a child were dashed.[24] In general, however, laws against illegal adoptions have been quite ineffective.[25]

Today, public agencies handle most adoptions; but most states also permit "independent" adoptions, which are basically unregulated.[26] About one-fifth of the domestic adoptions in 2002 were handled privately.[27] This opens the door to a whole new style of adoption, and more potential for abuse. About half the states expressly prohibit "baby-selling," but they do permit payment of the birth mother's medical expenses and the costs of early infant care, in addition to reasonable fees to cover court costs and lawyers' fees.[28] A typical adoptive couple spends \$15,000–\$20,000; sometimes as much as \$100,000.[29] Couples today who want to adopt use all sorts of means of finding babies. They run ads in local newspapers, touting their virtues. There are websites on the Internet, for matching up adoptive parents with children; parents advertise themselves "in spunky performances on videotapes, in lush scrapbooks," and in smiling professional portraits.[30]

THE PURPOSE OF ADOPTION

In the late nineteenth century, adoption was a tool of the controversial child-saving movement. Charles Loring Brace and his "Orphan Train" took hordes of poor New York children—many of them Catholic, and often without the consent of their parents—and shipped them off to adoptive (Protestant) homes in the Midwest. Adoption was also used to take children from poor families or minority families or unfit parents and give them to strangers.[31]

In general, however, adoption served to place unwanted or orphaned children with families that would take them in—often families of blood relations. A study of adoptions in Alameda County (Oakland), California over a twenty-year period at the turn of the twentieth century showed three types of adoptions: family preservation adoption (those by a relative after a parent died or abandoned a child); family creation adoptions (by a childless couple); and family re-recreation adoptions (by a stepparent).[32] Two-thirds of the adoptions were "unrelated" adoptions—a childless married couple adopting one or more children. Family preservation and re-creation adoptions had once dominated; but now family creation adoptions were becoming the norm.[33] Many of these children were "dependent"—they had no fit biological parents, and were wards of the state or charitable institutions. Others were abandoned with friends, relatives, or strangers by parents who could not care for them. The *San Francisco Chronicle* reported on November 9, 1904 that a "tiny baby girl, about one month old, well-clothed and securely wrapped in a basket, was left by unknown hands on the doorsteps of J. Reed ... A note pinned to the clothes of the infant" explained that the parents were too poor to bring up the child respectably.[34] Only 12 percent of the adoptions in the Alameda County study involved step-parent adoptions, which became more common as the rate of divorce and remarriage increased in the twentieth century. As many as half of all adoptions between 1951 and 1981 were under-taken by stepparents, reflecting the rise of the "blended" family.[35] In 2002, "unrelated" adoptions accounted for 58 percent of all domestic adoptions.[36]

RACE AND RELIGION

Among the early adoption statutes, four expressly mentioned race.[37] Texas refused to permit white children to be adopted by black parents and vice versa; Nevada excluded "Mongolians" from the adoption law altogether; Louisiana permitted single adults or married couples to "petition to adopt any child of his or their race," and Montana had a similar requirement.[38] Today such laws are obviously invalid; this kind of racial classification is unconstitutional.[39] But whether race can play any role in adoption is a more complicated question.

In *Palmore v. Sidoti* (1984), a Florida case, a father sought a change in custody because his white ex-wife lived with, and later married, a black man. His ostensible motive was to protect his daughter from the social difficulties an interracial household might bring. The trial court agreed; the child would inevitably be "more vulnerable to peer pressures," and suffer from "social stigmatization." The Supreme Court, however, reversed. A child was not to be taken from its mother even though racial bias was real enough, and might possibly inflict "injury" on the child. The "Constitution cannot control such prejudices but neither can it tolerate them."[40] The *Palmore* case did not, however, rule out any role for race in particular custody or adoption cases.[41] *Palmore* left room for courts to consider, case by case, how to balance constitu-tional norms outlawing "race-conscious decisionmaking" against the "sometimes compelling needs of individual children."[42]

During the first half of the twentieth century, it was very uncommon for parents of one race to adopt a child of another. Transracial adoption began after World War II and increased substantially in the 1960s.[43] The decline in racism played a role; but the strongest force driving the trend was the fact that the supply of Caucasian babies was drying up. The "shortage" is stark: in 1989, an estimated 1 million people were seeking to adopt, and only 30,000 white infants were available that year.[44]

After the Korean War, American families adopted thousands of war orphans or abandoned Korean children. The largest group of children adopted internationally and living in the United States are South Korean; 10 percent of all Korean American citizens arrived here via adoption. From 1953 to 2007, around 160,000 Korean children were adopted out of Korea; the vast majority ended up in the United States. The adoption of Korean children by white American families never created much controversy, although many of the children have struggled with issues of racial identity.[45] Seventy-eight percent of those surveyed perceived themselves as actually white or wanted to be white as children; 61 percent made a trip to Korea either to learn about their native culture or to search for their birth parents.[46]

Other types of multiracial adoption, in contrast, have been plagued with controversy.[47] It became common beginning in the 1950s and 1960s for white families to adopt American Indian and black children.[48] The Native American adoptions were condemned as a form of genocide. Investigations in the 1970s did reveal scandalous conditions. One in four Native American children spent time in a foster home or in a boarding home run by the Bureau of Indian Affairs. Tribal representatives called it child stealing, plain and simple. In response, Congress took the unusual step of passing a law to regulate adoptions of Native American children. The Indian Child Welfare Act (ICWA) of 1978 was designed to prevent "the breakup of Indian families."[49] Under the Act, tribes were given jurisdiction to resolve custody disputes between tribal members. But perhaps more importantly, the Act made it more difficult to place a child for adoption with non-Indian parents. Prospective placements were ranked in order of priority—a child's extended family was given first choice, then members of the child's tribe, then "other Indian families." Note the commitment to the concept of "pan-ethnicity": the idea that the native peoples, despite differences in culture, religion, language, and ways of life, have some sort of overarching unity. The bias against "assimilation" extended, then, to native peoples, collectively, as well as to each individual tribal nation. And underlying this, in turn, was the rise of plural equality, and with it the emphasis on ethnicity and "roots." ICWA is perhaps unique in focusing on the rights and well-being of Native American tribes as a whole, rather than on the best interests of individual children. After this, Indian children were no longer removed from their birth homes at high rates. More Indian children in foster care were ultimately placed in Indian homes. Fewer Indian children were removed from homes because of neglect. By 1986, the adoption rate for Indian children was similar to that of non-Indian children.[50]

In a 1972 position paper, the National Association of Black Social Workers (NABSW) took a "vehement stand against the placement of black children in white homes for any reason." The association argued that transracial adoption constituted a kind of cultural genocide; and that black children adopted by white families suffered psychological and physical harm.[51] "Only a black family can transmit the emotional and sensitive subtleties of perception and reaction essential for a black child's survival in a racist society," NABSW argued. That white adoptive parents took pains to learn about black culture and the needs of black children simply confirmed for the association the "unnatural character of transracial adoption."

NABSW's opposition did have an effect—after a threefold increase from 1968 to 1971, the number of black children adopted by white families dropped back down to 1968 levels (about 1 percent of adoptions) by 1975.[52] But race-matching was controversial, too. Efforts to race-match caused delays in the placement of children, and sometimes resulted in placing black children in black, but unsuitable, homes.[53] Studies also showed that black children adopted by white parents were generally well-adjusted and able to develop a healthy racial identity.[54] Transracial adoptees did well on "measures of self-esteem and identity." And "delays in and denials of permanent placement have devastating effects on children."[55] The debate reflected, in Twila Perry's words, two distinct perspectives—"liberal colorblind individualism," which militated in favor of transracial adoption, and "color and community consciousness," which counseled against it.[56] The two perspectives reflect two different assessments of the state of racism in America and the best means for dealing with the legacy of discrimination and racial segregation.[57]

Congress, in sharp contrast to the way it reacted to Native American adoptions, intervened against race-matching. Under the Multiethnic Placement Act of 1994 (MEPA), federally funded entities were not permitted to "delay or deny" an adoptive placement because of race, nor to "categorically deny" any adult the opportunity to be an adoptive or foster parent "solely on the basis of ... race." But MEPA did not bar consideration of race entirely. It expressly permitted agencies to consider "the cultural, ethnic, or racial background of the child and the capacity of the prospective foster ... parents to meet the needs of the child."[58] But even this mild invitation to consider race did not last. In 1996, Congress passed the Interethnic Placement Act, which amended MEPA to prohibit consideration of the race of adoptive parent or child.[59] (Congress expressly exempted Indian children from this provision.) The Adoption and Safe Families Act, adopted in 1997, tries to encourage states to speed up decisions on children in foster care, either to reunite them with their birth parents, or to put them up for adoption.[60] This has the effect, whether this was intended or not, of making transracial adoption more likely; agencies have less time to look for a same-race placement. But neither of these laws applies to the many adoptions arranged by private agencies or brokers, who have much more leeway to accommodate racial preferences of the birth mother and the adoptive parents.[61]

There is no question that barriers to transracial adoption have mostly come down. The federal government has tried to enforce the ban on race-matching. The Department of Health and Human Services (HHS) has fined public adoption agencies in two states for relying on race in placing children for adoption. An Ohio county was fined $1.8 million for illegitimately considering race in a series of placements, including, for one special needs child, turning down a very promising potential placement with a white family from Alaska in favor of placement with a local black woman that never materialized. A South Carolina agency was fined for subjecting prospective parents to additional scrutiny if they sought to adopt children of a different race.[62] But transracial adoption remains a flashpoint, even though the numbers of families involved is small. Some state and federal courts still interpret *Palmore* to permit consideration of race as one factor in custody disputes,[63] and some advocates still contend that same-race placements are preferable. Race remains a "sensitive and complex" issue.[64]

Efforts have also been made to match adoptive parents and children by religion. Even though religious beliefs are hardly hereditary, many statutes insisted that children be placed with parents who shared the religion of their birth mothers, if at all possible. The baby of a Catholic woman was to be placed with a Catholic family. Statutes today allow courts to consider whether a religious match is relevant to the "best interests" of the child. New York law expressly includes a preference for same-religion placements.[65] And virtually every state permits religion to play a role in an adoption proceeding, if either the birth parent or the adoptive child so requested. Many adoption agencies have religious affiliations and make no secret of their preference for "intrareligious" placements.[66]

Matching principles in adoption law were designed to create "as if" families—"families in which children to all appearances might have been born to the adoptive parents."[67] Limits on the age of adoptive mothers served this same function, by preserving the plausibility of biological motherhood.[68] But the trend has been away from this principle—for example, in limitations on race-matching. Adoptions today are more open, more diverse, and less easily passed off as identical to genetic family ties.

The Nature of the Adoptive Relationship

Are adoptive children treated legally the same as blood children? A formal adoption cuts the ties between a child and his birth family, and replaces them with ties to the adoptive family. The 1892 California Code, for example, provided that adoptive parents and child gained "towards each other the legal relation of parent and child" with all the rights and duties of that relationship; the biological parents, at the same moment, were "relieved of all parental duties towards, and all responsibility for, the child so adopted."[69]

But, despite laws like the one just quoted, adopted children were not, at the beginning of the century, *exactly* like other children in the eyes of the law. In some jurisdictions, for example, an adopted child could inherit from her adopted parents directly, but not through them from the extended family. The adopted child was the child only of the adoptive parents—but no further, for inheritance purposes.[70] And in some jurisdictions, an adopted child retained the right to inherit from his or her birth parents, at least in certain circumstances.

Over the course of the twentieth century, however, adoptive relationships did ripen into a more or less complete *substitution* for the relationship between the adopted child and her biological parents. This substitution means that an adopted child inherits fully from her adoptive family, but not at all from her birth family.[71] Provisions in wills and trusts for "children" or "issue" are routinely interpreted to include adopted children. If a stepparent adopts a child, however, in some states the child may retain inheritance rights from the kin of the other birth parent.[72] Some courts have carried very far the idea that adoption severs all biological ties. In an Indiana case, Robert Fischer was accused of criminal incest; his sex partner, his biological son, had been adopted by another family at age four. The appellate court ruled that the victim was not Fischer's "child" within the meaning of the incest law, since, "for all legal and practical purposes the adopted child is the same as dead to its parents."[73] But this precedent was overruled by the state's highest court three years later.[74]

Shrouded in Secrecy

Although adoptions under the earliest statutes were open, they became shrouded in secrecy during the twentieth century. States, over time, tried to give adopted parents and children, in essence, a blank slate.[75] They did this first through confidentiality—sealing the proceedings from third parties—and later through anonymity. The Minnesota code of 1917 required adoption records to be sealed. A 1930s Illinois law granted adoptive parents the right to a "clean" birth certificate, listing them as the legal parents. The law also prohibited the registrar of records from indicating adoption or illegitimacy on a birth certificate.[76] Every other state followed suit by the 1950s. Thus, adoption in the twentieth century was characterized by "exclusivity, secrecy, and transposition";

the child was "taken from one family and given to another"; all traces of the first family disappeared, records were sealed, and everyone ventured forth "as if the first family never existed and the second was created through an act of nature."[77] By the middle of the twentieth century, virtually all "unrelated" adoptions were not only confidential, but anonymous.[78] The process of placing a child with adoptive parents involved "no disclosure or sharing of the identity" among the parties.[79]

But adopted children, and sometimes their adoptive parents, began to demand information. Children wanted to find their roots—their "real" parents and "real" identities. Adopted children wanted to know about their genes and about the medical history of the birth family. Adoptive parents wanted to understand why the healthy infant they adopted struggled terribly in school or had behavioral problems. And, as illegitimacy became more common and less stigmatized, the desperate need to keep the facts of birth secret began to diminish.

In the late 1970s, there was a movement by adopted children in several states to gain access to their original birth certificates, and the names of their birth parents. As a legal matter, the movement basically failed. A New Jersey court, for example, in *Mills v. Atlantic City Dep't of Vital Statistics* (1976), upheld a law forbidding disclosure of birth records of adopted children, except for good cause and under court order.[80] As one witness in the case had said: "We want to be like everyone else. We didn't come out of an agency. We came out of a human being. It meant a lot to me just to have a name."[81] The court in *Mills* ruled, however, that the state had the power to impose rules which would protect the parties to an adoption. Sealed records, in the court's view, protect the child "from any possible stigma of illegitimacy" and protected a "loving and cohesive" relationship from the "invasion" of a "natural parent who later wishes to intrude into the relationship"; meanwhile, the birth parents are "free to move on and attempt to rebuild their lives" while the adoptive parents will be able to raise the child "without fear of interference" or the adverse effects of illegitimacy. The language assumes a particular psychological view of adoption. But social norms were changing. In the 1970s, a California task force recommended allowing access by adults to their original birth certificates. Still, the only change the state did make at the time was to permit birth parents who surrendered a child for adoption in 1984 or later to consent to disclosure if the adopted child requests it, at age twenty-one.[82]

The issue continues to be controversial. The Adoptees' Liberty Movement Association has the largest registry for matching adopted children with their birth parents. Bastard Nation, a radical group formed in 1996, has made unsealing adoption records its central mission. Birth parents created their own organization in 1976, called Concerned United Birthparents (CUB). The group's logo depicts a mother bear peeking backwards at her cub.[83] One woman, who, as a teenager, gave up a child for adoption, was active in this group and then went on to form a foundation, dedicated to facilitating adoption reunions. She claims to have matched up five hundred adopted children and birth parents, but was convicted of fraud and conspiracy for using illegal means to gain access to Social Security and medical records.[84] She described her actions as a form of "civil disobedience," and compared herself to Rosa Parks for standing up to the "immoral, unconscionable laws" that require sealing of adoption records.

Concrete legal change came only at the very end of the twentieth century. In 1998, Oregon voters passed Measure 58, an initiative that gives "any adopted person 21 years of age or older born in the state of Oregon" the right to request a copy of his or her original birth certificate, with the names and addresses of their birth parents, as well as other identifying information.[85] The referendum survived a lawsuit by seven birth mothers; they wanted to keep their names secret, and argued that confidentiality had been promised to them when they gave up their children for adoption.[86] In the first year after the initiative took effect, 5,721 adult adoptees filed disclosure requests.[87]

A handful of other states changed their laws around the same time to allow adoption records to be unsealed, once children reach adulthood.[88] In many states, voluntary adoption registries are available, where contact information can be exchanged if the child wishes it, and a birth parent indicates an interest in being "found." In 2010, Illinois passed a law to allow adult adoptive children to obtain their original certificates unless their birth parents object. The law was to take effect in eighteen months, during which time the state will notify birth parents of the impending disclosure and ask whether they want their names blacked out when the original birth certificate is revealed.[89] Several foreign jurisdictions, including England, Scotland, and Australia, have moved to permit disclosure of adoption information.

Perhaps an even more significant result of the adoption rights movement has been the innovation of "open adoptions." These adoptions range from limited sharing of identifying information to an arrangement where the birth mother handpicks adoptive parents who agree that she may remain a presence in the child's life. Although hard data are not available, all reports suggest a clear trend toward open adoption as the most common arrangement.[90]

There has also been at least a limited parallel push for "open sperm donation."[91] Traditionally, sperm donation has been anonymous, and donors are not considered fathers in any legal sense of the word.[92] Women choosing sperm never see a photograph of the donor, nor learn his name, picking instead a numbered donor based on a list of characteristics. But some children conceived with donor sperm have fought the traditional model. One enterprising teenage boy managed to track down his biological father by cross-checking his own DNA against a genetic database available on the Internet, and using information from a genealogy service to narrow down the field to a single man with the right Y chromosome and the right birth date and birth place.[93] Mothers have also made use of private networks and information to discover their children's half-siblings. The Donor Sibling Registry has facilitated over seven thousand matches between donor-conceived half siblings or donors and their offspring.[94] The secrecy model is thus threatened not only by policy arguments, but by the very difficulty of keeping such secrets, in the modern information age. Several European countries have banned anonymous sperm donation or passed laws to permit donor-children to discover the identity of their donors upon reaching adulthood.[95] But these kinds of restrictions have consequences; the store of donated sperm has all but disappeared in England, which banned anonymous donations in 2005, leaving women with up to a two-year wait.[96]

Although tens of thousands of children are born every year as a result of gamete donation (eggs, sperm, or embryos), the practice is all but completely unregulated. Entities like the American Society for Reproductive Medicine suggest "best practices," but they are not binding on doctors. Some states do allow courts to order release of information surrounding gamete donations "for good cause shown," but information is not released very often.[97] In response to pressures for information, though, several of the leading cryobanks have begun to offer women a choice between anonymous and non-anonymous sperm.[98] The latter is pricier and offers fewer choices. But it provides a way for children to benefit from updated medical histories as their donor-fathers get older and may show signs of inheritable disease. It also fills the "emotional void" some donor-children, like children adopted under a secrecy model, may experience.[99] Advocates for more openness have proposed establishing the "National Gamete Donor Registry," which would preserve donor records, provide a mechanism for preventing accidental incest, and offer updated health information, without necessarily revealing the identity of the donor.[100] Other proposals would allow donor-conceived children to learn the identity of their donors once they reach adulthood, a right some states provide to adopted children.[101]

Many prospective parents still might prefer the old-style, secret adoption process. But because adoptable infants are scarce, birth mothers often have the upper hand. An episode of ABC's *20/20* with Barbara Walters featured a very pregnant sixteen-year-old girl choosing among five would-be adoptive couples.[102] The promotional spots for "Be My Baby," one of which promised the "ultimate reality show," provoked outrage, including public condemnation by Bastard Nation. This organization claimed the show "exploits, degrades and demeans adopted persons of all ages, portraying us as prizes for 'desperate couples' in the great adoption duck shoot."[103]

Open adoptions have advantages—and also disadvantages.[104] Open adoptions can mean significant contact with the birth mother (and maybe the father, too), or just the occasional exchange of pictures and letters. The law is moving to support open adoptions, since many birth parents prefer it.[105] As of 2009, twenty-four states had statutes that make agreements on the post-adoption relationship between birth parents and adoptive parents enforceable, at least in some circumstances.[106] Unlike other types of contracts, however, post-adoption contracts must generally be approved by the court, and are subject to a number of restrictions, concerning eligible parties, acceptable terms, and available remedies. In North Carolina, for example, while parties may enter into a "postadoption contact agreement," consent to the agreement cannot be a condition of the adoption and, in any event, it is not enforceable.[107]

ADOPTION TRENDS: A SNAPSHOT

The rate of adoptions skyrocketed after the Second World War. Three times as many petitions to adopt were filed in 1944 as in 1934.[108] The number doubled between 1951 and 1982.[109] More recent data, from 2001, reported that there were currently 1.4 million adopted minor children in the United States.[110] The number of adoptions per year seems to have peaked in 1970, with nearly 180,000, and then leveled off between 125,000 and 150,000 per year.

We should point out, however, that these figures on adoption are not foolproof because they are generally based on survey responses, rather than on legal records, or based on an amalgamation of data from different sources. Adoption proceedings are still typically sealed, so that it is hard to gather even basic data on the number of adoptions, much less about the criteria used in granting or denying petitions to adopt.[111] Informal adoptions are even more difficult to measure, but research suggests that they are more common, for example, among blacks and Hispanics than among whites or Asians.[112]

International adoptions have increased steadily in popularity since the 1950s. In recent times, most of these children come from Asia, South America, and Africa, in that order.[113] The vast majority of foreign infants come from China or Korea; among those from China, girls outnumber boys 20 to 1.[114] Most older adopted children come from Europe. There were around 22,000 international adoptions by U.S. couples in 2004. Celebrities like Angelina Jolie and Madonna have adopted internationally.

Torry Ann Hansen, a registered nurse from Tennessee, sparked an international controversy in 2010 when she placed the seven-year-old boy she had adopted from Russia on a plane, alone, bound for his homeland. She claimed he was "violent and has severe psychopathic issues" and that she was "lied to and misled by the Russian orphanage workers." On the plane, he carried a backpack filled with magic markers and snacks—and a note from Hansen explaining that "[a]fter giving my best to this child, I am sorry to say that for the safety of my family, friends and myself, I no longer wish to parent this child." Russian officials took custody of the boy, and the Russian government soon afterwards suspended adoption of Russian children by American families until "safeguards could be put in place."[115] This would cut off a major source for American parents; Russia ranked third in 2009, behind China and Ethiopia, and has sent more than 50,000 children to be adopted by American families since 1991. In 2005, Romania passed a new child welfare law that all but completely bans international adoptions. A partial ban had been instituted years earlier, but the new law left "many families without children they had counted as theirs" and "thousands of abandoned Romanian children stranded indefinitely in institutions or foster care."[116] In 2007, China imposed new restrictions on foreign adoptions, including a ban on adoptions by adults who are single, obese or older than fifty.[117]

Compared with children in general, adopted children are more likely to live in a two-parent household. In part, this reflects the legal and other obstacles that stand in the way of a single adult who wishes to adopt. Eighty-three percent of adopted children live with two parents—relatively evenly split between those living with two adoptive parents and those living with one adoptive and one biological parent. Thus, adoption continues to play a role in recreating families, as well as in a modern form of "child saving"; though more and more, the balance has tipped toward adoption as a response to infertility.[118]

ADOPTION AND THE FORMATION
OF GAY AND LESBIAN FAMILIES

We have discussed the ongoing battle over same-sex marriage; the legal issues raised by gay and lesbian parenting have followed a somewhat different path. The law, more or less, has developed a tolerant approach to same-sex parenting, often taking the view that two parents are better than one, whether or not those parents fit the image of a traditional family.

Recently, more same-sex couples have been openly raising children, whether the children came from one partner's prior heterosexual relationship or as part of "planned gay father" or "planned lesbian" families.[119] For lesbian couples, these families emerged in large numbers beginning in the 1980s, as artificial insemination became popular. There was a movement to promote "self-insemination"; women became pregnant using sperm from a donor friend (sometimes shipped on dry ice) and a turkey baster. The result was a genuine "lesbian baby boom."[120]

Today, doctors perform most inseminations, using anonymous sperm donors, although a number of recent cases and studies have shown that lesbians have far less access to fertility services than straight single or married women. A surprising number of medical providers explicitly discriminate against patients based on marital status or sexual orientation, and, in most states, this is legal. Most state laws do not reach these forms of discrimination. California's Unruh Act is unusual in its scope—ladies' day at the car wash is illegal in California—and has been interpreted to invalidate common restrictions imposed by fertility doctors.[121]

For gay male couples, the planned family has always been more difficult to achieve. Some gay men have made co-parenting arrangements with lesbian mothers; some "have become known sperm donors for lesbian mothers; while others have no genetic connection with children they co-parent."[122] Increasingly, today, gay men rely on surrogacy in order to have children.[123] But, as we saw, surrogacy contracts face a good deal of legal uncertainty. Gay men thus have tended to rely on adoption of unrelated children. Since the 1980s, as April Martin put it, "an entirely new family structure, unparalleled in human history" has emerged. Gay people "in large numbers are setting out consciously, deliberately, proudly, openly, to bear and adopt children."[124]

According to 2000 census data, nearly 600,000 American households are anchored by a same-sex couple, and nearly a quarter of them are raising children. Up to 9 million children in the United States have at least one gay parent. Many of these children were conceived within a heterosexual relationship or marriage.[125] Of adopted minor children, 65,500 are living with a gay or lesbian parent.[126] Still, in some states, there is doubt as to whether a single, gay person can legally adopt a child. Or whether a gay couple can jointly adopt a child. Or whether one partner in a gay couple may adopt the other partner's child.

A Florida statute bans all gays and lesbians from adopting children. The Florida law was enacted in 1977, a result of a nationwide campaign by anti-gay activist and former Miss America Anita Bryant, to roll back civil rights for gays and lesbians. The law provides, simply, that "No person eligible to adopt under this statute may adopt if that person is a homosexual."[127] The statute does not single out any other class of people; even felons can potentially adopt.

This law was, of course, challenged, in part based on *Lawrence v. Texas* (see chapter 5). In 2004, Steven Lofton, a registered male nurse, wanted to adopt a boy, born HIV-positive, who had been in his care since infancy. A federal appellate court upheld Florida's categorical ban on adoption by homosexuals, refusing to interpret *Lawrence*'s ban on sodomy laws, and the sexual rights of homosexuals, to give a gay man the right to adopt a child.[128] The U.S. Supreme Court declined to review the case. A trial court in Florida did, later, strike down the statute, observing that "[i]t is clear that sexual orientation is not a predictor of a person's ability to parent."[129] This ruling was affirmed on appeal in 2010, and the state's attorney general has declined to appeal to the state's highest court.[130] Thus the law, though still on the books, is effectively dead.

A few other states make clear their distaste for gay adoption, or make it quite difficult. Arkansas voters, by referendum, decided to prevent gays and lesbians from adopting children. The new law accomplishes this result indirectly: no individual who is "cohabiting with a sexual partner" outside of marriage can adopt or become a foster parent to a child.[131] Since same-sex marriage is not legal in Arkansas, gay and lesbian *couples* cannot adopt. Mississippi bans adoptions by same-sex couples, and Utah bans adoption by all unmarried couples.[132]

As of 2010, however, these laws are outliers. Quietly, gays and lesbians have been granted rights to adopt, alone and jointly, in more than half of the states. In 1993, the highest courts in Vermont and Massachusetts approved of adoptions that resulted in a child with two legally recognized mothers.[133] In *Adoption of Tammy* (1993), two successful doctors, Susan Love, a nationally known breast cancer surgeon, and Helen Cooksey, decided to have and raise a child. Helen had first tried to conceive a child using sperm donated by Susan's brother. After that failed, Susan became pregnant through artificial insemination, using sperm donated by Helen's cousin, thus enabling both women to have a genetic link to their daughter, Tammy. The donor surrendered his parental rights, so there was no legal father. By a 4–3 vote, the Massachusetts Supreme Judicial Court granted a joint petition for Helen and Susan to adopt Tammy. The local statute did not explicitly say that an unmarried couple (of any sex) could not adopt a child.[134] The court allowed the adoption, which was, the court felt, in the best interests of Tammy. Many witnesses, including psychologists, teachers, a priest, and a nun, testified that both women were involved as parents and had created a stable family unit. Both "mama" and "mommy" would be treated as Tammy's legal parents.[135]

Since 1993, four states have passed legislation to permit so-called second-parent adoption (adoption by a same-sex partner of a parent),[136] and appellate courts in seven others have issued rulings that allow such adoptions. In many other states, lower courts have allowed adoptions by unmarried, same-sex couples.[137] By the time the California Supreme Court gave the official green light to second-parent adoptions in 2003 in *Sharon S. v. Superior Court*, it was retrospectively validating more than 20,000 adoptions already approved by lower courts.[138] (And the popular children's book, *Heather Has Two Mommies*, by Leslea Newman, was already fourteen years old.) Many states also allow same-sex couples to adopt a child jointly, even though the child is biologically related to neither of them.[139]

Some states do not allow second-parent adoptions. In addition to the four states discussed above that directly or indirectly prohibit gay couples from adopting by statute, appellate courts in three additional states—Nebraska, Ohio, and Wisconsin—have ruled expressly that second-parent adoptions are not allowed, even if the adults are not same sex.[140] For a second adult to adopt a child, he or she must be married to one of the biological parents, and the other biological parent must be out of the picture. But the scales, legally speaking, are definitely tipping in favor of allowing gay and lesbian co-parents. Courts and legislatures have recognized that it is beneficial to treat functional co-parents as legal ones. These men and women will have ties and obligations to the child, even if the two "parents" break up. Recognizing the functional parent protects the child, who gets to keep emotional and financial support from a second parent. It also protects the second parent herself. She does not run the risk of exclusion from the child's life, if and when the adult relationship ends.

Intent to Parent: The Newest Frontier

Some courts have recognized the parental rights of same-sex partners even without the benefit of adoption. In a somewhat surprising set of decisions in 2005, the California Supreme Court held, in essence, that a lesbian woman who agrees, with her partner, to bring a child into the world, but is not the child's biological mother, has the same rights and obligations as other legal parents. These cases emphasized the importance of *intent* to parent in creating a parent-child relationship.

In *Elisa B. v. Superior Court* (2005), a woman named Emily was artificially inseminated with sperm from an anonymous donor and gave birth to twins.[141] (Her partner, Elisa, had become pregnant the same way, with sperm from the same donor, a few months earlier.) In every respect, Emily and Elisa became parents together. They had lived for several years as partners, had commingled their lives financially and in other ways, and, together, had decided to have children. They were present for each other's inseminations, prenatal medical appointments, and deliveries. Emily and Elisa each breast-fed all three children and they identified themselves, in many contexts, as co-parents. Emily stayed home with the children, one of whom has Down's syndrome, and Elisa fully supported the five-member family. The couple separated when the children were toddlers. Elisa eventually ceased providing financial support for Emily and the twins and, when sued for child support, insisted she was mother only to the child she had given birth to.

The California Supreme Court rejected Elisa's argument. A child could have two legal mothers. By openly receiving the twins into her home and holding them out as her "natural" children, Elisa gained the status of "presumed parent." She had "actively consented to, and participated in, the artificial insemination of her partner with the understanding that she and Emily would raise the children as co-parents, and since they did act as co-parents for a substantial period of time," she could not rebut that presumption.

In another case, K.M. donated eggs to her registered domestic partner, E.G., to use for in vitro fertilization.[142] One woman was the "egg mother"; the other was the "womb mother"; at the time of the egg donation, K.M. signed a standard form relinquishing any claim to any resulting offspring. Later, she petitioned to be a legal mother of the twins to whom E.G. had given birth. Whether both women intended to be legal parents of these twins is less clear than in *Elisa B.* K.M. claims that they planned to raise any children together, but E.G. says she always intended to be a "single parent" with a "supportive" partner. In fact, they raised the children together for five years, with intertwined lives, before splitting up.

In this case, the woman who asked for the legal status of a mother did have a biological connection to the twins: she was the egg donor. A man who merely donates sperm to a woman other than his wife is *not* the father of any resulting child; should that principle apply to K.M.?[143] The California Supreme Court upheld the rights of K.M. Since she supplied eggs to her lesbian partner "in order to produce children who would be raised in their joint home," rules about sperm donors were not to be used to block her status as a parent. It would be illogical, the court held, to apply the rules about sperm donors to a woman who intended to play a role in the children's lives. Both K.M. and E.G. were entitled to the status of parent.

Finally, in *Kristine H. v. Lisa R.* (2005), two women had filed a petition to affirm the parental rights of the "second mother," while one of them was pregnant.[144] This permitted both women to be listed on the child's birth certificate. But when the women separated two years later, Kristine, the biological mother, sought to vacate Lisa's parental status. The California court, however, held that she was "estopped" from changing her mind about Lisa's rights. Courts generally do not permit individuals to renounce parental status by agreement, because this can adversely affect the child. But the court held simply, here, that Kristine could not take inconsistent positions in the same matter, in court, simply because of the passage of time.

California is ahead of most states in willingness to adapt traditional rules of parentage to same-sex couples. As we saw in chapter 12, New York does permit second-parent adoptions for same-sex couples, but does not recognize functional parent-child ties in the absence of a formal decree. Adoption is therefore the most secure way to solidify the ties between same-sex co-parents and children. Even states that expressly prohibit same-sex couples from adopting jointly will give effect to an out-of-state adoption under principles of full faith and credit. Unlike same-sex marriage, adoption decrees are legal judgments, and thus entitled to the most exacting kind of deference by sister states.

An appellate court in Florida—the state most hostile to gay and lesbian parenting—recently honored a same-sex adoption from Washington State. Kimberly Ryan gave birth to a daughter; her partner Lara Embry adopted the child soon after birth. They eventually broke up and entered into a custody and visitation agreement. But the arrangement deteriorated; Ryan refused to allow Embry to have any contact with their daughter. Before they broke up, they had moved to Florida, so when Embry petitioned a Florida court for parental rights, Ryan pointed to the state's notorious statute against same-sex adoptions. But the court did not bite. It ruled that, regardless of the state's public policy, an adoption decree issued by another court was entitled to full effect in Florida.[145]

Same-sex couples have had more success in earning legal protection for parenting than in the right to marry. Courts—and the public—have always been biased in favor of tying parents to children. Same-sex parenting issues also arise by and large case by case; they do not require (or entice) the legislature to act. The states that ban same-sex marriage claim they want to promote the "optimal" environment for childrearing: a household anchored by a married, heterosexual couple. But the few studies of gay parenting tend to find little difference between children raised by homosexual rather than heterosexual parents.[146] The Iowa Supreme Court, in striking down the state's ban on same-sex marriage in 2009, dismissed the state's argument as "largely unsupported by reliable scientific studies"; the plaintiffs who sought the right to marry, on the other hand, had "presented an abundance of evidence and research" that "the interests of children are served equally by same-sex parents and opposite-sex parents."[147] As early as 1976, the American Psychological Association took the position that sexual orientation should not be the "sole or primary variable considered in custody or placement cases."[148] In 2005, it concluded that "there is no evidence to suggest that lesbian women or gay men are unfit to be parents" or that "psychosocial development" among the children of gay or lesbian parents is "compromised relative to that among offspring of heterosexual parents."[149]

In 2002, the American Academy of Pediatrics (AAP) came out in favor of gay adoption, at least where a homosexual individual has either given birth to or adopted a child and wants the partner to become a legal co-parent.[150] Studies demonstrate, according to the AAP, that children are "more influenced by the nature of the relationships and interactions within the family than by the particular structural form it takes." The AAP also argued that the legal recognition of co-parents benefits the children. Many of these benefits are economic in nature—inheritance rights, health insurance coverage, Social Security survivor benefits, and a right of child support from both parents in the event of a separation. But perhaps as important, legal recognition of a co-parent gives that co-parent the right to maintain the parent-child relationship whether or not the relationship between the parents survives. The American Bar Association also adopted a resolution of support for gay and lesbian adoption.[151]

Public opposition to same-sex parenting is not as severe as it is to same-sex marriage. But opposition is far from dead. After more than a century of doing adoptions, Catholic Charities of Boston announced in 2006 that it would cease its "founding mission" rather than comply with a Massachusetts law prohibiting discrimination against gays and lesbians because it views the placement of children in gay adoptive homes as "immoral."[152]

.   .   .   .   .

It is no surprise that adoption law has been unable to escape involvement in some of America's most intractable issues—issues of race, for example; and the squabbles over the role of gay and lesbian couples in family law (and family life). And adoption also reflects—no surprise here too—the major cultural trends in American life. Americans generally, in the age of expressive individualism, try desperately to fashion for themselves unique and satisfying selves; and discover, in a sense, who they really are. For adopted children, this can include a search for their "real" parents, and the discovery of their true genetic code. Men and women can decide to have children or not. Adopted children, uniquely, have in a way the right to decide to have parents or not, or more accurately, to decide which parents to cling to.

Into the Void

IN THIS BOOK, we have explored the complex and fascinating world of family law—which in turn reflects the complicated and fascinating world of the family. In the twentieth century, families and family law underwent massive changes; and this book has tried to describe these changes, and (as best we can) to explain them.

In some ways, these changes seem consistent with one another, seem to go in one direction, and to move steadily along one particular path. Traditional morality has suffered serious defeats. Living in sin is no longer a sin for most people. Illegitimacy has lost its bite. Sodomy laws are history. Tough divorce laws have given way to no-fault. Gay marriage seems to be just beyond the horizon. All of this, in hindsight, has the smell of the inevitable; of course, no legal change occurred without a battle, sometimes a bitter one. But there were winners and losers. The losers, the people who were against radical change, now seem old-fashioned, misinformed, or, even worse, troglodytes, bigots, rearguard warriors, or even King Canute commanding the waves. Of course these "losers" have a radically different view of the situation.

And, in fact, no changes were inevitable. And in no case was it absolutely clear at the time who would win and who would lose. Suppose, in 1900, you asked an intelligent American—preferably middle-class, white, and male—to make predictions about the future of family law. We doubt if anybody would have predicted no-fault divorce; or the collapse of restrictions on marriage, or gay rights. This was, after all, the age of eugenics and a kind of panic over reproductive rights. Tough restrictions on marriage, and on illicit sex, seemed like the right way to go—the progressive way, in fact. Our intelligent American might predict that as civilization advanced, such blemishes and throwbacks as prostitution, sodomy, and the like would gradually retreat. *Marvin v. Marvin*, the millions of people who cohabit, and gay marriage, would have been simply unthinkable.

If our American came back to life, he would be amazed, not only by computers and jet airplanes, but also by no-fault divorce, domestic partnerships, surrogate motherhood, and the validation of all sexual relations among consenting adults. We, however, have the benefit of hindsight. We know how the story unfolded; and how the various battles came out. The sexual revolution—cause and effect of the decline of traditional values—and a radical strength of forms of expressive individualism, have worked their spell on families and family law. The result has been, among other things, a vast expansion of the family "menu." There is no longer a single form of legitimate marriage, but a variety of forms. There are now myriad paths to legal parenthood. Social change and new technology have both played a role in reshaping what the family is—and what "family" means.

But we are as helpless in predicting the future as our poor creature of 1900 was, and perhaps as likely to be wrong, if we try. In truth, what we see ahead is nothing but a giant void, more mysterious and unknowable than the distant galaxies. Where is technology taking us? There is no way of knowing. In the future, will parents simply clone children from prototypes? Perhaps children will clone parents. Or not. Today we take the sexual revolution for granted; but some kind of cataclysm of consciousness, some new Great Awakening, may bring back indissoluble marriage and strict regulation of family life and sexuality. We *think* this is impossible, but only because we are prisoners of our own times and our own mind-sets. In fact, nothing is impossible.

So we will resist the temptation to step into the darkness of the future. We have tried to explain how we got to where we are, and why, and what the steps were along the way. It is an interesting, and important, story. But there is no ending. This book comes to an end; but the story does not. The story of life goes on, into the void. And so too of the story of the law.

* *NOTES* *.

Introduction

1. On the scope of "family law," see Jill Elaine Hasday, "The Canon of Family Law," 57 *Stan. L. Rev.* 825 (2004).

2. For a wonderful explication of this point, see Stephanie Coontz, *The Way We Never Were: American Families and the Nostalgia Trap* (2000).

3. See John H. Langbein, "The Twentieth-Century Revolution in Family Wealth Transmission," 86 *Mich. L. Rev.* 722 (1988).

4. Lawrence Stone, *The Past and Present Revisited* (2d ed. 1988), p. 338.

5. This term is coined in Robert Bellah et al., *Habits of the Heart: Individualism and Commitment in America* (1985); see also Lawrence M. Friedman, *The Horizontal Society* (1999), pp. 70–79.

6. 557 P.2d 106 (Cal. 1976).

7. 539 U.S. 558 (2003).

8. Andrew J. Cherlin, "The Deinstitutionalization of American Marriage," 66 *J. of Marriage & Fam.* 848 (2004), pp. 848–61; Andrew Cherlin, *The Marriage-Go-Round: Marriage and the State of the Family in America Today* (2009), pp. 87–115.

9. Herbert Jacob, *Silent Revolution: The Transformation of Divorce Law in the United States* (1988).

10. James Boswell, *The Life of Samuel Johnson, LL.D, Vol. 1* (1791), p. 295.

11. 391 U.S. 68 (1968).

12. See Brady E. Hamilton et al., "Births: Preliminary Data for 2008," 58 *Nat'l Vital Stats. Rep.* 16 (2010), p. 6, table 1.

13. Cherlin, *The Marriage-Go-Round*, pp. 16–17.

14. Mary Ann Glendon, *Abortion and Divorce in Western Law* (1987), p. 135.

Chapter One
Marriage and the State

1. Loving v. Virginia, 388 U.S. 1 (1967); *N.Y. Times*, May 5, 2008 (obituary).

2. Scott Anderson, "The Polygamists: An Exclusive Look Inside the FLDS," *National Geographic* (Feb. 2010), p. 45.

3. See Sarah Barringer Gordon, *The Mormon Question: Polygamy and Constitutional Conflict in Nineteenth Century America* (2002).

4. Anti-Polygamy Acts, ch. 126, 12 Stat. 501 (1862), repealed 1910. On the history of polygamy laws, see Martha M. Ertman, "Race Treason: The Untold Story of America's Ban on Polygamy," 19 *Colum. J. Gender & L.* 257 (2010).

5. Reynolds v. United States, 98 U.S. 145 (1878).

6. Utah Enabling Act, ch. 138, 28 Stat. 107 (1894); Utah Const., Art. III, sec. 1. See also Potter v. Murray City, 760 F.2d 1065 (10th Cir. 1985), p. 67; Jill Elaine Hasday, "Federalism and the Family Reconstructed," 45 *UCLA L. Rev.* 1297 (1998), p. 1364.

7. See Martha Sonntag Bradley, *Kidnapped from that Land: The Government Raids on the Short Creek Polygamists* (1993).

8. *Wash. Post*, Sept. 29, 1935, p. B9; Dec. 8, 1935, p. SA5.

9. See Michael Janofsky, "Mormon Leader Is Survived by 33 Sons and a Void," *N.Y. Times*, Sept. 15, 2002.

10. Anderson, "The Polygamists," pp. 34–61.

11. Ibid., pp. 34, 36.

12. See State v. Green, 99 P.3d 820 (Utah 2004), affirming Green's bigamy convictions; see also "A Utah Man with 5 Wives Is Convicted of Bigamy," *N.Y. Times*, May 20, 2001; Michael Janofsky, "Utahan Is Sentenced to 5 Years in Prison in Polygamy Case," *N.Y. Times*, Aug. 25, 2001.

13. See Ryan D. Tenney, "Tom Green, Common-Law Marriage, and the Illegality of Putative Polygamy," 17 *B.Y.U. J. Pub. L.* 141 (2002), pp. 142–44.

14. See Timothy Egan, "The Persistence of Polygamy," *N.Y. Times Mag.*, Feb. 28, 1999, p. 51.

15. Green's child-rape conviction was also affirmed by the Utah Supreme Court. State v. Green, 108 P.3d 710 (Utah 2005).

16. See "Utah: Polygamist Freed after 6 Years," *N.Y. Times*, Aug. 8, 2007.

17. James C. McKinley, Jr., "Difficulties for Prosecutors in Trial of Sect Leader," *N.Y. Times*, Nov. 4, 2009, p. A14; James C. McKinley, Jr., "Polygamist Sect Leader Convicted of Sexual Assault," *N.Y. Times*, Nov. 6, 2009, p. A19.

18. See Utah Code Ann. sec. 76-7-101 (2010); Colo. Rev. Stat. Ann. sec. 18-6-201 (2010). We discuss the validity of this and other sexual regulation laws in the wake of *Lawrence v. Texas*, 539 U.S. 558 (2003), in chapter 5.

19. See Joanna L. Grossman and Lawrence M. Friedman, "'Sister Wives': Will Reality Show Stars Face Prosecution for Polygamy in Utah?" *FindLaw's Writ*, Oct. 4, 2010, available at http://writ.news.findlaw.com/grossman/20101004.html (visited Nov. 1, 2010).

20. On the practice of polygamy in South Africa, see Tracy E. Higgins et al., "Gender Equality and Customary Marriage: Bargaining in

the Shadow of Post-Apartheid Legal Pluralism," 30 *Fordham Int'l L. J.* 1653 (2007).

21. Megan Friedman, "Kenyan Polygamist Dies, Leaving 100 Widows," Oct. 5, 2010, available at http://newsfeed.time.com/2010/10/05/kenyan-polygamist-dies-leaving-100-widows/?hpt=C2 (visited Nov. 1, 2010).

22. Anderson, "The Polygamists," p. 56.

23. McKinley, "Polygamist Sect Leader Convicted."

24. Jeffs' conviction was recently reversed and remanded for a new trial because of an erroneous jury instruction. See State v. Jeffs, 243 P.3d 1250 (Utah 2010).

25. On the much rarer practice of polyandry, see, for example, Lydia Polgreen, "One Bride for 2 Brothers: A Custom Fades in India," *N.Y. Times*, July 16, 2010, p. A4.

26. On miscegenation laws in general, see Peggy Pascoe, *What Comes Naturally: Miscegenation Law and the Making of Race in America* (2009); Randall Kennedy, *Interracial Intimacies: Sex, Marriage, Identity, and Adoption* (2003), pp. 214–80; Rachel F. Moran, *Interracial Intimacy: The Regulation of Race and Romance* (2001).

27. Edward Stein catalogues anti-miscegenation laws in "Past and Present Proposed Amendments to the United States Constitution Regarding Marriage," 82 *Wash. U.L.Q.* 611 (2004). A few states have never had bans on interracial marriage, including Connecticut, Illinois, and Wisconsin.

28. See Va. Code Ann. secs. 20-54, 1-14 (repealed 1968); see also Walter Wadlington, "The *Loving* Case: Virginia's Anti-Miscegenation Statute in Historical Perspective," 52 *Va. L. Rev.* 1189 (1966).

29. Neb. Rev. Stat. sec. 491 (1922).

30. Ore. Rev. Stat. sec. 1999 (1901); see also Dudley O. McGovney, "Naturalization of the Mixed-Blood. A Dictum," 22 *Cal. L. Rev.* 377 (1934), p. 390 n. 49. On the laws against white-Asian marriages in the late nineteenth and early twentieth centuries, see Deenesh Sohoni, "Unsuitable Suitors: Anti-Miscegenation Laws, Naturalization Laws, and the Construction of Asian Identities," 41 *Law & Soc'y Rev.* 587 (2007).

31. See 1933 Cal. Stat. 561, which added this particular ban to the state's marriage code.

32. On the danger of "amalgamation," see Dr. W. A. Plecker, State Registrar of Vital Statistics of Virginia, quoted in "Shall We All be Mulattoes?" *Literary Digest*, March 7, 1925, p. 23. On relations between masters and slaves, see, for example, Annette Gordon-Reed, *The Hemingses of Monticello: An American Family* (2008).

33. *N.Y. Times*, Dec. 12, 1912, p. 24.

34. Cong. Rec. Vol. XLIX, 62nd Cong., 3d Sess., Dec. 11, 1912, pp. 502, 504.

35. Ann Hagedorn, *Savage Peace: Hope and Fear in America, 1919* (2007), pp. 249–61.

36. Ibid., p. 438.

37. The case is discussed in Earl Lewis and Heidi Ardizzone, *Love on Trial: An American Scandal in Black and White* (2001); Angela Onwuachi-Willig, "A Beautiful Lie: Exploring *Rhinelander v. Rhinelander* as a Formative Lesson on Race, Identity, Marriage, and Family," 95 *Cal. L. Rev.* 2393 (2007). See also Bela August Walker, "Fractured Bonds: Policing Whiteness and Womanhood Through Race-Based Marriage Annulments," 58 *DePaul L. Rev.* 1 (2008).

38. 198 P.2d 17 (Cal. 1948).

39. Kennedy, *Interracial Intimacies*, p. 258.

40. See Warren Weaver, Jr., "Air Force Drops Marriage Query," *N.Y. Times*, July 3, 1963, p. 12; "Democrats Asked to Oppose Antimiscegenation Laws," *N.Y. Times*, Oct. 14, 1965, p. 30.

41. "Ban on Interracial Couples Assailed by Catholic Group," *N.Y. Times*, Nov. 24 1963, p. 16.

42. George Dugan, "Presbyterians Urged to Oppose Bans on Interracial Marriages," *N.Y. Times*, May 22, 1965, p. 20.

43. 379 U.S. 184 (1964).

44. *Loving*. See Phyl Newbeck, *Virginia Hasn't Always Been for Lovers: Interracial Marriage Bans and the Case of Richard and Mildred Loving* (2004).

45. David Margolick, "A Mixed Marriage's 25th Anniversary of Legality," *N.Y. Times*, June 12, 1992, p. B20. On the *Loving* case generally, see John DeWitt Gregory and Joanna Grossman, "The Legacy of *Loving*," 51 *How. L. J.* 15 (2007); see also Loving v. Virginia: *Rethinking Race, Sex and Marriage in a "Post-Racial" World* (Kevin Maillard and Rose Cuison Villazor, eds., forthcoming, 2011).

46. See "Virginia Ban Struck Down, Has an Interracial Wedding," *N.Y. Times*, Aug. 13, 1967, p. 31.

47. See "Negro and White Wed in Nashville," *N.Y. Times*, July 22, 1967, p. 11.

48. See Susie Parker, "Erasing a Remnant of Jim Crow South from Law Books," *Christian Sci. Monitor*, Mar. 23, 1999, p. 2.

49. See Somini Sengupta, "Removing a Relic of the Old South," *N.Y. Times*, Nov. 5, 2000, p. D5.

50. Newbeck, *Virginia Hasn't Always Been for Lovers*, pp. 206–13.

51. "Man's Halt of Interracial Marriage Sparks Outrage," *N.Y Times*, Oct. 16, 2009.

52. "Interracial Couple Denied Marriage License by Louisiana Justice of the Peace," *Huffington Post*, Oct. 15, 2009, http://www

.huffingtonpost.com/2009/10/15/interracial-couple-denied_n_322784 .html (visited Aug. 1, 2010).

53. Simeon Booker, "The Couple That Rocked the Courts," *Ebony*, Sept. 1967, p. 78.

54. See, for example, M. Annella, "Interracial Marriages in Washington D.C.," 36 *J. Negro Educ.* 428 (1967); David M. Herr, "Negro-White Marriages in the United States," 28 *J. Marriage & Fam. L.* 262 (1966) p. 273, finding a similar trend.

55. See Zhenchao Qian and Daniel T. Lichter, "Social Boundaries and Marital Assimilation: Interpreting Trends in Racial and Ethnic Intermarriage," 72 *Am. Soc. Rev.* 68 (2007).

56. See ibid., p. 69.

57. See ibid., p. 90.

58. See ibid.; see also Raymond Fisman et al., "Racial Preferences in Dating," 75 *Rev. Econ. Stud.* 117 (2008); Kevin Johnson, "The Legacy of. Jim Crow: The Enduring Taboo of Black-White Romance," 84 *Tex L. Rev.* 739 (2006).

59. Moran, *Interracial Intimacy*, p. 99.

60. See, for example, Williams v. North Carolina, 317 U.S. 287 (1942). Estin v. Estin, 334 U.S. 541 (1948). See Joanna L. Grossman, "Fear and Loathing in Massachusetts: Same-Sex Marriage and Some Lessons from the History of Marriage and Divorce," 14 *B.U. Pub. Int. L.J.* 87 (2004), on the history of interstate conflict over marriage and divorce.

61. See, in general, Joanna L. Grossman, "Resurrecting Comity: Revisiting the Problem of Non-Uniform Marriage Laws," 84 *Or. L. Rev.* 433 (2005).

62. 125 U.S. 190 (1888), p. 205.

63. See Jill Hasday, "The Canon of Family Law," 57 *Stan. L. Rev.* 825 (2004), p. 831.

64. *Loving*, p. 8.

65. Ibid.

66. Ibid., p. 11, citing Korematsu v. United States, 323 U.S. 214 (1944), p. 216.

67. Ibid., pp. 11–12.

68. 316 U.S. 535 (1942). *Skinner* is discussed in greater detail in chapter 5.

69. *Loving*, p. 12.

70. 434 U.S. 374 (1978).

71. See, for example, Roe v. Wade, 410 U.S. 113 (1973), on the right to seek an abortion; Moore v. City of E. Cleveland, 431 U.S. 494 (1977), on the right to live with non-nuclear family members; Eisenstadt v. Baird, 405 U.S. 438 (1972), on the right of single people to obtain contraceptives.

72. *Zablocki*, pp. 383, 386. On the scope of the "right to marry," see Cass R. Sunstein, "The Right to Marry," 26 *Cardozo L. Rev.* 2081 (2005), p. 2087.

73. See also Mark Strasser, "*Loving* in the New Millennium: On Equal Protection and the Right to Marry," 7 *U. Chi. L. Sch. Roundtable* 61 (2000).

74. 482 U.S. 78 (1987).

75. Ibid., p. 82.

76. Ibid., p. 95.

77. See, in general, Michael Grossberg, "Guarding the Altar: Physiological Restrictions and the Rise of State Intervention in Matrimony," 26 *Am. J. Leg. Hist.* 197 (1982), pp. 217–24.

78. Chester G. Vernier, *American Family Laws*, Vol. I (1931), p. 189.

79. Ibid., p. 197. We discuss annulment law in chapter 8.

80. 1909 Wash. Sess. Laws, ch. 174.

81. 61 A. 604 (Conn. 1905).

82. See, for example, Wis. Stat. Ann. sec. 765.035 (2010), validating marriages "to which either party was an epileptic person." See also Frank A. Morland, *Keezer on the Law of Marriage and Divorce* (3d ed. 1946), pp. 200–201.

83. Note, "Pre-Marital Tests for Venereal Disease," 53 *Harv. L. Rev.* 309 (1939).

84. "Bennett's Trials with 'Damaged Goods,'" *Chic. Daily Trib.*, Sep. 28, 1913, p. B4. The English version can be found in *Three Plays by Brieux* (1907), with a preface by George Bernard Shaw.

85. "Syphilis and Marriage," *Chic. Defender*, May 18, 1918, p. 16.

86. 147 N.W. 966 (Wis. 1914).

87. The court had to deal with a number of other issues. The plaintiffs claimed that the statute was totally unreasonable; it allowed a fee of $3 for the clinical tests, and this was grossly inadequate, at least with regard to the Wassermann test for syphilis. The court, however, construed the statute not to require this particular test, but only "tests recognized and used" by ordinary doctors.

88. Ohio Rev. Code sec. 3101.5 (1972).

89. Miss. Code Ann. sec. 93-1-5(e) (2010).

90. Idaho Code Ann. sec. 32-412A (2010); see also Georgia Code Ann. sec. 19-3-35.1 (2010).

91. See Isabel Wilkerson, "Illinoisans Fault Prenuptial AIDS Tests," *N.Y. Times*, Apr. 16, 1988, p. 6.

92. Michael Closen et al., "Mandatory Premarital HIV Testing: Political Exploitation of the AIDS Epidemic," 69 *Tul. L. Rev.* 71 (1994), pp. 98–99.

93. See Margaret Brinig and Steven L. Nock, "Marry Me, Bill: Should Cohabitation be the (Legal) Default Option?" 64 *La. L. Rev.* 403 (2004), p. 442 n. 76.

94. Pa. Cons. Stat. Ann. secs. 23-1304 and 1305 contained the requirement until abolition. See Okla. Laws 2004, c. 333, sec. 3, which repealed 43 Okla. St. sec. 31; D.C. Law 15-154 (2003).

95. Ohio Rev. Code Ann. sec. 3101.08 (2010).

96. N.Y. Dom. Rel. sec. 11 (2010). Information about the Society can be found at http://www.nysec.org (visited Aug. 1, 2010).

97. See, for example, R.I. Gen. Laws sec. 15-3-6 (2010), which recognizes marriages solemnized "among the people called Quakers, or Friends, in the manner and form used or practiced in their societies, or among persons professing the Jewish religion, according to their rites and ceremonies, or by a local spiritual assembly of the Baha'is according to the usage of the religious community."

98. See www.ulc.net (visited Aug. 1, 2010).

99. Miss. Code Ann. sec. 93-1-17 (2010).

100. *In re* Will of Blackwell, 531 So. 2d 1193 (Miss. 1988); see also *In re* O'Neill, 2008 Pa. Dist. & Cty. Dec. LEXIS 135 (2008), validating a ULC marriage under Pennsylvania law.

101. See Rubino v. City of New York, 480 N.Y.S.2d 971 (1984); Ravenal v. Ravenal, 338 N.Y.S.2d 324 (1972); Cramer v. Commonwealth, 202 S.E.2d 911 (Va. 1974). Virginia's marriage law requires a minister to show "proof of ordination and of his being in regular communion with the religious society of which he is a reputed member." Va. Code Ann. secs. 20–23 (2010).

102. State v. Lynch, 272 S.E.2d 349 (N.C. 1980).

103. See N.C. Gen. Stat. sec. 51-1.1 (adopted 1981).

104. ULC v. Utah, 189 F. Supp. 2d 1302 (D. Utah 2002).

105. Wis. Stat. sec. 765.03(2) (2010).

106. Neb. Rev. Stat. secs. 1490, 1493 (1922).

107. N.M. Stat. Ann. sec. 3431 (1915).

108. S.C. Code secs. 20-24 (1962). For a chart of state statutes on marriage rules respecting age, see Morland, *Keezer on the Law of Marriage and Divorce*, pp. 210–11.

109. See, for example, Moe v. Dinkins, 669 F.2d 67 (2d Cir. 1982).

110. Without an applicable statute, courts rely on the common-law age minimums of twelve for girls and fourteen for boys.

111. The marriage law did not specify any minimum age for marriage before 2006, but courts had enforced the common-law ages.

112. Jodi Wilgoren, "Rape Charge Follows Marriage to a 14-year-old," *N.Y. Times*, Aug. 30, 2005.

113. See Colleen Kenney, "Koso Set to Come Home from Prison," *Lincoln Journal Star*, May 5, 2007, p. A1.

114. Kan. Stat. Ann. sec. 23-106 (2010), amended 2006.

115. See, for example, Fla. Stat. sec. 741.0405 (2010), which gives judges the discretion to allow a female of any age to marry if she has

a child or is pregnant. For a useful summary, see Legal Information Institute, *Marriage Laws of the Fifty States, District of Columbia and Puerto Rico*, available at http://topics.law.cornell.edu/wex/table_marriage (visited Aug. 1, 2010).

116. See Miss. Code 93-1-5 (2010), which permits boys to marry at seventeen and girls at fifteen without parental consent. For parties under age twenty-one, however, the code requires a three-day delay between application for and issuance of a marriage license, during which time the county clerk must send a copy of the application to the parents.

117. Margaret Mead, *Anomalies in American Post-Divorce Relationships* (1970).

118. Claude Levi-Strauss, *The Elementary Structures of Kinship* (Rodney Needham, ed., 1969), p. 479.

119. Vernier, *American Family Laws*, Vol. 1, pp. 178–82.

120. For a list of state laws regarding first-cousin marriages, see National Conference of State Legislatures, State Laws Regarding Marriage Between First Cousins, http://www.ncsl.org/default.aspx?tabid=4266 (visited Aug. 1, 2010).

121. Utah Code Ann. sec. 30-1-1(2) (2010).

122. On cousin marriage in the Muslim world, see Nikki Keddie and Lois Beck, *Introduction to Women in the Muslim World* (1978), pp. 27–28.

123. See Denise Grady, "Few Risks Seen to the Children of 1st Cousins," *N.Y. Times*, Apr. 4, 2002, p. A1; Robin L. Bennet et al., "Genetic Counseling and Screening of Consanguineous Couples and Their Offspring: Recommendations of the National Society of Genetic Counselors," 11 *J. Genetic Counseling* 97 (2002).

124. Israel v. Allen, 577 P.2d 762 (Colo. 1978).

125. See http://www.weekirk.com/ (visited Aug. 1, 2010).

126. See http://www.shalimarweddingchapel.com/gc.html (visited Aug. 1, 2009).

127. Marnie Hunter, "Hit the Road to Cut Wedding Stress," CNN. com, May 5, 2006, http://www.cnn.com/2006/TRAVEL/ADVISOR /05/05/destination.weddings/index.html (visited Aug. 1, 2010).

128. "Popping the Question has Popped in Price," Brides.com, Feb. 23, 2009, http://press.brides.com/Bridescom/PressReleases/Article2073 .htm (visited Aug. 1, 2010).

129. See Mary E. Richmond and Fred S. Hall, *Marriage and the State* (1929), p. 202.

130. See "Report of the Committee on Marriage and Divorce," in *Proceedings of the Seventeenth Annual Conference of Commissioners on Uniform State Laws* (1907), p. 122.

131. The Commissioners' notes to the age provision report that, at the time, thirty states had raised the requisite age above the common-law

minimums. See Unif. Marriage and Marriage License Act sec. 5, 9 U.L.A. 257 (1911).

132. See, for example, An Act Providing for Return of Marriage Statistics (1907); Marriage License Application Act (1950); Unif. Marital Property Act (1983); Unif. Premarital Agreement Act (1983).

133. See Stein, "Past and Present Proposed Amendments to the United States Constitution Regarding Marriage," pp. 15–21.

134. See, for example, Estate of May, 114 N.E.2d 4 (N.Y. 1953), discussed below. In *Zwerling v. Zwerling*, 244 S.E.2d 311 (1978), a woman got a Mexican divorce, and then married Zwerling in New York. Later they moved to South Carolina, which would not have recognized the Mexican divorce—and thus not have viewed the woman as eligible to remarry. But because the marriage was valid in New York, it was recognized in South Carolina.

135. Pennegar v. State, 10 S.W.2d 305 (Tenn. 1888); Morland, *Keezer on the Law of Marriage and Divorce*, pp. 20–21.

136. See P. H. Vartanian, "Recognition of Foreign Marriage as Affected by Local Miscegenation Law," 3 *A.L.R.* 2d 240 (1949), p. 242; see also Andrew Koppelman, "Same-Sex Marriage, Choice of Law, and Public Policy," 76 *Tex. L. Rev.* 921 (1998), 952–54.

137. See Vartanian, "Recognition of Foreign Marriage as Affected by Local Miscegenation Law," p. 240; Koppelman, "Same-Sex Marriage, Choice of Law, and Public Policy," pp. 954–62.

138. Burns Ind. Ann. Stat. sec. 9877 (1926).

139. Unif. Marriage Evasion Act, sec. 1, in *Proceedings of the Twenty-Second Annual Conference of Commissioners on Uniform State Laws* 127 (1912). Other states adopted statutes that dealt in other ways with evasive marriage, too. See, in general, Koppelman, "Same-Sex Marriage, Choice of Law, and Public Policy," p. 923 n.2; see, for example, Morland, *Keezer on the Law of Marriage and Divorce*, pp. 20–21.

140. 114 N.E.2d 4 (N.Y. 1953).

141. R.I. Gen. Laws sec. 36-415-4 (1938). On recognition of incestuous marriages generally, see Deborah M. Henson, "Will Same-Sex Marriages Be Recognized in Sister States?: Full Faith and Credit and Due Process Limitations on States' Choice of Law Regarding the Status and Incidents of Homosexual Marriages Following Hawaii's *Baehr v. Lewin*," 32 *U. Louisville J. Fam. L.* 551 (1994), pp. 567–71.

142. See, for example, Mason v. Mason, 775 N.E.2d 706 (Ct. App. Ind. 2002); *In re* Estate of Loughmiller, 629 P.2d 156 (Kan. 1981). Although the modern trend is towards recognition, some older cases refused recognition to cousin-marriages. See, for example, Arado v. Arado, 117 N.E. 816 (Ill. 1917).

143. See Miller v. Lucks, 36 So. 2d 140, 142 (Miss. 1948); see also *In re* Lenherr's Estate, 314 A.2d 255 (Pa. 1974), permitting a wife who married in another state to avoid a law restricting remarriage to claim a marital exemption from an inheritance tax when her husband died. For a discussion of cases recognizing marriages for limited purposes, see Herma Hill Kay, "Same-Sex Divorce in the Conflict of Laws," 15 *King's C. L. J.* 63 (2004).

144. See Legal Information Institute, *Marriage Laws of the Fifty States, District of Columbia and Puerto Rico*, available at http://topics.law.cornell.edu/wex/table_marriage (visited Aug. 1, 2010); Guide to Legal Impediments to Marriage for 57 Registration Jurisdictions (July 30, 2004), http://www.mass.gov/dph/bhsre/rvr/impediments1%20.pdf (visited Aug. 1, 2010).

CHAPTER TWO
MARRIAGE, LAW, AND SOCIETY: A TANGLED WEB

1. Jeff Strickler, "To have and to hold ... for 83 years and Counting," *Star Trib.*, Feb. 18, 2008.

2. Mike Celizic, "Couple, Married 83 Years, Share Their Secret," TODAYShow.com, Mar. 17, 2008, http://today.msnbc.msn.com/id/23671580/ (visited Aug. 1, 2010). Once Clarence died later that year, they lost the record for "longest living marriage." The record for the longest marriage *ever* is held by a Taiwanese couple, who were married for eighty-five years.

3. Leslie Bennetts, "It's a Mad, Mad Zsa Zsa World," VanityFair.com, Oct. 2007, http://www.vanityfair.com/fame/features/2007/10/zsazsa200710 (visited Aug. 1, 2010).

4. On divorce rates, see, for example, Matthew D. Bramlett and William D. Mosher, "First Marriage Dissolution, Divorce, and Remarriage: United States," 323 *Advance Data* (May 31, 2001). On ages at first marriage and median length of marriages that end in divorce, see Rose M. Kreider, U.S. Census Bureau, Current Population Reports, *Number, Timing, and Duration of Marriages and Divorces: 2001* (Feb. 2005), http://www.census.gov/prod/2005pubs/p70-97.pdf (visited Aug. 1, 2010); Paula Goodwin et al., "Who Marries and When? Age at First Marriage in the United States: 2002," 19 *NCHS Data Brief* (June 2009), http://www.cdc.gov/nchs/data/databriefs/db19.pdf (visited Aug. 1, 2010). On birth rates, see Brady E. Hamilton et al., "Births: Preliminary Data for 2007," 57 *Nat'l Vital Stats. Rep.* 1 (Mar. 2009), http://www.cdc.gov/nchs/data/nvsr/nvsr57/nvsr57_12.pdf (visited Aug. 1, 2010).

5. On general marriage trends in the twentieth century, see Andrew J. Cherlin, *Marriage, Divorce, Remarriage* (1992); Stephanie Coontz, *The Way We Never Were: American Families and the Nostalgia Trap* (1992); Stephanie Coontz, *Marriage, A History: How Love Conquered Marriage* (2006).

6. See U.S. Census Bureau, Current Population Survey, March and Annual Social and Economic Supplements, Table MS-2: Estimated Median Age at First Marriage, by Sex: 1890 to the Present, available at http://www.census.gov/population/www/socdemo/hh-fam.html#ht (visited Aug. 1, 2010).

7. On the delay in marriage, see, for example, *State of the Union: America in the 1990s*, vol. 2 (Reynolds Farley, ed., 1995), pp. 6–8.

8. Patricia Cohen, "Long Road to Adulthood Is Growing Even Longer," *N.Y. Times*, June 11, 2010, p. A1. A volume released by Princeton University and the Brookings Institution explores the factors contributing to delayed adulthood and the consequences of this demographic change. See "Transition to Adulthood," 20 *The Future of Children* 3 (Spring 2010). Frank Furstenberg examines the effects of this long transition on families in "On a New Schedule: Transitions to Adulthood and Family Change," 20 *The Future of Children* 67 (Spring 2010).

9. See Arthur J. Norton and Louisa F. Miller, U.S. Census Bureau, Current Population Reports, *Marriage, Divorce, and Remarriage in the 1990s*, P23-180, Figs. 1 and 2, p. 2.

10. Daniel T. Lichter and Zhenchao Qian, Census 2000, *Marriage and Family in a Multiracial Society* (2004), p. 5.

11. Norton and Miller, *Marriage, Divorce, and Remarriage in the 1990s*, p. 3, table B.

12. See Lichter and Qian, *Marriage and Family in a Multiracial Society*, p. 5.

13. See, for example, Lawrence M. Friedman, "A Dead Language: Divorce Law and Practice Before No-Fault," 86 *Va. L. Rev.* 1497 (2000), pp. 1502–03.

14. See T. Castro Martin and Larry L. Bumpass, "Recent Trends and Differentials in Marital Disruption," 26 *Demography* 37 (1989).

15. For a description and explication of divorce rates, see Ira Mark Ellman, "The Misguided Movement to Revive Fault Divorce, and Why Reformers Should Look Instead to the American Law Institute," 11 *Int'l J.L. Pol'y & Fam.* 216 (1997).

16. Norton and Miller, *Marriage, Divorce, and Remarriage in the 1990s*, p. 6.

17. See Naomi Cahn and June Carbone, *Red Families v. Blue Families: Legal Polarization and the Creation of Culture* (2010), on regional variations in family structure.

18. This calculator is available at http://www.divorce360.com /content/divorcecalcresults.aspx (visited Aug. 1, 2010).

19. Norton and Miller, *Marriage, Divorce, and Remarriage in the 1990s*, p. 5.

20. These and other data points are compiled in National Healthy Marriage Resource Center, *Remarriage Trends in the United States*, available at www.healthymarriageinfo.org (visited Aug. 1, 2010).

21. Ibid., p. 1.

22. Miller, *Marriage, Divorce, and Remarriage in the 1990s*, p. 6.

23. Andrew Cherlin, *The Marriage-Go-Round: The State of Marriage and the Family in America Today* (2009), p. 15.

24. Pew Research Center, *The Decline of Marriage and the Rise of New Families* (2010), p. 1.

25. Interview with Tera Hunter, Princeton University, Department of History, "Slave Marriages, Families Were Often Shattered by Auction Block," NPR, Feb. 11, 2010; see also *The African American Urban Experience: Perspectives from the Colonial Period to the Present* (Joe W. Trotter et al., eds., 2004).

26. Ibid.

27. *The Decline in Marriage Among African Americans: Causes, Consequences, and Policy Implications* (M. Belinda Tucker and Claudia Mitchell-Kernan, eds., 1995), p. xvii.

28. See, for example, Lichter and Qian, *Marriage and Family in a Multiracial Society*, p. 11 table 1; see also R. S. Oropesa and Nancy S. Landale, "The Future Marriage and Hispanics," 66 *J. Marriage & Fam.* 901 (Nov. 2004).

29. See, for example, U.S. Dept. of Labor, *The Negro Family: The Case for National Action* (1965), a report authored by Daniel Patrick Moynihan; see also William Julius Wilson, *The Truly Disadvantaged* (1987); Charles Murray, *Losing Ground* (1984); see also *The Urban Underclass* (Christopher Jencks and Paul E. Peterson, eds., 1991).

30. Racial variations in marriage and divorce have been reported and analyzed extensively. See, for example, Andrew J. Cherlin, "Marriage and Marital Dissolution Among Black Americans," 29 *J. Comp. Fam. Stud.* 147 (2003); Robert Joseph Taylor et al., "Recent Demographic Trends in African American Family Structure," in *Family Life in Black America* (Robert Joseph Taylor et al., eds., 1997), pp. 14, 47–51; Lichter and Qian, *Marriage and Family in a Multiracial Society*, pp. 8–18; Robert D. Mare and Christopher Winship, "Socioeconomic Change and the Decline of Marriage for Blacks and Whites," in *The Urban Underclass* (Jencks and Peterson, eds.), p. 175; R. S. Oropesa and Bridget K. Gorman, "Ethnicity, Immigration, and Beliefs about Marriage as a 'Tie That Binds'," in *The Ties That Bind: Perspectives on Marriage and Cohabitation*

(Linda J. Waite, ed., 2000), p. 188. See also Ralph Richard Banks, *Is Marriage for White People?: How the African American Marriage Decline Affects Everyone* (2011).

31. See Kristen Harknett and Sara S. McLanahan, "Racial and Ethnic Differences in Marriage After the Birth of a Child," 69 *Am. Soc. Rev.* 790 (Dec. 2004). Other results are available through the study's website at http://www.fragilefamilies.princeton.edu (visited Aug. 1, 2010).

32. James A. Sweet and Larry L. Bumpass, *American Families and Households* (1987), p. 57.

33. Ibid., p. 66 table 3.4 and p. 68 table 3.5.

34. Lichter and Qian, *Marriage and Family in a Multiracial Society*, p. 11 table 1.

35. U.S. Census Bureau, Current Population Survey, *2009 Annual Social and Economic Supplement* (2010), table A1.

36. See, for example, Sharon Sassler and Robert Schoen, "The Effect of Attitudes and Economic Activity on Marriage," 61 *J. Marriage & Fam.* 147 (1999), pp. 152, 157.

37. Robert Schoen, "The Widening Gap Between Black and White Marriages Rates: Context and Implications," in *The Decline in Marriage Among African Americans: Causes, Consequences, and Policy Implications* (Tucker and Mitchell-Kernan, eds.), p. 103; Lichter and Qian, *Marriage and Family in a Multiracial Society*, p. 26, Box 5; Harknett and McLanahan, "Racial and Ethnic Differences in Marriage After the Birth of a Child," discussing marriage markets for African American women.

38. See R. Richard Banks and Su Jin Gatlin, "African American Intimacy: The Racial Gap in Marriage," 11 *Mich. J. Race & L.* 115 (2005), pp. 129–32.

39. Sam Roberts, "Black Women See Fewer Black Men at the Altar," *N.Y. Times*, June 3, 2010, p. A12.

40. See Neil G. Bennett et al., "The Divergence of Black and White Marriage Patterns," 95 *Am. J. Soc.* 692 (1989), pp. 700–701; Cherlin, "Marriage and Marital Dissolution Among Black Americans," p. 150.

41. See, for example, Harknett and McLanahan, "Racial and Ethnic Differences in Marriage After the Birth of a Child"; Wilson, *The Truly Disadvantaged*; Mare and Winship, "Socioeconomic Change and the Decline of Marriage for Blacks and Whites"; Bennett et al., "The Divergence of Black and White Marriage Patterns," pp. 705–8. Richard A. Bulcroft and Kris A. Bulcroft, "Race Differences in Attitudinal and Motivational Factors in the Decision to Marry," 55 *J. Marriage & Fam.* 338 (1993), p. 352, concludes that one reason for the decline in marriage among blacks is "a lack of available black males who can meet black women's high expectations for male family headship (i.e., greater resources)."

42. Cherlin, "Marriage and Marital Dissolution Among Black Americans," p. 150.

43. See Bennett et al., "The Divergence of Black and White Marriage Patterns," pp. 711–14.

44. Pew Research Center, *The Decline of Marriage and the Rise of New Families*, pp. 2–3.

45. See Cherlin, *The Marriage-Go-Round*, pp. 63–86. On the evolution of marriage, see Coontz, *Marriage, A History*.

46. Coontz, *The Way We Never Were*, pp. 11–12.

47. Ibid., p. 68.

48. William L. O'Neill, *Divorce in the Progressive Era* (1967), pp. 17–18.

49. On the pressure of greater marital expectations, see Robert L. Griswold, *Family and Divorce in California, 1850–1890* (1982); Elaine Tyler May, *Great Expectations: Marriage and Divorce in Post-Victorian America* (1980), p. 4.

50. On the impact of this type of individualism on marriage, see Cherlin, *The Marriage-Go-Round*, pp. 29–30, 90–96.

51. Cherlin, *The Marriage-Go-Round*, p. 88. Cherlin calls this new phase "individualized" marriage.

52. Stephanie Coontz, "Too Close for Comfort," *N.Y. Times*, Nov. 7, 2006, p. A21.

53. We are indebted to Andrew Shupanitz for help with some of the research in this section.

54. William Blackstone's *Commentaries on the Law* (1765–1769); see also James Kent, *Commentaries on American Law* (1826); Tapping Reeve, *The Law of Baron and Femme* (1816).

55. Kent, *Commentaries*, Vol. II (2d ed. 1832), p. 106.

56. See, for example, Forbush v. Wallace, 341 F. Supp. 217 (1971), which upheld an unwritten Alabama policy that prohibited married women from obtaining a driver's license under their maiden names. The ruling was affirmed without opinion by the U.S. Supreme Court. 405 U.S. 970 (1972). On the history of marital naming laws and practices, see, in general, Suzanne A. Kim, "Marital Naming/Naming Marriage: Language and Status in Family Law," 85 *Ind. L.J.* 893 (2010); Elizabeth F. Emens, "Changing Name Changing: Framing Rules and the Future of Marital Names," 74 *U. Chi. L. Rev.* 761 (2007).

57. Bradwell v. Illinois, 83 U.S. 130 (1872) (Bradley, J., concurring), p. 139.

58. These devices are discussed in Hendrik Hartog, *Man and Wife in America: A History* (2000); Joanna L. Grossman, "Separated Spouses," 53 *Stan. L. Rev.* 1613 (2001), pp. 1627–29; Norma Basch, "Relief in the Premises: Divorce as a Woman's Remedy in New York and Indiana, 1815–1870," 8 *Law & Hist. Rev.* 1 (1990), p. 9; Marylynn Salmon, *Women and the Law of Property in Early America* (1986), p. 116.

59. On these acts generally, see Richard Chused, "Married Women's Property Law, 1800–1859," 71 *Geo. L. J.* 1359 (1983); Joan Hoff, *Law,*

Gender and Injustice: A Legal History of U.S. Women (1991), pp. 377–82, which lists the date of adoption for each married women's property act and the specific rights it granted.

60. Lawrence M. Friedman, *A History of American Law* (3d ed. 2005), p. 147.

61. Ind. Code Ann. sec. 2866 (1929).

62. Cal. Penal Code sec. 270a (1907).

63. Cal. Penal Code sec. 270a (2010, as amended in 1976).

64. 299 N.W.2d 219 (Wis. 1980).

65. 33 F. Supp. 936 (E.D. Mich. 1940).

66. Ibid., p. 938.

67. Favrot v. Barnes, 332 So. 2d 873 (La. App. 1976).

68. The rule in *Graham* was also followed by the American Law Institute's *First Restatement of Contracts* (1923), which gave the example of a married couple's agreement "to forego sexual intercourse" as an obviously "illegal" bargain.

69. 59 N.W.2d 336 (Neb. 1953).

70. Ibid., p. 342.

71. See, for example, *In re* Marriage of Mathiasen, 219 Cal. App. 3d 1428 (1990), where the court refused to enforce an agreement regulating financial support during marriage; see also James Herbie DiFonzo, "Customized Marriage," 75 *Ind. L.J.* 875 (2000), p. 935, noting that "[c]ourts have to date only infrequently considered—and generally declined to enforce—prenuptial agreements regulating the parties' behavior during marriage "; Judith T. Younger, "Perspectives on Antenuptial Agreements: An Update," 8 *J. Am. Acad. Matrimonial L.* 1 (1992), p. 8.

72. See Rodney Thrash, "So it Wasn't Love, Actually," *St. Petersburg Times,* Jan. 17, 2006.

73. Lee E. Teitelbaum, "Family History and Family Law," 1985 *Wis. L. Rev.* 1135 (1985), pp. 1144–47. But see Mary Ann Glendon, "Power and Authority in the Family: New Legal Patterns as Reflections of Changing Ideologies," 23 *Am. J. Comp. L.* 1 (1975), p. 9.

74. 9B U.L.A. 373 (1983). The list of states that have adopted or are considering adoption of the UPAA is available at http://nccusl.org (visited Aug. 1, 2010). We discuss the law regarding prenuptial agreements further in chapter 9.

75. Laura P. Graham, "The Uniform Premarital Agreement Act and Modern Social Policy: The Enforceability of Premarital Agreements Regulating the Ongoing Marriage," 28 *Wake Forest L. Rev.* 1037 (1993), p. 1043. See also DiFonzo, "Customized Marriage," p. 935.

76. Martha L. Fineman, "Implementing Equality: Ideology, Contradiction and Social Change. A Study of Rhetoric and Results in the Regulation of the Consequences of Divorce," 1983 *Wis. L. Rev.* 789 (1983), p. 796; see also DiFonzo, "Customized Marriage"; Mary Ann Glendon,

The New Family and the New Property (1981), p. 107; Michael Grossberg, "Guarding the Altar: Physiological Restrictions and the Rise of State Intervention in Matrimony," 26 *Am. J. Legal Hist.* (1982), p. 197.

77. Hartog, *Man and Wife in America*, pp. 95–96.

78. On this point, see, in general, Naomi Cahn, "Looking at Marriage," 98 *Mich. L. Rev.* 1766 (2000), p. 1770; Jana B. Singer, "The Privatization of Family Law," 1992 *Wis. L. Rev.* 1443 (1992), p. 1444; Teitelbaum, "Family History and Family Law," p. 1137.

79. 218 U.S. 611 (1910); see also Nancy Cott, *Public Vows: A History of Marriage and the Nation* (2000), pp. 161–62.

80. Aldrich v. Tracy, 269 N.W. 30 (Iowa 1936).

81. William L. Prosser, *Handbook of the Law of Torts* (1941), pp. 901–4.

82. 618 So. 2d 1360 (Fla. 1993).

83. Beatie v. Beatie, 630 A.2d 1096 (Del. 1993).

84. See, for example, Hill v. Hill, 415 So. 2d 20 (Fla. 1982), which reaffirmed the traditional doctrine to "protect the family unit" from "any intrusion that adversely affects the family relationship or the family resources." On the interspousal tort immunity then and now, see William E. McCurdy, "Torts Between Persons in Domestic Relation," 43 *Harv. L. Rev.* 1030 (1930); Carl Tobias, "Interspousal Tort Immunity in America," 23 *Ga. L. Rev.* 359 (1989).

85. 34 Stat. 1228 sec. 3 (act of March 2, 1907).

86. Nancy Cott, "Marriage and Women's Citizenship in the United States, 1830–1934," 103 *Am Hist. Rev.* 1440 (1998), pp. 1462–63.

87. Mackenzie v. Hare, 239 U.S. 299 (1915).

88. 42 Stat. 1021 (act of Sept. 22, 1922).

89. See Leti Volpp, "Divesting Citizenship: On Asian American History and the Loss of Citizenship through Marriage," 53 *UCLA L. Rev.* 405 (2005).

90. Arguments and Hearings before Elections Committee No. 1, Contested Election Case of *William C. Lawson v. Ruth Bryan Owen*, H.R., 71st Cong. 2d Sess. (1930), pp. 59, 61.

91. Kirk Semple, "Senate Measure Gives Rights to Widows of Citizens," *N.Y. Times*, Oct. 21, 2009, p. A19. On the gendered effects of a purportedly neutral immigration and naturalization system, see Kerry Abrams, "Becoming a Citizen: Marriage, Immigration, and Assimilation," in *Gender Equality: Dimensions of Women's Equal Citizenship* (Linda C. McClain and Joanna L. Grossman, eds., 2009), p. 39; Kerry Abrams, "Immigration Law and the Regulation of Marriage," 91 *Minn. L. Rev.* 1625 (2007).

92. 344 U.S. 604 (1953).

93. The easy case is when a husband leaves money outright to his wife (or she to him). There are also complex arrangements that allow spouses to tie up money in certain trust arrangements, and still gain the benefit of the marital deduction.

94. 72nd Congress, Sess. I, ch. 314, sec. 213 (act of June 30, 1932).

95. See 42 U.S.C. secs. 402(c),(d) and 416(d) (2010).

96. See 29 U.S.C. secs. 205(c)(2) and 1055(c)(2) (2010). This can, in some cases, be waived.

97. Family and Medical Leave Act of 1993, Pub. L. No. 103-03, 107 Stat. 6 (codified as amended at 29 U.S.C. secs. 2612-2654 (2000)).

98. See, for example, Langan v. St. Vincent's Hosp., 25 A.D.3d 90 (N.Y. App. Div. 2005).

99. See Reed v. Reed, 404 U.S. 71 (1971); Frontiero v. Richardson, 411 U.S. 677 (1973); Craig v. Boren, 429 U.S. 190 (1976).

100. See Title VII of the Civil Rights Act of 1964, 42 U.S. secs. 2000e to 2000e-17; Title IX of the Education Amendments of 1972, 20 U.S.C. sec. 1681 (1972).

101. See, in general, Herma Hill Kay, "From the Second Sex to the Joint Venture: An Overview of Women's Rights and Family Law in the United States During the Twentieth Century," 88 *Cal. L. Rev.* 2017 (2000).

102. 440 U.S. 268 (1979).

103. It is hard to reconcile the ruling in *Sharpe Furniture Co. v. Buckstaff*, discussed above, with the Supreme Court's rulings on sex-based classifications.

104. Dunn v. Palermo, 522 S.W.2d 679 (Tenn. 1975).

105. Ibid., p. 689.

106. See Claudia Goldin and Maria Shim, "Making a Name: Women's Surnames at Marriage and Beyond," 18 *J. Econ. Persp.* 143 (2004); Kif Augustine-Adams, "The Beginning of Wisdom Is to Call Things by Their Right Names," 7 *S. Cal. Rev. L. & Women's Stud.* 1 (1998).

107. 381 U.S. 479 (1965).

108. See Reva B. Siegel, "'The Rule of Love': Wife Beating as Prerogative and Privacy," 105 *Yale L.J.* 1073 (1994), pp. 2154–61; Carolyn B. Ramsey, "Intimate Homicide: Gender and Crime Control, 1880–1920," 77 *U. Colo. L. Rev.* 101 (2006).

109. Elizabeth Pleck, *Domestic Tyranny: The Making of Social Policy against Family Violence from Colonial Times to the Present* (1987), p. 186.

110. Linda Gordon, *Heroes of Their Own Lives: The Politics and History of Family Violence: Boston, 1880–1960* (1988), p. 260.

111. Janet A. Geller and James C. Walsh, "Spouse Abuse: Data from the National Crime Survey," in *Victimology* 2 (1977–78), p. 632.

112. 1976 Pa. Laws ch. 218.

113. See the discussion of fault-based divorce in chapter 8.

114. We discuss the decline of "crimes against morality" in chapter 5.

115. Alfred C. Kinsey et al., *Sexual Behavior in the Human Female* (1953), p. 416.

116. Alfred C. Kinsey et al., *Sexual Behavior in the Human Male* (1948), p. 585.

117. Lawrence M. Friedman, *Crime and Punishment in American History* (1993), p. 399.

118. Psychologist Lenore Walker coined this term in *The Battered Woman* (1979). For a critique of battered woman syndrome, see Donald Alexander Downs, *More Than Victims: Battered Women, The Syndrome Society, and the Law* (1996).

119. There were other rationales: that vindictive wives would fabricate evidence, and that allowing the action would disrupt marriages.

120. People v. Meli, 193 N.Y.S. 365 (S. Ct., Chautauqua County, 1922).

121. New Jersey v. Smith, 426 A.2d 38 (N.J. 1981). The New Jersey statute on rape did not explicitly contain the marital rape doctrine; and the court decided that the doctrine simply did not exist in the state of New Jersey (and never had).

122. 474 N.E.2d 567 (N.Y. 1984).

123. On the history of marital rape law, see Jill Elaine Hasday, "Contest and Consent: A Legal History of Marital Rape," 88 *Cal. L. Rev.* 1373 (2000).

124. Cal. Penal Code, sec. 261.6 (2010).

125. Cal. Penal Code, sec. 262b (2010). However, this short statute of limitations does not apply "if the victim's allegation of the offense is corroborated by independent evidence that would otherwise be admissible during trial."

126. Diana E. H. Russell, *Rape in Marriage* (1990), pp. 24–25.

127. "Jury Selection Starts in Oregon Trial of Man Accused of Raping Wife," *N.Y. Times*, Dec. 20, 1978, p. A16; "2 Rape Trial Witnesses Declare Accuser Lied," *N.Y. Times*, Dec. 23, 1978, p. 10; Les Ledbetter, "Woman in Oregon Rape Trial Says Husband Beat Her," *N.Y. Times*, Dec. 28, 1978, p. A16; Les Ledbetter, "Oregon Man Found Not Guilty on a Charge of Raping His Wife," *N.Y. Times*, Dec. 28, 1978, p. A1.

128. "Battle of Sexes Joined in Case of a Mutilation," *N.Y. Times*, Nov. 8, 1993, p. A16.

129. "Man Found Guilty in Florida of Raping His Wife," *N.Y. Times*, Sept. 2, 1984, p. 32.

CHAPTER THREE
COMMON-LAW MARRIAGE

1. On the rise of the common-law marriage, see Michael Grossberg, *Governing the Hearth* (1985), pp. 69–75, 86–102; Lawrence M. Friedman, *Private Lives: Families, Individuals, and the Law* (2004), pp. 17–27.

2. Robert Black, "Common Law Marriage," 2 *U. Cin. L. Rev.* 113 (1928), p. 133.

3. Atypically, the current statute on informal marriage in Texas provides that if a proceeding to prove such a marriage is not instigated

"before the second anniversary of the date on which the parties separated and ceased living together," the court will rebuttably presume no agreement to marry was made. Practically speaking, this may eliminate the need to seek a divorce. See Tex. Fam. Code sec. 2.401 (2009).

4. On this point, see Ariela R. Dubler, "Wifely Behavior: A Legal History of Acting Married," 100 *Colum. L. Rev.* 957 (2000). Separation cases serve a similar function. See Hendrik Hartog, *Man and Wife in America: A History* (2000), pp. 136–66.

5. Askew v. Depree, 30 Ga. 173 (1860).

6. For an overview, see John B. Crawley, "Is the Honeymoon Over for Common-Law Marriage: A Consideration of the Continued Viability of the Common-Law Marriage Doctrine," 29 *Cumb. L. Rev.* 399 (1999).

7. Fla. Stat. Ann. sec. 741.211 (2010); Idaho Code, sec. 32-201, in force Jan. 1, 1996: "Consent alone will not constitute marriage; it must be followed by the issuance of a license and a solemnization as authorized and provided by law."

8. *In re* Estate of Erlanger, 259 N.Y.S. 2d 610 (Surr. Ct. 1932); "Miss Fixel Is Held Widow of Erlanger: Common-Law Marriage Found Proved," *N.Y. Times*, Aug. 2, 1932.

9. The states are: Alabama, Colorado, Iowa, Kansas, Montana, Rhode Island, South Carolina, Texas, Utah, and the District of Columbia.

10. Tex. Fam. Code sec. 2.401 (2010); White v. White, 142 So. 524 (Ala. 1932).

11. Kan. Stat. Ann. sec. 23-101 (2010).

12. See, for example, S.C. Code Ann. sec. 20-1-360 (2010), which provides that the marriage requirements do not "render illegal any marriage contracted without the issuance of a license."

13. New York, for example, abolished common-law marriage by statute in 1933, but continues to recognize common-law marriages validly established in other states. See *In re* Estate of Watts, 31 N.Y.2d 491 (1973).

14. *In re* Estate of Duval, 777 N.W.2d 380 (2010).

15. For media coverage of the case, see, for example, Celestine Bohlen, "Common-Law Marriage Takes Stage," *N.Y. Times*, June 21, 1989, p. B3; Marvine Howe, "Lawyer Opposing Hurt Fighting an 'Uphill Battle,'" *N.Y. Times*, June 26, 1989, p. B4.

16. Jennings v. Hurt, 1989 N.Y. Misc. LEXIS 868.

17. Craig Wolff, "William Hurt and Ex-Dancer Were Never Married, a Judge Rules," *N.Y. Times*, Oct. 4, 1989.

18. See Charlotte K. Goldberg, "The Schemes of Adventuresses: The Abolition and Revival of Common-Law Marriage," 13 *Wm. & Mary J. of Women & L.* 483 (2007).

19. See Cynthia Grant Bowman, "Social Science and Legal Policy: The Case of Heterosexual Cohabitation," 9 *J. L. Fam. Stud.* 1 (2007),

p. 38, citing Anne Barlow and Grace James, "Regulating Marriage and Cohabitation in 21st Century Britain," 67 *Mod. L. Rev.* 143 (2004), pp. 161–63.

20. So, in the 1980s, a lifer in San Quentin, Ray Cummings, tried to get permission for a conjugal visit from his partner, Susan; the Supreme Court of California denied his request. The newspapers referred to Susan as Ray's "common-law wife." *L.A. Times,* Feb. 18, 1982, p. A1. But the Supreme Court never used the phrase, since the justices were well aware that there was no such thing as common-law marriage in California. The petition stated that he had a "family relationship" with Susan, based on a "long-standing and mutual emotional, psychological, and financial commitment." *In re* Cummings, 650 P.2d 1101 (Cal. 1982).

21. Otto E. Koegel, "Common Law Marriage and Its Development in the United States," in *Eugenics in Race and State,* Vol. 2 (1923), pp. 252, 260.

22. Mary E. Richmond and Fred S. Hall, *Marriage and the State* (1929), pp. 293–94.

23. James C. Mohr, *Abortion in America: The Origins and Evolution of National Policy* (1978); Lawrence M. Friedman, *Guarding Life's Dark Secrets: Legal and Social Controls over Reputation, Propriety, and Privacy* (2007), pp. 179–82.

24. See Theodore Roosevelt, "A Letter from President Roosevelt on Race Suicide," 35 *Am. Monthly Rev. Revs.* 550 (1907). On the eugenics movement, see Mark H. Haller, *Eugenics: Hereditarian Attitudes in American Thought* (1963); Christine Rose, *Preaching Eugenics: Religious Leaders and the American Eugenics Movement* (1904).

25. Richard Dugdale, *"The Jukes": A Study in Crime, Pauperism, Disease, and Heredity* (1877).

26. See Henry Herbert Goddard, *The Kallikak Family* (1912); Ysabel Rennie, *The Search for Criminal Man: A Conceptual History of the Dangerous Offender* (1978); Lawrence M. Friedman, *Crime and Punishment in American History* (1993), pp. 335–39.

27. 1907 Ind. Acts ch. 15.

28. 1909 Cal. Stat. ch. 720.

29. See, in general, Philip R. Reilly, *The Surgical Solution: A History of Involuntary Sterilization in the United States* (1991).

30. *L.A. Times,* Jan. 15, 1935, p. 3.

31. *L.A. Times,* Jan. 16, 1935, p. 3.

32. *N.Y. Times,* Jan. 23, 1935, p. 13.

33. *N.Y. Times,* Jan. 24, 1935, p. 20.

34. *L.A. Times,* Apr. 24, 1935, p. 2.

35. In 1914, too, Ellen Golden, of Louisville, Kentucky, claimed to be the common-law wife of Louis P. Ewald, a millionaire ironmaster, who

left a huge estate. Ewald certainly lived at times with Ms. Golden; and he actually adopted her children (and left them, but not her, a fortune in his will). The man had a "mania for secrecy," and seldom left his house except to ride in a cab. He sometimes called himself "John P. Golden." The case was settled out of court, for a sizable amount. *Wash. Post*, Mar. 27, 1914, p. 1; Apr. 4, 1914, p. 2.

36. "Evil in Illinois' Marriage Statute," *Chi. Trib.*, Nov. 6, 1904, p. B8.

37. 1909 Ill. Laws p. 276. The Oklahoma legislature abolished common-law marriage in 1994, see 43 Okla. St. sec. 4 (2010), but courts seem to have missed that news. See Davis v. State, 103 P.3d 70 (2004), in which the court considered whether a criminal defendant could make use of a marital evidentiary privilege based on an alleged common-law marriage.

38. Common-law marriage also may survive in some tribal legal systems; it is, for example, allowed under the Navajo Tribal Code tit. 9, sec. 3E. A common-law marriage requires the parties to intend to be husband and wife, to consent to the status, to live together, and to hold themselves out "within their community," as a married couple. See Antoinette Sedillo Lopez, "Evolving Indigenous Law: Navajo Marriage— Cultural Traditions and Modern Challenges," 17 *Ariz. J. Int'l & Comp. L.* 283 (2000), p. 300.

39. Parkinson v. J & S Tool Co., 313 A.2d 609 (N.J. 1974).

40. N.J.S.A. sec. 37-1-10 (2010).

41. On the ways in which common-law marriage served to protect women who became economically dependent within non-marital relationships, see Cynthia Grant Bowman, "A Feminist Proposal to Bring Back Common Law Marriage," 75 *Or. L. Rev.* 709 (1996).

CHAPTER FOUR
THE END OF HEART BALM

1. 169 P. 119 (Ore. 1917).

2. So did the male plaintiff in Clark v. Kennedy, 297 P. 1087 (Wash. 1931).

3. We are indebted to Amiram Gill for this information.

4. See Stokes v. Mason, 81 A. 162 (Vt. 1911).

5. Frank H. Keezer, *A Treatise on the Law of Marriage and Divorce* (2d ed. 1923), p. 60.

6. 58 S.W. 126 (Tenn. 1900).

7. On appeal, the state's highest court set aside the verdict and ordered a new trial, at least in part because it suspected the jury had been "influenced by sympathy, passion or prejudice." 95 A. 409 (Me. 1915).

8. Clevenger v. Castle, 237 N.W. 542 (Mich. 1931).

9. "Six Cents Damages for Alienation," *N.Y. Times*, June 12, 1925.

10. In the operetta, the judge saves the day by offering to marry the defendant himself.

11. Robert C. Brown, "Breach of Promise Suits," 77 *U. Pa. L. Rev.* 474 (1929), pp. 492, 494.

12. Carney v. McGilvray, 119 So. 157 (Miss. 1928). The Supreme Court of Mississippi found the instructions to the jury faulty, however, and reversed and remanded.

13. See Susan Staves, "Money for Honor: Damages for Criminal Conversation," in *Studies in Eighteenth-Century Culture*, Vol. 11 (Harry C. Payne, ed., 1982), p. 279; Laura Hanft Korobkin, *Criminal Conversations: Sentimentality and Nineteenth-Century Legal Stories of Adultery* (1998). On criminal conversation in Canada, see Patrick Brode, *Courted and Abandoned* (2002), pp. 121–32.

14. "Jacob Vanderbilt Sued," *N.Y. Times*, Feb. 15, 1890, p. 8.

15. Doe v. Roe, 20 A. 83 (Me. 1890).

16. Sims v. Sims, 76 A. 1063 (N.J. 1910).

17. *N.Y. Times*, Aug. 29, 1930, p. 13. On this affair, see Tonie and Valmai Holt, *In Search of the Better 'Ole: A Biography of Captain Bruce Bairnsfather* (1985), p. 152.

18. We are indebted for this data to Lisa Lawrence, "Marriage and Emotion: Alienation of Affections in New York, 1880–1935," term paper, May 2005, on file with authors.

19. On this affair, see *N.Y. Times*, Nov. 9, 1927, p. 27; May 4, 1928, p. 14; May 5, 1928, p. 27.

20. *Chi. Trib.*, May 23, 1909, p. 3.

21. *N.Y. Times*, Aug. 13, 1922, p. 1.

22. *N.Y. Times*, Oct. 12, 1923; Oct. 4, 1925, p. 3; Jan. 15, 1926; May 30, 1929, p. 24.

23. *N.Y. Times*, Mar. 31, 1931, p. 33.

24. O'Brien v. Manning, 166 N.Y. Supp. 760 (1917).

25. *N.Y. Times*, Feb. 11, 1915, p. 6; on the dismissal of the case, *N.Y. Times*, Apr. 27, 1915, p. 1.

26. *N.Y. Times*, Apr. 12, 1936, p. 26. Frederick had been stupid enough to write love letters to Ms. Mandel. After the verdict, the trial judge threatened to set the verdict aside, unless Ms. Mandel agreed to a reduction of the award to $150,000. *N.Y. Times*, Apr. 16, 1936, p. 5.

27. *Atlanta Const.*, Aug. 9, 1930, p. 6.

28. See Mary Coombs, "Agency and Partnership: A Study of Breach of Promise Plaintiffs," 2 *Yale J. of L. & Fem.* 1 (1989).

29. *N.Y. Times*, Oct. 15, 1911, p. 11.

30. Robert C. Brown, "Breach of Promise Suits," 77 *U. Pa. L. Rev.* 474 (1929), p. 497.

31. Harriet Spiller Daggett, *Legal Essays on Family Law* (1935), pp. 91–92.

32. Kyle Graham, "Why Torts Die," 35 *Fla. St. U. L. Rev* 359 (2008), p. 410.

33. Ibid., p. 413.

34. See, for example, Nathan P. Feinsinger, "Legislative Attack on 'Heart Balm,'" 33 *Mich. L. Rev.* 979 (1935).

35. Laws Pa. 1935, no. 189, abolished both breach of promise and alienation of affections.

36. *Chi. Trib.*, Mar. 22, 1935, p. 18.

37. "Aching Hearts are Itching Palms, Says Woman Legislator as Men Gallantly Pass 'Love Bill,'" *Indianapolis News*, Feb. 1, 1935, p. 1.

38. *Chi. Trib.*, Apr. 3, 1933, p. 14.

39. *Chi. Trib.*, Apr. 18, 1935, p. 1.

40. Orville Dwyer, "Supreme Court Rules Love Can be Worth Money," *Chi. Trib.*, May 22, 1946, p. 3.

41. *740 Ill. Comp. Stat.* 15/3 (2010).

42. Tenn. Code Ann. secs. 36-3-401-404 (2010).

43. 1935 N.Y. Laws 263, codified as N.Y. Civ. R. sec. 80-a (2010).

44. Fearon v. Treanor, 5 N.E.2d 815 (N.Y. 1936), p. 817.

45. Feinsinger, "Legislative Attack on 'Heart Balm,'" p. 979.

46. "Blackmail, Says Cameron," *L.A. Times*, May 29, 1921, p. 13; Blaine P. Lamb, "'A Many Checkered Toga': Arizona Senator Ralph H. Cameron, 1921–1927," 19 *Ariz. & the West* 47 (1977), p. 53.

47. The campaign against heart balm helped the battle against common-law marriage as well. See discussion in chapter 3.

48. 1935 Ind. Acts ch. 208. Sections 4 and 5 of the act, ibid., made it unlawful, in a divorce or custody action, to file a pleading "naming or describing in such manner as to identify any person as co-respondent or participant in misconduct of the adverse party"; instead, "general language" had to be used. (On petition, a judge had discretion to allow identification.) Nor could one elicit the identification of the co-respondent through testimony or cross-examination.

49. Cal. Civ. Code sec. 43.5 (1939).

50. Naturally, some conservatives disagreed and defended breach of promise, in the 1930s. See Frederick L. Kane, "Heart Balm and Public Policy," 5 *Fordham L. Rev.* 63 (1936). Professor Kane, who taught at Fordham University, thought the evidence of blackmail flimsy; the "agitation" for "heart balm" laws was an "aspect of a movement to destroy the concept and ideal of marriage as an outmoded tradition."

51. David Margolick, "Lawyer, Hereafter Broken Heart, Sues to Mend it," *N.Y. Times*, Sept. 11, 1992, p. B8. The plaintiff, Frank D. Zaffere 3d, a "corporate lawyer" in Chicago, had been engaged to a "hostess in

an Italian restaurant." Zaffere claimed he still loved her and was still willing to marry her, under certain conditions.

52. For example, North Dakota abolished breach of promise, alienation of affections, criminal conversation, and the action for seduction in 1983. N.D. Cent. Code sec. 14.02.06 (2010).

53. See, for example, Irwin v. Coluccio, 648 P.2d 458 (Ct. App. Wash. 1982).

54. That case was Watkins v. Lord, 171 P. 1133 (1918). Lemuel Shaw brought an action against Thomas Lord for "debauching" Shaw's wife. A jury awarded damages of $2,500; and the Idaho Supreme Court affirmed.

55. Neal v. Neal, 871 P.2d. 874 (Idaho 1994). The lower courts had dismissed the case. The Supreme Court of Idaho basically agreed; but oddly enough, it did reverse and send the case back to be tried, on the theory that her consent to sex with her husband was "ineffective" because he had lied and cheated.

56. O'Neil v. Schuckardt, 733 P.2d 693 (Idaho 1986). The action was brought against officials of the wife's church, a fundamentalist group that had split off from the Catholic Church, for destroying the marriage and proselytizing the children.

57. Wyman v. Wallace, 549 P.2d 71 (Wash. 1976). The Supreme Court of Iowa, in 1981, went the same route: "Suits for alienation ... are useless as a means of preserving a family. They demean the parties and the courts. We abolish such a right of recovery." See Fundermann v. Mickelson, 304 N.W.2d 790 (Iowa 1981).

58. There were litigants who tried to find some way to get around the laws which abolished these causes of action—but usually unsuccessfully. See, for example, Cherepski v. Walker, 913 S.W.2d 761 (Ark. 1996). Cherepski accused a Catholic priest of having an affair with his wife, but tried in vain to cast his claim as intentional infliction of emotional distress rather than alienation of affections.

59. In *McCutchen v. McCutchen*, 624 S.E.2d 620 (N.C. 2006), the court allowed Patricia McCutchen to sue, over an affair that had begun years before she brought the lawsuit. The court held that the statute of limitations did not start to run until "after alienation is complete," a question for the jury. See also Sherry H. Everett, "The Law of Alienation of Affections after *McCutchen v. McCutchen*: Breaking up Just Got Harder to Do," 85 *N.C. L. Rev.* 1761 (2007).

60. Cited in Jill Jones, "Fanning an Old Flame: Alienation of Affections and Criminal Conversation Revisited," 26 *Pepp. L. Rev.* 61 (1998–1999).

61. Oddo v. Presser, 581 S.E.2d 123 (N.C. Ct. App. 2003). The appellate court, in its decision, thought there should be a new trial on the

issue of compensatory damages; but on this point the Supreme Court of North Carolina, 592 S.E.2d 195 (N.C. 2004), disagreed.

62. Julie Scelfo, "Heartbreak's Revenge: Some States Allow Suits for 'Alienation of Affection,'" *Newsweek*, Dec. 4, 2006.

63. Rosen Law Firm, http://www.rosen.com/divorce/divorce articles/alienation-of-affection-and-criminal-conversation/ (visited Aug. 1, 2010).

64. Alice Gomstyn and Lee Ferran, "Wife's $9M Message to Mistresses: 'Lay Off'," abcnews.com, Mar. 23, 2010.

65. On this potential lawsuit, see Joanna L. Grossman and Lawrence M. Friedman, "Elizabeth Edwards v. Andrew Young: Can He Be Held Liable for Contributing to the Failure of the Edwardses' Marriage?" *FindLaw's Writ*, Feb. 19, 2010, available at http://writ.news.findlaw .com/grossman/20100219.html (visited Aug. 1, 2010).

66. See Hodges v. Howell, 4 P.3d 803 (Utah App. 2000).

67. A statute in South Dakota, S.D. C.L. sec. 20-9-7 (2010), states that "the rights of personal relation forbid" the "enticement" of a spouse. See Michele Crissman, "Alienation of Affections: An Ancient Tort—But Still Alive in South Dakota," 48 *So. Dak. L. Rev.* 518 (2003).

68. Saunders v. Alford, 607 So. 2d 1214 (Miss. 1992).

69. Fitch v. Valentine, 959 So. 2d 1012 (Miss. 2007).

70. In Canada, by the 1930s, seduction and breach of promise "had all but fallen into disuse"; as Patrick Brode put it, in "true Canadian fashion, seduction seems to have gone away quietly instead of in a blaze of glory." Brode, *Courted and Abandoned*, p. 186. The Family Law Reform Act of 1978 ended all the "heart balm" torts in Ontario. In Manitoba, the Equality of Status Act of 1982 did the same. The last province (Saskatchewan) abolished seduction as a cause of action in 1990. Ibid., pp. 188–89. English developments ran along parallel lines, and had a certain influence in Canada. In England, a statute of 1970 provided that an "agreement between two persons to marry one another shall not … have effect as a contract giving rise to legal rights"; and "no action shall lie … for breach of such an agreement." Law Reform (Miscellaneous Provisions) Act, 1970, ch. 33, sec. 1.

71. 555 S.E.2d 22 (Ga. 2001).

72. The source here is a story in the *Gainesville Times*, http://www .gainesvilletimes.com/news/archive/7296 (visited Aug. 1, 2010); see also Verdict, Shell v. Gibbs, 2007CV1638B, Ga. Super. Ct. (July 23, 2008). The verdict was not appealed.

73. See Emily Wagster Pettus, "Wife: Pickering Affair Destroyed Their Marriage," *Mobile Register*, July 17, 2009, p. A4. On modern alienation of affection lawsuits, see Wayne Drash, "Beware Cheaters: Your Lover's Spouse Can Sue You," CNN.com, http://www.cnn.com/2009

/LIVING/12/08/cheating.spouses.lawsuits/index.html (visited Aug. 1, 2010).

74. Quoted in Jones, "Fanning an Old Flame," p. 62. Jones herself was not unsympathetic to the causes of action: "the majority of objections to both alienation of affections and criminal conversation rest upon moral and philosophical viewpoints that are not common to all citizens." Ibid., p. 88. True enough, but they do seem to be common to *most* citizens.

75. N.Y. Civil Rights Law sec. 80-b (2010) (enacted 1965).

76. 272 N.E.2d 471 (N.Y. 1971), p. 476.

77. Lindh v. Surman, 742 A.2d 643 (Pa. 1999); Heiman v. Parrish, 942 P.2d 631 (Kan. 1997); Vigil v. Haber, 888 P.2d 455 (N.M. 1994). Older cases—still good law in many states—take a different approach. In "modified fault" jurisdictions, the ring must be returned if the woman called off the wedding. This would "deter mercenary women." See Rebecca Tushnet, "Rules of Engagement," 107 *Yale L.J.* 2583 (1998), p. 2592. In "strict fault" jurisdictions, the ring must be returned if the woman either called off the wedding *or* behaved in a way that it needed to be called off. This enmeshes a court in the complicated business of pinpointing the cause of a failed relationship.

78. Marcy Blum, "How to Cancel a Wedding," Forbes.com, http://www.forbes.com/2008/06/06/wedding-expense-refund-oped-cx_mb_0606cancel.html (visited Aug. 1, 2010). On the costs and legal remedies for cancelled weddings, see Neil G. Williams, "What to Do When There's No 'I Do': A Model for Awarding Damages Under Promissory Estoppel," 70 *Wash. L. Rev.* 1019 (1995), pp. 1059–60.

79. Ibid.

80. N.Y. Civ. Rights Law sec. 80-b (2010).

81. DeFina v. Scott, 755 N.Y.S.2d 587 (Sup. Ct. 2003), p. 592.

82. *Gaden*, p. 476.

83. Tushnet, "Rules of Engagement," p. 2611.

84. *DeFina*, p. 591. The "mandatory ring-return rules and the denial of women's claims for restitution have combined to make premarital law unfavorable to women." See Tushnet, "Rules of Engagement," p. 2618.

85. Rachel F. Moran, "Law and Emotion, Love and Hate," *J. Contemp. Leg. Issues* 747 (2001), p. 781.

Chapter Five
The Rise of Sexual Freedom

1. See, in general, Lawrence M. Friedman, *Crime and Punishment in American History* (1993), pp. 324–41.

2. 36 Stat. 825 (1910). This statute was codified as amended at 18 U.S.C. secs. 2421–2424 (2010). The Supreme Court upheld the original version of the Mann Act in *Hoke v. United States*, 227 U.S. 308 (1913).

3. On the "war against sex," see, in general, Lawrence M. Friedman, *Guarding Life's Dark Secrets* (2007), pp. 182–91. On criminal regulation of the family, see Melissa Murray, "Strange Bedfellows: Criminal Law, Family Law, and the Legal Construction of Intimate Life," 94 *Iowa L. Rev.* 1253 (2009).

4. We take up the effects of reproductive technology on the law of parentage in chapter 13.

5. Ariela Dubler considers the history of state efforts "to use marriage to locate and police the boundary between the categories of licit and illicit sex," in "Immoral Purposes: Marriage and the Genus of Illicit Sex," 115 *Yale L.J.* 756 (2006), p. 127.

6. Lawrence M. Friedman and Paul Tabor, "A Pacific Rim: Crime and Punishment in Santa Clara County, 1922," 10 *L. & Hist. Rev.* 131 (1992), p. 148. The article describes cases from a criminal docket that involved "crimes against family relations."

7. On these developments, see Lawrence M. Friedman, *American Law in the Twentieth Century* (2001), pp. 231–37.

8. Condom sales nationwide were at $100 million as early as 1950. The Food and Drug Administration approved oral contraception—the pill—for the first time in 1960. See, in general, Andrea Tone, *Devices and Desires: A History of Contraceptives in America* (2001), pp. 200, 203.

9. 316 U.S. 535 (1942). See Victoria F. Nourse, *In Reckless Hands:* Skinner v. Oklahoma *and the Near Triumph of American Eugenics* (2008).

10. 1907 Ind. Acts ch. 215; 1909 Cal. Stat. ch. 720. See, in general, Mark H. Haller, *Eugenics: Hereditarian Attitudes in American Thought* (1963).

11. 274 U.S. 300 (1927).

12. Apparently, the decision was not only callous, but based on wrong facts; none of the women involved were in fact defective. See Paul A. Lombardo, "Three Generations, No Imbeciles: New Light on *Buck v. Bell*," 60 *N.Y.U. L. Rev.* 30 (1985); *N.Y. Times*, Feb. 23, 1980, p. 6; Mar. 7, 1980, p. A16.

13. Today, about a quarter of the states permit involuntary sterilization of the mentally disabled under narrow circumstances; in others, courts will grant petitions for involuntary sterilization if certain criteria are met. Through either mechanism, however, the justification for the procedure is not rooted in the desire to control the state's gene pool. Rather, involuntary sterilization will be ordered under a "substituted judgment" standard (the individual would choose sterilization if capable of giving informed consent); best interests of the individual (the individual would be best served—in terms of habilitation or other needs

by undergoing sterilization—or medical necessity, that is the individual has a therapeutic need for sterilization). For a modern statute regulating involuntary sterilization, see, for example, Cal. Prob. Code sec. 1950 *et seq.* (2010).

14. 381 U.S. 479 (1965). See John W. Johnson, Griswold v. Connecticut: *Birth Control and the Constitutional Right of Privacy* (2005).

15. Ibid., pp. 485–86.

16. 405 U.S. 438 (1972).

17. 410 U.S. 113 (1973). There is, of course, a huge literature on this case. See, for example, David J. Garrow, *Liberty and Sexuality: The Right to Privacy and the Making of* Roe v. Wade (1998).

18. *Planned Parenthood v. Casey*, 505 U.S. 833 (1992), changed the framework to make abortion restrictions invalid only if they posed an "undue burden" on a woman's fundamental right to choose. *Gonzales v. Carhart*, 550 U.S. 124 (2007), upheld a federal law banning a particular method of abortion, deemed "partial-birth abortion" by opponents.

19. See, in general, Thomas C. Grey, "Eros, Civilization, and the Burger Court," 43 *L. & Contemp. Probs.* 83 (1980).

20. 478 U.S. 186 (1986).

21. Ruth Marcus, "Powell Regrets Backing Sodomy Laws," *Wash. Post*, Oct. 26, 1990, p. A3.

22. Powell v. State, 510 S.E.2d 18 (Ga. 1998), pp. 23–25. In *Commonwealth v. Wasson*, 842 S.W.2d 487 (Ky. 1992), pp. 501–2, the Kentucky Supreme Court also found protection for consensual homosexual activity in the state constitution.

23. 539 U.S. 558 (2003).

24. Tex. Penal Code Ann. sec. 21.06(a) (2003).

25. *Lawrence*, p. 567.

26. Much has been written on the meaning of *Lawrence*. See, for example, David D. Meyer, "Domesticating *Lawrence*," 2004 *U. Chi. Legal F.* 453 (2004), p. 454, arguing that *Lawrence* "is best understood as expanding the boundaries of the fundamental right of privacy, and that the linchpin of this expansion is a broadening conception of family." See also Cass R. Sunstein, "What Did *Lawrence* Hold? Of Autonomy, Desuetude, Sexuality, and Marriage," 2003 *Sup. Ct. Rev.* 27; Ariela R. Dubler, "From *McLaughlin v. Florida* to *Lawrence v. Texas*: Sexual Freedom and the Road to Marriage," 106 *Colum. L. Rev.* 1165 (2006); William N. Eskridge, Jr., "*Lawrence v. Texas* and the Constitution of Disgust and Contagion," 57 *Fla. L. Rev.* 1011 (2005); Katherine M. Franke, "The Domestic Liberty of *Lawrence v. Texas*," 104 *Colum. L. Rev.* 1399 (2004).

27. *Lawrence*, p. 578.

28. For a comprehensive list of criminal sexual morality laws as of 2005, see Sara Sun Beale, "From Morals and Mattress Tags to

Overfederalization," 54 *Am. U. L. Rev.* 747 (2005), pp. 752–53. On criminal laws today based on family status, see Dan Markel et al., *Privilege or Punish: Criminal Justice and the Challenge of Family Ties* (2009).

29. See Elimination of Outdated Crimes Amendment of 2003, D.C. Law 15-154 (effective Apr. 29, 2004). This law repealed, among other provisions, D.C. Law 22-201 sec. 3(B), which criminalized adultery.

30. Va. Code Ann. sec. 18.2-344 (2005).

31. Martin v. Ziherl, 607 S.E.2d 367 (Va. 2005), p. 370.

32. See http://www.passionparties.com (visited Aug. 1, 2010).

33. Tex. Penal Code secs. 43.21, 43.23 (2010).

34. Kristin Fasullo, "Beyond *Lawrence v. Texas*: Crafting a Fundamental Right to Sexual Privacy," 77 *Fordham L. Rev.* 2997 (2009), p. 3016.

35. Brenda Cossman, "Sexual Citizens: Freedom, Vibrators, and Belonging," in *Gender Equality: Dimensions of Women's Equal Citizenship* (Linda C. McClain and Joanna L. Grossman, eds., 2009), pp. 289–90. See also "The Turtle and the Hare," *Sex and the City*, television broadcast (HBO, Aug. 2, 1998).

36. Cossman, "Sexual Citizens," p. 290.

37. 517 F.3d 738 (5th Cir. 2008).

38. 478 F.3d 1316 (11th Cir. 2007).

39. 1568 Montgomery Highway, Inc. v. City of Hoover, 45 So. 3d 319 (2010).

40. Kan. Stat. Ann. sec. 21-3522 (2010).

41. Limon v. Kansas, 539 U.S. 955 (2003).

42. State v. Limon, 122 P.3d 22 (Kan. 2005).

43. State v. Holm, 137 P.3d 726 (Utah 2006).

44. See Utah Code Ann. sec. 76-7-101 (2010).

45. *Holm*, p. 777 (Durham, C.J., concurring in part and dissenting in part).

46. Muth v. Frank, 412 F.3d 808 (7th Cir. 2005), p. 818.

47. John F. Kelly, "Va. Man Challenges State's Adultery Law," *Wash. Post*, Feb. 26, 2004, p. B8.

48. Calvin R. Trice, "Adultery Case against Ex-Official Halted," *Richmond Times Dispatch*, Aug. 27, 2004, p. B4.

49. Danny Hakim and Trymaine Lee, "New Governor and Wife Talk of Past Affairs," *N.Y. Times*, Mar. 19, 2008, p. A1. On Eliot Spitzer's downfall, see Danny Hakim and William K. Rashbaum, "Spitzer is Linked to Prostitution Ring," *N.Y. Times*, Mar. 10, 2008.

50. NY CLS Penal sec. 255.17 (2008). See Nicholas Confessore and Jeremy W. Peters, "The Spitzer Scandal," *N.Y. Times*, Mar. 13, 2008, p. B1.

51. Robbie Brown and Shaila Dewan, "Mysteries Remain After Governor Admits an Affair," *N.Y. Times*, June 24, 2009, p. A1.

52. Robbie Brown, "Sanford's Wife Files for Divorce," *N.Y. Times*, Dec. 11, 2009, p. A10.

CHAPTER SIX
COHABITATION

1. N.C. Gen. Stat. sec. 14-184 (2010).
2. People v. C. H. Hamilton, No. 17701 (San Diego Sup. Ct., Jan. 1912).
3. Long v. State, 22 So. 725 (Fla. 1897).
4. Ibid., pp. 441–42.
5. See Martha L. Fineman, "Law and Changing Patterns of Behavior: Sanctions of Non-Marital Cohabitation," 1981 *Wis. L. Rev.* 275, p. 277.
6. Mass. Gen. Laws Ann. ch. 272, sec 16 (2010).
7. Fla. Stat. sec. 798.02 (2009); Mich. Comp. Law & Serv. sec. 750.335 (2010). Michigan amended this law in 2002 to increase the potential fine from $500 to $1,000.
8. Fineman, "Law and Changing Patterns of Behavior," pp. 287–98.
9. Fort v. Fort, 425 N.E.2d 754 (Mass. App. 1981), p. 758.
10. Jarrett v. Jarrett, 400 N.E.2d 421 (Ill. 1979).
11. Ibid., p. 426.
12. Burns v. Burns, 560 S.E.2d 47 (Ga. 2002).
13. See, for example, *In re* Marriage of Dwyer, 825 P.2d 1018 (Colo. Ct. App. 1991), pp. 1019–20.
14. Shahar v. Bowers, 114 F.3d 1097 (11th Cir. 1997). The sodomy ban was struck down the following year by the Georgia Supreme Court. See Powell v. State, 510 S.E.2d 18 (Ga. 1998).
15. *Shahar*, p. 1105.
16. 539 U.S. 558 (2003).
17. Hobbs v. Smith, No. 05 CVS 267 (N.C. Super. Ct. 2006).
18. Data-gathering on cohabitation did not begin in earnest until the 1980s, so little can accurately be said about its prevalence in earlier decades. See Pamela J. Smock, "Cohabitation in the United States: An Appraisal of Research Themes, Findings, and Implications," 26 *Ann. Rev. of Soc.* 1 (2000), p. 2.
19. U.S. Census Bureau, *Married-Couple and Unmarried-Partner Households: 2000* (February 2003), p. 1.
20. Ibid., p. 3.
21. Larry Bumpass and Hsien-Hen Lu, "Trends in Cohabitation and Implication for Children's Family Contexts in the United States," 54 *Population Stud.* 29 (2000), p. 29.
22. Smock, "Cohabitation in the United States," p. 3.
23. Ibid., p. 4.
24. Ibid., p. 3.

25. Ibid., p. 6.

26. Larry L. Bumpass and James A. Sweet, "National Estimates of Cohabitation," 26 *Demography* 615 (1989), p. 621.

27. Smock, "Cohabitation in the United States," p. 7.

28. Bumpass and Lu, "Trends in Cohabitation," p. 32.

29. Smock, "Cohabitation in the United States," p. 3.

30. Cynthia Grant Bowman, "Social Science and Legal Policy: The Case of Heterosexual Cohabitation," 9 *J. L & Fam. Stud.* 1 (2007), p. 16, summarizing studies. See also Bumpass and Sweet, "National Estimates of Cohabitation," pp. 620–21.

31. Smock, "Cohabitation in the United States," p. 10.

32. Bumpass and Sweet, "National Estimates of Cohabitation," pp. 616, noting that the "social disapproval" cohabitants once faced because "their living arrangements flaunted their sexual intimacy" has become "largely irrelevant now that sexual relationships are common regardless of living arrangements."

33. Arland Thornton and Linda Young-DeMarco, "Four Decades of Trends in Attitudes Toward Family Issues in the United States: The 1960s Through the 1990s," 63 *J. Marriage & Fam.* 1009 (2001).

34. Ibid., p. 1024, table 5.

35. Pew Research Center, *The Decline of Marriage and Rise of New Families*, Nov. 18, 2010.

36. See Smock, "Cohabitation in the United States," p. 5.

37. Ibid., p. 5. For further research on reasons for cohabitation, see Marin Clarkberg et al., "Attitudes, Values, and Entrance into Cohabitational versus Marital Unions," 74 *Soc. Forces* 609 (Dec. 1995).

38. See, for example, Swanner v. Anchorage Equal Rights Commission, 874 P.2d 274 (Alaska 1994), which interpreted Alaska's marital-status discrimination law, Alaska Stat. sec. 18.80.240 (2010), to protect unmarried cohabitants. It also rejected the landlord's claim that being forced to rent to unmarried couples violates his right to the free exercise of religion.

39. 436 F. Supp. 1328 (W.D. Pa. 1977), aff'd mem., 578 F.2d 1374 (3d Cir. 1978).

40. Ladue v. Horn, 720 S.W.2d 745 (1986). For a case reaching a different result, see Hann v. Housing Authority, 709 F. Supp. 605 (E.D. Pa. 1989), in which an unmarried couple living with their children was deemed a "single family" for purposes of qualifying for subsidized federal housing.

41. 431 U.S. 494 (1977).

42. 416 U.S. 1 (1974).

43. Hewitt v. Hewitt, 394 N.E.2d 1204 (Ill. 1979).

44. Ibid., p. 1207.

45. Ibid., p. 1211.

46. Marvin v. Marvin, 18 Cal. 3d 660 (1976), p. 666.

47. Ibid., p. 664.

48. Ibid., p. 669.

49. Marvin v. Marvin, 5 Fam. L. Rep. (BNA) 3077 (Cal. Super. Ct. 1979); see also Ann Laquer Estin, "Unmarried Partners and the Legacy of *Marvin v. Marvin*: Ordinary Cohabitation," 76 *Notre Dame L. Rev.* 1381 (2001).

50. Marvin v. Marvin, 122 Cal. App. 3d 871 (1981).

51. Anahad O'Connor, "Michelle Triola Marvin, of Landmark Palimony Suit, Dies at 76," *N.Y. Times*, Oct. 30, 2009, p. A22.

52. Boland v. Catalano, 521 A.2d 142 (Wash. 1987), p. 146, noted the "decided trend" to enforce agreements between unmarried cohabitants; Beal v. Beal, 577 P.2d 507 (Or. 1978), permitted enforcement of express or implied property-sharing agreements between cohabitants; see also Hay v. Hay, 678 P.2d 672 (Nev. 1984).

53. *In re* Estate of Steffes, 290 N.W.2d 697 (1980).

54. Ibid., p. 699.

55. See, for example, Minn. Stat. Ann. sec. 513.075 (West 2008). Contracts made "in consideration of" marriage must be in writing to comply with the Statute of Frauds, a statute that dictates the required formality for certain kinds of contracts. Cohabitation agreements are not generally covered by the Statute of Frauds, however, and thus can be made orally unless a state statute or judicial decision requires otherwise. Texas, for example, includes contracts made in consideration of "nonmarital conjugal cohabitation" in its Statute of Frauds. See Tex. Bus. & Com. Code sec. 26.01 (2010).

56. Wallender v. Wallender, 870 P.2d 232 (Or. 1994), p. 234.

57. New York refuses to enforce implied contracts in the cohabitation context because they are "conceptually so amorphous as practically to defy equitable enforcement" and inconsistent with the state's abolition of common-law marriage. See Morone v. Morone, 413 N.E.2d 1154 (N.Y. 1980). In *Tapley v. Tapley*, 449 A.2d 1218 (N.H. 1982), the court refused to recognize contract implied from rendition and acceptance of "housewifely services." See also Featherston v. Steinhoff, 575 N.W.2d 6 (Mich. 1997).

58. 78 Cal. Rptr. 2d 101 (App. 1998).

59. See Rehak v. Mathis, 238 S.E.2d 81 (Ga. 1977), p. 82; *Hewitt*.

60. Estin, "Ordinary Cohabitation," pp. 1383, 1384; see also Bowman, "Social Science and Legal Policy."

61. Hay v. Hay, 678 P.2d 672 (Nev. 1984), p. 674.

62. *In re* Estate of Roccamonte, 808 A.2d 838 (N.J. 2002).

63. Devaney v. L'Esperance, 949 A.2d 743 (N.J. 2008).

64. Ibid., quoting Levine v. Konvitz, 383 N.J. Super. 1 (App. Div. 2006).

65. See "An Act Concerning Palimony and Amending R.S. 25:1-5," N.J.S. Bill 2091, signed into law January 19, 2010.

66. See Elizabeth A. Pope, "Cohabitation: What to Do When Couples Cannot or Do Not Marry," D.C.B.A. Brief (Dec. 2007), advising lawyers how to draft cohabitation agreements.

67. The rule granting legal status to cohabiting couples was first announced in In re Marriage of Lindsey, 678 P.2d 328 (Wash. 1984).

68. 898 P.2d 831 (Wash. 1995), p. 834.

69. Wash. Rev. Code sec. 26.09.080 (2010).

70. See Olver v. Fowler, 168 P.3d 348 (Wash. 2007).

71. See Western States Constr., Inc. v. Michoff, 840 P.2d 1220 (Nev. 1992), p. 1222.

72. Olver v. Fowler, 126 P.3d 69 (2006) aff'd, 168 P.3d 348 (Wash. 2007).

73. American Law Institute, Principles of the Law of Family Dissolution: Analysis and Recommendations (2002).

74. On this point, see Bowman, "Social Science and Legal Policy," pp. 20–26.

75. An individual can bequeath property to an unmarried partner, but these wills are somewhat more vulnerable to will contests than more "natural" wills. In one Mississippi case, for example, the doctrine of "undue influence" was used to strike down a bequest to a woman's young and attractive lover. See In re Will of Moses, 227 So. 2d 829 (Miss. 1969).

76. See, for example, Estate of Cooper, 564 N.Y.S.2d 684 (Surr. Ct. 1990).

77. Steven L. Nock, "A Comparison of Marriages and Cohabiting Relationships," 16 J. Fam. Issues 53 (1995), p. 74.

78. Bowman, "Social Science and Legal Policy," p. 2.

Chapter Seven
Same-Sex Relationships

1. Minn. Stat. sec. 517 (1972).

2. See William N. Eskridge, Jr. and Darren R. Spedale, Gay Marriage: For Better or for Worse? (2006), pp. 14–15; see also Randy Shilts, And the Band Played On: Politics, People, and the AIDS Epidemic (1987).

3. Eskridge and Spedale, Gay Marriage, p. 16.

4. See, for example, Baker v. Nelson, 191 N.W.2d 185 (Minn. 1971), pp. 185–86, in which the court gave to the word "marriage" its common usage, as defined in the dictionary: "the state of being united to a person of the opposite sex as husband or wife."

5. Jones v. Hallahan, 501 S.W.2d 588 (Ky. Ct. App. 1973).

6. *Baker*, p. 187; see also *Jones*, p. 590; Anonymous v. Anonymous, 325 N.Y.S.2d 499 (1971). The court in *Singer v. Hara*, 11 Wash. App. 247 (1974), concluded simply that the plaintiffs were "being denied entry into the marriage relationship because of the recognized definition of that relationship."

7. The brief, though ostensibly on the question of jurisdiction, came out strongly against same-sex marriage, arguing that "it is patently obvious that to permit same sex marriages would create absolute chaos in our system of jurisprudence, government and culture." Appellee's Motion to Dismiss Appeal and Brief, *Baker v. Nelson*, No. 71-1027.

8. Baker v. Nelson, 409 U.S. 810 (1972).

9. Jurisdictional Statement, Baker v. Nelson, No. 71-1027.

10. Ibid., p. 8.

11. Eskridge and Spedale, *Gay Marriage*, p. 12.

12. See Cal. Civ. Code sec. 4100, enacted by Amended Stat. Ch. 339 sec. 1 (1977), and superseded by Cal. Fam. Code sec. 300 (2008).

13. See Jack Cheevers, "Coast City Set to Give Gay Couples Legal Status," *Boston Globe*, Dec. 6, 1982.

14. "The Family Changes Shape," *USA Today*, Apr. 13, 1987, at 1A.

15. Pew Research Center, *The Decline of Marriage and the Rise of New Families* (2010), p. 40.

16. 852 P.2d 44 (Haw. 1993).

17. *Baehr*, p. 63.

18. Loving v. Virginia, 388 U.S. 1 (1967), p. 3, quoting trial judge.

19. *Baehr*, p. 63.

20. *Loving*, pp. 7–8. See Andrew Koppelman, "Note, The Miscegenation Analogy: Sodomy Law as Sex Discrimination," 98 *Yale L.J.* 145 (1988), p. 147, which argues that just as miscegenation laws were designed to maintain white supremacy, "sodomy laws discriminate on the basis of sex—for example, permitting men, but not women, to have sex with women—in order to impose traditional sex roles."

21. *Baehr*, pp. 67–68.

22. Ibid.

23. The standard of review under the federal constitution is nominally lower than under the Hawaii constitution. See Craig v. Boren, 429 U.S. 190 (1976), establishing "intermediate scrutiny" as the standard of review for sex-based classifications; United States v. Virginia, 518 U.S. 515 (1996), requiring an "exceedingly persuasive justification" for a sex-based classification.

24. See Baehr v. Miike, 1996 WL 694235, p. *21 (Haw. Cir. Ct. Dec. 3, 1996), *aff'd*, 950 P.2d 1234 (Haw. 1997).

25. See Haw. Const. art. I, sec. 23; Haw. Rev. Stat. sec. 572-1 (Supp. 2004).

26. 1997 Haw. Sess. Laws, Act 383 (H.B. 118); S.B. 232, 26th Leg., Reg. Sess. (Hi 2011).

27. See Patrick J. Borchers, *"Baker v. General Motors*: Implications for Interjurisdictional Recognition of Non-Traditional Marriages," 32 *Creighton L. Rev.* 147 (1998), pp.152–53. For a sampling of the many articles perpetuating this idea, see "Editorial, The Freedom to Marry," *N.Y. Times*, Apr. 7, 1996, p. 10; Melissa Healy, "House Backs Curbs on Gay Marriages," *L.A. Times*, July 13, 1996, p. 1; George de Lama, "Hawaii May Lead Way On Same-Sex Marriage," *Chi. Trib.*, May 15, 1994, p. 21.

28. Evan Wolfson, "Fighting to Win and Keep the Freedom to Marry: The Legal, Political, and Cultural Challenges Ahead," *Nat'l J. of Sexual Orientation L.* 259 (1995), p. 262, http://www.ibiblio.org/gaylaw/issue2/wolfson.html (visited Aug. 1, 2010).

29. See, for example, 142 Cong. Rec. H7480, H7484 (1996), statement of Rep. Sensenbrenner.

30. President George W. Bush, President's Radio Address (July 10, 2004), audio and transcript available at www.presidency.ucsb.edu/mediaplay.php?id=25141$admin=43 (visited Aug. 1, 2010).

31. Katharine Q. Seelye, "Conservatives Mobilize Against Ruling on Gay Marriage," *N.Y. Times*, Nov. 20, 2003, p. A29.

32. See Dean E. Murphy, "San Francisco Married 4,037 Same-Sex Pairs From 46 States," *N.Y. Times*, Mar. 18, 2004, p. A26; Thomas J. Lueck, "Police Charge New Paltz Mayor for Marrying Same-Sex Couples," *N.Y. Times*, Mar. 3, 2004, p. B4.

33. See Defense of Marriage Act of 1996, Pub. L. No. 104-199, 119 Stat. 2419.

34. Statement of Senator Trent Lott, 142 Cong. Rec. S10100 (1996), emphasis added. For more on DOMA's legislative history, see Joanna L. Grossman, "Resurrecting Comity: Revisiting the Problem of Non-Uniform Marriage Laws," 84 *Or. L. Rev.* 433 (2005).

35. See Defense of Marriage Act sec. 3(a), codified at 1 U.S.C. sec. 7 (2004).

36. See Defense of Marriage Act sec. 2(a), codified at 28 U.S.C. sec. 1738C (2004).

37. One federal district court recently held this provision unconstitutional in two companion cases. See Gill v. Office of Personnel Management, 699 F. Supp. 2d 374 (D. Mass. 2010); Commonwealth of Mass. v. U.S. D.H.H.S., 698 F. Supp. 2d 234 (D. Mass. 2010).

38. See, for example, Baker v. General Motors Corp., 522 U.S. 222 (1998), p. 233; see also Fauntleroy v. Lum, 210 U.S. 230 (1908), p. 234,

which required Mississippi to give full faith and credit to a Missouri judgment to enforce a futures contract despite a Mississippi statute declaring that such a contract "shall not be enforced by any court."

39. 317 U.S. 287 (1942) (*Williams I*).

40. Ibid., p. 319; see also Williams v. North Carolina, 325 U.S. 226 (1945), p. 239; Estin v. Estin, 334 U.S. 541 (1948).

41. Wells v. Simonds Abrasive Co., 345 U.S. 514 (1953), p. 516.

42. Phillips Petroleum v. Shutts, 472 U.S. 797 (1985), p. 818, quoting Allstate Ins. Co. v. Hague, 449 U.S. 302 (1981), pp. 312–13; see also *Williams*, p. 298; Magnolia Petroleum Co. v. Hunt, 320 U.S. 430 (1943), p. 436.

43. See, for example, Defense of Marriage Act: Hearing on S. 1740 Before the S. Comm. on the Judiciary, 104th Cong., 42–43 (1996), hereinafter *Hearing on S. 1740*. During the hearings, Cass R. Sunstein discussed various examples in which full faith and credit principles were not applied to marriages.

44. Martinez v. City of Monroe, 50 A.D.3d 189 (N.Y. App. Div. 2008), recognizing a Canadian marriage for employment benefit purposes; Godfrey v. Spano, 892 N.Y.S.2d 272 (2009), upholding two governmental orders requiring recognition of same-sex marriages validly celebrated out of state; 95 Md. Op. Atty. Gen. 3 (2010).

45. Baker v. State, 744 A.2d 864 (Vt. 1999), p. 887.

46. Ibid.; see also Vt. Const., Ch. I, art 7.

47. See Report of the Vermont Commission on Family Recognition and Protection, http://www.leg.state.vt.us/workgroups/Family Commission (visited Aug. 1, 2010); The Legal, Medical, Economic & Social Consequences of New Jersey's Civil Union Law, http://www .nj.gov/lps/dcr/downloads/CURC-Final-Report-.pdf (visited Aug. 1, 2010).

48. 806 A.2d 1066 (Conn. 2002); see also Chambers v. Ormiston, 935 A.2d 956 (R.I. 2007).

49. Burns v. Burns, 560 S.E.2d 47 (Ga. 2002).

50. Langan v. St. Vincent's Hosp., 25 A.D.3d 90 (N.Y. 2005), *appeal dismissed by* 850 N.E.2d 672 (N.Y. 2006).

51. Goodridge v. Dep't of Public Health, 798 N.E.2d 941 (Mass. 2003).

52. Opinion of the Justices to the Senate, 802 N.E.2d 565 (Mass. 2004).

53. ALM GL ch. 207, sec. 11 (2004) (repealed).

54. Cote-Whitacre v. Dep't of Public Health, 2006 Mass. Super. LEXIS 670.

55. Cote-Whitacre v. Dep't of Public Health, 844 N.E.2d 623 (Mass. 2006); An Act Relative to Certain Marriage Laws, 2008 Mass. ALS 216; 2007 Mass. S.B. 800, repealing marriage evasion law.

56. See Kerrigan v. Comm'r of Public Health, 957 A.2d 407 (Conn. 2008); *In re* Marriage Cases, 183 P.3d 384 (Cal. 2008).

57. Strauss v. Horton, 46 Cal. 4th 364 (2009).

58. Perry v. Schwarzenegger, 704 F. Supp. 2d 921 (N.D. Cal. 2010).

59. See Varnum v. Brien, 763 N.W.2d 862 (Iowa 2009).

60. See An Act to Protect Religious Freedom and Recognize Equality in Civil Marriage, Vt. S.B. 115 (2009); An Act Affirming Religious Freedom Protections with Regard to Marriage and Prohibiting the Establishment of Civil Unions On or After January 1, 2010, N.H. H.B. 73 (2009); An Act to End Discrimination in Civil Marriage and Affirm Religious Freedom, L.D. 1020 (2009).

61. Maine Same-Sex Marriage People's Veto, Question 1 (2009).

62. See Religious Freedom and Civil Marriage Equality Amendment Act of 2009, D.C. Law 18-110.

63. See, for example, Cal. Fam. Code sec. 297 et seq. (2010); D.C. Code secs. 32-701 et seq. (2010); Wash. Rev. Code Ann. secs. 26.60.020 et seq.; Oregon Family Fairness Act, ch. 99, 2007 Or. Laws 607. An interactive map tracking developments on the same-sex marriage front is available at http://www.freedomtomarry.org/states/ (visited Aug. 1, 2010).

64. Illinois Religious Freedom Protection and Civil Union Act, SB 1716 (enacted 2010); 750 Ill. Comp. Stat. Ann. 75/1–90 (2011)

65. Poll data on attitudes about same-sex marriage and civil unions are available at www.pollingreport.com/civil.htm (visited Aug. 1, 2010).

66. See http://www.foxnews.com/story/0,2933,509733,00.html (visited Aug. 1, 2010).

67. See Hernandez v. Robles, 855 N.E.2d 1 (N.Y. 2006); Andersen v. King County, 18 P.3d 963 (Wash. 2006); Conaway v. Deane, 932 A.2d 571 (Md. 2007); Lewis v. Harris, 908 A.2d 196 (N.J. 2006). Legislative adoption of same-sex marriage in New York seemed for a time likely, but the Senate recently voted down a bill that would have legalized it. See Jeremy W. Peters, "New York State Senate Votes Down Gay Marriage Bill," *N.Y. Times*, Dec. 2, 2009, p. A1.

68. See Thomas Stoddard, "Why Gay People Should Seek the Right to Marry," *Out/Look* 8-12 (Autumn 1989); Paula Ettelbrick, "Since When is Marriage a Path to Liberation?" *Out/Look* 8-12 (Autumn 1989); see also William N. Eskridge, Jr., *The Case for Same-Sex Marriage: From Sexual Liberty to Civilized Commitment* (1996). For more recent explications of the "internal" gay marriage critique, see Nancy Polikoff, *Beyond (Straight and Gay) Marriage*, pp. 98–100 (2008); Ruthann Robson & S. E. Valentine, "Lov(h)ers: Lesbians as Intimate Partners and Lesbian Legal Theory," 63 *Temp. L. Rev.* 511, 540 (1990).

69. See, for example, Martha Albertson Fineman, "The Meaning of Marriage," in *Marriage Proposals* 29, 30 (Anita Bernstein, ed., 2006). Edward A. Zelinsky, "Deregulating Marriage: The Pro-Marriage Case for Abolishing Civil Marriage," 27 *Cardozo L. Rev.* 1161 (2006); Mary Lyndon

Shanley and Linda McClain, "Should States Abolish Marriage?" *Legal Affairs*, May, 16, 2005, http://www.legalaffairs.org/webexclusive/debateclub_m0505.msp.

70. Jane S. Schacter, "The Other Same-Sex Marriage Debate," 84 *Chi-Kent L. Rev.* 379 (2009).

71. See *In re* Estate of Gardiner, 42 P.3d 120 (Kan. 2002); Littleton v. Prange, 9 S.W.3d 223 (Tex. App. 1999).

72. Kan. Stat. Ann. sec. 23-101 (2010).

Chapter Eight
Untying the Knot: Divorce and Annulment

1. Fla. Stat. sec. 3190 (1920), in Chester G. Vernier, *American Family Laws*, Vol. II, (1932), p. 242: "No divorce shall be from bed and board, but every divorce shall be from the bonds of matrimony."

2. Ibid., p. 341.

3. Leon C. Marshall and Geoffrey May, *The Divorce Court: Maryland*, Vol. I (1932), p. 235. On the role and prevalence of marital separation in the nineteenth century, see Hendrik Hartog, *Man and Wife in America: A History* (2000).

4. Straub v. Straub, 208 A.D. 663 (N.Y. 1924).

5. There is a rich literature on the history of divorce in the United States. See, for example, Glenda Riley, *Divorce: an American Tradition* (1991); Nelson Blake, *The Road to Reno: A History of Divorce in the United States* (1962); Lawrence M. Friedman, "Rights of Passage: Divorce Law in Historical Perspective," 63 *Or. L. Rev.* 649 (1984).

6. The General Assembly, in 1947, proposed an amendment to the Constitution. Under this proposal, divorces could be granted on grounds of "adultery, desertion ... physical cruelty, or habitual drunkenness." The voters ratified this proposal. The divorce law went into effect on April 15, 1949. Paul H. Jacobson, *American Marriage and Divorce* (1959), p. 111.

7. For a state-by-state breakdown as of 1930 or so, see Isabel Drummond, *Getting a Divorce* (1930); see also Vernier, *American Family Laws*, Vol. II.

8. Fla. Stat. sec. 3191 (5) (1920).

9. Ala. Code sec. 34-20-5 (1940).

10. Tenn. Code sec. 8426 (7) (1932).

11. N.H. Rev. Stat. sec. 458:7 (8) (1968).

12. Kan. Stat. Ann., sec. 60-1501 (1935).

13. Md. Ann. Code art. 16, sec. 38 (1924).

14. N.M. Stat. Ann. sec. 68-501 (6) (1929).

15. Vernier, *American Family Laws*, Vol. II, p. 89.

16. Pa. Stat. Ann. sec. 9191 (1920).

17. Alberto Brandt Lopez, "Divorce and Annulment in San Mateo County, California, 1950–1957," unpublished J.S.D. dissertation, Stanford Law School, 2005, p. 90. See also Robert L. Griswold, "Law, Sex, Cruelty, and Divorce in Victorian America, 1840–1900," 38 *Am. Q.* 721 (1986), p. 722.

18. Or. Rev. Stat. sec. 6-907 (1930).

19. Cal. Civ. Code sec. 94 (Deering 1931).

20. Alfred Cahen, *Statistical Analysis of American Divorce* (1932), p. 15; William O'Neill, *Divorce in the Progressive Era* (1967).

21. Cahen, *Statistical Analysis,* p. 21.

22. U.S. Dep't Health & Hum. Servs., 54 *Nat'l Vital Stats. Rep.,* No. 20, July 21, 2006; *Statistical Abstract of the United States 2010,* p. 65, table 78.

23. William N. Gemmill, "Divorce as a Sign of Degeneracy or of Progress," 6 *Ill. L. Rev.* 32 (1914).

24. William T. Nelson, *Divorce and Annulment,* 2d ed., Vol. I (1945), p. 358.

25. N. P. Feinsinger and Kimball Young, "Recrimination and Related Doctrines in the Wisconsin Law of Divorce as Administered in Dane County," 6 *Wis. L. Rev.* 195 (1930), p. 210.

26. Ibid., p. 212.

27. Tenn. Code Ann. sec. 121 (1915).

28. See Charles S. Connolly, "Divorce Proctors," 34 *B.U. L. Rev.* 1 (1954).

29. W. Va. Code sec. 48-2-24 (1931). See McNinch v. McNinch, 188 S.E. 231 (W. Va. 1936). Here the husband sued for divorce, charging adultery, and asked for custody of a child. The wife denied the accusation, and charged plaintiff with "cruel and inhuman treatment"; she also asked for a divorce and custody. But then she agreed not to contest, in exchange for an agreement to get custody for three months during school vacations. The trial court granted the divorce and custody to the husband. The appeal court reversed, saying that the trial court shall have "delayed the hearing for investigation by the divorce commissioner." But this must have been unusual.

30. O'Neill, *Divorce in the Progressive Era,* p. 79.

31. In Wayne County, Michigan, there was an official called the "Friend of the Court." A description of the work of the "Friend" is found in George Squire, "Divorce and the Friend of the Court," 29 *Mich. St. Bar J.* 15 (1950). Squire's piece avoids the issue of collusion entirely.

32. Maxine B. Virtue, *Family Cases in Court* (1956), pp. 90–91.

33. Ibid., pp. 118, 140.

34. William J. Goode, *After Divorce* (1956), p. 133.

35. Joseph Epstein, "Divorce: Part One: Coming Apart in Chicago," *Chi. Trib.,* Nov. 5, 1972, p. 126.

36. Marshall and May, *The Divorce Court: Maryland*, pp. 199–200.

37. Jacobson, *American Marriage and Divorce*, p. 120.

38. Lopez, *Divorce and Annulment*, p. 58.

39. Lawrence M. Friedman and Robert V. Percival, "Who Sues for Divorce? From Fault through Fiction to Freedom," 5 *J. Legal Studies* 61 (1976).

40. U.S. Dept. of Health, Education and Welfare, *100 Years of Marriage and Divorce Statistics, United States, 1867–1967*, table 21, p. 50.

41. Lopez, *Divorce and Annulment*, p. 57.

42. Jacobson, *American Marriage and Divorce*, p. 121.

43. Lawrence M. Friedman, "A Dead Language: Divorce Law and Practice Before No-Fault," 86 *Va. L. Rev.* 1497 (2000), pp. 1524, 1525.

44. Dorothy Thompson, "The Barbarism of Divorce Laws," *Ladies' Home Journal*, Feb. 1949, p. 11.

45. See Reed v. Littleton, 289 N.Y. Supp. 798 (Sup. Ct. 1936).

46. *New York Sunday Mirror*, Feb. 25, 1934 (magazine), cited in Note, "Collusive and Consensual Divorce and the New York Anomaly," 36 *Colum. L. Rev.* 1121 (1936), p. 1131.

47. Leon C. Marshall and Geoffrey May, *The Divorce Court: Ohio*, Vol. II, p. 312.

48. Note, "The Administration of Divorce: A Philadelphia Study," 101 *U. Pa. L. Rev.* 101 (1953), p. 1204.

49. Riley, *Divorce*, pp. 147–51.

50. "Notice by the Probate Courts to the District Attorney in Adultery Cases," 4 *Mass. L.Q.*, pp. 45–46 (1947). The repeal was Laws Mass. 1948, ch. 279, sec. 1. The judge could still, at his discretion, inform the district attorney. We doubt that this happened very often.

51. Riley, *Divorce*, pp. 136–37.

52. Marshall and May, *The Divorce Court: Ohio*, p. 28.

53. Jacobson, *American Marriage and Divorce*, p. 100, table 48.

54. J. Herbie DiFonzo, *Beneath the Fault Line: The Popular and Legal Culture of Divorce in Twentieth Century America* (1997), p. 88.

55. Nelson Manfred Blake, *The Road to Reno: A History of Divorce in the United States* (1977), pp. 1–4.

56. Williams v. North Carolina, 317 U.S. 287 (1942). This case overruled *Haddock v. Haddock*, 201 U.S. 562 (1906). In *Haddock*, the husband moved to Connecticut, and got a divorce. His wife lived in New York. She was never served with process. The Supreme Court held that New York did not have to recognize the Connecticut decree.

57. Williams v. North Carolina, 325 U.S. 226 (1945).

58. Cahen, *Statistical Analysis*, p. 65. Apparently a small number of couples also got divorces in Paris. And Havana, Cuba, according to Cahen, also "opened a divorce mill to cater to wealthy American patrons."

Cahen reports that the traffic was not entirely one way: Canadians, fleeing from their own very strict laws, sometimes came to the United States to get their divorces. Ibid., pp. 66–67.

59. "Had Spat? Just Write to Mexico and Get Divorce," *Wash. Post,* Aug. 29, 1929, p. 12.

60. "The Perils of Mexican Divorce," *Time,* Dec. 27, 1963.

61. Ry Cooder, "Mexican Divorce" (1987).

62. Jacobson, *American Marriage and Divorce,* pp. 105–6.

63. 349 U.S. 553 (1955).

64. Ibid., p. 568.

65. Joseph B. Treaster, "A Weekend in Haiti can Include a Divorce," *N.Y. Times,* July 12, 1986.

66. *Wash. Post,* Apr. 26, 1979, p. DC13.

67. The website of Moroni Law Offices, P.C., http://guamdivorces. com/advantage_over_foreign_divorce.htm (visited Aug. 1, 2010).

68. 334 U.S. 541 (1948).

69. N.Y. Laws ch. 254 (1966); the statute also added, as grounds, abandonment, and two years of living separately under a decree or agreement of separation.

70. DiFonzo, *Beneath the Fault Line,* pp. 75–81; see also Herma Hill Kay, "Equality and Difference: A Perspective on No-Fault Divorce and its Aftermath," 56 *U. Cin. L. Rev.* 1 (1987), pp. 4–14.

71. North Carolina was an exception. Its divorce law, as strict as New York's had been, basically only allowed divorce for adultery—*except* for the provision on living apart; in 1948, this provision accounted for 91 percent of the divorces in the state. DiFonzo, *Beneath the Fault Line,* p. 81; see N.C. Gen. Stat. sec. 50-5 (1976).

72. N.M. Stat. sec 62-1 (1933).

73. N.M. Stat. sec. 319 (1973).

74. Max Rheinstein, *Marriage Stability, Divorce, and the Law* (1972), p. 251.

75. Hubert J. O'Gorman, *Lawyers and Matrimonial Cases: A Study of Informal Pressures in Private Professional Practice* (1963), pp. 26, 28. O'Gorman studied a sample of New York family laws. Only a handful approved of New York's laws. As one of them said, "Ninety percent of the undefended matrimonials are based on perjury.... We all know this. The judges know it. It's embarrassing." Ibid., p. 33.

76. Michael Clark, "Six Arrested Here in Divorce Racket as Inquiry Opens," *N.Y. Times,* Dec. 1, 1948, p. L1.

77. Joseph Epstein, *Divorced in America: Marriage in an Age of Possibility* (1974), p. 82.

78. Thompson, "The Barbarism of Divorce Laws," pp. 11, 12.

79. See Paul W. Alexander, "Foreword to Virtue," in Virtue, *Family Cases in Court*, pp. xxix, xxxi.

80. Judge Louis H. Burke, "Conciliation—A New Approach to the Divorce Problem," 30 *J. State Bar Cal.* 199 (1955), p. 205.

81. Louis H. Burke, *With This Ring* (1958), pp. 273–80.

82. John Bartlow Martin, "A Little Nest of Hate," *Saturday Evening Post*, Nov. 22, 1958, pp. 36, 121.

83. Vernier, *American Family Laws*, Vol II, pp. 150–56.

84. "Years Wait in Divorces Will Stand," *L.A. Times*, Mar. 30, 1933, p. 1.

85. Martin, "A Little Nest of Hate."

86. See, in general, Milton C. Regan, Jr., *Family Law and the Pursuit of Intimacy* (1993).

87. On the various stages of divorce reform in the twentieth century, see Herma Hill Kay, "From the Second Sex to the Joint Venture: An Overview of Women's Rights and Family Law in the United States During the Twentieth Century," *88 Calif. L. Rev.* 2017 (2000), pp. 2040–57.

88. (Former) Cal. Civ. Code sec. 4506. On the background of this statute, see Herbert Jacob, *Silent Revolution: The Transformation of Divorce Law in the United States* (1988).

89. (Former) Cal. Civ. Code sec. 4506.

90. (Former) Cal. Civ. Code sec. 4508 (a).

91. Minn. Stat. sec. 518.06 (2009).

92. See, for example, N.H. Rev. Stat. Ann. secs. 458.7, 458.7-a (2010).

93. Nev. Laws ch. 500 (1973). This statute also provided that if both husband and wife "have been guilty of a wrong," a court can nonetheless in its discretion grant a divorce—to the "party least in fault," if both of them want a divorce; otherwise to the petitioner, even if the petitioner was the most at fault.

94. 23 Pa. Cons. Stat. secs. 3301 (c) & (d) (2010).

95. In a few states, in contested divorces, courts did examine the facts. See, for example, Marriage of Mitchell, 545 S.W.2d 313 (Mo. App. 1976).

96. Alan H. Frank et al., "No Fault Divorce and the Divorce Rate: The Nebraska Experience—An Interrupted Time Series Analysis and Commentary," 58 *Neb. L. Rev.* 1 (1978), p. 66.

97. Stephen L. Sass, "The Iowa No-Fault Dissolution of Marriage Law in Action," 18 *S.D. L. Rev.* 629 (1973), p. 641.

98. Ibid., pp. 6–7.

99. N.Y. Dom. Rel. sec. 170 (2009).

100. Davis v. Davis, 2009 N.Y. Slip Op 8579. In 1926, the state's highest court interpreted abandonment—as a ground for legal separation,

since it was not yet grounds for divorce—to include sexual abandonment; sexual relations were one of the "basic obligations" of marriage. Mirizio v. Mirizio, 150 N.E. 605 (N.Y. 1926), p. 607. Diemer v. Diemer, 168 N.E.2d 654 (N.Y. 1960), applied this rule to a proceeding for divorce.

101. Ozkan v. Ozkan, *N.Y.L.J.* Aug. 12, 2004, p. 19 col. 3; Omahen v. Omahen, 769 N.E.2d 353 (N.Y. 2001).

102. Senate Bill 3890 (signed Aug. 15, 2010). On prior reform efforts, see Joanna L. Grossman, "Will New York Finally Adopt True No-Fault Divorce?" *FindLaw's Writ*, available at http://writ.news.findlaw.com/grossman/20041020.html (visited Aug. 1, 2010); J. Herbie DiFonzo and Ruth C. Stern, "Addicted to Fault: Why Divorce Reform Has Lagged in New York," 27 *Pace L. Rev.* 559 (2007).

103. Advertisement online for "3Step Divorce," one of a number of such companies, http://www.3stepdivorce.com/states/California.shtml (visited Aug. 1, 2010). The service is available for other states, too, for example, Pennsylvania.

104. See Harvey J. Sepler, "Measuring the Effects of No-Fault Divorce Laws Across Fifty States: Quantifying a Zeitgeist," 15 *Fam. L. Q.* 69 (1981); Frank et al., "No Fault Divorce and the Divorce Rate."

105. See Pierre Hegy and Joseph Martos, eds., *Catholic Divorce: The Deception of Annulments* (2000), p. 2; see also data at http://www.divorcereform.org/rates.html (visited Aug. 1, 2010).

106. Herbert F. Goodrich, "Jurisdiction to Annul a Marriage," 32 *Harv. L. Rev.* 806 (1918–19), pp. 807–8.

107. Or. Rev. Stat. sec. 6-902 (1930).

108. *L.A. Times*, Sep. 18, 1935, p. A3.

109. *L.A. Times*, June 4, 1943, p. 18.

110. Or. Rev. Stat. sec. 6-903 (1930).

111. "Drugged and Wed, Young Woman Says: Seeks Annulment," *Atlanta Const.*, July 10, 1924, p. 3.

112. Moyers v. Moyers, San Mateo Case 59684, filed October 21, 1952; in Lopez, *Divorce and Annulment*, p. 38. Eugene too was befuddled by drink and sedatives at the time. Eugene wanted money in exchange for defaulting the case; and when he was not paid, filed a motion to set aside the default. But Linda got her annulment. Ibid., p. 120.

113. *N.Y. Times*, March 7, 1908, p. 1.

114. Spears v. Alexander, District Court, Clark County, Nevada, Case No. D311371, filed Jan. 5, 2004.

115. In Alameda County, California, at the turn of the twentieth century, marriages ending in annulment typically lasted less than three years. Joanna Grossman and Chris Guthrie, "The Road Less Taken: Annulment at the Turn of the Century," 40 *Am. J. Legal Hist.* 307 (1996), p. 312.

116. *L.A. Times*, May 31, 1931, p. A2. A more cynical observer might wonder whether Herman had found somebody else to share his life with, after all those years.

117. See, for example, Cal. Civ. Code sec. 83.1 (Pomeroy 1901).

118. "Bridegroom Goes Free," *Oakland Trib.*, May 21, 1900, p. 4.

119. In Raia v. Raia, 108 So. 11 (Ala. 1926), the groom was seventeen, the bride was fifteen. He lied about his age when getting the license, and gave a false name. This would not normally seem to be grounds for an annulment. But the bride was not more than a block from the courthouse when she "sent word to her father" about what had happened; and he came and got her. There had been, it was alleged, no sex as yet. The appeal court overruled a demurrer to the case: "a marriage procured by fraud of such character as to go to the essence of the marriage ... may be annulled, provided application for annulment be made before the consummation of the marriage."

120. This and other cases from a study of annulments in Alameda County, California between 1895 and 1906 are described in Grossman and Guthrie, "The Road Less Taken."

121. *L.A. Times*, Jan. 21, 1930, p. II 1.

122. See Lawrence A. Frolik and Mary F. Radford, "'Sufficient' Capacity: The Contrasting Capacity Requirements for Different Documents," 2 NAELA J. 303 (2006).

123. See, for example, Edmund v. Edwards, 287 N.W.2d 420 (Neb. 1980).

124. Grossman and Guthrie, "The Road Less Taken," p. 307.

125. Marshall and May, *The Divorce Court: Maryland*, p. 235; Marshall and May, *The Divorce Court: Ohio*, p. 302.

126. Sass, "The Iowa No-Fault Dissolution of Marriage Law in Action," p. 636.

127. Lopez, *Divorce and Annulment*, p. 40.

128. Ibid., p. 57.

129. Hanson v. Hanson, 191 N.E. 673 (Mass. 1934).

130. Note, "Annulments for Fraud—New York's Answer to Reno?" 48 *Colum. L. Rev.* 900, (1948), p. 902.

131. *N.Y. Times*, June 25, 1919, p. 5. At the time, as we noted, an American woman who married a foreigner lost her citizenship.

132. Note, "Annulments for Fraud," pp. 905–6.

133. John W. Moreland, *Keezer on the Law of Marriage and Divorce*, 3d ed. (1946), p. 270.

134. In her book, *Are Men Necessary?: When Sexes Collide* (2006), Maureen Dowd claims that it is standard practice for women to "Google" their dates ahead of time to learn about their net worth, past indiscretions, and other tidbits that might not be revealed in person.

135. Marshall v. Marshall, 300 P. 816 (Cal. 1931).

136. Reynolds v. Reynolds, 85 Mass. 605 (1862).

137. Radochonski v. Radochonski, 1998 Wash. App. LEXIS 765, p. 4. In this case, the wife allegedly lied about her past—and her relationship with another man. Supposedly she married to get permanent residency status in the United States. But the husband was unable to prove that he relied on anything she said. Lies about the other man were not enough for an annulment. The husband denied any sexual relations; but the court did not believe him.

138. 389 N.E.2d 1143 (Ill. 1979).

139. 228 P.3d 267 (Colo. 2010), p. 270.

140. See, for example, Meagher v. Maleki, 131 Cal. App. 4th 1 (2005), which refused to grant an annulment based on fraud related to financial matters because that is not "a matter which the state deems vital to the marriage relationship."

141. And, to a lesser degree, in California, at the time when divorces did not become final for a year after the interlocutory decree.

142. Sass, "The Iowa No-Fault Dissolution of Marriage Law in Action," p. 637.

143. The ad is http://www.annulmentnevada.com/library/annulment -info.php (visited on Aug. 1, 2010). The ad spells out the "Reasons allowed for Annulment," which include "You married the Defendant due to Defendant's fraud"; also, a "marriage may be annulled for any cause which is a ground for annulling or declaring void a contract in a court of equity."

144. La. Rev. Stat. Ann. sec. 272. There is a large literature on the subject. See, for example, Amy L. Stewart, "Covenant Marriage: Legislating Family Values," 32 Ind. L. Rev. 509 (1999).

145. Ariz. Rev. Stat. sec. 25-901 (2010); Ark. Code sec. 9-11-1801 (2010).

146. For a list and discussion of some of the post-Louisiana proposals in other states, see Lynne Marie Kohm, "A Comparative Survey of Covenant Marriage Proposals in the United States," 12 Regent U. L. Rev. 31 (1999).

147. Laura Sanchez, "The Implementation of Covenant Marriage in Louisiana," 9 Va. J. Soc. Pol'y & L. 192 (2001).

148. See Lynn A. Baker and Robert E. Emery, "When Every Relationship Is Above Average: Perceptions and Expectations of Divorce at the Time of Marriage," 17 L. & Hum. Behav. 439, 443 (1993).

149. Kristin Netterstrom, "Area Residents Take Advantage of Covenant Marriage Alternative," http://www.nwaonline.net/articles /2005/02/14/news/bentonville/01cov.txt (visited Jan. 26, 2009).

150. Rick Lyman, "Trying to Strengthen an 'I Do' With a More Binding Legal Tie," N.Y. Times, Feb. 15, 2005, p. A16.

151. The website is http://www.covenantmarriage.com/aboutus/ php (visited Aug. 1, 2010).

152. Stewart, "Covenant Marriage: Legislating Family Values," p. 532.

153. S. Car. Code Ann. 20-1-230 (b) (2010).

154. Mackenzie Brown, "The State of our Unions," *Redbook*, June 1, 2008, p. 154.

155. Laura Sanchez et al., "Is Covenant Marriage a Policy that Preaches to the Choir? A Comparison of Covenant and Standard Married Newlywed Couples in Louisiana," Working Paper Series 02-06, Bowling Green State University, Center for Family and Demographic Research, pp. 1, 32.

156. Institute for American Values, *The Marriage Movement: A Statement of Principle* (2000).

157. This advertisement, as well as others in the National Healthy Marriage Research Center's media campaign, is available at http:// www.healthymarriageinfo.org/images/NHMRC-Print-PSA-1B_full2 .jpg (visited Aug. 1, 2010).

158. Administration for Children and Families, *Healthy Marriage Matters*, http://www.acf.hhs.gov/healthymarriage/about/factsheets_ hm_matters (visited Aug. 1, 2010).

159. Linda C. McClain, *The Place of Families* (2007), p. 117.

160. Ibid., p. 118.

161. Pub. L. 104-193 sec. 101 (1996).

162. MaClain, *The Place of Families*, p. 121. See Theodora Odoms et al., Center for Law and Social Policy, *Beyond Marriage Licenses: Efforts in States to Strengthen Marriage and Two Parent Families* (2004).

163. Legislation proposed by Senator Charles Grassley, 109th Cong., S. 667, Mar. 17, 2005.

164. Pub. L. 109-171 (2006).

165. The initiative is described in detail on the ACF website, http:// www.acf.hhs.gov/healthymarriage (visited Aug. 1, 2010).

CHAPTER NINE
DOLLARS AND SENSE: THE ECONOMIC CONSEQUENCES OF DIVORCE

1. Sanford N. Katz, *Family Law in America* (2003), p. 86.

2. James Kent, *Commentaries on American Law*, Vol. II (2d ed. 1832), p. 106. See discussion in chapter 2.

3. See, for example, McGuire v. McGuire, 59 N.W.2d 336 (Neb. 1953), which we discuss in chapter 2.

4. On women's rights regarding property from 1750 to 1830, see Marylynn Salmon, *Women and the Law of Property in Early America* (1986).

5. Hendrik Hartog, *Man and Wife in America: A History* (2000), pp. 29–39; see also Lawrence J. Golden, *Equitable Distribution of Property* (1983), p. 7.

6. Arizona, California, Idaho, Louisiana, Nevada, New Mexico, Texas, and Washington have always followed community property rules. Wisconsin adopted a very similar, but not identical approach based on the Uniform Marital Property Act in 1983. Alaska permits married couples to elect to hold their property as community property.

7. On community property generally, see W. S. McClanahan, *Community Property Law in the United States* (1982).

8. California, Louisiana, and New Mexico.

9. Arizona, Idaho, Nevada, Texas, and Washington.

10. See Chester G. Vernier, *American Family Laws*, Vol. II (1932), p. 260. Fifteen states also authorized alimony for husbands by this time, but such awards were extremely rare. Ibid., p. 262.

11. Ibid., p. 259.

12. On the traditional justification for alimony, see, for example, Herbert Jacob, *Silent Revolution: The Transformation of Divorce Law in the United States* (1988), p. 112. In cases of legal separation, an award of support was often called "separate maintenance."

13. Katz, *Family Law in America*, p. 95.

14. Ibid., p. 98.

15. Vernier, *American Family Laws*, Vol. II, p. 260; see also Mary Ann Glendon, *The New Family and New Property* (1981), p. 53.

16. Okla. Comp. Stat. sec. 508 (1921).

17. Vernier, *American Family Laws*, Vol. II, p. 261. See, for example, Neb. Rev. Stat. sec. 42 (1929).

18. Edward W. Cooey, "The Exercise of Judicial Discretion in the Award of Alimony," 6 *L. & Contemp. Probs.* 213 (1939), p. 220.

19. Cal. Civ. Code secs. 139, 142 (1929).

20. See, for example, Colo. Rev. Stat. sec. 5599 (1921); Cal. Civ. Code secs. 139, 142 (1929).

21. Vernier, *American Family Laws*, Vol. II, p. 283.

22. Jacob, *Silent Revolution*, p. 114. Mary Ann Glendon has also noted, with respect to alimony awards, the "well-known difficulties with … enforcement." Glendon, *The New Family and the New Property*, p. 53.

23. Carroll D. Wright, U.S. Dep't. of Labor, *A Report on Marriage and Divorce in the United States, 1867 to 1886* (rev. ed. 1891), pp. 211–12.

24. See Paul Jacobson, *American Marriage and Divorce* (1959), p. 126, noting that between 9 percent and 15 percent of divorcing wives were awarded alimony according to census data collected between 1887 and 1922.

25. See Cooey, "The Exercise of Judicial Discretion in the Award of Alimony," p. 214.

26. See Joanna Grossman and Chris Guthrie, "The Road Less Taken: Annulment at the Turn of the Century," 40 *Am. J. Legal Hist.* 307 (1996), p. 328.

27. Equitable distribution is a move away from the common-law rule that "no rights to property arise by virtue of the marriage." Golden, *Equitable Distribution of Property*, pp. 4–5.

28. Ibid., p. 3.

29. Ibid., p. 27.

30. 639 So. 2d 921 (Miss. 1994).

31. Ibid., pp. 929–30.

32. Ibid., p. 926.

33. See Doris Jonas Freed and Henry H. Foster, Jr., "Divorce in the Fifty States: An Overview as of 1978," 13 *Fam. L. Q.* 105 (1979), p. 114.

34. The Supreme Court of New Jersey held that the local equitable distribution law was a reasonable exercise of police power. Rothman v. Rothman, 320 A.2d 496 (N.J. 1974), p. 501.

35. Bureau of the Census, *Married Couples by Labor Force Status of Spouses: 1986 to Present* (Table MC-1) (2008); see also Bureau of the Census, Current Population Reports, Series P60-203, *Measuring 50 Years of Economic Change Using the March Current Population Survey* (1998), p. 27 (fig. 2.5a).

36. See Bureau of Labor Statistics, U.S. Dep't. of Labor, *Charting the U.S. Labor Market in 2006*, p. 66, chart 6-5 (2007), http://www.bls.gov/cps/labor2006/chartbook.pdf (visited Aug. 1, 2010). For a comprehensive analysis of women's current role in the workforce, see "The Shriver Report: A Woman's Nation Changes Everything," http://www.awomansnation.com/ (visited Aug. 1, 2010).

37. See, for example, Catherine Rampell, *As Layoffs Surge, Women May Pass Men in Job Force, N.Y. Times*, Feb. 6, 2009, p. A1.

38. Ibid.

39. Pew Research Center, "From 1997 to 2007: Fewer Mothers Prefer Full-time Work" (Aug. 1, 2007), available at http://pewresearch.org/assets/social/pdf/WomenWorking.pdf (visited Aug. 1, 2010).

40. Bureau of the Census, Table SHP-1, *Parents and Children in Stay-At-Home Parent Family Groups: 1994 to Present (July 2008)*, http://www.census.gov/population/www/socdemo/hh-fam.html (visited Aug. 1, 2010). In 1995, there were 22.9 million married-couple households, 4.4 million of which included a stay-at-home mother and 64,000 of which included a stay-at-home father. Ibid.

41. See Bureau of Labor Statistics, U.S. Dep't. of Labor, *Highlights of Women's Earnings in 2003*, pp. 29, 31, tables 12 and 14 (Sept. 2004), reporting that women's median weekly earnings were 79.5 percent of men's in 2003, but only 73.6 percent for college graduates.

42. See ibid., p. 3, chart 2, reporting median usual weekly earnings of $715 for white men, $567 for white women, $491 for black or African American women, and $410 for Hispanic or Latino women; compare Amy Caiazza et al., Inst. for Women's Pol'y Res., *The Status of Women in the States, Women's Economic Status in the States: Wide Disparities by Race, Ethnicity, and Region* (Apr. 2004), pp. 24–25, finding wide variation in Asian American women's wages.

43. See Daniel H. Weinberg, U.S. Dep't. of Commerce, Census 2000 Special Reports, *Evidence from Census 2000 About Earnings by Detailed Occupation for Men and Women*, pp. 7, 12, table 5 (May 2004).

44. See Michael Selmi, "Family Leave and the Gender Wage Gap," 78 *N.C. L. Rev.* 707 (2000), p. 715.

45. See, for example, Bureau of Labor Statistics, *Highlights of Women's Earnings in 2003*, p. 11, table 1; Francine D. Blau et al., *The Economics of Women, Men, and Work* (5th ed. 2006), p. 150.

46. See Stephen J. Rose and Heidi I. Hartmann, *Still a Man's Labor Market: The Long-Term Earnings Gap*, Inst. for Women's Pol'y Res. (2004), p. 9.

47. See Selmi, "Family Leave and the Gender Wage Gap," pp. 719–43.

48. Ibid., pp. 745–50; compare Nev. Dep't of Human Res. v. Hibbs, 538 U.S. 721, 730 (2003), discussing employer reliance on "stereotype-based beliefs about the allocation of family duties" as a form of sex discrimination.

49. See Selmi, "Family Leave and the Gender Wage Gap," p. 726.

50. See Linda R. Hirshman, *Get to Work: A Manifesto for Women of the World* (2006).

51. Leslie Bennetts, *The Feminine Mistake: Are We Giving Up Too Much?* (2007).

52. Katz, *Family Law in America*, p. 93. For a survey of current property division rules, see John DeWitt Gregory et al., *Property Division in Divorce Proceedings: A Fifty State Guide* (2003).

53. Uniform Marriage and Divorce Act (UMDA), 9A U.L.A. 159 (1970, amended 1973). The initial version incorporated a "dual property" approach, but in 1973 it was amended to permit division of separate and marital property.

54. Summary, Uniform Marital Property Act, http://nccusl.org (visited Aug. 1, 2010). The Uniform Marital Property Act (UMPA), adopted in 1983, proposed a system that was, essentially, a community property system. But only one state, Wisconsin, enacted the UMPA.

55. Katz, *Family Law in America*, p. 93.

56. See, for example, Marsha Garrison, "Good Intentions Gone Awry: The Impact of New York's Equitable Distribution Law Upon Divorce Outcomes," 57 *Brook. L. Rev.* 621 (1991), p. 681, table 24; James B.

McLindon, "Separate but Unequal: The Economic Disaster of Divorce for Women and Children," 21 *Fam. L. Q.* 351 (1987–88), p. 351.

57. On divorce lawyering in general, see Hubert J. O'Gorman, *Lawyers and Matrimonial Cases: A Study of Informal Pressures in Private Professional Practice* (1963); Austin Sarat and William L. F. Felstiner, *Divorce Lawyers and Their Clients: Power and Meaning in the Legal Process* (1995); Lynn Mather et al., *Divorce Lawyers at Work: Varieties of Professionalism in Practice* (2001); Howard S. Erlanger et al., "Participation and Flexibility in Informal Processes: Cautions from the Divorce Context," 21 *L. & Soc'y Rev.* 585 (1987); Kenneth Kressel, *The Process of Divorce: How Professionals and Couples Negotiate Settlements* (1985).

58. See Golden, *Equitable Distribution of Property*, p. 13.

59. *Ferguson*, p. 933.

60. Judith H. Dobrzynski, "A Corporate Wife Holds Out for a 50-50 Split of Assets," *N.Y. Times*, Jan. 24, 1997.

61. Wendt v. Wendt, 1998 Conn. Super. LEXIS 1023, pp. * 55–56.

62. Dobrzynski, "A Corporate Wife Holds Out for a 50-50 Split of Assets."

63. Ibid.

64. See Betsy Morris, "It's Her Job, Too: Lorna Wendt's $20 Million Divorce Case is the Shot Heard 'Round the Water Cooler," *Fortune*, Feb. 2, 1998, p. 65.

65. Her story is profiled on her own website, lornawendt.com (visited July 23, 2009). See also Ann Crittenden, *The Price of Motherhood* (2001), pp. 131–48.

66. 440 U.S. 268 (1979).

67. Glendon, *The New Family and the New Property*, p. 52.

68. Turner v. Turner, 385 A.2d 1280 (N.J. 1978), pp. 1281–82.

69. See, for example, McLindon, "Separate but Unequal," p. 364, finding, in a study of Connecticut divorces, a drastic reduction in the number of permanent alimony awards between the 1970s and the 1980s.

70. *Turner*, p. 1282. Katz, *Family Law in America*, p. 96.

71. McLindon, "Separate but Unequal," p. 365.

72. Lenore Weitzman, *The Divorce Revolution* (1985), p. 339; Lenore Weitzman, "The Economics of Divorce: Social and Economic Consequences of Property, Alimony and Child Support Awards," 28 *UCLA L. Rev.* 1181 (1981).

73. Herma Hill Kay, "Equality and Difference: A Perspective on No-Fault Divorce and its Aftermath," 56 *U. Cinn. L. Rev.* 1 (1987), p. 61 n. 311, notes the attention this statistic attracted in both academic and popular venues.

74. See, for example, Heather Ruth Wishik, "Economics of Divorce: An Exploratory Study," 20 *Fam. L. Q.* 79 (1986–87), p. 98, finding, based

on a review of divorces in 1982–83, that divorce was even more "economically damaging to women and children" in Vermont than in other parts of the country. Vermont convened a Commission on the Status of Women in 1982, charged, in part, to look at the "financial impact of divorce on women and children." Ibid., pp. 80–81. See also Paul Hoffman and John Holmes, *Husbands, Wives and Divorce in Five Thousand American Families—Patterns of Economic Progress* (1976), pp. 27, 31, reporting that men experience a 17 percent increase in standard of living after divorce, while women suffer a 29 percent decrease; McLindon, "Separate but Unequal," summarizing data from a variety of studies, pp. 80–81.

75. Marygold S. Melli, "Constructing a Social Problem: The Post-Divorce Plight of Women and Children," 1986 *Am. B. Found. Res. J.* 759 (1986), p. 770.

76. Bureau of the Census, Current Population Reports Series P-60, No. 173, *Child Support and Alimony: 1989*, p. 12.

77. Ibid., p. 13.

78. Marsha Garrison, "The Economic Consequences of Divorce," 32 *Fam. & Conciliation Cts. Rev.* 10 (1994), p. 11.

79. *In re* the Marriage of Larocque, 406 N.W.2d 736 (Wis. 1987).

80. See UMDA sec. 308 for a typical list of factors.

81. American Law Institute, in its *Principles of the Law of Family Dissolution* (2002), secs. 5.01–5.07.

82. Charles E. Welch, III and Sharon Price-Bonham, "A Decade of No-Fault Divorce Revisited: California, Georgia, and Washington," *J. Marriage & Family* (May 1983), p. 415, table 2. In Spokane County, Washington, alimony was awarded in 9.7 percent of cases in 1970 (pre-no-fault), but only in 7 percent of cases in 1980 (post-no-fault). The median award dropped from $125 per month to $94 per month. McLindon, "Separate but Unequal," p. 360.

83. Wishik, "Economics of Divorce," p. 85.

84. Bureau of the Census, U.S. Department of Commerce, *Child Support and Alimony: 1981* (Advance Report), Current Population Reports, Special Studies Series P-23, No. 124 (1984), pp. 24, 32.

85. McLindon, "Separate but Unequal," p. 363.

86. Bureau of the Census, U.S. Department of Commerce, Current Population Reports, Series P-60, No. 173, *Child Support and Alimony: 1989*, p. 12 and table K.

87. Ibid.

88. Freed and Foster, "Divorce in the Fifty States," p. 128.

89. See Employment Retirement Income Security Act of 1974, Pub. L. No. 93-406, 88 Stat. 829 (1974); Retirement Equity Act of 1984, Pub. L. No. 98-397, 98 Stat. 1426 (1984).

90. 489 N.E.2d 712 (N.Y. 1985).

91. Mahoney v. Mahoney, 453 A.2d 527 (N.J. 1982); Kuder v. Schroeder, 430 S.E.2d 271 (Ct. App. N.C. 1993).

92. Havell v. Islam, 301 A.D.2d 339 (N.Y. App. Div. 2002).

93. See Linda D. Elrod and Robert G. Spector, "A Review of the Year in Family Law," 42 *Fam. L. Q.* 713 (2009), chart 5; see also Keathley v. Keathley, 61 S.W.3d 219 (Ark. 2001). Sometimes too the misconduct affects the relative needs of the parties. An injured and abused wife may have lost some of her earning power.

94. American Law Institute, Principles of the Law of Family Dissolution; see also Brett R. Turner, "The Role of Marital Misconduct in Dividing Property upon Divorce," 15 *Divorce Litigation* 117 (July 2003), noting that twenty-seven states exclude consideration of fault. A 1979 state survey found that fifteen states excluded consideration of fault. See Freed and Foster, "Divorce in the Fifty States," p. 115.

95. UMDA, p. 161, prefatory note.

96. N.Y. Dom. Rel. sec. 236B.

97. The "shock the conscience" standard was set out in *Blickstein v. Blickstein*, 99 A.D.2d 287 (N.Y. App. Div. 1984), and applied in *Wenzel v. Wenzel*, 472 N.Y.S.2d 830 (S. Ct. 1984) and *Thompson v. Thompson*, N.Y.L.J., Jan. 5, 1990, p. 28.

98. DeSilva v. DeSilva, 2006 N.Y. Misc. LEXIS 2489 (Sup. Ct. N.Y.).

99. See Howard S. v Lillian S., 62 A.D.3d 187 (N.Y. App. Div. 2009).

100. Some studies report even higher rates of "quasi-marital" children. See Mary R. Anderlik and Mark A. Rothstein, "DNA-Based Identity Testing and the Future of the Family: A Research Agenda," 28 *Am. J. L. & Med.* 215 (2002), p. 222.

101. American Law Institute, *Principles of the Law of Family Dissolution.*

102. Mani v. Mani, 841 A.2d 91 (N. J. 2004). The list of factors to be considered does not include marital misconduct; but court can take into account "any other factor." New Jersey retains fault-based divorce as an alternative method; here fault may be considered in fixing the amount of alimony. The New Jersey State Bar Association filed a brief urging the court to exclude fault; the worry was opening the floodgates to litigation.

103. N.C. Gen. Stat. sec. 50-16.3A (2009).

104. See Freed and Foster, "Divorce in the Fifty States," p. 115, noting that in 1979, nine states treated some types of marital fault as an absolute bar to the receipt of alimony.

105. Ibid.

106. On fixed marital roles, see chapter 2.

107. 581 A.2d 162 (Pa. 1990).

108. On *Simeone* and the contractual approach to prenuptial agreements, see Brian Bix, "Bargaining in the Shadow of Love: The Enforcement of Premarital Agreements and How We Think About Marriage," 40 *Wm. & Mary L. Rev.* 145 (1998).

109. 9B U.L.A. 373 (1983). For the list of states which adopted or are considering adopting UPAA, see http://nccusl.org (visited Aug. 1, 2010). For discussion of the UPAA, see Judith T. Younger, "Perspectives on Antenuptial Agreements: An Update," 8 *J. Am. Acad. Matrimonial L.* 1 (1992); Gail F. Brod, "Premarital Agreements and Gender Justice," 6 *Yale J. L. & Feminism* 229 (1994).

110. The only limitation is, if enforcing the contract would put the poorer spouse on welfare, a court can order the richer spouse to provide minimal support.

111. *In re* Marriage of Shanks, 758 N.W.2d 506 (Iowa 2008).

112. California requires, as a condition of enforceability, that each party be represented by counsel. See Cal. Fam. Code sec. 1612(c) (2010). On the "minimum decencies" in the process that should be required before enforcement, see Judith T. Younger, "Lovers' Contracts in the Courts: Forsaking the Minimum Decencies," 13 *Wm. & Mary J. Women & L.* 349 (2007), 419–20.

113. American Law Institute, *Principles of the Law of Family Dissolution*, secs. 7.04, 7.05.

114. 929 N.E.2d 955 (Mass. 2010).

115. See Bratton v. Bratton, 136 S.W.3d 595 (Tenn. 2004); Casto v. Casto, 508 So. 2d 330 (Fla. 1987); N.Y. Dom. Rel. L. sec. 236(B)(3) (2010), which provides that an "agreement by the parties, made before or during the marriage, shall be valid and enforceable in a matrimonial action if such agreement is in writing, subscribed by the parties, and acknowledged or proven in the manner required to entitle a deed to be recorded"; Cal. Fam. Code sec. 1500 (2010). Ohio seems to be the only state that expressly bans postnuptial agreements. Ohio Rev. Code Ann. sec. 3103.06 (2010) provides that a "husband and wife cannot, by any contract with each other, alter their legal relations, except that they may agree to an immediate separation and make provisions for the support of either of them during the separation." Many states treat premarital and postmarital agreements the same, but *Ansin* requires greater scrutiny for the latter, as do the ALI Principles of Family Dissolution, sec. 7.01 cmt. e.

116. *In re* Marriage of Cooper, 769 N.W.2d 582 (Iowa 2009).

117. Ibid., p. 586.

118. On the history of the enforceability of separation agreements, see Sally Burnett Sharp, "Fairness Standards and Separation Agreements: A Word of Caution on Contractual Freedom," 132 *U. Pa. L. Rev.* 1399 (1984).

119. So provided in the UMDA sec. 306.

120. Robert H. Mnookin and Lewis Kornhauser, "Bargaining in the Shadow of the Law: The Case of Divorce," 88 *Yale L.J.* 950 (1979). ALI Principles, drafted later than the UMDA, recommend less deference to separation agreements. Such agreements are unenforceable if they "impair the economic well-being" of the custodial parent, or one with less money.

121. Ibid.

122. See Homer C. Clark, Jr., *The Law of Domestic Relations in the United States* (2d ed. 1988), p. 755.

123. Joann Loviglio, "Attorney Freed After Being Jailed 14 Years for Contempt in Divorce Case" (July 13, 2009), http://www.law.com/jsp/article.jsp?id=1202432191681 (visited Aug. 1, 2010).

124. Welch and Price-Bonham, "A Decade of No-Fault Divorce Revisited: California, Georgia, and Washington," p. 411.

125. Census Brief: Children with Single Parents—How They Fare, CENBR/97-1, p. 1, available at http://www.census.gov/prod/3/97pubs/cb-9701.pdf. Data from 2008 reveal that over half of families living in poverty are headed by a woman with no husband. See U.S. Census Bureau, Current Population Survey, 2008 and 2009 Annual Social and Economic Supplements, Table 4, available at http://www.census.gov/hhes/www/poverty/data/incpovhlth/2008/table4.pdf.

126. Garrison, "The Economic Consequences of Divorce," pp. 18–19.

CHAPTER TEN
COLLATERAL DAMAGE: THE CHILDREN OF DIVORCE

1. For a thoughtful analysis of this default approach, see David Meyer, "The Constitutional Rights of Non-Custodial Parents," 34 *Hofstra L. Rev.* 1461 (2006).

2. June Carbone argues, in *From Partners to Parents* (2000), that the centrality of custody determinations to divorce proceedings is part of a larger shift in family law from an emphasis on adult relationships to one on parent-child relationships.

3. Michael Grossberg, *Governing the Hearth: Law and the Family in Nineteenth Century America* (1985), p. 235.

4. See, in general, Mary Ann Mason, *From Father's Property to Children's Rights: The History of Child Custody in the United States* (1994).

5. See Elizabeth Cady Stanton et al., eds., *Declaration of Sentiments* (1848), reprinted in 1 *History of Woman Suffrage* 70–71, (1881), photo reprint 1985.

6. Grossberg, *Governing the Hearth*.

7. Painter v. Bannister, 140 N.W.2d 152 (Iowa 1966).

8. For another psychiatric perspective on this case, see Anna Freud, "*Painter v. Bannister*: Postscript by a Psychoanalyst," 7 *The Writings of Anna Freud* 247 (1966–70).

9. Harold Painter, *Mark, I Love You* (1980). The book was also turned into a made-for-television movie. Information is available at http://www.imdb.com/title/tt0081129/ (visited Aug. 1, 2010).

10. See Barbara A. Atwood, "The Child's Voice in Custody Litigation: An Empirical Survey and Suggestions for Reform," 45 *Ariz. L. Rev.* 629 (2003).

11. See, for example, Pusey v. Pusey, 728 1d 117 (Utah 1986).

12. Ibid., p. 120.

13. Watts v. Watts, 350 N.Y.S.2d 285 (1973), p. 290.

14. See, for example, Garska v. McCoy, 278 S.E.2d 357 (W. Va. 1981).

15. See, for example, Kathryn L. Mercer, "A Content Analysis of Judicial Decision-Making—How Judges Use the Primary Caretaker Standard to Make a Custody Determination," 5 *Wm. & Mary J. of Women & L.* 1 (1998), which examines the role continuity of care plays in custody decision-making.

16. See, for example, Squires v. Squires, 854 S.W.2d 765 (Ky. 1993). The Uniform Marriage and Divorce Act bars any modification within two years of the initial order unless there is present danger to the child. Even after two years, the status quo is strongly presumed to be the best situation. See Unif. Marriage & Divorce Act sec. 409 (1970, amended 1973).

17. See Jody Heymann, *The Widening Gap: Why America's Working Families Are in Jeopardy and What Can Be Done About It* (2000).

18. Available data on current patterns of household work are available at http://mothersandmore.org/press_room/statistics.shtml (visited Aug. 1, 2010).

19. See Eleanor Maccoby and Robert Mnookin, *Dividing the Child: Social and Legal Dilemmas of Custody* (1992), p. 284; see also Wendy Reiboldt and Sharon Seiling, "Factors Related to Men's Award of Custody," 15 *Fam. Advoc.* 42 (1993).

20. Karen Czapanskiy, "Volunteers and Draftees: The Struggle for Parental Equality," 38 *UCLA L. Rev.* 1415 (1991).

21. Ireland v. Smith, 547 N.W.2d 686 (Mich. 1996).

22. See, for example, Burchard v. Garay, 724 P.2d 486 (Cal. 1986).

23. Simpson was acquitted of the criminal charges, but later found liable in civil court for the "wrongful death" of both victims. For an account and timeline of both proceedings, see B. Drummond Ayres, Jr., "Civil Jury Finds Simpson Liable in Pair of Killings," *N.Y. Times*, Feb. 5, 1997, p. A16.

24. Tamar Lewin, "Demands of Simpson Case Land Prosecutor in Custody Fight," *N.Y. Times*, Mar. 3, 1995, p. B8.

25. Alice Hector initially lost custody of her two daughters primarily because she worked long hours and her husband did not. This ruling, however, was vacated after a rehearing by the court of appeals. See Young v. Hector, 740 So. 2d 1153 (Ct. App. Fla. 1999); Melody Petersen, "Working Mother Regains Custody of Two Children," *N.Y. Times*, July 15, 1999, p. C10.

26. The Prost case and other similar ones are discussed in Melody Petersen, "The Short End of Long Hours; A Female Lawyer's Job Puts Child Custody at Risk," *N.Y. Times*, July 18, 1998, p. D1.

27. On reforms necessary to reduce conflict in custody disputes, see Andrew I. Schepard, *Children, Courts, and Custody: Interdisciplinary Models for Divorcing Families* (2004).

28. On these devices, see *Psychological Testing in Custody Cases*, http://www.divorcenet.com/states/nationwide/psychological_testing _in_custody_cases (visited Aug. 1, 2010).

29. See, for example, Ellis v. Ellis, 952 So. 2d 982 (2007). On the controversy, see Barbara Jo Fidler and Nicholas Bala, "Children Resisting Postseparation Contact with a Parent: Concepts, Controversies, and Conundrums," 48 *Fam. Ct. Rev.* 10 (2010); Richard A. Warshak, "Bringing Sense to Parental Alienation: A Look at the Disputes and the Evidence," 37 *Fam. L. Q.* 273 (2003).

30. On the role of controversial parental beliefs and practices in custody determinations, see Eugene Volokh, "Parent-Child Speech and Child Custody Speech Restrictions," 81 *N.Y.U. L. Rev.* 631 (2006).

31. Jarrett v. Jarrett, 400 N.E.2d 421 (Ill. 1979).

32. Ibid., pp. 426–27.

33. Roe v. Roe, 324 S.E.2d 691 (Va. 1985), p. 727. A Louisiana court granted disproportionate joint custody time to the father over the lesbian mother "where the sexual preference is known and openly admitted, where there have been open, indiscreet displays of affection beyond mere friendship and where the child is of an age where gender identity is being formed." Lundin v. Lundin, 563 So. 2d 1273 (La. App. 1990), p. 1277. The difficulties faced by lesbian mothers and the grassroots movement that arose to protect them in custody cases are depicted artfully in a documentary, *Mom's Apple Pie: The Heart of the Lesbian Mothers' Custody Movement* (2007).

34. On this point, see the discussion of gay and lesbian parenting in chapter 12.

35. Pulliam v. Smith, 501 S.E.2d 898 (N.C. 1998).

36. Frank F. Furstenberg, Jr. and Christine W. Nord, "Parenting Apart: Patterns of Childrearing after Marital Disruption," 47 *J. Marriage & Family* 893 (1985), p. 902.

37. See, for example, Taylor v. Taylor, 508 A.2d 964 (Md. 1986).

38. For a critique of joint custody at its high point, see Jana B. Singer and William L. Reynolds, "A Dissent on Joint Custody," 47 *Md. L. Rev.* 497 (1988).

39. But see Eleanor Maccoby and Robert Mnookin, in their study of joint custody in California: Maccoby and Mnookin, *Dividing the Child*.

40. 507 N.W.2d 788 (Mich 1993).

41. See Maccoby and Mnookin, *Dividing the Child*; see also Margaret F. Brinig, "Does Parental Autonomy Require Equal Custody at Divorce?" 65 *La. L. Rev.* 1345 (2005).

42. See Martha Fineman, *The Autonomy Myth: A Theory of Dependency* (2004).

43. See American Law Institute, *Principles of the Law of Family Dissolution: Analysis and Recommendations* (2002), sec. 2.08; Marygold S. Melli, "The American Law Institute Principles of Family Dissolution, the Approximation Rule and Shared-Parenting," 25 *N. Ill. U. L. Rev.* 347 (2005).

44. For recent census data on living arrangements, see Rose M. Kreider and Diana B. Elliott, U.S. Census Bureau, *America's Families and Living Arrangements: 2007* (2009), p. 16, figure 9; see also Irwin Garfinkel et al., "Child Support Orders: A Perspective on Reform," 4 *The Future of Children: Children and Divorce* 84 (1994), p. 84; Patricia H. Shiono and Linda Sandham Quinn, "Epidemiology of Divorce," 4 *The Future of Children: Children and Divorce* (1994), p. 15. The marriage rate in the United States has declined over the course of the twentieth century from an all-time post–World War II high of 143 per 1,000 women to only 76 per 1,000 women in 1988.

45. Garfinkel et al., "Child Support Orders," p. 1, observe that "judicial discretion is giving way to administrative regularity" in matters of child support On this shift, see also Donna Schuele, "Origins and Development of the Law of Parental Child Support," 27 *J. Fam. L.* 807 (1988), pp. 825–26; Grossberg, *Governing the Hearth*, pp. 291–92.

46. Chester G. Vernier, *American Family Laws*, vol. IV (1936), p. 4. See also Schuele, "Origins and Development of the Law of Parental Child Support," pp. 809–16.

47. Schuele, "Origins and Development in the Law of Parental Child Support," p. 825.

48. Vernier, *American Family Laws*, Vol. IV, p. 5; Nan D. Hunter, "Child Support Law and Policy: The Systematic Imposition of Costs on Women," 6 *Harv. Women's L. J.* 1 (1983), p. 3.

49. Cal. Civ. Code. secs. 206-7 (1933), in Vernier, *American Family Laws*, Vol. IV, p. 67.

50. Iowa Code sec. 13230 (1927), in Vernier, *American Family Laws*, Vol. IV, p. 72.

51. Ibid., p. 5.

52. On the low rate of child support awards in the early part of the twentieth century, see J. Schouler, *A Treatise on the Law of Marriage, Divorce, Separation and Domestic Relations* (1921), pp. 880–85; William Goode, *After Divorce* (1956), p. 222.

53. Garfinkel et al., "Child Support Orders: A Perspective on Reform," p. 85.

54. Ibid. On the structure and inadequacies of the child support system as of 1981, see Harry Krause, *Child Support in America: The Legal Perspective* (1981).

55. Garfinkel et al., "Child Support Orders: A Perspective on Reform," p. 85. On typical child support laws as of 1983, see Hunter, "Child Support Law and Policy," pp. 5–6.

56. On the difficulties of using common-law mechanisms for collecting past due support, see Schuele, "Origins and Development of the Law of Parental Child Support," pp. 826–39.

57. See, for example, Hunter, "Child Support Law and Policy," pp. 15–17.

58. Ibid., p. 15.

59. See Child Support Enforcement Amendments of 1984, Pub. L. No. 98-378, codified at 42 U.S.C. sec. 667 (1984).

60. See Family Support Act of 1988, pub. L. No. 100-485, codified as 42 U.S.C. sec. 667(b)(2) (1988).

61. See Maureen A. Pirog et al., "Interstate Comparisons of Child Support Orders Using State Guidelines," 47 *Fam. Rel.* 289 (1998), p. 289, citing CSR, Inc., *Evaluating Child Support Guidelines: Report to the Office of Child Support Enforcement* (1996).

62. Thomas B. v. Lydia D., 69 A.D.3d 24 (N.Y. App. Div. 2009).

63. See Chen v. Warner, 695 N.W.2d 758 (Wis. 2005).

64. Lopez v. Ajose, 2005 *N.Y.L.J.*, April 5, 2005, p. 19, col. 1.

65. See discussion of women and wage-earning in chapter 9.

66. In most jurisdictions, child support awards can be reviewed periodically for cost-of-living adjustments, but unless circumstances change substantially, the awards will not be recalculated (apart from the cost-of-living adjustments). See, for example, Ky. Rev. Stat. Ann., sec. 403.213 (2010). On the custodial parent's freedom to relocate, see Lucy S. McGough, "Starting Over: The Heuristics of Family Relocation Decision Making," 77 *St. John's L. Rev.* 291 (2003).

67. *In re* Vrban, 293 N.W.2d 198 (Iowa 1980).

68. La. Rev. Stat. Ann. sec. 9:315.11 (2009). Similarly, the ALI recommends against imputing income, based on earning capacity, to a custodial parent with young children. *Principles of the Law of Family Dissolution* secs. 3.14(5), 3.15(1)(a). Wisconsin permits judges to use actual rather than imputed income in figuring support payments,

if the voluntary reduction in income is reasonable under the circumstances.

69. Pirog et al., "Interstate Comparisons of Child Support Orders Using State Guidelines," p. 291.

70. Mike Tierney, "With Nine Mouths to Feed, Travis Henry Says He's Broke," *N.Y. Times*, Mar. 12, 2009, p. B14.

71. See Henry v. Beacham, 686 S.E.2d 892 (Ga. App. 2009).

72. See, in general, Garfinkel et al., "Child Support Orders," p. 90. The ALI Principles provide that a noncustodial parent's income base for determining support is reduced by child support payments he already owes to other children. American Law Institute, *Principles of the Law of Family Dissolution*, sec. 3.14(3).

73. See Ann Nichols-Casebolt and Irwin Garfinkel, "Trends in Paternity Adjudications and Child Support Awards," 72 *Soc. Science Q.* 83 (1991), p. 84. On the structure and effectiveness of incentives and penalties under federal child support enforcement law, see Judith H. Cassetty and Royce Hutson, "Effectiveness of Federal Incentives in Shaping Child Support Enforcement Outcomes," 27 *Child. & Youth Servs. Rev.* 271 (2005).

74. Blaine Harden, "Finding Common Ground on Poor Deadbeat Dads," *N.Y. Times*, Feb. 3, 2002, p. D3.

75. Karen DeMasters, "Deadbeat Dads (and Moms) Are Rounded Up in Raids," *N.Y. Times*, May 17, 1998, p. M6.

76. Robert Pear, "U.S. Agents Arrest Dozens of Fathers in Support Cases," *N.Y. Times*, Aug. 19, 2002.

77. Prior to 1996, federal law mandated that states grant a $50 disregard per month, which meant that a mother receiving public assistance could keep the first $50 collected in child support, before making any welfare reimbursement. The 1996 welfare reform repealed that mandate; it was now up to the states to decide whether to do this, and in what amount. See Personal Responsibility and Work Opportunity Reconciliation Act, Pub. L. No. 104-193, 110 Stat. 2105 (1996).

78. Harden, "Finding Common Ground."

79. See U.S. Census Bureau, Current Population Reports, Special Studies, Series 9-23, *Child Support and Alimony: 1981* (1985), p. 2, table A.

80. U.S. Census Bureau, Current Population Reports, Series P-60, *Child Support and Alimony: 1989*, p. 4, table B. On general trends, see Nichols-Casebolt and Garfinkel, "Trends in Paternity Adjudications and Child Support Awards."

81. Timothy S. Grall, Current Population Reports, *Custodial Mothers and Fathers and Their Child Support: 1981*, P60-225 (2003), p. 2, table A. On reasons why so many women do not have child support in place, see Chien-Chung Huang, "'Why Doesn't She Have a Support Order?'

Personal Choice or Objective Constraint," 54 *Fam. Rel.* 547 (2005), which found that a majority of women without an order faced an "objective constraint" to getting one.

82. Ibid.

83. See Ira Mark Ellman, "Should Visitation Denial Affect the Obligation to Pay Support?" 36 *Ariz. St. L. J.* 661 (2004).

84. According to a 1989 census report, 90.2 percent of fathers with joint custody pay child support, versus 79.1 percent with only visitation privileges, and 44.5 percent with neither joint custody nor visitation rights. See Gordon H. Lester, Current Population Reports, Series P-60 No. 173, U.S. Census, *Child Support and Alimony: 1989* (1991), p. 7; see also Chien-Chung Huang, "Mothers' Reports of Nonresident Fathers' Involvement with Their Children: Revisiting the Relationship Between Child Support Payment and Visitation," 58 *Fam. Rel.* 54 (2009); Judith A. Seltzer et al., "Family Ties After Divorce: The Relationship Between Visiting and Paying Child Support," 51 *J. Marriage & Fam.* (1989), p. 1013. Marygold Melli argues that child support guidelines should have specific formulas to reflect different time-sharing arrangements, in "Guideline Review: Child Support and Time Sharing by Parents," 33 *Fam. L. Q.* 219 (1999).

85. See Lydia Scoon-Rogers and Gordon H. Lester, Current Population Reports, Series P60-187, Bureau of the Census, *Child Support for Custodial Mothers and Fathers: 1991*, (1995); see also Hunter, "Child Support Law and Policy," p. 2.

86. Grall, "Custodial Mothers and Fathers," p. 1.

87. Ibid., p. 3.

88. On the adverse effects of the child support system on women, see, in general, Hunter, "Child Support Law and Policy"; Judi Bartfeld, "Child Support and the Postdivorce Economic Well-Being of Mothers, Fathers, and Children," 37 *Demography* 203 (2000), pp. 203–4.

89. See, for example, Pirog et al., "Interstate Comparisons of Child Support Orders Using State Guidelines," p. 293.

90. Bartfeld, "Child Support and the Postdivorce Economic Well-Being of Mothers, Fathers, and Children," p. 211.

91. Donald T. Oellerich et al., "Private Child Support: Current and Potential Impacts," 18 *J. Soc. & Soc. Welfare* 3 (1991), p. 3.

Chapter Eleven
The Extended Family: Elder Law and the Law of Inheritance

1. For more detail, see Lawrence M. Friedman, *Dead Hands: A Social History of Wills, Trusts, and Inheritance Law* (2009).

2. On these figures, see ibid., p. 60.

3. Fla. Stat. sec. 732.102 (2010).

4. In other states, the surviving spouse gets a lump sum plus one-half of the balance of the estate if there are surviving descendants. See, for example, Fla. Stat. sec. 732.103.

5. See Friedman, *Dead Hands*, pp. 86–87.

6. Unif. Probate Code secs. 2-103, 2-105 (1990, amended 2008). See also Ala. Rev. Code sec. 43-8-42 (2009); N.M. Stat. sec. 45-2-103 (2010); W.Va. Code sec. 42-1-3a (2010).

7. See chapter 14.

8. On the historical treatment of illegitimate children, see John Witte, Jr., "Ishmael's Bane: The Sin and Crime of Illegitimacy Reconsidered," 5 *Punishment & Soc'y* 327 (2003).

9. Probate Act of Illinois, 1953, ch. 12.

10. 391 U.S. 68 (1968). Legal ties between non-marital children and their fathers are also reinforced by a series of cases recognizing the constitutional parental rights of unwed fathers. See discussion in chapter 13.

11. Solangel Maldonado drew our attention to an unusual case in which the Iowa Supreme Court upheld a statute expressly authorizing courts to force divorced parents, but not never-married parents, to contribute to a child's college tuition. See Johnson v. Louis, 654 N.W.2d 886 (Iowa 2002), explaining that the "educational benefit is a quid pro quo for the loss of stability resulting from divorce," while non-marital children "cannot claim the loss of stability such change in status brings." Ibid., p. 891.

12. Ala. Code sec. 43-8-48(2) (2010).

13. Wash. Rev. Code sec. 11.04.081 (2010).

14. See, for example, United Kingdom Inheritance (Provisions for Family and Dependants) Act 1975. On the merits of a discretionary distribution system, see Frances Foster, "Linking Support and Inheritance: A New Model From China," 1999 *Wis. L. Rev.* 1199; Ronald Chester, "Disinheritance and the American Child: An Alternative From British Columbia," 1998 *Utah L. Rev.* 1; Helene S. Shapo, "A Tale of Two Systems: Anglo-American Problems in the Modernization of Inheritance Legislation," 60 *Tenn. L. Rev.* 707 (1993).

15. On the complex story of cases seeking compensation for caretaking of elderly relatives, see Hendrik Hartog, "Someday All This Will Be Yours: Inheritance, Adoption, and Obligation in Capitalist America," 79 *Ind. L.J.* 345 (2004).

16. See Ralph C. Brasier, *Inheritance and the Evolving Family* (2004), p. 87.

17. See Cal. Fam. Code sec. 297.5(c) (2010).

18. Estate of Cooper, 187 A.D.2d 128 (N.Y. App. Div. 1993). John Langan was similarly deprived of standing to bring a wrongful death claim

against a hospital allegedly responsible for his partner's death, even though they were joined in a civil union. Langan v. St. Vincent's Hosp., 850 N.E.2d 672 (N.Y. 2006). The same court, however, allowed a man to take over tenancy of his same-sex partner's rent-controlled apartment, a right typically reserved for legal relatives. Braschi v. Stahl Associates, 543 N.E.2d 49 (N.Y. 1989).

19. See Martinez v. City of Monroe, 50 A.D. 3d 189 (N.Y. App. Div. 2008), recognizing a Canadian marriage for employment benefit purposes; Godfrey v. Spano, 107 Fair Empl. Prac. Cas. (BNA) 1358 (2009), upholding two governmental orders requiring recognition of same-sex marriages validly celebrated out of state. See also our discussion of the legal rights of same-sex couples in chapter 7.

20. Wills are formal documents. They have to be executed just so: they need two witnesses, and a certain form of ceremony. In about half the states, however, you can dispense with witnesses and ceremony, so long as the will you execute is entirely in your handwriting, and signed—a so-called holographic will.

21. Ga. Code Ann. sec. 53-4-1 (2010).

22. Recall the discussion of marital property laws in chapter 9.

23. "Strauss Will Fight Seen," *N.Y. Times*, July 25, 1934, p. 35.

24. Newman v. Dore, 9 N.E.2d 966 (N.Y. 1937).

25. New York was the first state to adopt such a system. See N.Y. EPTL sec. 5-1.1 (2010).

26. Wis. Stat. sec. 169.3935 (1915).

27. The older statute was Cal. Prob. Code sec. 640; the present statute is sec. 6602.

28. Conn. Gen. Stat. sec. 45a-320c (2010).

29. Okla. Stats, tit. 58, sec. 311 (2010).

30. See N.Y. EPTL sec. 5-3.1 (2010).

31. Wyo. Stat. Ann. sec. 2-7-508 (2010).

32. Fla. Stat. sec. 732-4015 (2010). The right was substantially pared down as of October 1, 2010.

33. Cal. Prob. Code sec. 6524 (2010).

34. (Former) Cal. Civ. Code sec. 1307.

35. See, for example, N.Y. EPTL sec. 5-3.2 (2010).

36. La. Civ. Code sec. 1493 (2010).

37. See, for example, Nev. Rev. Stat. sec. 125B.1309 (2010).

38. For more on the lack of inheritance protection for children, see Friedman, *Dead Hands*, pp. 36–44.

39. Lawrence Friedman et al., "The Inheritance Process in San Bernardino County, California, 1964: A Research Note," 43 *Hous. L. Rev.* 1445 (2007), p. 1462.

40. Carole Shammas et al., *Inheritance in America: From Colonial Times to the Present* (1987), p. 184.

41. Friedman, *Dead Hands*, p. 141.

42. The story is told in David Margolick, *Undue Influence: The Epic Battle for the Johnson & Johnson Fortune* (1994).

43. See "The Forbes 400 Richest Americans 2009," available at http://www.forbes.com/lists/2009/54/rich-list-09_Barbara-Piasecka-Johnson_709C.html (visited Aug. 1, 2010).

44. A will can only be contested by someone with a pecuniary stake in the outcome. Close family members are often the only ones with standing, because they will usually inherit through intestacy, if the will in question is declared invalid.

45. "Olcott Will Probated," *N.Y. Times*, July 15, 1903, p. 1.

46. "A Man's Will's His Will," *Wash. Post*, Jan. 5, 1906, p. 3.

47. *In re* Estate of Strittmater, 53 A.2d 205 (N.J. 1947).

48. Matter of Kaufmann, 20 A.D.2d 464 (N.Y. App. Div. 1964), aff'd, 205 N.E.2d 864 (1965).

49. The poll was conducted by the Indiana University Center for Survey Research, on behalf of an organization called "Indiana Equality." Interestingly, although a majority favored giving these couples inheritance rights, it was a weaker majority than on other issues—74 percent thought these couples should have hospital visitation rights, for example.

50. S.C. Code Ann. sec. 8695 (1932).

51. Ind. Code sec 29-1-2-14 (2010); and yet, see n. 49 above, on the attitude of the good people of Indiana toward inheritance rights for same-sex partners.

52. See N.C. Gen. Stat. sec. 31A-1 (2010).

53. N.Y. EPTL sec. 5-1.2; see also Pa. Cons. Stat. sec. 20-2106 (2010).

54. See Restatement (Third) of Property: Wills and Other Donative Transfers sec. 9.7 (2003); see also, for example, Shriners Hospitals for Crippled Children v. Zrillic, 563 So. 2d 64 (Fla. 1990).

55. The most famous volume in this literature is Norman F. Dacey, *How to Avoid Probate* (1965). Although the book sold millions of copies, Dacey was sued multiple times for allegedly engaging in the unauthorized practice of law. See Richard D. Lyons, "Obituary, Norman Dacey, 85; Advised His Readers to Avoid Probate," *N.Y. Times*, Mar. 19, 1994.

56. The first case recognizing this arrangement was Matter of Totten, 71 N.E. 748 (N.Y. 1904). It is now codified and regulated by statute in New York. See N.Y. EPTL secs. 7-5.1 *et seq.* (2010).

57. John H. Langbein, "The Twentieth-Century Revolution in Family Wealth Transmission," 86 *Mich. L. Rev.* 722 (1988).

58. Shapira v. Union Nat'l Bank, 315 N.E.2d 825 (Ohio Ct. Common Pleas 1974). In most states, will or trust provisions imposing complete restraints on marriage or providing incentives to divorce are invalid, but partial restraints are tolerated.

59. 25 Del. C. sec. 503 (2010). See Jesse Dukeminier and James E. Krier, "The Rise of the Perpetual Trust," 50 *UCLA L. Rev.* 1303 (2003).

60. We are indebted to Micah G. Block, J.D., Stanford, 2009, for some of the references in this section; and also to Andrew Shupanitz, Stanford Law School, for help with the research.

61. N.D. Cent. Code sec. 14-09-10 (2010).

62. Ann Britton, "America's Best Kept Secret: An Adult Child's Duty to Support Aged Parents," 26 *Cal. W. L. Rev.* 351 (1990).

63. "California Doctor Plans Old Age Utopia," *N.Y. Times*, Dec. 22, 1934, p. 15.

64. "Townsend Group Queries Congress," *N.Y. Times*, Dec. 15, 1935, p. 1.

65. I. M. Rubinow, *The Quest for Security* (1934), pp. 222–23.

66. Ibid., p. 238.

67. 79 Cong. Rec. 5,594 (1935).

68. Terrance A. Kline, "A Rational Role for Filial Responsibility Laws in Modern Society?" 26 *Fam. L. Q.* 195 (1992), p. 199.

69. Edward A. Gargan, "House Panel Finds Widespread and Growing Abuse of the Elderly," *N.Y. Times*, Apr. 3, 1981, p. A12.

70. Eleanor Nelson, "Battered Elders—a Growing 'Unseen' Problem," *Chi. Trib.*, Dec. 1, 1982, p. B3.

71. Billingslea v. Texas, 780 S.W.2d 271 (Tex. Crim. App. 1989).

72. National Center on Elder Abuse, http://www.ncea.aoa.gov/NCEAroot/Main_Site/Index.aspx (visited Aug. 1, 2010).

73. Cal. Prob. Code sec. 259 (2010).

74. *In re* Estate of Malbrough, 768 N.E.2d 120 (Ill. App. 2002).

75. American Bar Association and American Psychological Association, *Assessment of Older Adults with Diminished Capacity: A Handbook for Psychologists* (2008), p. 11.

76. N.Y. Mental Hyg. Law sec. 81.02 (a) (2) (2010).

77. 528 N.W.2d 567 (Iowa 1995).

78. 1977 Cal. Stat. ch. 453.

79. Lawrence M. Friedman and June O. Starr, "Losing It in California: Conservatorship and the Social Organization of Aging," 73 *Wash. U. L. Q.* 1501 (1995).

80. See Steve Stoliar, *Raised Eyebrows: My Years Inside Groucho's House* (1996), p. 26; Stefan Kanfer, *Groucho: The Life and Times of Julius Henry Marx* (2000), p. 411.

81. Roxana Robinson, *Georgia O'Keefe: A Life* (1989), p. 523.

82. Ibid., p. 558.

83. Lisa Anderson, "Tragic Opera: Sir Rudolf Bing, Wife Are in a Drama of Dignity Lost," *Chi. Trib.*, May 15, 1988, p. C1; Timothy Clifford, "Bings Are Single Again," *Newsday*, Sept. 7, 1989, p. 6.

CHAPTER TWELVE
PARENTS AND CHILDREN: RIGHTS AND DUTIES

1. B. F. Skinner, *Walden Two* (2d ed. 1976), pp. 131–32.

2. Cited in Meyer v. Nebraska, 262 U.S. 390 (1923), pp. 401–2.

3. The Supreme Court, in *Mormon Church v. United States*, 136 U.S. 1 (1890), described the parens patriae doctrine as "inherent in the supreme power of every state, ... a most beneficient function, and often necessary to be exercised in the interests of humanity, and for the prevention of injury to those who can protect themselves." See also Joseph Story, *Commentaries on Equity Jurisprudence* (3d ed. 1843), sec. 1341, describing the state's right to interfere when a father "acts in a manner injurious to the morals or interests of his children."

4. On the argument that the state should provide more affirmative support to families, see Maxine Eichner, *The Supportive State: Families, Government, and America's Political Ideals* (2010); Linda C. McClain, *The Place of Families: Fostering Capacity, Equality, and Responsibility* (2006).

5. 262 U.S. 390 (1923).

6. Ibid., pp. 402–3.

7. 268 U.S. 510 (1925).

8. Ibid., p. 534.

9. Ibid., p. 535.

10. 321 U.S. 158 (1944).

11. Marvin Ventrell, "Evolution of the Dependency Component of the Juvenile Court," 19 *Child. Legal Rts. J.* 2 (1999), p. 16.

12. See, in general, Maxine Eichner, "Who Should Control Children's Education?: Parents, Children, and the State," 75 *U. Cin. L. Rev.* 1339 (2007).

13. See Michael S. Katz, *A History of Compulsory Education Laws* (1976). For a survey of current compulsory education laws, see Eric A. DeGroff, "State Regulation of Nonpublic Schools: Does the Tie Still Bind?," 2003 *B.Y.U. Educ. & L.J.* 363.

14. 406 U.S. 205 (1972).

15. For a critique of this exclusive focus on curricular standards, see Emily Buss, "The Adolescent's Stake in the Allocation of Educational Control between Parent and State," 67 *U. Chi. L. Rev.* 1233 (2000).

16. On home schooling, see, in general, Kimberly A. Yuracko, "Education Off the Grid: Constitutional Constraints on Homeschooling," 96 *Cal. L. Rev.* 123 (2008).

17. *In re* Rachel L., 73 Cal. Rptr. 3d 77 (2008), vacated and replaced by Jonathan L. v. Super. Ct., 165 Cal. App. 4th 1074 (2008). The Michigan Supreme Court ruled in 1993 that the state could require teacher certification for home schooling that was not undertaken for religious reasons. See Michigan v. Bennett, 501 N.W.2d 106 (Mich. 1993).

18. 197 U.S. 11 (1905).

19. Zucht v. King, 260 U.S. 174 (1922).

20. On this controversy, see Sylvia Law, "Human Papillomavirus Vaccination, Private Choice, and Public Health," 41 *U.C. Davis L. Rev.* 1731 (2008); Tracy Solomon Dowling, "Mandating a Human Papillomavirus Vaccine," 34 *Am. J. L. & Med.* 65 (2008).

21. See, in general, James Keith Colgrove, *Vaccination Policy, Politics and Law in the Twentieth Century* (2004); Note, "Toward a Twenty-First Century *Jacobson v. Massachusetts*," 121 *Harv. L. Rev.* 1820 (2008). On current exemptions in state law, see Sean Coletti, Note, "Taking Account of Partial Exemptors in Vaccination Law, Policy, and Practice," 46 *Conn. L. Rev.* 1341 (2004), pp. 1370–75.

22. *In re* Hofbauer, 47 N.Y.2d 648, 656 (1979).

23. "Study Says Laetrile Is Not Effective as Cancer Cure," *N.Y. Times,* May 1, 1981; Harold M. Schmeck, Jr., "Final Report on U.S. Laetrile Study Says Drug Has No Value," *N.Y. Times,* Jan. 28, 1982.

24. See Walter H. Waggoner, "Boy, 10, in Laetrile Case," *N.Y. Times,* July 18, 1990.

25. Ibid. Patients had tried to force the government to allow them access to Laetrile. The Supreme Court upheld the right of the Food and Drug Administration to keep Laetrile off the market. See United States v. Rutherford, 442 U.S. 544 (1979).

26. On this issue, see, in general, Elizabeth A. Lingle, "Treating Children by Faith: Colliding Constitutional Issues," 17 *J. Legal Med.* 301 (1996); James G. Dwyer, "The Children We Abandon: Religious Exemptions to Child Welfare and Education Laws as Denials of Equal Protection to Children of Religious Objectors," 74 *N.C. L. Rev.* 1321 (1996).

27. See 42 U.S.C. sec. 5106i(a) (2010).

28. Compare, for example, *In re* Sampson, 278 N.E.2d 918 (N.Y. 1972), upholding a court order for surgery to correct a teenager's facial deformities, with *In re* Seiferth, 127 N.E.2d 820 (N.Y. 1955), refusing to override parent's objection to surgery to correct a cleft palate and hairlip.

29. See Emma Graves Fitzsimmons, "Wisconsin Couple Sentenced in Death of Their Sick Child," *N.Y. Times,* Oct. 8, 2009, p. A16. See, in general, Shawn Francis Peters, *When Prayer Fails: Faith Healing, Children, and the Law* (2007).

30. See U.S. Dep't. of Health and Human Svcs., *Child Maltreatment 2008*.

31. The case is discussed in Michele Bratcher Goodwin, "Baby Markets," in *Baby Markets: Money and the New Politics of Creating Families* (Michele Bratcher Goodwin, ed., 2010), pp. 2, 8–9.

32. 25 U.S.C. sec. 1901ff (2010).

33. See Santosky v. Kramer, 455 U.S. 745 (1982).

34. See Sallie A. Watkins, "The Mary Ellen Myth: Correcting Child Welfare History," 35 *Social Work* 500 (1990).

35. Mary Ellen's story was retold in a recent article, Howard Markel, "Case Shined First Light on Abuse of Children," *N.Y. Times*, Dec. 15, 2009, p. D6.

36. "Mrs. Connolly, the Guardian, Found Guilty, and Sentenced to One Year's Imprisonment at Hard Labor," *N.Y. Times*, Apr. 28, 1874. On the case, see a series of articles under the tagline "Mary Ellen Wilson" in the *New York Times* on April 11, 12, and 14, 1874.

37. This history is discussed in great detail in Jill Elaine Hasday, "Parenthood Divided: A Legal History of the Bifurcated Law of Parental Relations," 90 *Geo. L.J.* 299 (2002), pp. 303–7 and 333–47.

38. See 42 U.S.C. sec. 191 (2010) (adopted April 9, 1912). The history of child welfare law in the United States is painstakingly described in Brenda G. McGowan, "Historical Evolution of Child Welfare Services," in *Child Welfare for the 21st Century: A Handbook of Practices, Policies & Programs* (Mallon and Hess, eds., 2005), pp. 10–44.

39. Social Security Act of 1935, 42 U.S.C. sec. 301 *et seq.*, tit. IV-B.

40. Child Abuse Prevention and Treatment Act, Pub. L. No. 93-247 (1974).

41. See, for example, N.Y. Soc. Serv. Law sec. 413(1) (2010).

42. Key enactments after CAPTA include: Adoption Assistance and Child Welfare Act of 1980, Pub.L. 96-272; Child Abuse Amendments of 1984, Pub. L. 98-457; Child Abuse Prevention and Treatment Amendments of 1996, Pub. L. 103-235; Adoption and Safe Families Act of 1997, Pub. L. 105-89; Child Abuse Prevention and Enforcement Act of 2000, Pub. L. 106-177.

43. Current state laws are described in Child Welfare Information Gateway, *Definitions of Child Abuse and Neglect* (2009), available at www .childwelfare.gov/systemwide/laws_policies/statutes/defineall.cfm (visited Aug. 1, 2010).

44. Jean Koh Peters, "How Children Are Heard in Child Protective Proceedings, in the United States and Around the World in 2005: Survey Findings, Initial Observations, and Areas for Further Study," 6 *Nev. L.J.* 966 (2006).

45. Nicholson v. Williams, 203 F. Supp. 2d 153 (E.D.N.Y. 2002), p. 163.

46. 820 N.E.2d 840 (N.Y. 2004).

47. Matter of St. George, *N.Y.L.J.*, Nov. 13, 2000, p. 28, col. 1 (Fam. Ct. Monroe Co.).

48. On the line between reasonable discipline and physical abuse, see Scott A. Davidson, "When is Parental Discipline Child Abuse?—The Vagueness of Child Abuse Laws," 34 *U. Louisville J. Fam. L.* 403 (1996).

49. Adoption and Safe Families Act, Pub. L. No. 105-89 (1997).

50. U.S. Department of Health and Human Services, Child Welfare Information Gateway, "Foster Care Statistics," www.childwelfare.gov/pubs/factsheets/foster.cfm (visited Aug. 1, 2010).

51. Her foster parents, Joel Steinberg and Hedda Nussbaum, were charged with murder. In 1987, according to reports, 108 children died of abuse or neglect in New York City. In many cases, the problems of the families were known to child abuse agencies; yet the death occurred. Sam Robert, "Long After Lisa, Tragedy of Abuse Can Still Happen," *N.Y. Times*, Feb. 8, 1988.

52. DeShaney v. Winnebago Cty. Dep't of Soc. Servs., 489 U.S. 189 (1989).

53. Linda Goldston and Mark Gomez, "South Bay Sex-abuse Lawsuit: Ex-foster Child Awarded $30 Million," *Mercury News*, Aug. 5, 2010.

54. James Barron, "Decision Whether to Charge Prom Mother Awaits Tests," *N.Y. Times*, June 10, 1997, p. B2.

55. Robert Hanley, "Woman Gets 15 Years in Death of Newborn at Prom," *N.Y. Times*, Oct. 30, 1998, p. B1; Karen Demasters, "'Prom Mom' Released," *N.Y. Times*, Dec. 2, 2001, p. 14NJ-6.

56. Robert D. McFadden, "Teen-Age Sweethearts Charged with Murdering Their Baby," *N.Y. Times*, Nov. 18, 1996, p. B1; Robert Hanley, "Teen-Agers Get Terms in Prison in Baby's Death," *N.Y. Times*, July 10, 1998, p. A1.

57. Joseph P. Fried, "Trial Begins for Woman in the Death of Her Baby," *N.Y. Times*, Jan. 7, 1998, p. B3.

58. Carol Sanger, "Infant Safe Haven Laws: Legislating in the Culture of Life," 106 *Colum. L. Rev.* 753 (2006), p. 754.

59. Tex. Fam. Code Ann. sec. 262.301, et seq. (2009).

60. See Margaret Graham Tebo, "Texas Idea Takes Off: States Look to Safe Haven Laws as a Protection for Abandoned Infants," *A.B.A. J.*, Sept. 2001, p. 30. On the current safe haven landscape, see Guttmacher Institute, *State Policies in Brief: Infant Abandonment* (July 1, 2010), available at http://www.guttmacher.org/statecenter/spibs/spib_IA.pdf (visited Aug. 1, 2010).

61. In the Bible, Moses' mother abandons him in a reed basket in the Nile; Pharaoh's daughter rescues him.

62. Sanger, "Infant Safe Haven Laws," p. 756.

63. A description of the various safe haven laws is provided in U.S. Department of Health and Human Services, Child Welfare

InformationGateway,"InfantSafeHavenLaws,"www.childwelfare.gov/systemwide/laws_policies/statutes/safehaven.cfm (visited Aug. 1, 2010).

64. Wendy Koch, "Nebraska 'Safe Haven' Law for Kids Has Unintended Results," *USA Today*, Sept. 9, 2008.

65. Neb. Rev. Stat. sec. 29-121 (2009).

66. Susan Ayres, "Kairos and Safe Havens: The Timing and Calamity of Unwanted Birth," 15 *Wm. & Mary J. Women & L.* 227 (2009), p. 228. In comparison to more than 100 babies abandoned in public places in 1998, more than 31,000 babies were delivered and "abandoned" in hospitals by being left without any arrangements for care.

67. Some states deal with this problem by giving the "anonymous" mother a bracelet that connects her to the abandoned infant, and can give her standing to appear later in court if she chooses to drop her anonymity.

68. Enforcement of support obligations in various contexts is discussed in chapters 10, 12, and 13.

69. Sanger, "Infant Safe Haven Laws," pp. 781–88.

70. Sanger, ibid., pp. 788–800, surveys the data, along with possible explanations, for the relative ineffectiveness of safe haven laws.

71. See Wendy Grossman, "Rock-A-Baby Bye-Bye," *Houston Press*, April 25, 2002. Houston received its first "safe haven" drop-offs only after a public official spent $100,000 of his own money to publicize the law.

72. Cara Buckley, "Safe-Haven Laws Fail to End Discarding of Babies," *N.Y. Times*, Jan. 13, 2007, p. B1; see also Abandoned Infant Protection Act, N.Y. Penal Law 260.03.15(2) (2009).

73. Tina Kelley, "Parents in Crisis Have Many Options for Giving Babies Haven," *N.Y. Times*, Mar. 5, 2008, p. B1.

74. Evan B. Donaldson Adoption Institute, *Unintended Consequences:"Safe Haven" Laws Are Causing Problems, Not Solving Them*, available at: http://www.adoptioninstitute.org/whowe/Lastreport.pdf (2003) (visited Aug. 1, 2010). These "unintended consequences" include encouraging abandonment, and the concealment of important medical history.

75. Sanger, "Infant Safe Haven Laws," p. 758. This was probably a more serious problem in the past. It was serious in late nineteenth-century England. In those days, an unmarried servant girl who gave birth faced loss of her job—and perhaps starvation.

76. Hasday, "Parenthood Divided."

77. 247 U.S. 251 (1918). This was a 5 to 4 decision.

78. Quoted in Grace Abbott, *The Child and the State*, vol. 1 (1938), pp. 546–48.

79. Quoted in Hasday, "Parenthood Divided," at 363.

80. See, for example, Linda Greenhouse, "Justices Deny Grandparents Visiting Rights," *N.Y. Times*, June 6, 2000.

81. For more on the parties in this case, see Timothy Egan, "After Seven Years: Couple Is Defeated," *N.Y. Times*, June 6, 2000.

82. See Wash. Rev. Code secs. 26.09.240, 26.10.160(3) (2010).

83. 530 U.S. 57 (2000).

84. N.Y. Dom. Rel. sec. 72 (2010).

85. See Hertz v. Hertz, 291 A.D. 2d 91 (N.Y. App. Div. 2002).

86. Ohio Rev. Code Ann. sec. 3109.11 (2010).

87. Harrold v. Collier, 836 N.E.2d 1165 (Ohio 2005). For other cases upholding third-party visitation laws, see *In re* Harris, 96 P.3d 141 (Cal. 2004); Blixt v. Blixt, 774 N.E.2d 1052 (Mass. 2002). For a case striking one down, see Santi v. Santi, 633 N.W.2d 312 (Iowa 2001), which characterized the invalid law as substituting "sentimentality for constitutionality." See, in general, John DeWitt Gregory, "Defining the Family in the Millennium: The *Troxel* Follies," 32 *U. Mem. L. Rev.* 687 (2002).

88. Rules for determining legal parentage are covered in chapter 13, adoption in chapter 14.

89. *In re* Parentage of L.B., 122 P.3d 161 (Wash. 2005).

90. See, for example, K.M. v. E.G., 117 P.3d 673 (Cal. 2005); *In re* Parentage of A.B., 837 N.E.2d 965 (Ind. 2005); C.E.W. v. D.E.W., 845 A.2d 1146 (Me. 2004); T.B. v. L.R.M., 786 A.2d 913 (Penn. 2001); V.C. v. M.J.B., 748 A.2d 539 (N.J. 2000); E.N.O. v. L.M.M., 711 N.E.2d 886 (Mass. 1999); *In re* the Custody of H.S.H.-K., 533 N.W.2d 419 (Wis. 1995).

91. See, for example, Jones v. Barlow, 154 P.3d 808 (Utah 2007); *In re* Bonfield, 780 N.E.2d 241 (Ohio 2002).

92. 930 N.E.2d 184 (N.Y. 2010).

93. Matter of Alison D. v. Virginia M., 572 N.E.2d 27 (N. Y. 1991).

94. *Debra H.*, pp. 191–92.

95. Cal. Fam. Code sec. 3101 (2010).

96. Corbin v. Reimen, 228 P.3d 1270 (Wash. 2010).

97. See also Lewis v. Goetz, 203 Cal. App. 3d 514 (1988).

98. U.N. Convention on the Rights of the Child, G.A. Res. 44/25, U.N. Doc. A/RES/44/25 (Nov. 20, 1989), at Art. 12.

99. Martha Albertson Fineman, "What Is Right for Children? Introduction," in *What Is Right for Children? The Competing Paradigms of Religion and Human Rights* (Martha Albertson Fineman and Karen Worthington, eds., 2009), pp. 1–2.

100. On modern conceptions of "children's rights," see, in general, Martin Guggenheim, *What's Wrong with Children's Rights* (2007); James G. Dwyer, *The Relationship Rights of Children* (2006); Nancy E. Walker, *Children's Rights in the United States* (1999); Martha Minow, "What Ever

Happened to Children's Rights?" 80 *Minn. L. Rev.* 267 (1995); Lee E. Teitelbaum, "Children's Rights and the Problem of Equal Respect," 27 *Hofstra L. Rev.* 799 (1999).

101. See, for example, Moe v. Dinkins, 669 F.2d 67 (2d Cir. 1982).

102. See Ohio Rev. Code Ann. sec. 3101.05 (2010).

103. 750 Ill. Comp. Stat. 5/203 (2010).

104. *In re* Barbara Haven, 86 Pa. D. & C. 141 (Orphans' Ct. 1953).

105. 428 U.S. 52 (1976). We discuss the cases establishing a woman's right to abortion in chapter 5.

106. 443 U.S. 622 (1979), p. 647. The right was revisited in a series of subsequent cases. See H.L. v. Matheson, 450 U.S. 398 (1981); Hodgson v. Minnesota, 497 U.S. 417 (1990); Ohio v. Akron Center for Reproductive Health, 497 U.S. 502 (1990).

107. On the implementation of these laws, see Carol Sanger, "Regulating Teenage Abortion in the United States: Politics and Policy," 18 *Int'l J. L. Pol'y & Family* 305 (2004).

108. See *Guttmacher Institute, State Policies in Brief: Parental Involvement in Minors' Abortions* (July 1, 2010), available at http://www.guttmacher .org/statecenter/spibs/spib_PIMA.pdf. Most of these statutes make exceptions for medical emergency, and some in cases of incest, assault, or parental neglect.

109. See Carey v. Population Svcs. Int'l, 431 U.S. 678 (1977).

110. On medical decision-making by minors, Guttmacher Institute, *State Policies in Brief: Minors' Access to STI Services* (July 1, 2010), available at http://www.guttmacher.org/statecenter/spibs/spib_MASS. pdf (visited Aug. 1, 2010); Guttmacher Institute, *An Overview of Minor's Consent Law* (July 1, 2010), available at http://www.guttmacher.org/ statecenter/spibs/spib_OMCL.pdf (visited Aug. 1, 2010), which notes the minor's ability to "consent to a range of sensitive health care services" has "expanded dramatically over the last 30 years." See also Jennifer L. Rosato, "The End of Adolescence: Let's Get Real: Quilting a Principled Approach to Adolescent Empowerment in Health Care Decision-Making," 51 *DePaul L. Rev.* 769 (2002).

111. For typical emancipation statutes, see N.C. Gen. Stat. sec. 7B-3500-09 (2010); 750 Ill. Comp. Stat. 30/1-11 (2010). For a fifty-state survey, see "Emancipation of Minors—Laws," Legal Information Institute, available at http://topics.law.cornell.edu/wex/table_emancipation (visited Aug. 1, 2010).

112. On the Moceanu case, which included many allegations of wrongful conduct like squandering her earnings, see Jere Longman, "Gymnast Moceanu Gets Order of Protection against Father," *N.Y. Times*, Dec. 1, 1998.

113. Anthony DePalma, "Court Grants Boy's Wish to Pick His Parents," *N.Y. Times*, Sep. 26, 1992, p. 1.

114. John J. O'Connor, "Harsh Worlds Encroach on TV's Glossy Land," *N.Y. Times*, Feb. 8, 1993, p. C16.

115. On the history of juvenile courts, see Lawrence M. Friedman, *Crime and Punishment in American History* (1993), pp. 413–17; Steven L. Schlossman, *Love and the American Delinquent: The Theory and Practice of 'Progressive' Juvenile Justice, 1825–1920* (1977).

116. *In re* Gault, 387 U.S. 1 (1967).

117. 393 U.S. 503 (1969).

118. The case is *Davis v. Meek*, 344 F. Supp. 298 (N.D. Ohio 1972). The dress code cases, and the student rights cases in general, are discussed in Lawrence M. Friedman, "Limited Monarchy: The Rise and Fall of Student Rights," in *School Days, Rule Days: The Legalization and Regulation of Education* (David L. Kirp and Donald N. Jensen, eds., 1986), p. 238.

Chapter Thirteen
Whom Do We Belong To? Parentage and the Law

1. See "Worth the Wait!" *People*, Aug. 17, 2009, p. 96; "Healthy Baby Born 22 Years after Father's Sperm Was Frozen," *Medical News*, http://www.news-medical.net/news/2009/04/15/48357.aspx (visited Aug. 1, 2010).

2. See "Twins Born at 66; World's Oldest Mother Dies," *Gold Coast Bulletin*, July 17, 2009.

3. See Stephanie J. Ventura, "Changing Patterns of Nonmarital Childbearing in the United States," *National Center for Health Statistics*, Data Brief No. 18 (2009), p. 2.

4. See Lucy Carnie, "Sperm Wail by Donor: Must Pay Support 18 Yrs. Later," *N.Y. Post*, Dec. 2, 2007.

5. "Woman Gives Birth to Baby Conceived Outside the Body," *N.Y. Times*, July 26, 1978, p. A1.

6. See "Profile: Louise Brown," BBC News, http://news.bbc.co.uk/2/hi/health/3091241.stm (visited Aug. 1, 2010).

7. We take up the issue of co-parent adoption in chapter 14.

8. On some of the legal and public policy issues presented by reproductive technology, see Naomi Cahn, *Test Tube Families: Why the Fertility Market Needs Regulation* (2009); Mary Lyndon Shanley, *Making Babies, Making Families: What Matters Most in an Age of Reproductive Technologies, Surrogacy, Adoption, and Same-sex and Unwed Parents* (2001); Janet L. Dolgin, *Defining the Family: Law, Technology, and Reproduction in an Uneasy Age* (1999).

9. See Mary Ann Mason, *From Father's Property to Children's Rights* (1994), p. 24.

10. Chester G. Vernier, *American Family Laws*, Vol. IV (1936), p. 207; Mason, *From Father's Property to Children's Rights*, p. 25.

11. Ark. Code Ann. sec. 772-85 (1921), in Vernier, *American Family Laws*, Vol. IV, p. 222.

12. The Uniform Illegitimacy Act of 1922 tried to provide for more support of illegitimate children—more obligations, and more effective enforcement mechanisms. The Act was later withdrawn. See Prefatory Note, Uniform Parentage Act, 9B U.L.A. 287 (1987).

13. Mary Ann Mason notes this as a "reversal of the colonial practice, where fathers could choose to raise the child rather than pay support to the mother." Mason, *From Father's Property to Children's Rights*, p. 70.

14. Ibid.

15. Ventura, "Changing Patterns of Nonmarital Childbearing in the United States," p. 1.

16. Mason, *From Father's Property to Children's Rights*, pp. 99–100.

17. See Leslie Harris et al., *Family Law* (4th ed. 2010), p. 887. In England, a husband was conclusively presumed to be the father of his wife's children, unless he had been out of the kingdom for more than nine months.

18. Prochnow v. Prochnow, 80 N.W.2d 278 (Wis. 1957).

19. 491 U.S. 114 (1989).

20. See, in general, June Carbone and Naomi Cahn, "Which Ties Bind? Redefining the Parent-Child Relationship in an Age of Genetic Certainty," 11 *Wm. & Mary Bill Rts. J.* 1011 (2003), p. 1044.

21. Parker v. Parker, 950 So. 2d 388 (Fla. 2007).

22. See, for example, Chris W. Altenbernd, "Quasi-Marital Children: The Common Law's Failure in *Privette* and *Daniel* Calls for Statutory Reform," 26 *Fla. St. U. L. Rev.* 219 (1999), pp. 227–28, which cites a study in the 1940s finding that 10 percent of children born to married women were conceived in adultery.

23. Unif. Parentage Act sec. 101, 9B U.L.A. 299 (2001). Under the original 1973 version of the UPA, a father could seek to disestablish paternity within five years of the child's birth. Unif. Parentage Act sec. 6 (1973).

24. The child of a married couple is still presumed to be the husband's child. But this can be rebutted if he, the wife, and the biological father agree to this effect. And it can be rebutted in a suit to disestablish paternity, as long as the suit is filed within two years of the child's birth. The husband can act later, but only if he can prove that he did not have sex with the mother during the necessary period, and that he did not hold the child out as his own. Unif. Parentage Act secs. 204, 607 (2002).

25. See Millicent A. Tanner, "Case Note: Paternity," 32 *U. Louisville J. Fam. L.* 189 (1993); see also Brie S. Rogers, "The Presumption of

Paternity in Child Support Cases: A Triumph of Law Over Biology," 70 *U. Cinn. L. Rev.* 1151 (2002); Judy N. Tabb, "Family Law—Louisiana's Presumption of Legitimacy—Methods of Disavowal—Sterility," 44 *Tul. L. Rev.* 598 (1970).

26. See, in general, Paula Roberts, "Questioning the Paternity of Marital Children," www.clasp.org (visited Sept. 19, 2009).

27. The National Center For Men, Home Page, http://www.nationalcenterformen.org/ (visited Aug. 1, 2010); see Ronald K. Henry, "The Innocent Third Party: Victims of Paternity Fraud," http://www.defaultpaternity.org/pdf/flq-0706.pdf (Aug. 1, 2010); see Melanie B. Jacobs, "When Daddy Doesn't Want to be Daddy Anymore: An Argument Against Paternity Fraud Claims," 16 *Yale J.L. & Feminism* 193 (2004).

28. Selwyn Duke, "Abortion, Authority and Responsibility," http://mensnewsdaily.com/2006/03/17/abortion-authority-and-responsibility/?cp=1 (visited Aug. 1, 2010).

29. See Dubay v. Wells, 442 F. Supp. 2d 404 (E.D. Mich. 2006), aff'd, 506 F.3d 422 (6th Cir. 2007).

30. Dubay, 442 F. Supp. 2d 404, p. 413; Dubay, 506 F.3d 422, p. 430.

31. See N.E. v. Hedges, 391 F.3d 832 (6th Cir. 2004).

32. See Rivera v. Minnich, 483 U.S. 574 (U.S. 1987), p. 579.

33. Pamela P. v. Frank S., 59 N.Y.2d 1 (1983), p. 7.

34. Pamela P., ibid., allowed defense of fraud but called it a "limited defense" in that it did not relieve the man of support obligations; see also Pinhas Shifman, "Involuntary Parenthood: Misrepresentation as to Use of Contraceptives," 4 *Int'l J. L. Pol'y & the Fam.* 279 (1990), pp. 279–96.

35. See Brown v. Wyatt 202 S.W.3d 555 (Ark. Ct. App. 2005).

36. See David J. Mack, "Note: Cleansing the System: A Fresh Approach to Liability for the Negligent or Fraudulent Transmission of Sexually Transmitted Diseases," 30 *U. Tol. L. Rev.* 647 (1999); see also DeVall v. Strunk, 96 S.W.2d 245 (Tex. Civ. App. 1936); Kathleen K. v. Robert B., 150 Cal. App. 3d 992 (1983); Maharam v. Maharam, 123 A.D.2d 165 (N.Y. App. 1986).

37. See Ventura, "Changing Patterns of Nonmarital Childbearing in the United States," p. 2. There is significant racial variation in the rate of non-marital childbearing. Although the overall rate is 40 percent, 72 percent of births to African American women were non-marital, versus only 17 percent to Asian or Pacific Islander women. See Brady E. Hamilton et al., "Births: Preliminary Data for 2008," 58 *Nat'l Vital Stats. Rep.* 16, Apr. 6, 2010, p. 6 table 1.

38. See Stanley v. Illinois, 405 U.S. 645 (1972), p. 646.

39. Ibid., p. 651.

40. 391 U.S. 68 (1968).

41. Later cases cemented the view that illegitimate children were entitled to the benefits of a parent-child relationship. In 1977, the Supreme Court struck down an Illinois code provision that permitted illegitimate children to inherit only from their mothers, a common (but not universal) rule. Trimble v. Gordon, 430 U.S. 762 (1977). For other cases establishing the rights of illegitimate children, see Jimenez v. Weinberger, 417 U.S. 628 (1974); Weber v. Aetna Casualty & Surety Co., 406 U.S. 164 (1972).

42. "Male Lib: No Relief for the Chauvinist Pigs," *N.Y. Times*, Apr. 9, 1972, p. E9; Fred P. Graham, "Court Backs Rights of Unwed Fathers: Says a State Cannot Take Children From Man Just Because Mother Dies," *N.Y. Times*, Apr. 4, 1972, p. 1.

43. 441 U.S. 378 (1979).

44. Ibid., p. 388.

45. 463 U.S. 248 (1983).

46. See N.Y. Soc. Serv. Law sec. 372-c (1983).

47. *Lehr*, p. 262.

48. See Mary Beck and Lindsay Biesterfeld, "A National Putative Father Registry," 36 *Cap. U. L. Rev* 295 (2007); see also Donna L. Moore, "Implementing a National Putative Father Registry by Utilizing Existing Federal/State Collaborative Databases," 36 *J. Marshall L. Rev.* 1033 (2003).

49. See *In re* Petition of Kirchner, 649 N.E.2d 324 (Ill. 1995).

50. See *In re* B.C.G., 496 N.W.2d 239 (Iowa 1992); *In re* Baby Girl Clausen, 502 N.W.2d 649 (Mich. 1993).

51. The movie, which one reviewer described as containing "lots of appropriate weeping," first aired on ABC in September 1993. See John J. O'Connor, "Dramatizing the Battle to Bring Up Baby Jessica," *N.Y. Times*, Sept. 24, 1993.

52. See "Adoptive Parents Divorce after Custody Fight Loss," *N.Y. Times*, Oct. 24, 1999.

53. Iowa Code Ann. sec. 600A.9 (2010).

54. See Uniform Adoption Act, Prefatory Note. See also Susan Chira, "Law Proposed to End Adoption Horror Stories," *N.Y. Times*, Aug. 24, 1994. Under the Uniform Adoption Act, proposed in 1994, unwed fathers, to thwart a pending adoption, had to speak up quickly, and also demonstrate potential for good parenting.

55. See Fla. Stat. sec. 63.087, 63.088(5) (2003) (repealed). See Nicholas Ciappetta, "Note: Florida's Scarlet Letter Repealed: A Retrospective Analysis of the Constitutionality of the Florida Adoption Notification Provision and a Commentary on the Future of the Right to Privacy," 32 *Hofstra L. Rev.* 675 (2003).

56. Jon Burstein, "Moms Challenge New Adoption Law: Women Fear Ads Naming Sex Partners," *Sun-Sentinel* (Fort Lauderdale, FL), Aug. 7, 2002, p. 1A; "Scarlet Letter," *Playboy*, Jan. 1, 2003.

57. G.P. v. Florida, 842 So. 2d 1059 (Fla. Ct. App. 2003).

58. See, for example, Tamar Lewin, "Unwed Fathers Fight for Babies Placed for Adoption by Mothers," *N.Y. Times*, Mar. 19, 2006, p. 1. See, in general, Laura Oren, "Thwarted Fathers or Pop-Up Pops?: How to Determine When Putative Fathers Can Block the Adoption of Their Newborn Children," 40 *Fam. L. Q.* 153 (2006).

59. Ibid.

60. See Lori B. Andrews, "The Aftermath of Baby M: Proposed State Laws on Surrogate Motherhood," *Hastings Center Report* (Nov. 1987), p. 31.

61. Unif. Parentage Act, 9B U.L.A. 287 (1973, amended 2002).

62. Ibid., sec. 5.

63. Ibid., sec. 4.

64. Unif. Parentage Act sec. 703 (2002). On the judicial approaches to artificial insemination cases, see Gaia Bernstein, "The Socio-Legal Acceptance of New Technologies: A Close Look at Artificial Insemination," 77 *Wash. L. Rev.* 1035 (2002); Marsha Garrison, "Law Making for Baby Making: An Interpretive Approach to the Determination of Legal Parenthood," 113 *Harv. L. Rev.* 835 (2000). In states with no specific law on the status of sperm donors, courts have relied on equitable or other principles to assign rights and obligations.

65. See Alice J. Carlson, "Trade in Reproductive Human Biota: Our Quest for Babies," http://www1.american.edu/TED/reproductive -trade.htm#r5, (visited Aug. 1, 2010); see also Karen Springen and David Noonan, "The Web Has Changed the Process of Looking for Donors. Jokes Aside, It's Become a Booming Business," *Newsweek*, Apr. 21, 2003, http://www.newsweek.com/id/59049 (visited Aug. 1, 2010).

66. See http://www.cryobank.com/Donor-Search/Look-A-Likes/ (visited Aug. 1, 2010).

67. See, for example, Ferguson v. McKiernan, 598 Pa. 78 (2007), which ordered a sperm donor to pay child support for resulting twins despite a contract relieving him of all parental rights and obligations.

68. See, for example, Roni Caryn Rabin, "As Demand for Donor Eggs Soars, High Prices Stir Ethical Concerns," *N.Y. Times*, May 15, 2007; Naomi Cahn, "Reproducing Dreams," in Goodwin, *Baby Markets*, pp. 147, 156–68; Nanette R. Elster, "Egg Donation for Research and Reproduction: The Compensation Conundrum," in Goodwin, *Baby Markets*, p. 226.

69. Janice C. Ciccarelli and Linda J. Beckman, "Navigating Rough Waters: An Overview of the Psychological Aspects of Surrogacy," 61 *J. Soc. Issues* (2005), p. 21.

70. See *In re* Baby M, 537 A.2d 1227 (N.J. 1988).

71. Ibid., p. 1235.

72. On the *Baby M* case in general, see Elizabeth S. Scott, "Surrogacy and the Politics of Commodification," 72 *L. Contemp. Prob.* 109 (2009); Carol Sanger, "Developing Markets in Baby-Making: *In the Matter of Baby M,*" 29 *Harv. J. L. & Gender* 67 (2007); Mark Rust, "Whose Baby Is It—Surrogate Motherhood after *Baby M,*" 73 *A.B.A. J.* 52 (1987).

73. In re *Baby M,* p. 1237.

74. Ibid., p. 1240.

75. Ibid., p. 1250.

76. Ibid., p. 1255.

77. Ibid., p. 1259.

78. Sanger, "Developing Markets in Baby-Making," p. 69. The initial ruling of the trial court, in favor of surrogacy, had already provoked debate. Betty Friedan saw "frightening implications for women," a "terrifying denial of what should be basic rights for women." James Barron, "Views on Surrogacy Harden after Baby M Ruling," *N.Y. Times,* April 2, 1987, p. A1.

79. Judith Areen, *"Baby M* Reconsidered," 76 *Georgetown L.J.* 1741 (1988); Ciccarelli and Beckman, "Navigating Rough Waters," p. 23, noting that "[s]urrogacy, like abortion, is controversial precisely because it evokes and often contradicts basic concepts about family, motherhood, and gender roles."

80. See, for example, J. Mahoney, "An Essay on Surrogacy and Feminist Thought," 16 *L. Med. & Health Care* 81 (1988).

81. "Poll Shows Most in U.S. Back Baby M Ruling," *N.Y. Times,* April 12, 1987, p. A39.

82. Ciccarelli and Beckman, "Navigating Rough Waters," p. 29.

83. A few cases prior to *Baby M* had considered the enforceability of surrogacy contracts. See, for example, Doe v. Kelley, 307 N.W.2d 438 (Mich. 1981); Surrogate Parenting Associates, Inc. v. Kentucky, 704 S.W.2d 209 (1986).

84. See Donald Janson, "Baby M Ruling Welcomed at Meeting of Surrogacy Experts," *N.Y. Times,* Feb. 5, 1987, p. B5.

85. These states include Arizona, Indiana, Louisiana, Michigan, Nebraska, North Dakota, and Utah. See, for example, Neb. Rev. Stat. sec. 25-21 (1988).

86. The Uniform Status of Children of Assisted Conception Act, promulgated in 1988, offered alternative provisions on surrogacy: one banning such arrangements, one allowing them. USCACA secs. 5, 10, 9C U.L.A. 363 (2001).

87. See N.Y. Dom. Rel. sec. 123 (2009). On these developments in New York, see Scott, "Surrogacy and the Politics of Commodification," pp. 119–20.

88. See, for example, Calvert v. Johnson, 851 P.2d 776 (Cal. 1993); Doe v. Roe, 717 A.2d 706 (Conn. 1998).

89. Scott, "Surrogacy and the Politics of Commodification," p. 120.

90. Robert Hanley, "Jersey Panel Backs Limits on Unpaid Surrogacy Pacts," *N.Y. Times*, Mar. 12, 1989, p. 38.

91. Ibid., p. 14; see also Sanger, "Developing Markets in Baby-Making," p. 79, citing *Resolve, The National Infertility Association, Fact Sheet 56: Surrogacy (Gestational Carrier)* (2004), p. 3.

92. Ciccarelli and Beckman, "Navigating Rough Waters," pp. 31–32.

93. Martha Field advocates a non-enforcement approach to surrogacy contracts, rather than one that expressly disallows or permits them. See Martha Field, "Reproductive Technologies and Surrogacy: Legal Issues," 25 *Creighton L. Rev.* 1589 (1992).

94. 750 Ill. Comp. Stat. Ann. sec. 47/5 (2009).

95. Ibid., sec. 47/20.

96. Ibid., sec. 47/15.

97. Scott, "Surrogacy and the Politics of Commodification," p. 109.

98. See, for example, Fla. Stat. sec. 742.15 (2010); N.H. Rev. Stat. secs. 168-B:1 et seq. (2010); Nev. Rev. Stat. sec. 126.045 (2010); Va. Code Ann. sec. 20-159 (2010).

99. Sophia J. Kleegman and Sherwin A. Kaufman, *Infertility in Women* (1966), p. 178, cited in Andrews, "The Aftermath of Baby M," p. 31.

100. See Ciccarelli and Beckman, "Navigating Rough Waters," pp. 23–24, describing the data collection issues surrounding surrogacy.

101. Ibid., p. 23.

102. Sara Rimer, "No Stork Involved, but Mom and Dad Had Help," *N.Y. Times*, July 12, 2009, p. A1.

103. Katherine T. Pratt, "Inconceivable? Deducting the Costs of Fertility Treatment," 89 *Cornell L. Rev.* 1121 (2004), p. 1136.

104. See Lori B. Andrews, "Surrogate Motherhood: The Challenge for Feminists," 16 *L. Med. & Health Care* 72 (1988), p. 74; Elizabeth Bartholet, "Guiding Principles for Picking Parents," 27 *Harv. Women's L. J.* 323 (2004), p. 328.

105. A recent article describes the complexity and legal uncertainty of some surrogacy arrangements. See Stephanie Saul, "Building a Baby, with Few Ground Rules," *N.Y. Times*, Dec. 13, 2009, p. A1.

106. A.G.R. v. D.R.H., No. FD-09-001838-07, Super. Ct. N.J. (Dec. 23, 2009); see also Joanna L. Grossman, "Time to Revisit *Baby M.?*" Find-Law's Writ, Jan. 19 (2010), available at http://writ.news.findlaw.com/grossman/20100119.html (visited Aug. 1, 2010).

107. See William Blackstone, *Commentaries on the Law* (1765–1769), Vol. 1, p. 130.

108. Section 204 of the Uniform Parentage Act uses a rebuttable presumption of parentage for births within 300 days of a man's death. Unif. Parentage Act sec. 204, 9B U.L.A. (2001).

109. "A Birth Spurs Debate on Using Sperm after Death," *N.Y. Times*, Mar. 27, 1999, A11.

110. Allison Sherry, "Doomed Man's Wife Succeeds in Effort to Have Sperm Saved," *Denver Post*, Oct. 22, 2003, p. A1.

111. The American Society for Reproductive Medicine cautiously supported posthumous reproduction in 2004, as long as guidelines on screening, disclosure, and consent were followed. See ASRM, "Posthumous Reproduction," 82 *Fertility & Sterility* 260 (2004). Legal questions can also be raised about ownership and use of sperm and embryos left behind after death. See, for example, Hecht v. Superior Court, 16 Cal. App. 4th 836 (1993), a dispute between a surviving girlfriend (she wanted to use the sperm to inseminate herself), and his children from a prior marriage (who wanted it destroyed).

112. On the developing law regarding posthumously conceived children, see, for example, Browne C. Lewis, "Dead Men Reproducing: Responding to the Existence of Afterdeath Children," 16 *Geo. Mason L. Rev.* 403 (2009); Raymond C. O'Brien, "The Momentum of Posthumous Conception: A Model Act," 25 *J. Contemp. Health L. & Pol'y* 332 (2009); Charles P. Kindregan, Jr., "Dead Dads: Thawing an Heir from the Freezer," 35 *Wm. Mitchell L. Rev.* 433 (2009); Ruth Zafran, "Dying to be a Father: Legal Paternity in Cases of Posthumous Conception," 8 *Hous. J. Health L. & Pol'y* 47 (2007).

113. 371 F.3d 593 (9th Cir. 2004); but see Khabbaz v. Comm'r, 930 A.2d 1180 (N.H. 2007), holding that a child conceived after the father's death in the state was not "surviving issue" for inheritance purposes and, therefore, not eligible for Social Security survivor's benefits.

114. Under federal law, "dependent children" are entitled to survivor's benefits under Social Security. Legitimate children are always considered "dependent."

115. See Vernoff v. Astrue, 568 F.3d 1102 (9th Cir. 2009).

116. 760 N.E.2d 257 (Mass. 2002).

117. La. Rev. Stat. 9:391.1 (2009). A Canadian law commission recently recommended that provinces create protections for posthumously conceived children, as long as they were conceived within two years of a parent's death. Manitoba Law Reform Commission, Rep. No. 118, Posthumously Conceived Children: Intestate Succession and Dependent's Relief, p. 30, http://www.gov.mb.ca/justice/mlrc/reports/118.pdf (visited Feb. 7, 2010).

118. See N.Y. EPTL sec. 5-3.2(b) (2010).

119. In a question about the rights of a posthumously conceived child, the Arkansas Supreme Court denied inheritance rights and concluded the opinion by "strongly encourage[ing] the general assembly to revisit the intestacy succession statutes to address the issues involved in the instant case and those that have not but will likely evolve." Finley v. Astrue, 270 S.W.3d 849 (Ark. 2008).

Chapter Fourteen
Chosen People: Adoption and the Law.

1. Stephen Cretney, *Family Law in the Twentieth Century: A History* (2003), p. 596.

2. See, in general, Stephen B. Presser, "The Historical Background of the American Law of Adoption," 11 *J. Fam. L.* 443 (1971), p. 443; Chris Guthrie and Joanna L. Grossman, "Adoption in the Progressive Era: Preserving, Creating, and Re-Creating Families," 43 *J. Am. Leg. Hist.* 235 (1999). On the informal arrangements that preceded the passage of the first adoption statutes, see Yasuhide Kawashima, "Adoption in Early America," 20 *J. Fam. L.* 677 (1981–82), p. 677; Presser, "The Historical Background of the American Law of Adoption," pp. 456–64; C.M.A. McCauliff, "The First English Adoption Law and its American Precursors," 15 *Seton Hall L. Rev.* 656 (1986).

3. 1846 Miss. Laws, ch. 60, Miss. Code (Hutchinson 1848) ch. 35, art. 2; Laws Mass. 1851, ch. 324, p. 815.

4. Kawashima, "Adoption in Early America," pp. 677–78.

5. Michael Grossberg, *Governing the Hearth: Law and the Family in Nineteenth Century America* (1985), p. 268; Jamil S. Zainaldin, "The Emergence of a Modern American Family Law: Child Custody, Adoption, and the Courts, 1796–1851," 73 *N.W. L. Rev.* 1038 (1979).

6. Guthrie and Grossman, "Adoption in the Progressive Era," p. 253.

7. Ibid., p. 237.

8. Chester G. Vernier, *American Family Laws*, Vol. IV (1936), pp. 279–80.

9. Cal. Civ. Code secs. 221-22 (Hart 1892), in ibid., p. 286.

10. Cal. Civ. Code secs. 223–225 (Hart 1892).

11. Cal. Civ. Code sec. 224 (Hart 1892).

12. 1917 Laws Minn. ch. 222.

13. Allen v. Allen, 330 P.2d 151 (Ore. 1958).

14. See Cal. Fam. Code sec. 9100 (2009).

15. See, for example, Unif. Adoption Act sec. 7-105 (1994); Danielle Saba Donner, "The Emerging Adoption Market: Child Welfare Agencies, Private Middlemen, and 'Consumer' Remedies," 35 *U. Louisville J. Fam. L.* 473 (1996), p. 518.

16. Burr v. Bd. of Cty. Commr's, 491 N.E.2d 1101(Ohio 1986); see also Meracle v. Children's Svc. Soc'y, 437 N.W.2d 532 (Wis. 1989), with similar facts; and Roe v. Catholic Charities, 588 N.E.2d 354 (Ill. 1992), where the agency had concealed information about children's severe psychological problems.

17. See the discussion in Mallette v. Children's Friend and Service, 661 A.2d 67 (R.I. 1995). On wrongful adoption generally, see D. Marianne Blair, "Getting the Whole Truth and Nothing But the Truth: The Limits of Liability for Wrongful Adoptions, 67 *Notre Dame L. Rev.* 851 (1992).

18. Compare Michael J. v. County of Los Angeles, 201 Cal. App. 3d 859 (1988), and Engstrom v. State, 461 N.W.2d 309 (Iowa 1990), which reject liability for negligence by adoption agencies, with McKinney v. State, 950 P.2d 461 (Wash. 1998), and Gibbs v. Ernst, 647 A.2d 882 (Pa. 1994), which allow it.

19. The wrongful adoption cases and the passage of disclosure statutes are discussed in Laura Morgan, "Telling the Truth in Adoption Proceedings: Tort Action for Wrongful Adoption," 10 *Divorce Litig.* 11 (Jan. 1998).

20. Ohio Rev. Code Ann. sec. 3107.017 (2010).

21. See Jacqueline Horner Plumez, "Adoption: Where Have All the Babies Gone?" *N.Y. Times*, April 13, 1980.

22. National Council on Adoption, *Adoption Factbook IV*, p. 10.

23. "3 Accused Here in Adoption Ring," *N.Y. Times*, Dec. 6, 1949.

24. Andrew Keshner, "Attorney Gets 10 to 20 Years for Adoption Scam," *N.Y.L.J.*, Dec. 8, 2010, p. 1.

25. Stuart W. Thayer, "Moppets on the Market: The Problem of Unregulated Adoption," 50 *Yale L.J.* 715 (1950).

26. National Council on Adoption, *Adoption Factbook IV*, p. 7.

27. Ibid., p. 6.

28. See, for example, Unif. Adoption Act sec. 7-103, 9 U.L.A. (pt. IA). On the general rules governing the adoption of children, see Susan Frelich Appleton and D. Kelly Weisberg, *Adoption and Assisted Reproduction* (2009).

29. Laura Masnerius, "Market Puts Price Tags on the Priceless," *N.Y. Times*, Oct. 26, 1998, p. A1.

30. Ibid.

31. Walter I. Trattner, *From Poor Law to Welfare State: A History of Social Welfare in America* 111 (5th ed. 1994).

32. The full results of this study are reported in Grossman and Guthrie, "Adoption in the Progressive Era."

33. Kawashima, "Adoption in Early America," p. 689, reporting that most colonial adoptions involved relatives.

34. "Baby Girl Abandoned by Unknown Parents," *S.F. Chron.*, July 7, 1908, p. 5. California was a hotbed of activity in the child-saving movement. See William H. Slingerland, *Child Welfare Work in California* (1916), p. 17; Michael B. Katz, *In the Shadow of the Poorhouse: A Social History of Welfare in America* (1986), pp. 113–45; Susan Tiffin, *In Whose Best Interest? Child Welfare Reform in the Progressive Era* (1982), pp. 38–39.

35. Homer H. Clark, Jr., *The Law of Domestic Relations in the United States*, (2d ed. 1988).

36. National Council on Adoption, *Adoption Factbook IV* (2007), p. 9.

37. Our thanks to Sarah Crabtree for some of the research in this section.

38. Vernier, *American Family Laws*, Vol. IV, p. 282; La. Rev. Stat. Ann. sec. 9:422 (1972).

39. See, for example, Compos v. McKeithen, 341 F. Supp. 264 (E.D. La. 1972) and *In re* Adoption of Gomez, 424 S.W.2d 656 (Tex. Civ. App. 1967), which both ruled that it was a violation of the Equal Protection Clause to prohibit transracial adoptions altogether.

40. 466 U.S. 429 (1984), pp. 432–33.

41. Mark C. Rahdert, "Transracial Adoption—A Constitutional Perspective," 68 *Temple L. Rev.* 1687 (1995), p. 1695; David D. Meyer, "*Palmore* Comes of Age: The Place of Race in the Placement of Children," 18 *U. Fla. J. L. & Pub. Pol'y* 183 (2007), p. 189. Meyer notes that for years "after *Palmore*, states continued to adhere to statutes or other legal guidelines establishing priorities or preferences for same-race placements, sometimes specifying the length of time children would be kept waiting while caseworkers searched for willing adoptive parents of the child's race." Meyer, p. 185.

42. Meyer, "*Palmore* Comes of Age," p. 187.

43. On this early history, see, for example, Randall Kennedy, *Interracial Intimacies: Sex, Marriage, Identity, and Adoption* (2003), p. 387; see also Twila L. Perry, "The Transracial Adoption Controversy: An Analysis of Discourse and Subordination," 21 *N.Y.U. Rev. L. & Soc. Change* 33 (1993).

44. Perry, "The Transracial Adoption Controversy," p. 42. On changing attitudes toward unwed motherhood, see, for example, Mary Lyndon Shanley, *Making Babies, Making Families: What Matters Most in an Age of Reproductive Technologies, Surrogacy, Adoption, and Same-Sex and Unwed Parents* (2001), pp. 16–17; E. Wayne Carp, *Family Matters: Secrecy and Disclosure in the History of Adoption* (1998).

45. See Hollee McGinnis et al., *Beyond Culture Camp: Promoting Healthy Identity Formation in Adoption* (Evan B. Donaldson Adoption Institute, 2009).

46. Ron Nixon, "Adopted from Korea and in Search of Identity," *N.Y. Times*, Nov. 9, 2009, p. A9.

47. See, in general, Perry, "The Transracial Adoption Controversy"; Elizabeth Bartholet, "Where Do Black Children Belong? The Politics of Race Matching in Adoption," 139 *U. Pa. L. Rev.* 1163 (1991).

48. See Ruth-Arlene W. Howe, "Adoption Practice, Issues, and Laws, 1958–1983," 17 *Fam. L. Q.* 273 (1983).

49. 92 Stat. 3069 (act of Nov. 8, 1978), 25 U.S.C. 1915 (2008).

50. Ann E. MacEachron et al., "The Effectiveness of the Indian Child Welfare Act of 1978," 70 *Soc. Science Rev.* 451 (1996), pp. 458–59.

51. Robert H. Bremner, *Children and Youth in America: A Documentary History* (1974), Vol. 3, pp. 777–80. William Merritt restated NABSW's opposition to transracial adoption in 1985—in just as stark terms— condemning it as a "hostile act against our community" and a "blatant form of race and cultural genocide." Testimony, Senate Comm. Labor & Human Resources, 99th Cong., 1st Sess., June 25, 1985, quoted in Perry, "The Transracial Adoption Controversy," p. 47.

52. Kenneth L. Karst, "Law, Cultural Conflict, and the Socialization of Children," 91 *Cal. L. Rev.* 967 (2003), pp. 982–83, citing Bartholet, "Where Do Black Children Belong?" 1178–80. Data after 1975 are scant because the federal government stopped collecting information about adoptions.

53. Patricia K. Jennings, "The Trouble with the Multiethnic Placement Act: An Empirical Look at Transracial Adoption," 49 *Soc. Persp.* 559 (2004), p. 561.

54. Ibid.; see also Evan B. Donaldson Institute, *Finding Families for African American Children: The Role of Race & Law in Adoption from Foster Care* (2008), p. 22.

55. Elizabeth Bartholet, "Race Separatism in the Family: More on the Transracial Adoption Debate," 2 *Duke J. L. & Pol'y* 99 (1995), p. 100.

56. Perry, "The Transracial Adoption Controversy," pp. 43–47.

57. See, for example, Shanley, *Making Babies, Making Families*, pp. 24–25.

58. Pub. L. No. 103-382, 108 Stat. 4056 (1994).

59. See Removal of Barriers to Interethnic Adoptions, Pub. L. 104-188, sec. 1808, 110 Stat. 1904 (1996) (codified as amended at 42 U.S.C. sec. 1996b (2010)). Under current law, federally funded entities must also "diligently recruit" foster and adoptive parents who reflect the diversity of children in need of placements. Jennings, "The Trouble with the Multiethnic Placement Act," p. 561. States have made efforts to recruit black adoptive parents, but even with similar adoption rates, transracial adoption is necessary because black children are so

disproportionately represented among would-be adoptees. See Bartholet, "Race Separatism in the Family," p. 101.

60. Pub. L. No. 105-89, 111 Stat. 2115 (codified as amended in scattered sections of 42 U.S.C.).

61. On the role of racial preferences, see R. Richard Banks, "The Color of Desire: Fulfilling Adoptive Parents' Racial Preferences through Discriminatory State Action," 107 *Yale L.J.* 875 (1998); Solangel Maldonado, "Discouraging Racial Preferences in Adoptions, 39 *U.C. Davis L. Rev.* 1415 (2006), pp. 1472–73.

62. These cases are recounted in more detail in Meyer, "*Palmore* Comes of Age," pp. 196–98.

63. See, for example, *In re* Marriage of Gambla, 853 N.W.2d 847 (Ill. App. Ct. 2006), which is discussed at length in Meyer, "*Palmore* Comes of Age," pp. 192–95. See also J.H.H. v. O'Hara, 878 F.2d 240 (8th Cir. 1989); *In re* R.M.G., 454 A.2d 776 (D.C. 1982); Drummond v. Fulton County Dep't of Family & Children's Svcs., 563 F.2d 1200 (5th Cir. 1977).

64. Twila L. Perry, "Book Review: Hawley Fogg-Davis, Power, Possibility and Choice: The Racial Identity of Transracially Adopted Children," 9 *Mich. J. Race & L.* 215 (2003), p. 233.

65. N.Y. Soc. Serv. Law sec. 373 (2009).

66. Perry, "The Transracial Adoption Controversy," p. 56. Perry notes that in 1954, forty-three states provided for religious-matching by statute, and seventeen still had such statutes in 1989.

67. Shanley, *Making Babies, Making Families*, p. 12.

68. See, for example, "Sample Letter to Families Applying for Infants Where the Woman is Over 40 Years of Age," (early 1940s), available at: http://www.uoregon.edu/~adoption/archive/SLFAIWWOFYA.htm, which explained that women forty and over were generally not eligible to adopt.

69. Cal. Civ. Code secs. 228–229 (Hart 1892).

70. Naomi Cahn describes the range of rules regarding inheritance by adopted children in the late nineteenth and early twentieth centuries in "Perfect Substitutes or the Real Thing?" 52 *Duke L. J.* 1077 (2003), pp. 1126–32. "No statute accorded adoptive children the same intestacy rights as biological children." Ibid., p. 1132.

71. Two states still allow inheritance from both sets of parents. See Tex. Prob. Code sec. 40 (2010). On the more typical approach, see Uniform Probate Code sec. 2-114 (2008).

72. See, for example, Unif. Prob. Code sec. 2-114 (2008); Hall v. Vallandingham, 540 A.2d 1162 (Ct. App. Md. 1988).

73. State v. Fischer, 493 N.E.2d 1265 (Ind. App. 1986).

74. Bohall v. State, 546 N.E.2d 1214 (Ind. 1989).

75. On the many factors fueling the movement toward secrecy, see Carp, *Family Matters*, pp. 102–37.

76. 1931 Laws Ill., p. 734; 1937 Laws Ill., p. 1006; Ill. Rev. Stat. 1939, ch. 111½, secs. 48a, 57.6.

77. Annette Ruth Appell, "Blending Families through Adoption: Implications for Collaborative Adoption Law and Practice," 75 *B.U. L. Rev.* 997 (1995); see also Adam Pertman, *Adoption Nation: How the Adoption Revolution is Transforming America* (2000); Carp, *Family Matters*.

78. On this history, see Elizabeth J. Samuels, "The Idea of Adoption: An Inquiry into the History of Adult Adoptee Access to Birth Records," 53 *Rutgers L. Rev.* 367 (2001).

79. Joel D. Tenenbaum, "Introducing the Uniform Adoption Act," 30 *Fam. L. Q.* 333 (1996–97), p. 334.

80. Mills v. Atlantic City Dep't of Vital Statistics, 372 A.2d 646 (N.J. 1977), p. 649.

81. Donald Janson, "Adopted Children Seeking Changes in Law on Finding Natural Parents," *N.Y. Times*, Oct. 27, 1976.

82. Cal. Fam. Code sec. 9203 (2009). On the history of adoption records law in California, see Kathleen Caswell, "Opening the Door to the Past," 32 *Golden Gate U. L. Rev.* 272 (2002), pp. 281–83; Everett R. Holles, "California Health Department Seeks to Open Adoption Records," *N.Y. Times*, Oct. 8, 1977, p. 34.

83. On this and other aspects of adoption in the United States, see The Adoption History Project, available at http://www.ureogen.edu /~adoption/people/CUB.htm (visited Aug. 1, 2010). On the advocacy efforts for birth parents, see also Nadine Brozan, "Parents Who Gave Up Babies Organize to Gain New Rights," *N.Y. Times*, Jan. 23, 1978.

84. Tamar Lewin, "Woman Convicted of Fraud in Efforts to Find Adoptees," *N.Y. Times*, July 30, 1993.

85. Oregon Ballot Measure 58 (1998).

86. Doe 1 v. State, 993 P.2d 822 (Ore. 1999).

87. Jim Robbins, "Where Adoption Is Suddenly an Open Book," *N.Y. Times*, May 17, 2001, p. F12.

88. See Alaska Stat. sec. 18.50.500 (2009); Kan. Stat. Ann. sec. 65-2423 (2008); Tenn. Code Ann. secs. 36-1-125 to -129 (1996); see also M. Christina Rueff, "A Comparison of Tennessee's Open Records Law with Relevant Laws in Other English-Speaking Countries," 37 *Brandeis L. J.* 453 (1998–99). Alabama granted a blanket right to see original birth certificates upon reaching adulthood; but then changed the law. Now there is an automatic right only to non-identifying information about background and circumstances of birth. Information revealing who the birth parents were, however, can be granted by court order or if the birth parents, after an intermediary contacts them, give their consent. Ala.

Code Ann. sec. 26-10A-31 (2009). On the movement to unseal adoption records, see Naomi Cahn and Jana Singer, "Adoption, Identity, and the Constitution: The Case for Opening Closed Records," 2 *U. Pa. J. Const. L.* 150 (1999).

89. 2009 Ill. H.B. 5428 (enacted May 21, 2010). Before this Act, an adoptee could find his or her birth parents only if the parents had signed up for the state's Adoption Registry and Medical Information Exchange.

90. See, for example, Susan Livingston Smith, Evan B. Donaldson Adoption Inst., *Safeguarding the Rights and Well Being of Birth Parents in the Adoption Process* (2007), http://www.adoptioninstitute .org/publications/2006, pp. 6 and 19 (visited Aug. 1, 2010).

91. See Margaret Talbot, "The Year in Ideas: A to Z; Open Sperm Donation," *N.Y. Times*, Dec. 9, 2001. On the parallels between secrecy in adoptions and sperm donations, see Naomi Cahn, "Necessary Subjects: The Need for a Mandatory National Donor Gamete Databank," 12 *DePaul J. Health Care L.* 203 (2009).

92. We discussed the parentage issues raised by sperm and egg donation in chapter 13.

93. Betsy Streisand, "Who's Your Daddy? Sperm Donors Rely on Anonymity; Now Donor Offspring (And their Moms) Are Breaking Down the Walls of Privacy," *U.S. News & World Report* (Feb. 5, 2006).

94. The registry is available at http://donorsiblingregistry.com/ (visited Aug. 1, 2010).

95. On the comparative law of gamete donation, see Lucy Frith, "Gamete Donation and Anonymity," 16 *Hum. Reprod.* 818 (2001).

96. Carey Goldberg, "The Search for DGM 2598," *Boston Globe*, Nov. 23, 2008.

97. See, for example, Cal. Fam. Code sec. 7613(a) (2007).

98. See, for example, the Fairfax Cryobank ID Option Donor Program, http://www.fairfaxcryobank.com/IDConsentDonor.shtml (visited Aug. 1, 2010).

99. Streisand, "Who's Your Daddy."

100. Goldberg, "The Search for DGM 2598"; see also Cahn, "Necessary Subjects."

101. On current regulations and proposals for change, see Michelle Dennison, "Revealing Your Sources: The Case for Non-Anonymous Gamete Donation," 21 *J. L. & Health* 1 (2007–08).

102. "Be My Baby," *20/20*, ABC News, aired Apr. 30, 2004.

103. "Bowling for Babies: Bastard Nation's Response to *20/20*'s Be My Baby Ad Campaign," http://www.bastards.org/activism/bowling -babies.html (visited Aug. 1, 2010).

104. See, for example, Esther B. Fein, "Secrecy and Stigma No Longer Clouding Adoptions," *N.Y. Times*, Oct. 25, 1998; Michael Winerip,

"With Open Adoption, A New Kind of Family," *N.Y. Times*, Feb. 24, 2008.

105. Mary Shanley notes that "[o]pen adoption developed in response to the realization of white birth mothers that 'the agencies needed them, rather than birth mothers needing the agencies.'" Shanley, *Making Babies, Making Families*, p. 21.

106. For a state law survey, see Child Welfare Information Gateway, "Postadoption Contact Agreements Between Birth and Adoptive Families: Summary of State Laws" (2009), available at www.childwelfare. gov; see also E. Gary Spitko, "Open Adoption, Inheritance, and the "Uncleing" Principle," 48 *Santa Clara L. Rev.* 765 (2008), p. 777.

107. N.C. Gen. Stat. sec. 48-3-610 (2010).

108. Thayer, "Moppets on the Market."

109. National Committee for Adoption, *Adoption Factbook: United States Data, Issues, Regulations, and Resources* (1985).

110. Rose M. Kreider and Jason Fields, "Living Arrangements of Children: 2001," *U.S. Census Bureau, Current Population Reports*, P70-104 (July 2005), pp. 6–7.

111. On data collection problems in this area, see Victor E. Flango, "Are Courts an Untapped Source of Adoption Statistics?," 11 *St. Court J.* 12 (1987), p. 13.

112. Christine A. Bachrach et al., "On the Path to Adoption: Adoption Seeking in the United States, 1988," 53 *J. Marriage & Fam.* 705 (1991), p. 705.

113. See National Council for Adoption, *Adoption Factbook IV*, p. 5. Among adoptions by strangers in the United States, the percentage of international adoptions more than doubled between 1992 (10.5 percent) and 2002 (21.7 percent).

114. Ibid., p. 13; see also Barbara Stark, "Baby Girls from China in New York: A Thrice-Told Tale," 2003 *Utah L. Rev.* 1231 (2003).

115. Clifford J. Levy, "Russia Calls for Halt on U.S. Adoptions," *N.Y. Times*, Apr. 9, 2010.

116. Elisabeth Rosenthal, "Law Backfires, Stranding Orphans in Romania," *Int'l Herald Trib.*, June 23, 2005.

117. See Jim Yardley, "China Tightens Adoption Rules, U.S. Agencies Say," Dec. 19, 2006.

118. For general background on modern adoption law, see Joan Hollinger and Naomi Cahn, *Families by Law: An Adoption Reader* (2004); Susan Frelich Appleton and D. Kelly Weisberg, *Adoption and Assisted Reproduction: Families under Construction* (2009).

119. See Nancy D. Polikoff, "The Social Construction of Parenthood in One Planned Lesbian Family," 22 *N.Y.U. Rev. L. & Soc. Change* 203 (1996).

120. Nancy Polikoff, Brief Amicus Curiae, R.-Y v. Robin Y., New York County Family Court Docket No. P3884/91, reprinted in 22 *N.Y.U. Rev. L. & Soc. Change* 213 (1996–97), pp. 219–20 n. 2, citing documentation of early lesbian planned families. See also Nan D. Hunter and Nancy D. Polikoff, "Custody Rights of Lesbian Mothers: Legal Theory and Litigation Strategy," 25 *Buff. L. Rev.* 691 (1976); Benna F. Armano, "Lesbian Mother: Her Right to Child Custody," 4 *Golden Gate U. L. Rev.* 1 (1973).

121. See North Coast Women's Care Medical Group, Inc. v. Superior Court, 189 P.3d 959 (Cal. 2008); Unruh Civil Rights Act, Cal. Civ. Code sec. 51 (2010). On the question whether fertility services should be more closely regulated, see Naomi Cahn, *Test Tube Families: Why the Fertility Market Needs Regulation* (2009).

122. See Charlotte Patterson and Fiona Tasker, "Research on Lesbian and Gay Parenting: Retrospect and Prospect," *J. GBLT Fam. Stud.*: Special Issue: Lesbian and Gay Parenting: New Directions (2006), p. 4.

123. See A. I. Lev, "Gay Dads: Choosing Surrogacy," 7 *Lesbian & Gay Psychol. Rev.* 73 (2006).

124. April Martin, "The Planned Lesbian and Gay Family: Parenthood and Children," cited in Polikoff, Brief Amicus Curiae, p. 219.

125. Judith Stacey and Timothy J. Biblarz, "(How) Does the Sexual Orientation of Parents Matter?" 66 *Am. Soc. Rev.* 159 (2001), pp. 164–65.

126. See Gary J. Gates et al., *Adoption and Foster Care by Gay and Lesbian Parents in the United States* (2007), available at http://www.law.ucla.edu/Williamsinstitute/publications/Policy-Adoption-index.html.

127. Fla. Stat. sec. 63-042(3) (2010).

128. 377 F.3d 1275 (11th Cir. 2004). The story of one of the plaintiffs in *Lofton* is portrayed in *Daddy and Papa* (2002), a documentary by Johnny Symons about gay fatherhood in America.

129. *In re* Adoption of Doe, 2008 WL 5006172 (Fla. Cir. Ct. Nov. 25, 2008).

130. *In re* Matter of Adoption of X.X.G. and N.R.G., 45 So. 3d 79 (Fla. App. 2010); see also Joanna L. Grossman, "Will Gays and Lesbians in Florida Finally Gain the Right to Adopt Children?" *FindLaw's Writ*, Oct. 26, 2010, available at http://writ.news.findlaw.com/grossman/20101026.html (visited Nov. 1, 2010).

131. Ark. Code Ann. sec. 9-8-304 (2009).

132. Miss. Code Ann. sec. 93-17-3(5) (2009): "Adoption by couples of the same gender is prohibited"; Utah Code Ann. sec. 78B-6-117 (2009): "A child may not be adopted by a person who is cohabiting in a relationship that is not a legally valid and binding marriage under the laws of the state"; "A child may be adopted by … adults who are legally married."

133. See Adoption of B.L.V.B., 628 A.2d 1271 (Vt. 1993); Adoption of Tammy, 619 N.E.2d 315 (Mass. 1993).

134. Mass. Gen. Laws ch. 210, sec. 1 (2009). The local statute provided that a "person of full age may petition the probate court ... to adopt as his child another person younger than himself, unless such other person is his or her wife or husband, or brother, sister, uncle or aunt, of the whole or half blood."

135. The statute did say that adoption has the effect of terminating legal ties between the adoptive child and her natural parents, but the court interpreted that provision not to apply to stepparent or second-parent adoptions, when one of the natural parents is a party to the adoption petition. Doris Sue Wong, "Lesbian Couple Allowed to Adopt," *Boston Globe*, Sept. 11, 1993.

136. See Cal. Fam. Code sec. 9000(f) (2004); Colo. Rev. Stat. secs. 9-5-203(1), 19-5-208(5), 19-5-210(1.5), 19-5-211(1.5) (2007); Conn. Gen. Stat. sec. 45a-724(3) (2004); Vt. Stat. Ann. tit. 15A, sec. 1-102(b) (2004). On second-parent adoptions generally, see Jane S. Schacter, "Constructing Families in a Democracy: Courts, Legislatures, and Second-Parent Adoption, 75 *Chi.-Kent L. Rev.* 933 (2000).

137. A complete list of current laws on second-parent adoption is available at: www.familyequality.org (visited Aug. 1, 2010).

138. 73 P.3d 554 (Cal. 2003); see also *In re* Jacob, 660 N.E.2d 397 (N.Y. 1995).

139. See, for example, *Jacob*.

140. Boseman v. Jarrell, 704 S.E. 2d 374 (N.C. 2010); *In re* Adoption of Luke, 640 N.W.2d 374 (Neb. 2002); *In re* Adoption of Doe, 719 N.E.2d 1071 (Ohio Ct. App. 1998); *In re* Angel Lace M., 516 N.W.2d 678 (Wis. 1994).

141. 117 P.3d 660 (Cal. 2005).

142. K.M. v. E.G., 117 P.3d 673 (Cal. 2005).

143. We discuss the legal treatment of sperm donors in chapter 13.

144. 117 P.3d 690 (2005).

145. Embry v. Ryan, 11 So. 3d 408 (Fla. App. 2009); see also Russell v. Bridgens, 647 N.W.2d 56 (Neb. 2002); Starr v. Erez, COA99-1534 (N.C. Ct. App. Nov. 27, 2000); Finstuen v. Edmonson, 496 F. Supp. 2d 1295 (W.D. Okla. 2006). A New York court allowed a same-sex couple to jointly adopt the biological child of one of the partners, even though the co-parent already had enforceable parental rights because the couple had legally married in the Netherlands. The court held that "the best interests of this child require a judgment that will ensure recognition of both Ingrid and Mona as his legal parents throughout the entire United States." *In re* Sebastian, No. 38-08, Surrogate's Court: County of New York (Apr. 9, 2009).

146. See, in general, Charlotte J. Patterson, "Adoption of Minor Children by Lesbian and Gay Adults: A Social Science Perspective," 2 *Duke J. Gender L. & Pol'y* 191 (1995); Richard E. Redding, "It's Really About Sex: Same-Sex Marriage, Lesbigay Parenting, and the Psychology of Disgust," 15 *Duke J. Gender L. & Pol'y* 127 (2008); Susan Golombok et al., "Children with Lesbian Parents: A Community Study," 39 *Dev. Psychol.* 20 (2003); Megan Fulcher et al., "Lesbian Mothers and Their Children," in *Sexual Orientation and Mental Health: Examining Identity and Development in Lesbian, Gay, and Bisexual People* (Allen M. Omoto and Howard S. Kurtzman, eds., 2006), p. 281.

147. Varnum v. O'Brien, 763 N.W.2d 862 (Iowa 2009).

148. The declaration is cited at http://www.nclrights.org/site /DocServer/adptn0204.pdf?docID=1221 (visited Aug. 1, 2010).

149. American Psychological Association, *Lesbian and Gay Parenting* (2005), p. 15.

150. American Academy of Pediatrics, Co-Parent or Second Parent Adoption by Same-Sex Parents, 109 *Pediatrics* 339 (2002).

151. American Bar Association, House of Delegates, Report 112A (2003), http://www.abanet.org/leadership/2003/journal/112.pdf (visited Aug. 1, 2010).

152. Patricia Wen, "Catholic Charities Stuns State, Ends Adoptions," *Boston Globe*, Mar. 11, 2006. For arguments against same-sex parenting, see also Lynn D. Wardle, "The Potential Impact of Homosexual Parenting on Children," 1997 *U. Ill. L. Rev.* 833 (1997). On the other end of the spectrum, we see lawyers and brokers who specialize in adoption for gays and lesbians, and a recent survey found that many non-specialized adoption agencies will accept gay men and lesbians as clients. D. M. Brodzinsky and Evan B. Donaldson Adoption Institute, *Adoptions by Lesbians and Gays: A National Survey of Adoption Agency Policies, Practices, and Attitudes* (2006), http://www.adoptioninstitute.org/whowe /Gay%20and%20Lesbian%20Adoption1.html (visited Aug. 1, 2010); see also Charlotte J. Patterson, "Lesbian and Gay Family Issues in the Context of Changing Legal and Social Policy Environments," in Bieschke et al., eds., *Handbook of Counseling and Psychotherapy with Lesbian, Gay, Bisexual, and Transgender Clients* (2007), p. 363.

Billingslea, Ray Edwin, 256
Bing, Sir Rudolph, 260
Blackadder, Idelia and John A., 181–82
Blackstone, William, 4, 59, 68
Blackwell, Cobert, 43
blended families: adoption and, 309–10,
    315; child support in, 228; rise of, 310;
    stepparents' rights, 278–79; will con-
    tests in, 246
blind credulity, 185
Blodgett, H. H., 87
blood tests, requirements for marriage,
    41–42
blood-typing, paternity, 288–89
Bobbitt, Lorena and John Wayne, 76
Boehler, Alfred, 74
Boland v. Catalano (1987), 364n52
Bowers v. Hardwick (1986), 114–15, 125
Brace, Charles Loring, 309
Bradkowski, Keith, 240
breach of promise: abolition of, 96–106,
    357n70; cause of action, 12, 90–93,
    355n50
Breitung, Juliet, 97
Brennen, William J., 113
Brethren of the United Order, 29
Bricklin Perceptual Scales, 219
Brieux, Eugene, 41
Brode, Patrick, 357n70
Brooks, Mary Lou, 132
Brougham, Ward, 95
Brown, Louise, 322
Brown, Robert C., 98
Brown v. Board of Education (1954), 152
Bryan, William Jennings, 66
Bryant, Anita, 143, 323
Buck, Carrie, 112
Buck v. Bell (1927), 112
Bureau of Indian Affairs, 311
Bureau of War Risk Insurance, 84
Burke, Louis, 174
Burns, Susan and Darian, 123–24, 151
Burr v. Burr (1986), 307, 413n16
Bush, George W., 148, 190

Caban, Abdiel, 293
Caban v. Mohammed (1979), 293

Cable Act of 1922, 66–67
California, laws and statutes on: adop-
    tion, 412n9, 305–6, 314; adoption
    records, 316; alimony, 61, 195, 379n10;
    annulment, 181–82, 185, 196, 375n115,
    376n119; child custody, 221–22; child
    support, 224; citizenship, 66; cohabita-
    tion, 10, 121–22, 131, 139; common-law
    marriage, 80, 83, 352n20; compulsory
    education, 265; conservatorships, 259;
    divorce, 14, 163, 175–76, 178, 377n141;
    domestic partnership, 240; eugenics
    movement, 86, 112; heart balm laws,
    100; inheritance rights, 243–45, 257;
    intent to parent, 325–27; interracial
    marriage, 32; marital age, 44, 110; mari-
    tal rape, 75; parentage, 289, 297, 299,
    303, 314; parental rights, 264–65, 277,
    279; prenuptial agreements, 385n112,
    385n115; property rights, 379n6; remar-
    riage waiting periods, 44, 169; same-sex
    adoption, 322; same-sex relationships,
    144–45, 150, 152–53; second-parent
    adoptions, 324; stepparents' rights, 279;
    sterilization, 86; surrogacy, 299
California Cryobank, 297
Cameron, Lucille, 33
Cameron, Ralph, 100
Canada, laws and statutes on: heart balm
    laws, 357n70; posthumously conceived
    children, 411n117; same-sex relation-
    ships/marriage in, 152, 394n19
CAPTA, 268, 399n42
Carbone, June, 386n2
Caribbean islands, divorce in, 171–72,
    372n58
Carney, Cordelia P., 93
Carr, Stanley, 183
Carvin, Sue Ellen, 278
Catholic Charities of Boston, 328
Catholic church, annulment and, 160, 164,
    177–78, 180–81, 185
Chadwick, H. Beatty, 213
Cheatham, Denty, 70
Chen, Jane, 226–27
Cherepski v. Walker (1996), 356n58
Cherlin, Andrew, 54, 178